HUMAN RESOURCE STRATEGY

McGraw-Hill Series in Management

CONSULTING EDITORS

Fred Luthans and Keith Davis

HUMAN RESOURCE STRATEGY

James W. Walker
The Walker Group, Phoenix

McGRAW-HILL, INC.
New York St. Louis San Francisco Auckland Bogotá
Caracas Lisbon London Madrid Mexico Milan Montreal
New Delhi Paris San Juan Singapore Sydney Tokyo Toronto

HUMAN RESOURCE STRATEGY

3 4 5 6 7 8 9 0 DOC DOC 9 0 9 8 7 6 5 4 3

ISBN 0-07-067846-4

This book was set in Times Roman by Better Graphics, Inc.
The editors were Alan Sachs, Dan Alpert, and Bernadette Boylan;
the production supervisor was Richard A. Ausburn.
The cover was designed by Nicholas Krenitsky.
R. R. Donnelley & Sons Company was printer and binder.

Library of Congress Cataloging-in-Publication Data

Walker, James W., (date).
  Human resource strategy / James W. Walker.
      p.   cm.—(McGraw-Hill series in management)
  Rev. ed. of: Human resource planning. c1980.
  Includes bibliographical references (p.   ) and indexes.
  ISBN 0-07-067846-4
  1. Personnel management.   2. Manpower planning.   I. Walker, James
W., (date). Human resource planning.   II. Title.   III. Series.
HF5549.W3116   1992
658.3'01—dc20
                                                        91-43285

ABOUT
THE AUTHOR

JAMES W. WALKER is a partner in The Walker Group, a strategy consulting organization based in Phoenix, Arizona. The firm helps international clients formulate business and human resource strategies and implement them through organization, staffing, development, performance management, and other aspects of the management of human resources.

Dr. Walker is widely known for his speaking, writing, and other professional activities in the human resource field. Jim was founder of the Human Resource Planning Society and served as its charter president. He is the author of many articles and seven books.

He earned an M.A. in Labor and Management and a Ph.D. in Business Administration from the University of Iowa. He then served on the business faculties at Indiana University and at San Diego State University. In 1971, Jim became a management consultant with Towers, Perrin, Forster & Crosby in Philadelphia and then moved to New York when the firm's corporate group relocated there. He took a leave of absence in 1977 to teach at Arizona State University and to write. He returned to Towers, Perrin in 1979 and was vice president and director of Human Resource Consulting Services until leaving to establish The Walker Group in 1986.

In addition to his work with clients, he and his colleagues created the *Human Resource Business School,* a one-week program conducted each April in Arizona. The program helps human resource professionals strengthen the business perspective required for their changing roles.

He is married with one son and resides in Phoenix, Arizona.

CONTENTS

PREFACE

The way we manage the people in our organizations needs to be aligned with our business strategies. The means for this alignment is human resource strategy—a directional plan for managing human resources that addresses important people-related business issues.

This book is written for students of management and for managers—line managers, staff managers, and managers in the human resource function. Its purpose is to examine how managers may implement more effectively the people-intensive strategies that are rapidly becoming a primary source of competitive advantage.

The management of human resources can no longer be viewed as an activity relegated to human resource staff, or even managed by staff. It is a core management activity, in the mainstream of formulating and implementing business strategy. Only by addressing human resource issues in the context of overall strategic management will managers and human resource staff together achieve the results needed to sustain and develop a business.

This book originated in response to a request from McGraw-Hill for an update of *Human Resource Planning,* which I completed in 1979. At that time, the idea of linking the management of human resources with business planning was just being developed and tested. Since then, however, so much has changed in the way we develop and implement business strategies and in the ways we manage people that more than a revision was required. This is a new book. Little was retained from the earlier work.

In the earlier book, I defined human resource planning as a management process of analyzing an organization's human resource needs under changing conditions and developing the activities necessary to satisfy these needs. This still holds true, but because plans are so discontinuous (they represent such rapid and marked change), *strategy* is a more relevant focus.

I believe there is a general acceptance in business that strategic management is necessary for a company to gain and sustain its competitive position. Management adds value to an enterprise by defining the right issues, charting the right course of action, and helping people implement these actions effectively. Sometimes management is more implicit than explicit, but successful companies point to managing strategic change as their hallmark.

As a result, the book is not merely descriptive. Like the previous work, it is intended to be pragmatic without being a "how-to" book. It is intended for use in advanced courses on strategic human resource planning and management. However, it is not an exhaustive reference to the research, techniques, and literature on the subject.

Since writing the previous book, I have had the privilege of working with a wide variety of companies in addressing the subjects discussed here. I am deeply indebted to these clients for the opportunities to develop and apply new ideas and approaches. Clearly, we have learned and advanced together as conditions and challenges have changed. Throughout the book, I have quoted from public materials and other companies. Without citing all of the sources, I would like to acknowledge them and thank them for the realism they add to the text.

I also acknowledge the great influence my professional colleagues in the Human Resource Planning Society have had in my learning and work. HRPS was getting established as I wrote my earlier book; its successful growth reflects how far we have progressed in the ensuing years.

Among my consulting colleagues, I thank Bob Armes, Christopher Shipp, Bob Eichinger, Andy Merryman, Karl Price, Scott Schenone, Carol Schreiber, Guillaume Franck, and Detlef Lehman for their ideas and comments, which they will see reflected in the book. I particularly thank my partners, Bill Reif and Tom Bechet, for their encouragement and for patiently debating with me what "truth" is in the 1990s.

I owe special thanks to my core reviewers, Lee Dyer, of Cornell University, and Randall Schuler, of New York University, for their detailed and thoughtful comments, suggestions, and criticisms of each chapter as it was written. Both Lee and Randy demonstrated great skill in encouraging me while asking very challenging questions. Sometimes I felt like I was writing my dissertation again. I am also very grateful to Ellen Ernst Kossek, Michigan State University and Pat Wright, Texas A&M University, for reviewing portions of the manuscript at various stages.

My thanks also go to Harriet, for encouraging me to work on the book when there were many other things to do on precious days and weekends between client travel. Her counsel was valuable, as always.

Finally, I owe my high optimism to my young son, Michael Scott Lazer Walker. I can only think the best of all of our future possibilities when he is near. To him and to his future, I dedicate this book.

James W. Walker

HUMAN RESOURCE STRATEGY

CHAPTER 1

INTRODUCTION

Strategy is defined as all the things necessary for the successful functioning of an organization as an adaptive mechanism.

Richard Pascale

Companies everywhere are changing the way they manage in order to be more competitive. A key measure of management in the 1990s and beyond lies in results attained relative to the opportunities and constraints created by rapid environmental change.

A primary way to gain competitive advantage is to manage people more effectively. Developing and implementing human resource strategies ensures that actions in managing human resources are aligned with competitive demands, as reflected in business strategies. To win in the global marketplace, companies are seeking to provide distinctly superior customer service, develop new capabilities and employee commitment, pursue innovation and creative initiative, and manage change through teamwork and cooperation. Most are striving to manage with fewer employees, fewer management levels, and more flexibility in management practices.

Senior executives acknowledge the importance of people as an asset—and of managing change effectively through people. They frequently speak with conviction about company values, vision, mission, and strategies—and expect the policies and programs will be put in place to guide and support effective management. They want their managers to do what is basically right. Surveys repeatedly affirm that CEOs consider human resource issues to be important to their businesses and want them addressed effectively by their managers and the human resource staff.

However, there remains a gap between the rhetoric and the reality in many companies. It is extremely difficult for companies to change the way people are managed. Inertia tends to continue past human resource practices. Policies and programs guiding human resources are not always current with changing business priorities. Many activities simply keep companies up with competitors and do not provide any competitive advantage.

1

Human resource strategy is important because it enables management to define and address "people-related business issues" in a practical way. In this introductory chapter we will address:

- How human resource strategies are formulated and implemented
- Why human resource strategy is important
- What it means to be a flexible organization and how this affects the management of human resources

Also, examples of company responses to people-related business issues are presented.

OVERVIEW OF THE PROCESS

The process of developing and implementing human resource strategies—the process of managing human resources in alignment with business strategy—is a management process. Human resource strategies are management strategies, developed and implemented by managing executives in the same manner as other functional strategies. Implicitly or explicitly, they are considered an important aspect of implementing business strategies.

Managers and human resource staff implement these human resource strategies through an ongoing process of activities: organization design, defining staffing needs, staffing, developing capabilities (and management talent), enabling performance, evaluating performance, and rewarding and recognizing performance. This management process, shown in Exhibit 1-1, is a series of activities through which managers successively define and address human resource issues on a continuing basis.

The challenge of managing human resources is to ensure that all activities are focused on business needs. All human resource activities should fit together as a system and be aligned with human resource strategies. These strategies, in turn, should be aligned with the business strategy.

Developing HR Strategies

Managers define the human resource issues important to their business. This requires assessment of the opportunities and threats posed by changes occurring in the environment and the relative strengths and weaknesses of the business itself. Issues derive from assessment of these changes, including changes in business strategies and objectives, new technology, mergers or acquisitions, changing customer requirements and expectations, restructuring, work force changes, and globalization of business. Chapter 2 examines how managers identify, define, and analyze human resource issues.

The urgency for change depends in large part on the imperatives implicit in business strategies. In some companies, human resource issues are included in the strategic business plans, along with financial, product, marketing, and other concerns. Changes are typically identified in broad terms, calling for new

---

EXHIBIT 1-1   ALIGNING THE MANAGEMENT OF HUMAN
RESOURCES WITH STRATEGY

Defining Human Resource Issues

Developing Human Resource Strategies

Aligning Employee Expectations with Strategy

Sharing Successes

Designing the Organization

Evaluating Performance

Defining Staffing Needs

Enabling Performance

Strategic Staffing

Developing Effective Managers

Developing Capabilities

Managing the Human Resource Function

---

organization structure, new incentive compensation programs, reduction of staffing or costs, or acquisition of new skills.

In other companies, business strategies stress other functional areas, not the management of human resources. Here, managers address human resource issues separately. They consider the implications of business strategies, issues emanating from changing external conditions, and issues relating to internal organization and management. They develop and implement human resource strategies as guides to action under changing conditions.

Managers shape human resource strategies to guide their actions. Strategies may be more or less explicit, near- or long-term, general or specific, depending on the approach used. However defined, they provide directional plans for managing people in flexible organizations. Chapter 3 examines the process for formulating human resource strategies.

Many well-intended strategies have little effect because management practices are not aligned with them. Plans need to be communicated, understood, and adopted as important guides to action. Managers, employees, and other stakeholders (e.g., vendors, distributors, contractors) need to share the vision, values, and mission of the business—as reflected in strategies. Ultimately, strategies need to be translated into organizational goals and objectives, and into specific unit and individual key result areas and objectives. Chapter 4 addresses the difficult process of shaping expectations and managing necessary change to implement strategies.

Building the Organization

Strategies call for changes in the way a company is managed. The capacity to manage change depends on the way the business is organized and staffed. As they become more flexible, companies need to improve continually and develop their basic capacity to perform. There is a saying that "IBM reorganizes only for a good business reason. If the organization hasn't changed in two years, that's a good business reason." Of course, structure and people are closely interrelated aspects of building an effective, flexible organization.

Companies are minimizing the levels and complexity of the organization structure and encouraging delegation, initiative, and innovation. Jobs, too, are often flexible. Companies change job responsibilities and activities to fit changing business needs and employee capacities and interests. They believe that this fosters innovation and flexibility in job performance. Roles of managers are changing under changing conditions (e.g., brokers, negotiators, coaches, consultants, individual contributors).

To be more flexible, many companies are encouraging informal, direct contacts across organizations (multiple, changing matrices of relationships). Communications are also more flexible, providing employees and managers the information they need to do their jobs and to feel that they are fully informed. Companies are providing new processes for employee involvement in communications and decisions.

When strategies change, structure needs to follow. Designing the organization for changing needs requires continual review and planning of formal organization structure (e.g., roles, responsibilities, and relationships) and the processes by which work is performed (e.g., delegation, decision making and approval, network relationships, teamwork). Particularly, the design of management functions requires reconsideration and change—as the demands on managers change rapidly. The challenges of designing and implementing organizational changes are discussed in Chapter 5.

People bring an organization to life. In Chapter 6 we address management practices in planning for future staffing in terms of numbers, skills mix, deployment, and retention. In the 1990s, strategic staffing, including recruiting and retaining needed talent, will be vital because of limited talent supply, increased competition for talent, and changing/increasing demands on talent. Approaches for staffing are addressed in Chapter 7.

Many companies are adopting flexible employment as a human resource strategy. They focus recruitment, retention, and development on a core of talent with critical skills required. They staff variable needs with talent on contingent employment arrangements—fixed term, temporary, part time.

Many services which do not require day-to-day company supervision are contracted out.

Developing Capabilities

The development of talent for future needs focuses on employees within the organization. In the 1990s, emphasis will be given to the continual improvement of individual talents through education, job-related training, job assignments, and coaching. Retention, utilization, and development of talent will be priorities. Chapter 8 focuses on the development of nonmanagerial employees, particularly professional and technical talent. Chapter 9 addresses changing requirements for managerial talent and ways companies may plan for succession and development of managers.

Companies are seeking ways to guide and support company efforts in developing managers as leaders for the new flat, lean, and flexible environment. General Electric, for example, believes that teamwork, companywide perspective, global insight, and customer orientation are critical attributes for its leaders.

With fewer managers and fewer management levels, management capabilities are more important. Providing challenging and broadening experiences is the key to developing flexible managers. However, in flat and lean organizations, job rotation and and mobility are difficult because there are fewer managers—and increased time pressures and demands on unit and individual performance. Business units have little slack and have difficulty releasing talented managers for broadening assignments, even temporary ones.

Companies are emphasizing flexible careers, fostering individual growth and learning through changing on-the-job experiences, assignments under different managers, and special projects. They are seeking to leverage training and education to address critical needs (not on curricula or career steps). Emphasis on company attention to career development is shifting to reliance on employee initiatives in job assignment changes and development activities.

Management appraisal, development, and succession planning processes typically address future, not current, requirements of key management positions targeted for staffing within the organization. Traditional replacement planning, concentrating on grooming candidates, falls short of needs in rapidly changing organizations. Flexible organizations find that fewer than half of all management positions are actually filled with individuals identified in advance as candidates. These organizations make the most of job vacancies as opportunities to give individuals new experiences and challenges. At the same time, flexible organizations recruit externally to fill key positions as well as staff within; rapidly changing needs often make it difficult to give internal candidates the chance to prepare for demanding assignments: everyone is stretched.

Management education and training programs, generally costly and time-consuming, are designed to achieve broader objectives in flexible organizations. Traditionally, classroom-type programs have concentrated on building knowledge, awareness, and basic individual skills relevant to management tasks. They have not always reached the managers who need the development the most; neither have they always been regarded as uniformly successful in changing behaviors. To address these concerns, many companies are now redesigning programs to support directly company strategies for change and to focus on specific issues, skills, and behaviors.

Managing Performance

Building the capacity to act is important, but the other major management task is managing performance for achievement of desired results. Although performance management has been a management concern for decades, few companies are satisfied that their process is effective. As noted, performance expectations (objectives, goals, standards, etc.) are defined by the strategic context. Implementation requires active management guidance and support, evaluation and feedback on performance, and rewards and recognitions for performance.

We will consider in Chapter 10 how managers may improve the ways they enable employees to perform, that is, how they lead and motivate employees, and provide the resources necessary for effective performance. Employees in the 1990s will respond best to a culture that supports performance—that focuses on strategic challenges (e.g., customer satisfaction, quality), that provides the resources needed (e.g., funds, information, tools), and that provides a high degree of involvement in the management of the business.

Performance evaluation has been a particularly difficult and frustrating challenge for companies. It is even more important in the lean, flexible, competitive, and demanding 1990s. Evalution is discussed in Chapter 11 as a process which includes company, business unit, team, and individual performance evaluation. Ways in which managers may evaluate performance and provide feedback to employees that is relevant to all of these levels of performance are examined.

Above all, employees and managers need to share in the success of the business. Recognizing and rewarding performance is the subject of Chapter 12. In the 1990s, salary increases, incentive awards, and other financial rewards are being complemented by a myriad of recognitions and innovative ways to celebrate accomplishments as businesses, teams, and individuals. The chapter also addresses the changing role of employee benefits, job security, and other perceived inducements to stay with a company and perform.

Flexible compensation is widely used to ensure competitiveness of rewards and to contain costs. Multiple compensation programs are widely used, emphasizing incentives, special awards and recognitions, and wide ranges for base pay levels and adjustments. Flexible benefits contain rising costs and respond to employee preferences for different types of benefits. To support compensation actions, companies are using varied formats and approaches in performance appraisal and are obtaining inputs from different sources (e.g., managers, peers, customers, etc.).

Managing the Human Resource Function

Managing human resources is a line management responsibility. It is management's job to define the strategic context, build the organization, develop capabilities, and manage performance. The challenge of the human resource staff function is to enable managers to fulfill this responsibility and pursue continual improvements in each of these areas, critical to competitive success. Companies are seeking more flexible practices for managing talent in varied and changing conditions. The human resource staff function itself operates more efficiently and flexibly, reflecting more effective use of information technology and broader capabilities of staff.

Accordingly, the roles of human resource staff are being redefined as human resource managers and professionals work as partners with managers in formulating and implementing human resource strategies. In flexible companies, human resource staff are energetic and capable members of the management team—working with managers as partners in addressing important human resource issues.

However, many human resource staff are, like managers, still unsure of their changing roles and priorities. They too, are influenced by the familiar practices of the past—what they are good at and interested in. Many staff lack sufficient experience, training, or skills relevant to their emerging challenges. Also, like other staff functions, many human resource staffs have been reduced in size and resources and have been decentralized, yet they are providing a large volume of ongoing administrative and service functions. Finally, human resource staffs continue to be viewed by some managers as primarily a support function, on the sidelines of the management process rather than directly participating on the management team.

In Chapter 13, we address ways to manage the changing human resource function. How can the function provide the basics *and* take active roles in managing change? How should the function be organized and staffed to work most effectively with management? How can capabilities of human resource staff be developed to meet changing demands?

WHY HUMAN RESOURCE STRATEGY?

Business organizations face challenges in achieving and maintaining a competitive edge in a rapidly changing world. These include managing growth and change in a global marketplace, introducing new technology, achieving and maintaining low costs, improving service/product quality, and balancing diversity and synergy.

Addressing these business challenges requires the talents, energies, and performance of employees. How effectively business strategies are implemented depends in large part on the management of human resources. In this book, references to employees include both managers and nonmanagers. On occasion, we will also address other people who contribute to the process as well, such as contractors, vendors, and distributors. Increasingly, fewer of the "people" who do the work of a business are actually employees.

Companies perceive human resource issues as important challenges in achieving desired business changes. Human resource issues and strategies are directly linked with business issues and strategies. They go hand in hand in reality, thus also in management thinking, planning, and action.

Strategic Context

Most companies have business strategies which define plans for future growth, development, and profitability of the business. They also have various kinds of specific functional or product business strategies—for financial management, product management and marketing, manufacturing and technology, materials management, and information management. These strategies define how a company will gain and sustain its competitive advantage in the marketplace.

"One can have strategies for tomorrow that anticipate the areas in which the greatest changes are likely to occur, strategies that enable a business or public service institution to take advantage of the unforeseen and unforseeable" (Drucker, 1980). Operational planning optimizes the trends evident today—the continuities; strategies aim to exploit new and different opportunities that are not yet apparent.

Strategic planning, the formulation part of strategic management, examines relevant external and internal factors in the business environment in relation to the current situation. Conclusions are then reached on business definition, mission, vision, strategic objectives, performance targets, and action plans.

As conditions change more rapidly, strategic planning is becoming increasingly tentative, short-term, and issue-focused. Planning has become useful more as a tool for provoking thinking and discussion than as a process of determining long-term objectives and courses of action. It is most valuable as an issue identification and diagnostic process and is necessary to foster management consideration of long-range vision, strategic direction, and values. In this way, the process helps managers think about long-term changes affecting near-term actions. Strategies are shaped as guides to help organizations recognize and address important changes and opportunities to manage them effectively.

Strategies Are People-Intensive

The capacity to implement changes called for in business strategies is dependent on people. People, not companies, innovate, make decisions, develop and produce new products, penetrate new markets, and serve customers more

---

EXHIBIT 1-2 STRATEGIC CONTEXT AT APPLE COMPUTER

Mission:

Help people transform the way they work, learn and communicate by providing exceptional personal computing products and innovative customer services.

- We will pioneer new directions and approaches, finding innovative ways to use computing technology to extend the bounds of human potential.
- Apple will make a difference: our products, services, and insights will help people around the world shape the ways business and education will be done in the 21st century.

Initiatives:

- Focus on satisfying customers: we will be known for our innovative products and services and for our satisfied customers.
- Become a more global company: we will develop our products and services using state-of-the-art technologies and ideas in the world to serve the people of the world.
- Build an integrated infrastructure: we will fully utilize the power of our technology to support our relationships with customers, third-party partners, and the people of Apple.

Source: Apple Computer Inc., used with permission.

effectively. Typically, human resource issues are central to strategy implementation.

For example, Apple Computer strives "to help transform the way people work, learn, and communicate." A statement of Apple's mission and key initiatives is presented in Exhibit 1-2. Apple focuses on two primary priorities:

- Develop new products resulting in a more balanced product portfolio, attending to customer needs at the low end, the middle, and the high end.
- Address use of these products across the business, educational, and government markets in three major geographic regions: the United States, Europe, and the Pacific.

In the course of addressing these priorities, Apple has restructured frequently, redeployed its management and technical talent, and gradually adapted its management processes to address growing competitive challenges. The rapid growth of the company has created demands for talent that have been met by recruiting and rapid advancement. Nearly half of Apple's employees in 1990 had only two years' tenure; bench strength in technical and managerial areas was considered insufficient.

The youthful idealism of Apple's culture is now yielding to a more pragmatic corporate culture focused on the challenges of maintaining leadership as a provider of trend-setting personal computers. Apple seeks to maintain its strong sense of values, informality, and individual initiative while seeking balance in the midst of continuing growth and change. Human resource plans, accordingly, focus on staffing and selection, assimilation and acculturation, learning and development, and managing change. In fact, in 1991, steps were taken to reduce overall staffing at Apple, signaling a shift of focus to more selective staffing and improvement in utilization.

Just as Apple's strategies have significant human resource implications, so do all other companies' strategies. Among the people-related business issues being addressed by companies today are the following:

• Achieving and sustaining cost competitiveness: personnel costs, utilization, downsizing, eliminating unnecessary work
• Achieving competitive differentiation through service and product quality: productivity, customer satisfaction, and other components of total quality
• Implementing organizational restructuring and mergers or acquisitions
• Increasing delegation of authority and responsibility: streamlined approval processes, increased employee involvement, risk/reward compensation, and empowerment to act
• Enhancing organizational effectiveness: team building, shared vision and values (culture), lateral relationships, etc.
• Developing leadership: staffing, appraisal, and development of managers
• Enhancing work force capability and motivation: staffing, retention, motivation and rewards, development, communications and involvement, work life issues

Companies have in common one fundamental human resource issue: How can the organization ensure that it will have people of the right types and numbers, organized appropriately, managed effectively, and focused on customer requirements?

Alignment

Human resource strategies define how a company will manage its people toward the achievement of business objectives—setting priorities for action. Like any strategy, a human resource strategy is a directional plan of action for managing change. It provides a business perspective of actions necessary to gain and sustain competitive advantage through the management of human resources—a *focus* on priorities in managing people in a changing environment.

Through human resource strategy, managers and human resource staff jointly define and resolve people-related business issues. The planning process adds value by helping managers identify the issues most critical to the organization's competitiveness and ultimately to its success. It helps management set priorities and define a vision of how it intends to manage its people.

As illustrated in Exhibit 1-3, the management of human resources is aligned with business strategy through the defined human resource issues and strategies. The clearer and more focused the issues and strategies, the closer the alignment.

Human resource strategies provide a basis for discussion and agreement among unit managers on priorities, activities, and allocation of time and resources. Where explicit business strategic planning is used by management, human resource strategies are developed as part of this process, with human

---

EXHIBIT 1-3 STRATEGIC ALIGNMENT

Business Strategy

External and Internal Environment:
Business-Related Changes/Issues

Business Mission, Vision, Values

Objectives and Strategies

Alignment

Human Resource Issues
Human Resource Strategies

**Implementation: Management
of Human Resources**

Human Resource Programs and Activities
Evaluation of Results

EXHIBIT 1-4 WHY HUMAN RESOURCE STRATEGY?

- Defines opportunities and barriers for achievement of business objectives
- Prompts new thinking about issues; orients and educates participants and provides a wider perspective
- Tests management commitment for actions; creates a process for allocating resources to specific programs and activities
- Develops a sense of urgency and commitment to action
- Establishes selected long-term courses of action considered high priority over the next two to three years
- Provides a strategic focus for managing the business and developing management talents

---

resource and management effectiveness issues addressed as any other business issues.

Human resource strategy helps focus, mobilize, and direct all human resource activities on the issues that most directly affect the business. It is the glue that binds all other human resource activities and makes sense of them from a management viewpoint. Benefits of human resource strategy are listed in Exhibit 1-4.

Human resource strategy also aligns management thinking and actions in managing human resources. It defines how managing human resources may be approached through a logical, coherent, strategy-focused process. It goes beyond human resource strategy formulation into strategy implementation, shaping how managers manage human resources for greater results. It defines how they will manage human resources in the 1990s and beyond—identifying and defining issues as needs and determining ways to address these through well-considered priorities and action plans.

THE RESULT: HR STRATEGIES

How do companies define their human resource issues and address them through human resource strategy? The following examples reflect typical company approaches.

Managing Growth and Change

Many companies are experiencing rapid business growth or change, particularly in worldwide markets. Their business strategies call for development of business units and transformation of business practices to anticipate competitive needs and respond to increasing business complexity. The human resource implications of these strategies often concentrate on staffing and changing the way staff are managed.

Companies experiencing these changes emphasize recruiting needed talent (both in numbers and in changing skills required) and replacement or retraining of those who do not match needs. Strategies also involve design of new compensation programs to attract and retain key talent and changes in the way the organization is managed to ensure a competitive, entrepreneurial spirit.

A major commercial bank, for example, shifted away from traditional corporate and retail banking services and toward investment banking and corporate financial services. This resulted in shifts toward autonomous banking units, the creation of many new incentive plans, widespread changes in staff, and new management planning and control processes. The bank evolved from a large, stable institution into a flexible, fast-paced, risk-oriented enterprise.

A retail food business, with both company-operated and franchised stores, has grown rapidly in recent years. As it has expanded, both domestically and internationally, strains on its management systems and on its people became evident. The human resource issue of strategic importance is to equip management with the capacity to sustain the targeted growth and profitability—not to let management talent or effectiveness be a barrier to continued expansion.

A fast-growing high-technology company is noted for its "family culture," its informality, youthful vigor, and creativity. As the company has expanded, nearly doubling in size every several years, the demands on recruiting, development, and effective integration of new talent into the culture have mounted. Additionally, pressures to become more "businesslike" are being balanced with the desire to retain the spirit of the company.

Introducing New Technology

Leading manufacturing companies are focusing on the introduction of new products and technology. Business strategies require shifts toward shorter product cycles, simultaneous engineering, and the use of new technology such as expert systems, artificial intelligence, fiber optics, computer-aided design and manfuacturing, and robotics. The human resource issue is essentially reskilling of the work force. Human resource strategies typically address needs for changes in recruiting, education and training, teamwork and technology transfer, organizational and staffing changes, project management and cross-discipline integration, and assessment of individual skills and development needs.

In an automobile company, for example, design and manfuacturing engineering organizations are being merged to address new technological needs and an "engineering college" has been established to provide expanded technical training. Other strategies include assessment of skills, forecasting of staffing and skill needs, and improved program management and organizational effectiveness.

A computer manufacturer is emphasizing cross-training, teamwork, and collaboration across units to improve engineering and technology transfer. Retraining, transfers, and recruiting are needed to ensure that the required new skills are available as needed to sustain the company's technological competitive advantage.

Achieving and Maintaining Low Costs

For many companies, becoming or remaining a low-cost producer is a key business objective. For them, lower direct product costs, minimized indirect/overhead expenses, and avoidance of future costs or extraordinary expenses are key concerns. The human resource implications are evident: reducing and managing personnel-related costs, downsizing (rightsizing), eliminating unnecessary work, reducing benefit costs, adopting pay-for-performance programs, improving productivity and efficiency, and avoiding costs resulting from litigation and regulatory demands.

A major manufacturer is seeking continual improvements in product costs. An across-the-board reduction in staff of 25% is being followed by more selective changes in staffing and organization. A cooperative strategy process involving the unions focuses on opportunities for further productivity gains.

A pharmaceutical company seeks to contain its rising expenses as a way to improve profitability. A level-by-level management review of staffing needs, tied to the drivers of work load, pointed toward actions that would improve utilization of current staffing. Elimination and automation of activities, reassignment of work and job redesign, and elimination of duplications were sought to help contain needs for additional staff and allow redeployment of current staff.

An office equipment company found itself a high-cost producer as it experienced increased foreign competition in its markets. It is gradually and steadily reducing its cost structure by identifying and addressing opportunities for improvements. Similarly, a steel company has reduced the scale of the organization by eliminating operations and downsizing the entire organization, while maintaining and strengthening the capabilities needed to achieve targeted profitability.

A poultry processor is facing an unusual business issue with significant human resource implications. Carpel tunnel syndrome, caused by repetitive motion, is increasing in attention and cost potential (fines and litigation costs). The condition and competition for employee talent are also increasing wage rates at company locations. The preferred strategy, increased use of automation, is constrained by the state of technology: the capacity to handle varying-sized chickens efficiently and the capacity to control salmonella contamination. In the absence of automation, strategies emphasize rotation and retraining of employees to minimize the effect of the syndrome.

Improving Quality

Enhancing the value or quality of products and services is a key objective in many companies for gaining competitive advantage over, or at least parity with, competitors. Companies are setting tougher performance requirements, seeking continual quality improvement in products/services, and strengthening the value chain involving vendors and distributors. For these companies, the overriding human resource issue is improving organizational effectiveness.

Strategies include streamlining the work (structure, delegation, activities) strengthening management for performance and service/quality, attracting and retaining needed talent, improving team effectiveness, and building employee involvement and commitment to changes supporting the company vision and values. Companies often adopt a process of "total quality management" to provide a broad approach to these concerns.

A lodging and food service company seeks to continue its rapid growth while sustaining profitability and cash flow. However, the industry is "overbuilt" and the economics are increasingly difficult to sustain. The available labor pool is diminishing (as a result of changing demographics), and turnover is rising in some segments of the business. Accordingly, the company is implementing strategies to improve employee retention, to be a more attractive employer (company of choice), and to improve employee capability and motivation to provide superior service.

To maintain its competitive superiority in business results, a pharmaceutical company seeks ways to sustain and improve performance in research, sales, manufacturing, and other functions. The company faces organizational blockages resulting from low turnover, flatter organization structures, age compression and postponed retirements, and an oversupply of promotable talent. Accordingly, human resource strategies address needs for tougher performance and productivity goals, increased employee understanding and support, and strengthened overall organization.

A computer manufacturer recognizes that to maintain its competitiveness in a rapidly changing market it needs to improve its focus on the customer. Effective customer service requires quicker responses, more effective information support, and lower overhead costs. Strategies address opportunities to redeploy and retrain talent, streamline internal communications and decision processes, and more directly support customer needs.

An electronics company includes quality and productivity improvement as a strategic requirement to remain competitive on a global basis. Every year, each business reviews its strategy, structure, management processes, and performance and identifies ways to improve organizational effectiveness. Over five years, each has planned and implemented a series of unique projects aimed at achieving breakthrough steps in these areas. Priorities have included competitive benchmarking, achieving total customer satisfaction, and reducing total cycle time. The organization effectiveness process itself is part of the strategy, because it is a shared learning experience involving a large number of managers and employees.

Balancing Autonomy and Synergy

Some companies are seeking to increase business unit competitiveness in diverse markets by managing business units as profit centers. At the same time, they are seeking to maintain the value added by the overall enterprise. The primary human resource challenge is to make flexibility work.

Typical strategies include clarifying management philosophy and policy, developing customized/flexible compensation and benefit programs, strengthening management capabilities/capacity to act, and building teamwork and organizational effectiveness.

An insurance company encourages initiatives in its diverse financial services and investment business units. Each business unit defines its own competitive requirements and priorities, including human resource issues. However, the overall enterprise monitors these priorities, provides coordination and integration on common concerns, and imposes issues of overriding corporate concern (such as affirmative action and management succession, and management incentive plan design).

A retailer is seeking to increase its competitiveness by organizing the business along product lines and then expanding its network of stores within each line rather than as integrated, full-service stores. Human resource strategies are being implemented for the ways employees are to be recruited, compensated, and managed differently in each business segment, according to its competitive environment.

A food products company acquired several unrelated businesses in recent years, but continued to manage them from the food products perspective. Now, it is further decentralizing management processes and the human resource function itself to respond to different subsidiary needs and bring accountability for human resource management into the businesses.

Unregulated subsidiaries of a telephone operating company are developing human resource strategies to address their unique human resource issues, such as technical staffing, sales effectiveness, and international staffing. At the same time, these strategies are formulated within the context of the far larger telephone company, which has different issues and concerns. The balancing of subsidiary and enterprise strategies is in itself an issue being addressed by the corporate and subsidiary executives.

SUMMARY

Managers need to focus their actions on the areas which will truly make a difference in a company's competitiveness. In times when there are far more "top priorities" than there is time to address them, *focus* is essential for managers. In managing human resources, there are so many ways to spend time and resources—most seemingly worthwhile. Managers need some basis for deciding what actions are most important for achieving business objectives.

Strategic management enables managers to respond to environmental changes based on a defined business mission, vision, and values. Strategies are directional plans that guide management actions in the pursuit of opportunities. In an environment of intense competition, management seeks to gain and sustain advantage, not merely keep up. Strategies point the way for the most promising changes.

Human resource strategies are directional plans addressing people-related business issues. They are functional management strategies developed and implemented by managers in the same way as other strategies. Human resource strategies are important because they help management determine how to manage people in support of the business strategies. They provide *alignment* of human resource practices and business strategy.

Human resource strategy provides a focus on human resource activities/programs necessary for the success of the business. It also focuses management attention on actions to a greater degree than traditional human resource planning: "What will be done to address key issues?" Managers need a sense of priorities if they are to manage people effectively in a rapidly changing environment.

It may seem faddish to use the term *strategy*, particularly in a book that succeeds one on human resource *planning*. Human resource plans may include strategies, but more typically they refer to operational courses of action, such as recruiting and staffing, management succession, or redeployment plans.

I believe that strategies will persist as guiding forces for companies seeking to manage necessary change in the 1990s and beyond. Strategy has been valued by managers for centuries, originating in military use. As companies seek to win decisively in increasingly competitive fields, strategy will become increasingly important. Managers will aggressively define their competitive threats and opportunities, build on their strengths, and build up their weaknesses. They will seek to manage human resources to ensure nimble, lean, quick, and flexible organizations.

In practice, many themes of change are implied strategies addressing people-related issues: total quality management, service quality and customer satisfaction, culture change, intrapreneurialism and creativity, or process management. I have no doubt that new themes will arise and will be valuable in guiding management action in the years ahead. However, strategy, as directional plans for change, continues to be important.

A. FOCUS ON MANAGING: THE FLEXIBLE ORGANIZATION

The relative stability and predictability of business are being replaced by uncertainty, complexity, and rapid change. Intense global competition, rapidly changing technology, shifting demography, economic fluctuations, and other dynamic conditions require companies to be adaptive and swift. Companies are stripping away long-standing management policies and practices impeding flexibility and are adopting new practices to foster desired initiative, innovation, and change.

In this rapid transformation, executives are asked to be more than managers; they are expected to be leaders of change. General Electric seeks leaders with the capacity to turn threats into opportunities and to excite others about a new vision of the future. Another company looks for "bold new leaders who can make things happen." In this era, said H. Ross Perot, "slow, gradual, evolutionary change is the same as none at all."

As a result of these strategic factors, companies face alternative ways to manage, relative to their strategic situations. In concept, there are four alternative situations that call for alignment with the complexity and rate of change of the business: institutional, flexible, entrepreneurial (garage), and niche. These are illustrated in Exhibit A-1.

Organizational
Complexity

High	Institutional	Flexible
Low	Niche	Entrepreneurial
	Slow	Rapid

Rate of Change

Human resource strategy helps define the direction, pace, and priorities for an organization to change, in the context of business strategies. This framework is used in the following chapters to help define flexible practices and differentiate them from the alternatives.

Institutional Organizations

Companies with strategies calling for slow change typically maintain an organization that promotes stability, caution, risk avoidance, and careful management action. Companies operating in regulated environments (such as electric utilities) or companies in mature markets with mature products (e.g., industrial equipment, railways) are often managed as institutions.

In traditional, institutional enterprises, management emphasizes control, consistency, and certainty. The organizations are complex, and the pace of change is slow. Planning emphasizes financial goals and measurements; risk is avoided or managed cautiously. Managers are typically developed and promoted from within; career paths are well defined. Careers emphasize mastery and progression through job assignments, supplemented by formal training. Rewards normally emphasize base salary, employee benefits, and job security.

The institutional model was the norm for most of this century, a period in which change was slow and the most respected businesses were the very largest and most complex, such as AT&T, General Motors, Exxon, U.S. Steel, Bank of America, and other leading corporations. The practices demonstrated by such companies were also the "gospel" according to leading business schools and management consulting firms. American management practices were at that time the envy of the world, in terms of optimizing the management of large, established businesses.

The organization structure is hierarchical, with single lines of authority and accountability. While a minimum number of levels is desired, the need for control and risk avoidance requires management oversight. Spans of management, too, may be too narrow for the same reason. Information flows vertically, with interactions among units intended to "go through channels," relying on key managers as the coordination points. Staff functions exist to assist, monitor, and control: "Line manages, staff advises." Also, managerial work is separated from other work, viewing management as a specialized function (Dougherty, 1989).

This type of organization, in its pure and perfect form a bureaucracy, is exactly what a slow-change, high-control strategy calls for. It is the traditional model of organization followed by business for decades, and upon which classic organization theory and principles are based. When appropriate and fully implemented, it is considered the most "efficient" form.

Entrepreneurial Organizations

At the other extreme are simple organizations that are fast-growing and changing. Most businesses begin as entrepreneurial enterprises, or "garages" (characterizing entrepreneurs as starting out in a garage, as did Hewlett and

Packard and others). Apple Computer epitomized the entrepreneurial organization in its early years—and continues to be regarded as such by many of its employees even as the company expands and grows complex.

Fast-growing, fast-changing, and simple organizations such as ventures and entrepreneurial enterprises are typically managed directly and informally. Management involves experimentation, action on immediate needs and tasks, and opportunism. Informal practices are sufficient because the businesses are typically small and not yet complex.

Managers fill various roles and functions, and "stretch" to meet expanding job demands. Staffing for growth is typically through external recruiting; few resources are devoted to development of talent from within, except by job challenges. Rewards include direct satisfaction from achievements, but also compensation through equity participation. The companies attract talent through the excitement of entrepreneurship, not principally through employee benefits, job security, or long-term career paths.

The seeming ideal organization to many managers is the entrepreneurship. Here is a small, simple venture (or "garage" business) that is full of excitement and change. The objective is to survive, prosper, and grow. And to do this, the enterprise needs to be nimble, creative, and efficient. It is the type of organization that Tom Peters must dream of: biased toward action, close to the customer, entrepreneurial and autonomous, hands-on, value-driven, simple, and lean (Peters & Waterman, 1982).

Whether an independent enterprise or a venture within a larger organization, an entrepreneurial organization acts small. The managers are the hubs of wheels, working closely with employees to get the work done. Management is on a first-name basis, open, and "shirtsleeves." There is a mutual respect among managers and employees; in fact, strong values and culture help keep it that way. Spans of management are wide, relationships are fluid, levels and accountabilities are not particularly relevant. There is a minimum of procedure, policy, and protocol. One of the "turn-ons" in a garage is the absence of such bureaucracy.

Usually providing only one or a few products or services, this type of organization does not have many alternative structures. Only as the business grows and becomes more complex does structure become important. These are organizations built around people.

Niche Organizations

Garages that do not grow and that experience little change become "niches." Franchises, "mom and pop" businesses, small but mature manufacturers and service firms, and other specialized firms are managed as relatively simple businesses without much need (or resources) for change. Franchisees, for example, are expected to manage the business "by the book," without variation, innovation, or major change in complexity of the business. Of course, most businesses in America are niches, employing more workers than any other type of business.

Flexible Organizations

A flexible organization, by contrast, is the most adaptable form for a complex enterprise. If they grow, garages become more complex but, hopefully, still rapidly changing organizations. Hewlett-Packard, PepsiCo, and Digital Equipment are three examples of "garages" that have become large and complex companies, still managed flexibly.

Managers in flexible organizations recognize the need for a balance between entrepreneurship and formal, disciplined management. Interest in innovation, creativity, initiative, and competitiveness reflects acceptance of the need for change, but in the context of maintaining the management coordination necessary in complex organizations.

To be flexible means balancing order and chaos. There must be enough latitude for business units to thrive in their marketplaces as entrepreneurial businesses, yet enough discipline to achieve the necessary benefits of large-scale integration and management value added in a highly competitive, global marketplace. Interest in innovation, creativity, initiative, and competitiveness reflects widespread acceptance of the need for change, but in the context of maintaining the management coordination necessary in complex organizations.

Managing effectively in a flexible organization requires adaptive management policies and practices, as well as collaborative management and human resource staff roles and responsibilities. Working with a formal hierarchy is a network of relationships that helps individuals work in teams and directly with each other. At IBM, for example, employees are encouraged to spend the first few weeks on any new job familiarizing themselves with their new surroundings, so that they can get to know the people and the resources available and establish the network they will work within.

The flexible form is becoming more common, because the strategic drivers in most companies impel management to seek increased flexibility. In a sense, flexible organizations are more difficult to manage, with dual or multiple reporting relationships, lateral relationships, increased teamwork, and empowered employees making decisions independently. It can drive a traditionally oriented manager crazy.

It is said there are no flexible organizations, only flexible people. If so, a flexible structure is one that merely doesn't impede behavior that will lead to desired results. Digital Equipment has been regarded as one of the best "non-managed companies" in America. The structure was sufficiently loose and flexible so that its professionals and managers could shape their organizations and tasks in the ways they considered most suitable.

Flexible structures are flat, lean, and changing. They are, essentially, always in transition. When people change jobs, the structure changes and the informal networks change as well. Staff and line are partners, working jointly toward achieving objectives. And teams are a vital force—whether focused as a work unit, or as temporary project or coordinating linkages across units or functions. Information flows freely in a flexible organization, aided by direct access to information systems and among employees.

The challenge for most organizations in the 1990s and beyond is to move toward the flexible mode of managing—to be sufficiently large and complex to have a marketplace impact, but also to be nimble, adaptive, and innovative. In sum, the challenge is to find the best of entrepreneurial and institutional management to fit the strategic challenges of a business.

Companies best representing these management practices include computer and software companies, financial service firms, high-technology manufacturers, and other businesses requiring a high degree of adaptability. While few companies have all these characteristics, most companies today have some flexible practices and are adopting others. Siemens, Europe's second largest electronics firm, typifies this important shift. "Siemens has been known for tight organization, loyal employees, financial conservatism, devotion to systems, and management led by engineers," noted *The Economist*. "But Siemens managers have now decided that their future lies in high-growth sectors where nimbleness is better rewarded than discipline. To prosper, they must develop new corporate skills."

Many businesses that are institutionally managed are trying to manage as more complex but flexible organizations. In virtually every aspect of managing human resources, companies seek to move away from rigid, closed, change-resistant approaches for managing and toward more adaptive, open, dynamic approaches.

PART ONE

DEFINING THE STRATEGIC CONTEXT

CHAPTER 2

FOCUSING ON HUMAN RESOURCE ISSUES

The key source of competitiveness in the '90s is that our people work more effectively than your people; our leaders are better than your leaders.

William E. Reif

Through strategic management, companies continually assess and address opportunities for gaining and sustaining competitive advantage. It is through this lens that human resource issues come into view. As business strategies are increasingly people-intensive, the human resource implications of planned business changes become prominent and command specific management attention.

In the 1990s and beyond, people will increasingly make the critical difference in enabling companies to win competitively. "As customers increasingly make choices on the basis of how people perform rather than how products perform, the management of human resources becomes a primary source of differentiation" (Reif, 1991). The emphasis will be on the abilities, skills, and performance of employees who satisfy customer needs 100% every time.

Human resource issues are gaps between the current situation and the desired situation. They represent opportunities for people to contribute more effectively to the achievement of business strategies. Definition of issues is the first step in the process of formulating human resource strategies and aligning human resource actions with business priorities.

This chapter examines how companies define human resource issues. It discusses:

• How companies identify, analyze, and select human resource issues which will be addressed through human resource strategies
• Current human resource issues that derive from business strategy and issues deriving from environmental changes affecting business strategy

Issues change as conditions change; however, the concerns represented here suggest the relevance of different types of issues to business strategy.

EXHIBIT 2-1 STEPS IN DEFINING ISSUES

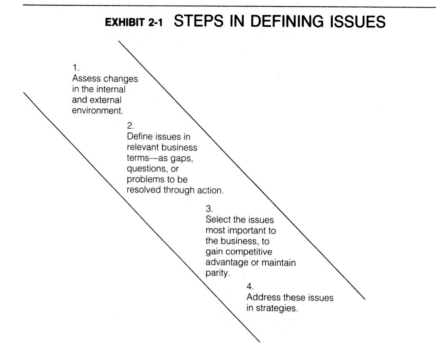

1.
Assess changes
in the internal
and external
environment.

2.
Define issues in
relevant business
terms—as gaps,
questions, or
problems to be
resolved through action.

3.
Select the issues
most important to
the business, to
gain competitive
advantage or maintain
parity.

4.
Address these issues
in strategies.

Four steps in defining issues are discussed: environmental assessment, definition of issues in business terms, selection of issues, and addressing these issues through strategies. These steps are illustrated in Exhibit 2-1.

ENVIRONMENTAL ASSESSMENT

The first step in defining human resource issues is an assessment of the changes in the internal and external environment of a business. Environmental assessment entails scanning a company's internal organization and realms outside the organization for information on changes that may affect the company's future performance. It is a fact-gathering exercise: collecting and examining data that suggest future trends and changes.

This activity may be integrated with an environmental assessment conducted for overall business strategy formulation or may be conducted separately and focused on human resource subjects. It may also be separate, but parallel, contributing to and drawing from other analysis efforts.

In this initial step, managers search out and consider all information that may be relevant in any way. Ninety percent of the information may not ultimately be acted upon, but unless the sweep is wide, the essential ten percent may be missed.

EXHIBIT 2-2 TWO APPROACHES FOR
ENVIRONMENTAL ASSESSMENT

FUTURE VISION
Desired Future Situation:
Where We Want To Be

Futures   GAPS   Change
Analysis   Analysis

TODAY
Current Situation:
Where We Are Today

There are two fundamental ways to look for noteworthy changes in the environment: from today toward the future and from the future back to today. The former represents analysis of incremental changes; the latter represents analysis of possible future conditions. These two approaches, often used in tandem, are illustrated in Exhibit 2-2.

Incremental Change Analysis

Most business focuses on the current situation, with changes defined on an iterative, cumulative basis. In this context, issues represent problems or opportunities for changes from the current situation. The gaps represent ways that a company may achieve or enhance a competitive edge (Greer, Jackson, & Fiorito, 1989; Ulrich, 1989).

The most common way to define issues is to assess the changes that are expected to occur. These are derived from either internal or external changes, intended by management or occurring as a result of uncontrolled forces (as in work force changes). Issues are identified in the way that people normally think—incrementally from the present toward the future.

In this process, managers identify and evaluate human resource issues by sorting through available strategic planning, competitive, and environmental information for evidence of changes having human resource implications—and then define human resource issues that may be addressed. Such analysis may examine employee productivity issues, service quality, staffing surpluses or shortfalls, succession needs, skill requirements, utilization, costs, turnover/retention patterns, or employee attitudes.

Managers also obtain and consider perspectives of relevant constituents, such as other managers and employees, vendors, suppliers, and customers.

Companies solicit inputs from managers at various levels through their participation in the planning process or through interviews, focus groups, or surveys with key managers. Many companies survey employees, either specifically for planning inputs or more broadly as an assessment of organizational climate and human resource practices. Companies may involve employees through interviews or focus groups to help define issues and alternative strategies. Some also interview or survey customers, contractors, and other business partners regarding human resource issues to be addressed.

Environmental scanning is used to identify prospective human resource issues deriving from changing external conditions. Scanning the many changes occurring in social, political, legislative, demographic, economic, technological and other areas yields a wide array of issues that may be considered. Some companies, such as General Electric, once collected extensive environmental scan information as input to human resource planning (Schreiber, 1982). Today, abundant information is readily available to companies from secondary sources (newspapers, magazines, research publications, consulting firm studies, ongoing data bases, industry or association studies, etc.) (Coates, 1987; London, Bassman, & Fernandez, 1990).

Companies identify implications of significant demographic, health and safety, legislative, and other external trends that influence organizational conditions, such as work force availability, labor mobility/turnover, union relations, employee attitudes and productivity, or substance abuse (Craft, Fleisher, & Schoenfeld, 1990; Schuler, 1989; Sweeney & Nussbaum, 1989).

Companies also assess their human resource practices relative to those of competitor companies. This involves examining the relative human resource strengths and vulnerabilities of the company and its key competitors as well as assessing the company's talent, management practices, and human resource systems and programs relative to other companies—to identify opportunities for improvement. "We may be doing as well as, or even better than, our competitors in various services, but that doesn't mean we can't create an even larger positive gap between us and them," said a GTE executive (Deutsch, 1990).

Benchmarking, the process of identifying and emulating companies that are best at a given activity, has become widely used since it was first introduced in the 1970s. Used initially to examine competitor product characteristics (e.g., copiers and automobiles), it is now used to model customer service, systems, training, and virtually any activity. Companies search for and examine the best practices in management among companies, not just in the industry but anywhere they exist.

Such benchmarking need not require broad surveys. Increasingly, companies zero in on just a few companies that are recognized as having "best practices" in a specific area of interest. For example, when L. L. Bean, a catalog distribution company, wanted to benchmark its management succession and development systems, it visited 3M, IBM, and Disney. "We're happy to share our information on distribution, and we've found that companies are happy to share information on the areas they're best at,'' said Austin Farrar, Bean's human resource vice president (Deutsch, 1990).

Where specific issues are identified, focused data analysis is often conducted, digging more deeply into the ramifications of identified changes. For example, forecasting of future staffing demand and supply within a company may be conducted through use of computer-based modeling. Once a major effort involving custom programming for a mainframe computer, such forecasting is now a desktop computer exercise. Data necessary for forecasting and analysis may be downloaded from mainframe data systems and processed using generally available software.

Companies often focus on issues of concern as subjects for special study— as a step preceding the development of a strategy or action plan. Once they identify substance abuse, AIDS testing, or applicant literacy as a possible concern, they collect additional information to help define the scope of the issue and alternative responses. The environmental assessment process, then, is iterative.

Futures Analysis

Environmental assessment may also focus on the longer-range future—through visioning or "futures analysis." Here, issues are identified and analyzed outside the context of the current situation (Choates, Coates, Jarratt, & Heinz, 1986; Schrenk, 1988). Companies define issues through a broader, more conceptual process of looking into the future.

Such analysis allows companies to project future conditions and set future objectives to be achieved. It represents a leap to the future rather than step-by-step progression from today's situation forward to the future. It allows managers to assess the future relevance of issues that appear important today and thereby identify important human resource issues.

In the late 1980s, many companies looked to the year 2000, to encourage forward thinking about how the world and their companies would be different at the turn of the century. Companies often position such analysis to look a decade ahead, farther than the current strategic planning time period. As we move through the 1990s, such a vision will need to extend into the twenty-first century.

Futures analysis is an inherent requirement for strategic thinking. It requires defining the forces shaping the future, evaluating alternative future states, setting objectives, and selecting courses of action that will yield needed changes in direction for the enterprise. While incremental change analysis looks at continuities, futures analysis looks at discontinuities (Drucker, 1980).

Future analysis provides at least a conceptual vision of the future that can help identify and define organizational or competitive requirements. For example, General Motors is seeking to implement its vision for the twenty-first century. The plan calls for GM to be the highest quality at the lowest cost; to be international in scope and make the most efficient use of resources; and to use the highest technology, the most innovative and creative people, and a very efficient supplier network. New qualities of leadership are also foreseen—"management with the vision to determine where the corporation should go, as well as the ability to involve the entire organization in that vision and to create enthusiasm and support for their ideas."

Northern Telecom, Ltd., a telecommunications equipment company, announced an objective in 1990 of expanding revenue five times within ten years, to $30 billion. To achieve the plan, called Vision 2000, the company must improve its international performance and capture about 10% of the projected $300 billion market for switching and transmission systems. The plan called for initiatives in its fiber-optic transmission systems and a network design concept called Fiber World. According to Paul Stern, the CEO, "By Vision 2000 we mean, What do we want to be when we grow up?"

In its simplest forms, futures analysis involves open thinking about future issues and options. Companies use brainstorming, visioning, or modified Delphi analysis (iterative survey of experts) to help define the future human resource issues that need to be addressed. It is an exercise that may involve many participants within the company as well as outside consultants or others.

Futurists, functioning on company planning staffs and as independent consultants, have helped assess the prospective futures in which companies would operate. Their value added appears to lie in their work on demographic, technological, and environmental futures. In other areas—such as sociopolitical changes worldwide, energy availability, economic conditions, or legislation—they have been less helpful because of significant, unexpected changes in these areas. Regarding human resource planning, the most valuable work has been in assessing the implications of trends and emerging developments for management practices, such as work force projections (Hallett, 1987; Johnston, 1989).

Sources of Issues

In conducting an environmental assessment, a company looks within the organization, to other organizations, and to the overall business environment to identify trends and conditions that may give rise to issues requiring attention (Certo & Peter, 1988; Wheelen & Hunger, 1987). Exhibit 2-3 illustrates these three sources of issues.

The internal environment includes the effectiveness of research, manufacturing, sales and marketing, human resources, and other functions affecting organizational performance. It also includes processes: the linked actions and decisions involving different functions or units, such as resource allocation, planning, management development, or customer service. Resources within the company—capital, technical, and people—are also a source of issues, as they may not be deployed optimally. And, of course, the organization struc-

---

EXHIBIT 2-3 SOURCES OF CHANGES PRODUCING ISSUES

Internal Environment	Other Organizations	External Environment
Functional effectiveness	Customers	Demographics
Processes	Competitors	Legal
Resources	Vendors/suppliers	Political
Organization	Business partners	Social
Employees and managers	Employed work force	Technology
	Labor organizations	International
		Economic

←——————— Business Strategy Formulation ———————→

---

ture, culture, and employee and management talent represent a source of opportunities for improvement.

Companies look to other organizations for indications of gaps or opportunities as well. The most important are customers (and prospective customers) and competitors. Other businesses that support the business are often relevant, as are employees in other companies and labor organizations.

By assessing changing competitive circumstances, companies identify current or future threats or opportunities created by actions of competitors. The pace of change continues to be rapid, driven by new technology, new products and shorter cycle times, aggressive competitive initiatives and more rapid responses, and more diverse, flexible actions in local markets.

To a varying degree, companies also scan the broader external environment for relevant demographic, legal, political, social, and technological trends. When there is a high public awareness of environmental changes, companies tend to give such changes more consideration. For example, demographic trends are driving significant changes in work force composition and attitudes by the year 2000. Also, companies striving to operate globally consider more closely relevant trends internationally and in specific countries and regions of the world.

As part of its environmental assessment for strategic planning, many companies organize their findings as an analysis of strengths, weaknesses, opportunities, and threats (SWOTs) for each business. This approach, which bridges the three levels of sources outlined, provides a succinct assessment of negative factors which need to be built up and positive factors which can be built upon. It is a useful frame of reference for examining human resource issues (Thompson & Strickland, 1987).

Environmental assessment is a critical step in strategic management because it provides an "outside in" flow of information and ideas. Competitive strategies need to be based on external changes, and not based on preconceived thinking about threats and opportunities. According to strategy guru Michael Porter, "The essence of formulating competitive strategy is relating a company to its environment. The best strategy for a given firm is ultimately a unique construction reflecting its particular circumstances" (Porter, 1980).

DEFINING HUMAN RESOURCE ISSUES

Changes are not necessarily people-related business issues. Political and economic changes in China may be significant but not relevant to a company or to its human resource management. New optical scanning technology may become widely available at low cost, but until it is adopted by a company, its use does not give rise to a human resource issue. Trends may suggest that employees will extend their careers and defer retirement, but if a company has a young work force, this trend has little effect.

As distinct gaps between the current situation and the desired future, issues represent an opportunity for improvement or a chance to gain new competitive advantage. In a negative sense, they are problems or shortcomings that must be resolved—a barrier or obstacle to performance that must be removed or, at best, avoided. Issues are sources of "pain or gain."

Specificity of Definition

Some human resource issues may easily be defined in specific, concrete terms, such as shortfalls of staffing relative to planned expansion needs or specific skills required to support new products or technology. Just from direct observation and experience, managers can see issues that need to be addressed. Other issues are more difficult to define, such as the challenge of becoming a more global business. Some are complex, with no easy solutions, such as health care cost containment. Many issues are interrelated and, hence, difficult to isolate one from another, such as work force skills, motivation, turnover, customer service, and employee involvement. As a result, it takes a company considerable time to fully define and resolve important issues (Heisler, Jones, & O'Benham, 1989).

Furthermore, some issues have value implications; they evoke different emotional responses from different people. And sometimes the reactions conflict, requiring trade-offs in resolving issues. For example, managing work force diversity is a social objective to some, a business necessity to others. Adopting more flexible management practices while yielding institutional traditions is also traumatic for some people. For example, treating people differently, according to business situations and performance, is not always perceived as treating people fairly and consistently. Accordingly, expert knowledge or data alone cannot define these issues.

Well-defined issues provide a clear focus on the gap that needs to be bridged. The following are several examples of actual issues identified by companies:

• Certain nationalities and women are underrepresented, particularly at senior levels (The World Bank).
• There are unrealized operating efficiencies that may be achieved by simplifying, consolidating, delegating, restructuring, automating, and eliminating work (Burroughs Wellcome Co.).

- With our decentralized operating strategy, we need to find ways to facilitate transfer of new technology/approaches for operations and customer service among stores, particularly from "R&D stores" (The Kroger Co.).
- In the next five years, we will lose many of our experienced professional and technical experts as staff retire or leave (The World Bank).
- Unisys has a diffuse set of subcultures rather than a corporate culture; many management practices conflict with our espoused core values, causing skepticism in the work force (Unisys).
- Personnel shortages in certain skill areas create work load imbalances, affect staff morale, and affect continuity of patient care (Kaiser Permanente).
- There is a gap between our Aspirations Statement and reality (see Exhibit 4-7) (Levi Strauss).

Issues are typically identified at each level of an organization. Divisional, decentralized companies assess people-related business issues in each business unit/situation and review them to identify commonalities and differences on a companywide basis. Implicitly, plans include overlaying company and business unit issues using a common framework.

What Issues Are Not

Many efforts to define human resource issues end up with statements that are anything but issues. They are too broad, too presumptive, too action-oriented, or too functional.

Some company statements of human resource issues are so broad that they could apply to any company and imply directional plans, challenges, or goals rather than business-related issues. For example:

- More effective utilization of our human resources
- A more risk-oriented, high-performance organization
- Managing a more diverse work force
- Skills obsolescence

In other cases, the issues are defined as "assumptions," which limits their definition as problems, opportunities, or gaps. As assumptions, they are facts, taken directly from environmental assessment and put into a plan.

- Fewer electronic engineers will graduate than will be required by employers.
- In the future, global executives will require fluency in at least one nonnative language.
- Increased stock ownership will enhance employee identification with company strategy and objectives.

Also, many human resource issues are overly action-oriented and functional. They state actions that relate to particular human resource functional activities, somehow implying inherent issues.

- Managers do not spend sufficient time managing their people; they are acting as individual contributors.
- A new, integrated human resource information/payroll system needs to be implemented.
- Performance management systems need to be redesigned.
- Market pricing for salary structure needs to be established.
- Employees need earlier and broader orientation to the company.

Needs may be relevant, but they are not people-related business issues that are addressed in a strategy. These may be responses to issues as part of near-term operating or action plans.

In such statements, there is no "pain" identified relevant to the company. The statements should be examined and redefined as gaps—opportunities or problems facing the company without presumed solutions.

SELECTING ISSUES

Managers prefer to focus on a few important, actionable concerns. They recognize a need to be selective and to concentrate management attention and limited resources. Accordingly, companies apply a screening process to limit issues to those which they believe have a direct business impact and are issues that can be addressed effectively.

Managers feel that they can take action on pragmatic, "real world" issues that have a significant near-term impact. One company considers an issue important when management of people can "make or break" achievement of business strategies. Companies also consider inherent conflicts and trade-offs among issues (e.g., low cost and high service, union avoidance and productivity). Of course, management interest, budget constraints, and available resources are usually influential factors.

Screening Criteria

Some human resource issues stand out as opportunities. The process of defining human resource issues ideally results in a clear focus on the issues that matter the most. Although there may be many important human resource issues, companies find it most effective to focus on a few, important, actionable concerns. This helps develop a sense of urgency and builds commitment to action. From the wide range of possibly important issues, management must select those that warrant attention.

Choices are made using various criteria. Often, the perceptions of managers or human resource staff drive priorities. These perceptions may reflect the business interest, but may also reflect limited perspective, local interests, personal agendas and preferences, and other factors that may not serve the best business interests. Budgeting processes may defer high-cost priorities, sustain initiatives that are already under way, and diminish those that cannot demonstrate a near-term return on investment.

Some companies formally rank issues and then develop management action plans for these selected issues. To prioritize issues, they consider the importance of each issue, the organization's capacity to address it, the urgency or timing of the issue, resource constraints, management perceptions, and current work in progress. At General Electric, a process was developed that screens issues by assessing (1) the probability of the issue occurring, (2) the impact on the business if it occurs, and (3) the company's ability to influence, manage, or control the issue. These factors represent an issue's relevance to the business (Schreiber, 1982).

All business issues have human resource implications. Any of the many changes occurring in a business has an impact on people—whether cost reduction actions, restructuring, new technology, business expansion, or restructuring. Successful implementation of business changes requires that human resource issues be addressed effectively.

Similarly, all relevant human resource issues are business issues. Wherever their source, and whoever is concerned with the issues, they are important because they affect a company's capacity to win competitively. Employee health care, changing employee attitudes, employee turnover, skill development, and managing work force diversity are important to management because they may have a positive impact on the business. To ignore these issues may adversely affect business performance.

Competitive Advantage

The most important criterion for screening issues is the prospective effect on competitive advantage. Increasingly, business strategies focus on opportunities to gain or sustain competitive advantage—a fundamentally advantageous position from which to compete. A competitive advantage involves a success factor in the market, substantial enough to make a difference and sustainable in the face of changing conditions and competitive actions. It is gained by focusing on variables that clearly differentiate a company from its competitors. Such advantage allows a company to increase volume, reduce costs, retain customers, and hence increase profitability.

Attaining such an advantage requires assessment of a company's strength (distinctive factors) and shortfalls relative to competitors. It also requires purposeful assessment of opportunities for innovation—ways to gain an edge in competitive practices. Hence the search for competitive advantage fits well with the process of defining human resource issues.

In the 1980s, many companies focused on two primary ways to gain and sustain competitive advantage: cost leadership and differentiation of products (Porter, 1980, 1985). Companies rushed to position their products and businesses to win competitively on these bases. Michael Porter and his followers relegated procurement, technology development, firm infrastructure, customer service, and human resource management to secondary or support roles in value creation.

Today, however, companies are quick to respond to competitive initiatives. As a result, cost leadership or product differentiation is difficult to gain or to sustain for more than a short time. Any attained advantage, then, may now bring companies only up to *parity* with competitors.

The most appropriate screen for human resource issues is the potential gain in competitive advantage. Limited resources and time need to be devoted to the issues that will yield the greatest gain for the business. In the 1990s and beyond, people will make the difference competitively.

Virtually any human resource factor may help differentiate a company from its competitors if it brings some perceived benefit to the customer, directly or indirectly. Managers increasingly see service, development and retention of staff, and organizational performance as primary factors (Reif, 1991). The choice of issues will change as conditions change, but there are always those that will yield the greatest benefit for competitive advantage.

In the 1991 Human Resource Business School program, human resource executives from twenty-five companies examined in depth their company SWOT, strategic plans and objectives, and human resource issues. In one exercise, they listed and discussed the human resource issues their companies, as a group, considered most important. These are listed in Exhibit 2-4.

EXHIBIT 2-4 HUMAN RESOURCE ISSUES: PARITY OR ADVANTAGE?

Competitive Parity

Normal compensation practices
Human resource information
Employee assistance
Management of diversity
Employee/work force literacy
Quality of work life initiatives
Flexible working hours
Legal and regulatory compliance
Relocation management
Employee selection
Benefits cost containment
Employee orientation
International human resource management

Competitive Advantage

A risk-reward business culture
Management focus and execution on critical issues
Communicating and acting more rapidly
Truly superior innovation
Competence in managing change
Teamwork and flexible, streamlined organization
Partnerships with school systems and universities
Redefined union relationships
Distinct cost advantage, superior productivity
Service quality
Superior employee skills

More significant, however, was their sorting of these issues into two classes: those that are necessary to maintain parity with competitors and those that will gain competitive advantage. Some issues which they had addressed initially for purposes of gaining an edge had become matters of maintaining parity (e.g., management of diversity, compensation programs). Others, still quite important and time-consuming, are required to maintain parity (e.g., benefits cost containment, international human resource management). The group perceived that the issues suggesting competitive advantage are typically more difficult to define and address.

ISSUES DERIVING FROM BUSINESS CHANGES

Typically, the most important human resource issues arise from changes in the business, usually in the context of business strategies and operational plans. Companies first examine their current business strategies to define human resource issues. Human resource issues derive from changes as organizations refocus, rebuild, and adjust to continuing, sometimes chaotic change. More broadly, issues reflect the current "drivers" of the business—the factors that determine changes occurring in the direction or pace of a business. Exhibit 2-5 lists some issues that derive from two major types of business change: improving business performance and managing business growth and change.

Maintaining Low Costs and Strong Cash Flow

Companies have become expert at finding ways to reduce personnel-related costs. Organizations are leaner and flatter, staffing levels are down, alternative staffing patterns have been adopted to lower costs and increase flexibility, benefits and compensation costs have been restructured, and information technology is replacing or reducing labor-intensive work. In the 1990s, the search

---

EXHIBIT 2-5 HUMAN RESOURCE ISSUES DERIVING FROM BUSINESS CHANGES

Improving Business Performance

    Maintaining low costs and strong cash flow
    Improving product and service quality
    Effectively introducing new technology
    Building superior capabilities
    Maintaining high employee commitment

Managing Growth and Change

    Meeting changing staffing needs
    Making a merger or acquisition work
    Effectively restructuring
    Becoming more global as a business

---

for ways to reduce costs and increase efficiency will continue and will be reflected in human resource issues defined as important to management.

Many costs are not people-related, such as raw material, energy costs, cost of capital (interest expense or dividends), capital equipment, facilities or rent, etc. But even in a capital-intensive business, such as an oil company, personnel costs are typically 30% or more of expenses.

High capital costs sharpen management focus on cost containment, revenue generation, and, therefore, profitable operations. High financial leverage (reflected in a high debt-to-equity ratio in a company's capital structure) drives management to optimize short-term profitability and cash flow for purposes of covering interest expenses.

Where leverage is relatively low (high equity), or where ownership is closely held (privately owned or with large proportions of stock held by a few owners or investors), management is more likely to focus on longer-term development of the business. Cash flow generated through operations may be invested for future development of the business instead of for debt service. Also, private ownership may be a distinct plus in that it protects the company from the Wall Street focus on immediate-term profitability.

Quality of Products and Services

Companies are continually seeking to upgrade or improve the quality of the products or services provided and reduce the time it takes to design, develop, produce, and deliver them.

Step-by-step improvements based on measures, feedback, and learning are imperative to a company's ability to compete. PepsiCo has overtaken McDonald's as the largest and fastest-growing operator of fast-food restaurants by continually introducing changes in products, systems, and organization that affect every aspect of its operations.

Areas of concern typically include:

- Streamlining and decentralizing organization to get "closer to the customer"
- Delegating authority and empowering employees to act more quickly to meet customer needs
- Improving the speed and availability of information needed to act
- Speeding production cycle times, achieving just-in-time deliveries and rapid response to market changes and customer requirements

For example, Motorola is widely known for its extraordinary success in reducing the time required to develop new products and bring them to market. This strategic objective, considered competitively vital, required intensive training of Motorola employees and restructuring of the way products are developed and produced.

New Technology

Companies are rapidly applying new technology. Every management function is being redefined through the development and use of new systems: research and engineering, manufacturing, materials management, sales and marketing, and communications.

Before he retired in 1989, Roger Smith of General Motors observed, "People are a bigger part of the automation equation than anyone could have predicted. And much more upfront education and training of people will be required to meet the higher levels of automation. It's my belief that with automation we may even have labor shortages—especially of trained people."

Information technologies are changing the way people communicate, work, and play. Information is not controlled by the management hierarchy, but is readily and quickly available to all employees, empowering them to be direct participants in the management of the business. Such changes are driven by advances in computers and microelectronics. As personal computers and computer networks become commonplace, employees gain a personal information access and processing capacity that is unprecedented.

Communications will become universally available, through the mobile communications environment that is rapidly developing: portable cellular phones, facsimile machines, wristwatch pagers, and computers with twenty-four-hour accessibility. Wristwatch telephones, with numbers assigned to individuals for life, are anticipated in the not-too-distant future.

Touch screens, digital sketch pads, voice-recognition systems, and optical scanners make computers easier to use. The computer, one observer noted, will be fully accepted once it is as easy to operate as a microwave oven. Information technology has the potential to be used increasingly as a teaching and learning aid.

Introduction of advanced technology provides only a temporary competitive advantage, as others quickly achieve parity by catching up. It is the effective *application* of the technology—the productivity through people—that yields an advantage.

General Electric found, for example, that "investment in product and process technology pays off best (as measured by the hard productivity numbers) when it is combined with employee training and new flexible work structures." CEO Jack Welch calls for "productivity growth and competitive advantage through people power, for company cultures to be guided by speed, simplicity, and self-confidence" (Doyle, 1989).

- Speed is the ability to anticipate and act, instead of review and react; it is the ability to see and seize competitive advantage first.
- Simplicity is clarity in understanding competitive facts and in articulating a competitive vision instead of resorting to complexity and sophistication for their own sake; simplicity is crucial for speed.
- Self-confidence is necessary for people to be willing to be simple and swift.

Companies need to consider the human resource implications of emerging technologies and their application.

Building Superior Capabilities

Advantage may come through distinctive capabilities of people in an organization such as competence developed by a core business, e.g., a technical competence (3M's competence in adhesives) or a management or processing competence (Banc One's skills in data processing and retail banking).

Even where the district competency of a company is anchored in technology, that technology is valuable only if it is transferred across units and product lines. Canon, for examaple, has special expertise in precision mechanics, fine optics, and microelectronics which it has effectively applied to cameras, printers, faxes, calculators, copiers, and other products.

Companies have sought to develop a superior capability in various ways, for example, by upgrading talent/capabilities through recruitment, training, and development of managers with multinational experience and capabilities. Transfers of talent across groups are essential for technology transfer. At Canon, "competence carriers" move regularly between the copier business and the professional optical-products business (Prahalad, 1990). In a sense, capabilities may enable a company to become a lower-cost producer of products and services.

Employee Commitment

Employee performance will be more critical to service quality and other aspects of competitive performance. Accordingly, a major issue for companies will be the need to empower employees to act in the company's best interests. Talented employees, in short supply and high demand, will be mobile. As GE's Frank Doyle observed, "If they feel unduly constrained and unable to control their work product and workplace, the growing scarcity of skilled people will allow them simply to vote with their feet and move from employer to employer" (Doyle, 1989).

Employee commitment helps differentiate a company from its competitors when it brings some perceived benefit to the customer, directly or indirectly. Creative incentive compensation plans, gainsharing, profit sharing, or ESOP programs may be a plus. Positive union relations (or the absence of unions), intense employee loyalty and retention, better trained or cross-trained staff, superior teamwork and communications, and an image of being a good employer may all be differentiating advantages for a company.

IBM recognized long ago that its "respect for people," reflected in extraordinary personnel relations policies and activities, contributes to IBM's performance as well as its image as a "good company" in the marketplace. It is not merely the company's technical excellence, products, marketing, sales, and size that give it advantages; it is its special commitment to people.

Employees expect to have a voice in the decisions that affect their work and their careers. As organizations have become flatter, less hierarchical, and more flexible, employees expect to have more responsibility and autonomy. Company cultures that were envisioned and talked about in the 1960s and 1970s are becoming the norm today. Employees believe that management should encourage their participation and that jobs should be designed to challenge and reward them.

The desire to be consulted, or at least to be informed, was reflected in legislation covering plant closings, environmental hazards such as toxic materials, and other conditions affecting employees. Employees are concerned with such business and environmental issues, hence making them human resource issues.

Changing Staffing Needs

While companies once hired employees with an assumption of lifetime careers, this is not typically the case today. As business needs and work requirements change, companies must redefine their staffing needs, both quantitatively and qualitatively.

The mass media have given a lot of coverage to the reductions of staff among companies. From 1985 to 1991, the top 100 companies in the United States reduced the number of staff required by nearly 200,000. However, while some companies, such as General Motors and IBM, contracted sharply, others continued to expand and grow. Also, below the surface level of head-count changes, there were many changes in job assignments. At the same time, many other businesses were on a rapid growth curve, as start-ups or entrepreneurial growth companies.

Changes in staffing needs accompany introduction of new technology, capital investments, restructuring, and other business changes. Introduction of technology is often assumed to reduce staffing requirements. On the contrary, it has generally had the effect of increasing staffing needs, although in different, usually higher-level, skill categories.

Mergers and Acquisitions

Many companies use mergers and acquisitions to achieve various objectives as part of a strategic approach to growth. Each year there are thousands of mergers among companies, large and small. Mergers help companies accelerate their growth by moving into new markets, gain market share, enhance technical expertise or knowledge, broaden products and services offered, or improve financial performance.

The success of such actions depends on the product, technical, marketing, and financial fit among the organizations coming together. Success also requires management fit—the accommodation of different organization structures, employee talents and expectations, and management practices. Mergers also affect customers, suppliers, shareholders, employees, and other groups. Exactly how the desired results are accomplished may be addressed as human resource issues.

Issues arise first during the planning phase of mergers or acquisitions. Human resource factors need to be considered in evaluating the feasibility of combinations and in planning for their implementation. Nearly a third of all mergers and acquisitions end in divestiture, typically because they were not well conceived, understood, or managed.

In the course of examining prospective partners or acquisitions, a management team conducts a "due diligence" review. In this exercise, risks are typically examined in terms of labor contract obligations, executive compensation contracts, retirement and other benefit plan commitments (including pension funding surpluses or shortfalls), and other financial concerns. Additionally, other human resource factors may be addressed: adequacy of current management talent, depth or bench strength of future management and technical talent, cultural fit, and potential conflicts that are difficult to resolve.

After the word is out that a company is being considered, there are important communications issues to be managed: What should employees in each company be told? How may rumors (which are rampant and usually unfounded) be confronted and limited? Management is typically reluctant, and legally constrained, to disclose very much information on the progress of deliberations and negotiations.

In the implementation process, practical human resource issues arise in terms of organization changes, management staffing changes, integration of work forces, communications, adoption of policies, orientation of employees and other constituents, etc. The strategy for implementing a merger depends on key decisions regarding the desired outcomes—the degree of integration intended. Relationships may remain very loose (operating as an independent subsidiary or a separate division), collaborative (with some changes to achieve synergies where appropriate), or tight (design of a new company, with integration) (Butler, Ferris, & Napier, 1991).

Restructuring

Companies are striving to make their organizations flatter, resulting in broader scope responsibilities of management at all levels. Middle management is redefined to take on more responsibility for translating strategy into operational business plans.

Organizations need to be leaner and more flexible as well. They may resemble a network, with a blend of hierarchy, entrepreneurial units, and decentralized structure. The aim is to increase the capacity to act swiftly, creatively, and efficiently to meet customer needs or competitive challenges. More work is performed through ad hoc teams involving people from different groups. The distinction between staff and line blurs.

Jobs are restructured and more fluid, changing more frequently to take advantage of individual employee talents, rather than forcing individuals into rigid job definitions. The emphasis is also on teamwork, rather than individual performance.

As a result, staffing requirements of organizations change. Most companies have reexamined their staffing needs in light of restructuring and have "right-sized" their work forces. Human resource issues are raised in the process of determining required staffing changes and when and how they will be implemented.

Companies are also restructuring their relationships externally, seeking collaboration with their partners—suppliers and contractors on the upstream side, and their distributors and customers on the downstream side. Forging stronger relationships with suppliers and distributors than competing companies have can be a potent form of competitive advantage. The strengths of the partners add to the company's strengths, creating a larger capacity.

Joint ventures, multi-national competition and collaboration, and alliances are sought as ways to enhance capability. Complex networks among companies are creating the U.S. equivalent of the Japanese *keiretsu*. At the same time, such arrangements create new demands for staffing these organizations, development of skills needed to work effectively through alliances, and developing effective working relationships across organizations that often have different cultures.

Becoming a Global Business

For many companies, expanding globally is a matter of survival, and it means radically changing the way people are managed. Global competition will intensify in the 1990s. Competitive practices in the triad of major economic powers—Europe, Japan, and North America—define how major corporations function competitively. No longer is a "home country" viewpoint adequate. These changes have significant human resource implications.

To pursue productivity and growth opportunities, companies will increasingly be structured with cross-border organizations and through alliances, joint ventures, mergers, and partnerships. The rush toward building Pan-European organizations to seize opportunities in 1992 illustrates this trend.

In Europe, employment and pay practices that vary among European Economic Community (EEC) member countries will need to be managed by companies. For example, high-pay economies (such as Germany) and low-pay economies (such as Spain or Greece) will need to be reconciled. Otherwise, talent will migrate to high-pay areas and work will migrate to the low-pay economies, creating dislocations. Benefits also vary widely and are institutionalized in some countries. How will these be changed or accommodated?

Political forces and labor unions dictate social issues in some economies. German unions seek to sustain and expand their strong "consultative" roles in management of companies. Labor standards, work rules, and other industrial relations differences will persist as reflections of different social values and approaches. Managing employees in countries with different labor practices and structures is particularly complex. Labor laws reflect differences in cultures and political balances that are difficult to change. Establishing and applying common labor practices internationally will certainly be an issue in the future.

As Japan pushes into "higher value" goods and faces stiffened competition from other Asian economies, it faces new competitive and cultural challenges. A major issue is the adaptability of its homogeneous, slowly changing society. Women are assuming larger economic and political roles. Young people are seeking greater flexibility and opportunity in the country's rigid educational system (which emphasizes science educations for a selected elite). Signs of consumerism are appearing, in an economy that has supported producers (and protected inefficient producers at the expense of consumers).

Companies doing business in and with Japan will need to develop and implement human resource strategies that respond to and support this adaptation process. Issues arise in operations in Japan and also in operations elsewhere in the world involving Japanese management and Japanese employees. Japanese operations and American joint ventures in the United States have discovered that developing the optimal blend of cultures is a difficult challenge, but one that can be met effectively.

As companies are challenged to "think globally," they seek opportunities for commonality and interchangeability across the world. Global companies are managed through a single global system or management process. Some companies are even striving to be transnational or "stateless" corporations, which ignore national boundaries and focus on markets. Here, the home country is treated as merely another host country; there is no "domestic" market. In concept, the company could be headquartered anywhere.

For example, Asea Brown Boveri (ABB) is widely regarded as a model of a stateless company. Through acquisitions, this firm became a leading electrical equipment company in European and world markets. ABB's stateless managers shuffle assets around the globe, keep the books in dollars, and conduct most business in English. Yet the companies that make up ABB are established domestic players in their local markets. Such corporate ingenuity is the blueprint for the future and a key competitive edge.

Such companies face a difficult task in managing human resources worldwide. They have to consider how they will use and manage talent in subsidiaries in multiple countries, including local host country nationals, third country nationals, and expatriates. The costs of using expatriates in other countries are high, and expatriates often experience lower living standards and difficulties in reentering mainstream careers. There always seem to be questions of incentive and fair treatment of home country staff relative to expatriates and other employees. Few companies are yet managing their talent globally, establishing common practices and management capabilities on a worldwide basis (Dowling & Schuler, 1990).

ISSUES DERIVING FROM SOCIAL AND DEMOGRAPHIC CHANGES

Among the external changes that generate human resource issues, the most visible are demographic and social changes. They have also been highly publicized in terms of a significantly different "work force 2000." Three sets of changes are noteworthy for the 1990s: work force changes, changes in work attitudes and expectations, and changes in health and family care. Some of the pertinent issues are presented in Exhibit 2-6.

In the 1970s and 1980s, it was a buyer's market for talent. There was ample talent in the work force, fed by new entrants in the baby boom bulge of the population. In the 1990s and beyond, entry-level talent is scarce; and the work force, like the population, is aging. The combination of these factors will result in shortages of talent in many areas. Companies need to act creatively to ensure that they will attract, retain, and effectively manage the talent they need. Companies may strive to be a preferred employer for the talent they need most.

At the same time, the work force is becoming more heterogeneous. At all levels, employment will be increasingly composed of minorities, women, and foreign workers. To meet the needs of entry-level workers, companies will have to develop literacy and basic job skills among workers and recruits. They will also need to equip and employ inner-city youth. Disabled persons will be increasingly represented in the work force as a source of talent and in com-

---

EXHIBIT 2-6 HUMAN RESOURCE ISSUES DERIVING FROM SOCIAL AND DEMOGRAPHIC CHANGES

Work Force Changes

Overcoming a shortage of entry-level talent
Overcoming skill shortfalls
Reaching disadvantaged youth
Managing work force diversity
Adapting to an aging work force
Adapting to women as a majority in the work force
Accommodating disabled workers

Work Attitudes and Expectations

Responding to changing career expectations
Responding to job security concerns
Managing pay expectations
Establishing preferred labor relations
Complying with laws and regulations

Health and Family Care

Containing health care costs
Containing substance abuse
Coping with AIDS
Responding to family care needs
Redefining retirement benefits

---

pliance with legislation. Work force changes that are a source of human resource issues are discussed in "Focus on Managing B."

Deriving from demographic shifts, economic conditions, and societal changes, employee attitudes toward work and careers are also changing. These influence individuals' relationships with their companies and result in human resource issues that may need to be addressed. In today's flexible organizations, employees may not fulfill expectations of lifetime employment, steady pay increases, or rapid career movement. Externally, labor relations and employment legislation and litigation also give rise to company issues. These changes are discussed in "Focus on Managing C."

An area of continuing management and public concern is health and family care. Providing adequate health care at a reasonable cost is a continuing elusive goal. Health care costs continue to rise, for both employees and retirees, directly affecting business expenses. To serve their diverse work force, companies face employee needs for child care and other services. They also strive to cope with substance abuse and AIDS. Health and family care changes that are a source of human resource issues are discussed in "Focus on Managing D."

SUMMARY

Focusing on the human resource implications of changes allows managers to define the issues that they need most to address. In this chapter we have reviewed many changes occurring within and outside a business which give rise to human resource issues, and therefore to the topic areas that managers should consider in identifying and defining pertinent issues. With an understanding of important human resource issues, they may chart future strategies to guide human resource practices, the subject of the next chapter.

The notion of focusing on issues as a basis for formulating strategy is not new. Yet in managing human resources, it has not been widely applied. In every aspect of human resources, attention has typically been on the development and application of new programs and policies in functional areas: compensation, employment, benefits, labor relations, communications, training, etc. Functional thinking is reinforced by much of the training, literature, professional associations, and even certifications available to human resource staff. The functional view establishes, at the outset, a framework for thinking that limits a business perspective or "outside in" thinking.

Focusing on issues also requires managers (and human resource staff) to think in terms of change. There is no perfect model to emulate. There is no standard list of topics to be addressed. Human resources, like other functions, is a potent, dynamic, and interesting aspect of management. Some issues may be clearer than others, but part of the challenge is figuring out what the fuzzier issues really mean and what can practically be done about them.

Above all, managers have the opportunity to decide which issues will be addressed. This is another chance to think through trade-offs (e.g., short-term and long-term, employee and management, company and public, cost and benefit) that influence decisions. It is an exciting opportunity to decide how people can—and will—help gain and sustain competitive advantage for the company.

B. FOCUS ON MANAGING: WORK FORCE CHANGES

The work force in North America will undergo major changes in its structure and composition that will affect how companies recruit, hire, retain, and manage their talent. Many of these changes result from the aging of the demographic "baby boom" bulge in the population. Other changes result from the rapid influx of foreign workers and the rapidly changing pattern of participation in the work force.

Shortages of Entry-Level Workers

After the very large baby boom generation was born (1946–1965), a period of significantly lower numbers of births prevailed until the late 1970s (when women of the baby boom generation began having children). As a result of the fewer births during the 1965–1978 period, the number of 16- to 24-year-olds in the population and in the work force began a decline in 1976 that will continue through the early 1990s. The overall labor force will grow by about 15 million in the 1990s, less than the 18 million growth in the 1980s and 24 million in the 1970s (Johnston & Packer, 1989; Kutscher, 1987).

Lower birthrates, a rising median age, and the bulge in the elderly population will have a significant impact on worker availability by the mid-1990s. The U.S. work force grew at an annual rate of 2.7% in the 1970s as baby boomers entered the work force. The rate will be barely 1% in the 1990s.

Already, companies are experiencing difficulties in filling entry-level staffing needs, such as service workers and secretarial-clerical jobs. A 1990 study by the Hudson Institute and Towers Perrin found that a majority of employers surveyed expected "some or great" difficulty finding the help they need.

As a result, employers will have to recruit talent more aggressively and make employment more attractive through higher wages and better working conditions. Fast-food chains have raised wages to attract hourly food service workers in tight labor markets. Companies such as Marriott, TRW, American Express, and IBM have stressed their positive image as good employers— "employers of choice."

Other countries—such as Germany, France, Britain, and Japan—are facing similar demographic and work force shifts. The unification of Germany and the opening of the Baltic countries have provided a source of needed talent. In the Far East, work is being shifted to countries with ample labor supply.

Skill Shortfalls

In the 1990s, five occupational groups are projected to experience faster employment growth: technicians, service workers, professional workers, sales workers, and executive and managerial employees.

The demand for technicians and professional workers, in the face of a diminishing supply, is resulting in a shortage of needed skills. New technology is raising the standards of skill, knowledge, and adaptability for workers. The rapid adoption of new information and process technologies by companies results in new, higher standards of skill, knowledge, and adaptability for workers. In high-technology environments, high-value work and performance require high-talent employees.

Furthermore, the service worker and sales worker jobs require skills that many prospective employees lack, particularly minorities and immigrants who are new entrants to the work force. There are fewer jobs that are totally "unskilled" or even where less than a high school education is required. Prospective workers need basic reading, comprehension, arithmetic, and other skills to perform. Schools are viewed as unable to equip individuals with the ability and incentive to learn—the essential ingredient for lifelong learning. Companies must either screen candidates diligently or provide remedial training needed to bring them up to par.

A survey of 400 companies by the Commission on Skills of the American Work Force found that few employers plan to provide remedial training for employees. Instead, many accept the fact of a low-skilled work force and are lowering the job requirements or "de-skilling" jobs through automation, cutting wages, and exporting production jobs to other countries. They are using automation to create very simple work tasks—jobs described by critics as "idiot-proof," with low wages and little responsibility. The commission study recommended a higher-wage, low-turnover, invest-in-training path to staffing for the future (Hoerr, 1990).

Although companies currently spend an estimated $30 billion annually on training and education, the challenges for the future are great. The 1990s may be the "decade of training," as companies invest heavily in developing the talent needed to meet rising needs. Companies will strive to be "learning organizations," considered good places for individuals to learn, grow, and develop their talents.

Work Force Diversity

Eighty percent of new entrants to the U.S. work force in the 1990s will be female or minority workers. Women account for 64% of the increased work force. Blacks, Hispanics, Asians, and other races are projected to account for 57% of work force growth. If non-Hispanic white women are included, the combined share of figure growth reaches more than 90%.

Growth of the U.S. work force will be increasingly dependent on immigration. The number of legal and illegal immigrants entering the United States will continue to increase, accounting for nearly 25% of the change in the work force in the 1986–2000 period. In large part due to immigration, the Hispanic group in our population is growing faster than any other. In the 1980s, the number grew 40%, to 23 million; by 2010, the number will reach 35 million. Hispanics may then outnumber blacks in the United States.

As a result, the work force will be increasingly multi-cultural and multi-lingual. Most immigrants will continue to come from Latin America and Asia. Because many are not English-speaking or lack the job skills which are in high demand, their integration in the work force is more difficult. Furthermore, their employment is impeded by their geographic concentration in California, Texas, and New York.

This is not to say that working white males will be extinct. In fact, changing the overall composition of the work force is a slow process. In 1990, white males constituted 47% of the work force; in the year 2000, that figure will be 45% (Perry, 1991).

Companies such as Digital Equipment, DuPont, AT&T, and Marriott have given this issue priority, with emphasis on Spanish and English language training and on the "valuing of differences." The companies seek to help employees acknowledge and appreciate cultural differences and to foster improved working relationships. "The diversity approach," according to Louis Griggs, a training expert in this area, "enables us to treat our differences without an 'us-them' antagonism because we all have our own cultural and ethnic identity. We all need to be understood by ourselves and each other" (Castelli, 1990). Experience is accruing so rapidly that a body of knowledge is developing on this issue (Fernandez & Dubois, 1990; Loden & Rosener, 1991).

Older Workers

Until the mid-1990s, the proportion of the U.S. population and work force over age 55 will decline, and the share of 35- to 54-year-olds will increase substantially. This results in a highly experienced, stable, and generally healthy work force—contributing to productivity. However, it may also mean less mobility; baby boomers in their middle age may be less willing to relocate for new opportunities. The bulge may result in higher labor costs (older workers cost more than younger ones) and blocked opportunities for advancement of younger workers.

In fact, the median age of the work force will rise to 38.9 in 2000, up from 35.3 in 1986 and a postwar low of 34.6 in 1980. As the population ages, more people will be in the ages which have had, and will likely continue to have, declining work force participation. The trend has been toward earlier retirement, encouraged by employee pension and retirement programs and the effects of employer retirement and staff reduction practices.

After the mid-1990s and into the next century, the proportion of the population over age 55 will increase rapidly. The question is whether they will participate in the work force or retire and become dependent. The health and vigor of these future older Americans (which is expected to be improved), their economic status (whether they, in fact, increase their savings rate during the 1990s), and the attractiveness of continued careers will influence their decision to continue working. Extended careers will also help companies contain costs associated with retirement, such as retiree medical benefit programs and postretirement increases in pension benefits.

To reverse the withdrawal from the work force in the future, companies will need to seek ways to induce talented employees to stay on—to extend their working careers as long as they can ably perform. Early retirement incentives, programs widely used in the 1970s and 1980s to thin the ranks of longer-service employees, will be less common.

At the same time, the political influence of older Americans will increase with their numbers. The elderly population (over age 75) will rise from 12% of the U.S. population in 1990 to nearly 22% in 2030. Their voice will undoubtedly result in protections for company retirement programs and for Social Security program benefits. Public concern about Social Security viability may result in increased demands on private employer retirement programs.

Working Women

Women have accounted for 60% of the work force growth for the past twenty years and will continue to do so in the future. By 2000, 61.5% of all women over age 16 will be in the work force, up from 55% in 1986, 50% in 1979, and 44% in 1972. Because so many women have already entered the work force, their participation growth rates will slow. By the year 2000, women will make up 47% or more of the work force, up from 45% in 1986 and 39% in 1972. In addition, the trend is for women to move into new higher-skill work classifications, including senior management positions.

Women in the European Community are also increasing their participation in the work force. They made up 40% of the work force in 1988, up from 37% in 1980. Equal opportunities legislation made it more possible for women to work outside the home, and adverse economic conditions encouraged them to do so. Also, women in Europe now have, on average, fewer children, giving them more freedom to work ("Europe's Women," 1990).

The rapid expansion of part-time jobs and flexible working arrangements has enabled women to combine paid work with child care. Women are more likely than men to use flexible schedules, including job sharing, regular part-time work, flextime, and home-based work (Christensen, 1990).

Disabled Workers

Handicapped Americans are being tapped by many companies as a source of talent. Prompted by the Americans with Disabilities Act (1990) and other federal and state legislation, employers are providing jobs or services to the handicapped. At least 43 million people (17% of the population) have disabilities, yet only one out of three is employed. The new laws ban discrimination against disabled persons who qualify for a job. The laws also require transportation systems and public facilities to be accessible to the disabled.

Marriott, Pizza Hut, Citicorp, McDonald's, and other companies have hired more disabled workers. Marriott has more than 8,000 disabled workers on its staff nationwide. The company reports that lower turnover makes up for any added training expense. In one year, Pizza Hut hired more than 1,000 disabled workers, mostly mentally retarded persons, through a program subsidized by the Department of Education (Naisbitt, 1990).

C. FOCUS ON MANAGING: CHANGING EMPLOYEE EXPECTATIONS

There has been a strong reaction to the many unilateral actions companies have taken regarding their employees. Workers are increasingly challenging the rights of management and are seeking to redefine their implicit "contract" with their employers.

Some companies—such as Citicorp, GE, and Marriott—have considered this issue so important that they have reexamined their commitment to employees and communicated newly strengthened statements of their philosophy. Marriott calls its commitment the "employee covenant"; it defines the company's promises to its employees—for fair treatment, training, job security, promotion opportunities, etc.

Changing Career Expectations

With fewer management levels and fewer jobs in companies, opportunities for career advancement (generally perceived as promotions) are becoming fewer. Companies are keeping employees longer in their jobs before promotions and are emphasizing rotation or lateral moves instead of higher-level jobs. They are also stressing development and satisfaction through growth and performance on the current job.

Career paths, once charted as road maps for employees, are now abbreviated and more tentative. With rapid organizational changes, jobs are in flux, and career paths are fluid. As a result, it's harder to look down the road at certain job opportunities. Systems to communicate information on job openings, such as job posting, are helping to make the internal job marketplace more open and "user-friendly."

Many employees, finding themselves "plateaued" in jobs where further advancement is unlikely, must adapt to their career realities or pursue new opportunities. Management will seek to maintain motivation, commitment, and performance—and make a slower career pace acceptable and positive.

Many employees are reconsidering their career objectives and values. The highly charged, stressful, competitive (albeit financially rewarding) careers sought in the 1980s are being reexamined. Employees are reacting to "the cumulative effect of too many challenges, contests, ambitions, doubts, failures, frustrations, successes, lapsed mentors, lapsed ideals, and lost expense-account slips . . . in short, what you've been doing with your work life and what your work life has been doing to you" (Grunwald, 1990).

Of course, different employee groups have different career expectations. Companies need to be sensitive to differences and adapt to them. It's not up to companies to master plan careers, as was once assumed in some large corporations, but rather to provide current and candid information on opportunities and encouragement for self-guided career planning and development.

Career Employment

When adverse events occur for even a few employees, the implied promise of job security is abruptly broken for all. Quite naturally, many employees feel that the rules of career employment have changed. Accordingly, companies are concerned with finding ways to redefine this implied contract to allow the more flexible staffing that is required by changing business requirements.

In some instances, employees are challenging the assumed absolute right of an employer to remove someone from a job or to terminate an individual's employment. They believe that they have a "right" to a job once they have been hired. Employees are seeking more formal employment contracts and explicit policies, as well as protection through legislation and court actions. Many court decisions have favored individual employees, especially where employee manuals, policies, or implicit agreements imply regular and continuing employment.

In this environment, many companies are seeking to retain the talent they have so carefully recruited and trained. They may change staffing configurations to meet changing needs, but they seek to implement them in ways that do not threaten the sense of security among their valued employees.

Pay Expectations

As promotion opportunities become more limited, so will compensation opportunities. Large pay increases used to come with promotions. Increasingly, pay changes reflect job responsibility, skills learned, and competitive pay levels in the community or industry. Annual pay rate adjustments reflect competitive practice, but are awarded to recognize merit. Inflation was a plus, in that it created a pot of money to spread around.

Even in times of high inflation, companies are likely to give increases for merit, not for cost of living. Also, to link pay to performance, companies will continue to seek creative ways to pay lump sum bonuses or incentive awards—for either individual or group accomplishments. Profit sharing and stock ownership, plans that allow broad participation by employees in the results of performance, will likely become more common.

Designing and implementing such compensation practices create difficult challenges for managment. Salary administration and incentive compensation remain an art, not a science. New computer applications may, however, streamline the administrative demands of the process.

Also, employees will increasingly challenge practices as inadequate and unfair. Pressures will continue on management to establish rational pay practices, consistent with the concept of equal pay for work of comparable worth— both within companies and through legislation.

In the 1990s and beyond, we may also expect pressures to reduce the vast differences in pay among employee groups. Executive pay has risen to a multiple of average employee pay that is widely regarded as unreasonable, if not obscene. Pay rates for similar work performed in different countries will also be challenged, both by the U.S. employees who have lost the work shifted elsewhere and by the local country employees who are paid a fraction of the U.S. rates.

Labor Relations

Labor unions in the United States will continue to influence management decisions regarding human resources. In representing member interests, they will be a force for flexibility and change, working with management, or a force for rigidity, sustaining practices that may be outmoded in a competitive environment (Lawler & Mohrman, 1987).

Unions no longer dominate entire industries—like automobiles, steel, and rubber—the way they once did. Imports and nonunion domestic competitors do not allow companies to pass on higher labor costs to consumers as they once did. And changes on the factory floor have given workers more discretion over how they do their jobs, making unions less important as intermediaries with management.

Nevertheless, there are signs of union strength in the 1990s. Unions are providing more services to members, such as financial and social services like credit cards, group purchasing, portable health care, health and safety information, and family counseling. They are taking tougher stands with companies on heaith care costs and benefits, job security provisions, and innovations in worker involvement plans.

Companies will continue to take different positions with unions, working with them either collaboratively or competitively through aggressive negotiations of new contract terms and even decertification efforts. Unions will continue to seek to expand and organize new workers, including high-skill workers, to sustain their influence.

Where union representation does not exist, companies will be alert to possible union organization activities, so as to avoid unions. With high employee expectations, companies that do not manage employee relations well may find themselves with unions to deal with in the future. Even where unions lack influence with employers, they find an audience in legislatures and Congress. Plant closing laws are one example, creating onerous demands on employers seeking to restructure operations.

Employment Legislation and Litigation

The U.S. Congress and state legislatures will continue to enact laws that affect the employee contract. Legislation and court cases in the fifty states and the District of Columbia address human resource concerns in the areas of employment at will, discrimination, testing, employee access to records, mandated leave, entitlements of terminated employees, toxic substance laws, and whistle-blower protection. In addition, state and federal laws govern taxation of compensation and benefits, regulation of benefit plans and protection of pensions, layoffs and plant closings, and other management programs and actions.

Increasing numbers of employees act as aggrieved parties to seek redress through lawsuits on such matters. The increasingly litigious nature of employment relationships suggests that management will face continuing difficulties in managing the terms and conditions of employment.

D. FOCUS ON MANAGING: HEALTH AND FAMILY CARE

Issues of public concern are business issues as well. These include health care, substance abuse, AIDS, family care, and retirement. These issues have their roots in changing demographic and health trends, rising costs of health care, and changing social attitudes and conditions. They are being addressed by a variety of institutions, including employers.

Health Care Benefits

Health care is a growing concern. The United States is facing a health care crisis involving both the cost and the quality of care. Other countries, such as Canada, are also seeking ways to redefine medical and health care services so that the maximum human benefit may be provided at affordable cost.

Three factors are driving up the costs of health care. New diagnostic and therapeutic procedures involving costly new technology are being developed and applied at a rapid pace. Second, routine aspects of health care services (facilities, feeding, nursing, etc.) have not significantly changed or improved in productivity. Finally, health care demands are growing as our population ages. These factors will not be abated unless major changes are implemented in health care delivery.

Companies are seeking to contain the cost of health care benefits. Health care is certainly a company human resource issue, typically requiring changes in benefits coverage and increased employee participation in costs. Employees will have more choice in their benefits, but will also bear an ever-increasing portion of the costs. A typical example is a flexible benefits program adopted by Bankers Trust Company (New York) called "Bankers' Choice," which puts employees in charge of managing their own benefits and benefit costs.

Most companies have implemented utilization review programs, in which costs and benefits are monitored. Also, many are adopting more aggressive "managed care" programs in which the employer selects the health services provider. Managed care, in combination with the flexible options, is a positive approach that will help hold down costs over the long term while minimizing the burden on employees.

Companies will also invest more time and money in wellness programs— efforts to develop healthy employees. Exercise programs, smoking cessation courses, health awareness programs, and stress counseling will become standard fare in companies. For example, Adolph Coors Company has had a wellness program in place for more than ten years. The program saves the company nearly $2 million annually in health care costs, workers' compensation claims, and substance abuse treatment costs (Caudron, 1990).

In a tight labor market, there is a risk, however, that employees will feel they are shortchanged. As limits are imposed on benefits—through cost sharing, cost reduction, and benefits reduction—employees will still expect or want more. In companies that have introduced new, flexible benefit programs, employees have widely perceived that they are intended to mask reductions ("Labor Letter," 1991). For some employees, health care plans may be an important recruitment and retention factor. Already, it is an issue for many part time employees who are not covered by any company plans.

Substance Abuse

The abuse of drugs and alcohol has become a large problem for companies, involving all occupations and employee levels. In the 1990s, the problem will continue to grow. One study estimated that as many as 15 million people, 14% of the work force, abuse drugs. About one-third of these people are referred for treatment (Heisler, Jones, & Benham, 1988).

Substance abuse is both a human resource problem and a legal problem. Employers must balance safety and productivity concerns with those of employee privacy and workplace morale. Abusers have three to four times as many accidents on the job and are absent up to three times as often as nonabusers. Medical costs and benefits are three times as high. Indirect effects include costs of replacing and retraining employees, higher workers' compensation costs, theft losses, product quality losses, and adverse effects on morale. Of course, there is the human suffering of the individuals and their families.

Companies are seeking to combat substance abuse in several ways. Managers need to be alert to abuse and need to act promptly on detected problems. To this end, many are conducting blood and urine tests for employment candidates and, subsequently, for employees where there is probable cause, after accidents, or (in some cases) randomly. Of course, the use of testing embroils a company in the justification of its policies and practices, including legal defense.

Employee assistance programs help rehabilitate employees suffering from drug or alcohol dependency. Usually, outside firms or agencies are used. Companies need to determine the extent to which rehabilitation assistance will be provided. While the programs help employees reduce their absenteeism and medical costs, they may not yield long-term cures for their dependency problems.

AIDS

Acquired immune deficiency syndrome (AIDS) has spread rapidly in the United States and in countries around the world. Most large companies have experienced AIDS problems and may expect more in the future. Nearly 1.5 million people in America carry the AIDS virus (HIV, LAV, and HTLV-III). Of these, 70% will develop the disease or AIDS-related complex (ARC) within five years. All those with the disease will die within seven years; there is no cure for AIDS. Most of those with ARC will be too ill to work on a continuing basis.

Medical costs will be high for treatment of patients with AIDS, further compounding efforts to contain health care costs. Costs for a typical AIDS patient are estimated to range from $50,000 to $150,000 (McAuliffe, 1987). As a result, companies, their insurers, patients, and their physicians are considering alternatives, such as home or hospice care, which are less costly and may provide greater comfort.

AIDS is also an issue for companies because of the fears and emotional reactions of employees—which may affect morale and productivity. Management needs to take informed and responsible actions to abate rumors, fears, and disruptions. Company policies on AIDS testing, fair treatment and accommodation of employees with AIDS, and education of employees about AIDS all require careful consideration.

Family Care

Child care and elder care will be more important in the future, as people seek to work while maintaining their family responsibilities. This is not a "women's issue," because it affects the productivity of all employees. Elder care for aging parents is just as important as child care.

To attract and retain talented employees, companies need to recognize the onerous demands of dependent children and of aging, dependent relatives. Increased absenteeism, stress, and lost productivity cost companies billions of dollars each year. Workable solutions to family-care situations require management initiatives and joint implementation projects involving care providers and community organizations.

Retirement Benefits

With fewer government and corporate funds available, employees will need to plan earlier and assume more personal responsibility for the financing of their own retirement. According to Helen Dennis, "As corporate retirement policies and programs become increasingly bottom-line driven, employees will need to design adaptable retirement plans that anticipate trends in the 1990s and beyond" (Dennis, 1990).

The shift in the 1980s from defined benefit pension programs toward defined contribution programs [e.g., 401(k) plans] will continue. Contributions to such programs are dependent on company financial performance. Payouts depend, additionally, on the investment performance of the funds accumulated in the plans. Employees benefit from such programs in that the contributions are clearly defined. Also, vesting and portability provisions have improved significantly, giving employees greater confidence in these plans as investments under their influence or control.

Companies are seeking to emphasize all three legs of the retirement stool: government benefits (Social Security), company programs, and personal savings and investment. This requires increased awareness, a sense of responsibility for retirement planning, and investment knowledge by employees.

Early retirement programs will continue to be offered to high-salaried, long-term employees as a way to trim personnel costs. The willingness of employees to opt for early retirement may be abated by an increased desire to continue working—for personal and economic reasons. With increased longevity and capability, employees may not wish to retire early; and companies such as Polaroid and IBM have adopted programs for retirees to go back to work.

One area of growing concern is retiree medical benefits. With continuing government and corporate cutbacks, some retirees may receive no medical benefits from their employers in the future and others will have to work longer to qualify for these benefits. Companies face decisions on whether to continue such programs, to establish different tiers of benefits (protecting provisions for past retirees but modifying terms for new retirees), or to shift the expenses. Some companies have already frozen or otherwise limited future retiree medical benefits and have made provisions to recognize the financial obligation.

CHAPTER 3

DEVELOPING HUMAN RESOURCE STRATEGIES

We have a business plan, but it's being revised almost before the ink dries.

Robert W. Baker, Senior Vice President, American Airlines

The rapid changes which make strategies more important then ever in managing an enterprise also make them more difficult to formulate. With many issues to consider and limited time and resources to give them, managers need to focus on and effectively address the truly important business issues, including human resource issues.

In this new environment, strategic management has gained increased attention. However, strategies have also become more tentative, short-term, and focused. Business planning is often more valuable as a tool for provoking thinking and discussion than as a process for defining long-term objectives and courses of action.

Business strategies are shaped as guides to help organizations recognize and address issues that call for changes and to give them the opportunity to manage these changes effectively. These strategies focus on the concerns of greatest importance and create a "window of opportunity" for bringing management to action. Strategic planning creates "air time" for discussion of key issues among managers.

Companies are recognizing that attention to the financial and technological side of the business must be balanced with attention to planning for human resources. Some companies address human resources as part of business strategic planning. These plans are similar to functional strategies for finance, marketing, technology, manfacturing, and information management developed in support of overall business strategies. In other cases, human resource strategies are developed separately, often with a focus on the roles and objectives of the human resource staff function. These strategies effectively support strategic priorities as well, as long as the issues addressed are relevant to the business.

In today's rapidly changing environment, a key purpose of human resource strategy is to guide development of a more flexible, adaptive organization. The capacity to implement business strategies requires implementation of human resource strategies focusing on people-related issues. Human resource strategy is more than a series of action plans relating to human resource management; it is an integrated, multi-faceted, long-term agenda for changing the very character of a company.

This chapter describes how companies develop human resource strategies, including:

- How planning for human resources has evolved
- How companies formulate human resource strategies
- How human resource strategy fits as part of overall strategic management
- How companies implement business and human resource strategies

While human resource strategies are logically part of a complete business strategy, in practice they are often developed separately. In whatever way they are developed, they serve to translate human resource issues into action plans; they position the management of human resources as the essence of business strategy implementation. They align the management of people with the overall management of the business.

EVOLUTION OF PLANNING FOR HUMAN RESOURCES

Planning for human resources has evolved over the past several decades from a process narrowly focused on staffing requirements to a process addressing broader people-related business issues. Broadly defined, human resource planning is "analyzing an organization's human resource needs under changing conditions and developing the activities necessary to satisfy these needs" (Walker, 1980).

Early forms of human resource planning were narrow in scope and operational. Some companies have developed human resource plans that address broad agendas for strategic change. However, most have emphasized more specialized, functional plans focusing on concerns such as future staffing, management succession and development, or work force management. Furthermore, many human resource plans were developed by and for the benefit of the human resource staff function rather than by managers for use in managing their business activities.

Origins

Planning for human resources has been a management activity since the origins of modern industrial organization. Economist Alfred Marshall observed in 1890 that "the head of a business must assure himself that his managers, clerks, and foremen are the right men for their work and are doing their work well." Division of labor, specialization, organization of management into levels, work simplification, and applications of standards for selecting employees and measuring their performance were all principles applied early in industrial management. They were also applied in large nonindustrial settings, including religious, governmental, and military organizations.

In the first part of this century, the focus in "manpower planning" was on the hourly production worker. The aim of improving efficiency through work engineering and early industrial psychology applications was consistent with the need to improve productivity and introduce greater objectivity to personnel practices.

During World War II and the postwar years, attention to employee productivity intensified. Concern was also great regarding the availability of competent management personnel, since there was a talent shortage as well as significant demand for goods and services. New technologies and interest in behavioral aspects of work added complexities to the planning task.

1960s and 1970s

Expanded demand for high-talent personnel resulted in the advancement of technology in the 1960s (e.g., the space race) and rapid corporate expansion and diversification. In response, planning focused on balancing supply of talent with demand, particularly for managerial, professional, and technical talent. The demographic shortage of men aged 30 to 40 and shortages of specific engineering and scientific skills were noteworthy during this period.

In the 1960s, manpower planning was defined as the process by which management determines how the organization should move from its current to its desired human resources position. Through planning, management sought to have the "right number and the right kinds of people, at the right places, at the right time, doing things that resulted in both the organization's and the individuals' maximum long-run benefits" (Vetter, 1967).

Flowing from this concept were five steps: identifying organizational objectives and plans, forecasting human resource requirements, assessing in-house skills and other internal supply characteristics, determining the net human resource requirements, and developing action plans and programs to ensure the right people at the right place. The process was conceived as linear—one in which the past was a basis for planning for the future.

The prevalent view of human resource planning, which persists in some approaches used by companies today, was that "companies forecast their needs for manpower into the future, forecast their internal labor supply for meeting these needs, and identify the gaps between what will be needed and what will be available." Plans led to programming for recruiting, selecting, and placing new employees; providing for training and development; and anticipating necessary promotions and transfers (Burack & Walker, 1972; Geisler, 1967; Wikstrom, 1971).

For example, at TRW, manpower planning was considered a necessary process for allocation of scarce resources. The process had as its prime objective the effective utilization of scarce or abundant talent in the interest of the individual employee and the company. "In its broadest sense, it is a matter of anticipating the future business environment and pattern of the organization, and then relating manpower requirements to these conditions. They are first stated grossly and then further defined in terms of disciplines, skills, and qualifications, all of which are related to time. Realistic plans for recruitment and development of the manpower resource are made after consideration of the external and internal factors affecting the manpower objectives of each organizational unit" (White, 1970).

It is noteworthy that at TRW, and many other companies at that time, such planning was the responsibility of line management, or of program planning and budgeting staff, not the human resource/personnel staff.

As new legislation, court decisions, and governmental regulations developed, planning addressed affirmative action and other aspects of compliance. Significant new regulations governed employment practices, safety, and pensions. Attention was also given to salary administration practices to ensure competitive and motivational compensation in an era of rapid inflation. Generally, these were unsettled times, during which managers coped with the energy crisis, uncertain costs and profits, the slowing of business expansion, and heightened employee concerns about women's liberation, reverse discrimination, and the "midlife crisis."

However, during these years, manpower planning became widely established as an activity in major business and governmental organizations. As it evolved, human resource planning assumed broader scope than supply-demand balancing or quantitative forecasting. Attention broadened to include "upstream" links with strategic planning and "downstream" links to action program planning. The term *human resource* gained favor as a way to minimize the sexist implication of *man*power and also to emphasize the positive view of employees as a basic corporate *resource* rather than an expense.

In 1977, the Human Resource Planning Society was founded to provide a forum for education and research in this emerging field of management. At its first conference, in Atlanta in 1978, a broad view of human resource planning was evident, with sessions addressing environmental scanning, forecasting and planning, career planning and development, performance, organization design, and other topics.

1980s

During the "awkward eighties," companies downsized substantially, many with multiple waves of reductions in force and early retirement "open window" programs. Companies sought to decentralize, reduce overhead, and become more lean and efficient. This resulted in considerable displacement of talent (alleviated somewhat by outplacement services, a booming new industry) and changes in the fundamental "social contract" implied between employers and employees.

There was less new legislation during the decade, particularly during the Reagan administration, but regulatory requirements and enforcement continued. Regulations, court decisions, and state legislation brought new challenges to employment at will, employee rights, comparable worth in job evaluation, and other human resource practices.

In the 1980s, interest heightened in career planning, flexible work arrangements (such as flextime and job sharing), and rewards related to performance. The contingent work force grew rapidly as companies sought to use part-time and short-term contract employees to meet staffing needs while reducing the regular long-term core group of employees. Companies experimented with new human resource practices in order to retain and motivate needed talent.

Human resource planning emphasized management succession planning, planning for staff reductions (rightsizing), implementation of restructuring and mergers/acquisitions, and development of changes in corporate culture to support achievement of new business priorities.

Approaches to human resource planning became more pragmatic, using such tests as perceived business need, cost-effectiveness, and potential impact on competitive advantage. A 1989 survey of 137 companies found a shift to human resource planning techniques more appropriate for relatively short planning horizons. The researchers found few companies using planning horizons of the length common a decade before. Also, detailed quantitative forecasts of supply and demand for talent were less common (Greer et al., 1989).

Companies began using a wider variety of planning tools and techniques, resulting in an untidy but apparently pragmatic approach to strategy formulation. Approaches for addressing human resource plans in conjunction with strategic plans were developed. Different planning tools were used in different situations and at different times. Companies pointed to valuable planning activities, but few had an established, comprehensive, consistently applied process (Craft, 1988; Dyer, 1986; Dyer & Holder, 1988; Manzini, 1986).

DEFINING HUMAN RESOURCE STRATEGIES

The crux of human resource planning is neither a particular set of techniques nor their relative sophistication, but rather their usefulness to managers in charting new directions. Human resource strategies are management responses to emerging issues; they are plans addressing opportunities to gain and sustain competitiveness through the management of people.

A human resource plan is *strategic* when it helps management anticipate and manage increasingly rapid, even tumultuous change. Human resource strategies are the means of aligning the management of human resources with the strategic context of the business. Accordingly, there is an intense focus on issues deriving from environmental assessment, as discussed in the previous chapter.

A business strategy (or strategic plan) addresses the overall direction of a business under conditions of change. A strategy involves multiple programs and activities, typically involving multiple functions and extending several years. Issues of strategic importance are not easily or speedily resolved.

Examples of HR Strategies

Human resource strategies share these same characteristics. They provide an overall direction, involve multiple programs or activities, involve multiple functions, and may extend more than one year.

The following overall strategy statements illustrate these characteristics. They correlate with the examples of issues presented in the previous chapter.

- Plan future staffing by examining utilization of current staff and projected changes in the work load (Burroughs Wellcome Co.).
- Control our demand for personnel in short supply, increase the supply of talent, and enhance recruitment and retention of needed talent (Kaiser Permanente).
- Utilize management education as a vehicle for promoting change (Unisys).
- Educate managers and employees about "Aspirations" and give them the skills, programs, and policies support to operate in the new environment (Levi Strauss).
- Expand the employee incentive program and employee ownership in the company (The Kroger Co.).
- Focus recruitment efforts in scarce skills areas and target nationalities (The World Bank).

By contrast, the following are examples of company human resource strategy statements that lack these characteristics:

- Conduct an audit of all human resource activities and determine which ones are valuable, what new activities are needed, and what can be dropped.
- Intensify our efforts to provide excellent service at all levels of the organization.
- Improve efficiency and productivity with the aid of technology.
- Promote a culture in which all employees have the opportunity to contribute to their fullest potential, in support of company objectives.

Strategies provide a focus for an implementation plan of action. Action plans include multiple activities and programs as required, with responsibility and timing specified for each. Also, financial and staff requirements are described, to the extent they are known, for near-term actions.

Human resource strategies are typically rolled out (top down) and rolled up (bottom up) in the context of both business plans and functional human resource plans (staff departmental plans) at each level of the organization. Management agreement on strategies is achieved in the same manner as for other functional plans and specific business objectives.

Different business units may have strategies addressing different issues. However, as these "roll up," common themes typically emerge which become corporatewide strategies. Conversely, senior management may determine a need which is addressed top-down, corporatewide. In both cases, there is an integration of strategies.

AT&T Human Resource Strategy

AT&T provides an excellent example of how a company's human resource priorities relate to its strategic priorities. The company is undergoing significant restructuring and competitive repositioning in the face of challenges in its deregulated markets.

AT&T's mission is to be the world leader in information movement and management. It will accomplish this mission by preserving and growing its core business, developing leadership in data networking services, and increasing its share in global markets. The company considers its competitive advantages to be its resources, financial strength, array of products and service offerings, research and development (Bell Laboratories), and quality.

The company operates through nineteen business units, each one focused on specific markets and responsible for everything from new products to pricing and marketing. Divisions, providing common support, are aligned to one or more units. Across the company, core activities continue to include basic research, human resource policies, and financial systems.

Under deregulation, AT&T has faced intense competition in all of its markets. To remain competitive, the consumer products business moved its manufacturing offshore to Singapore, streamlined the organization (reduced staff, reduced management levels to four, cut bureaucracy), and focused on costs and quality. AT&T is aggressively pursuing international markets to offset competitive intrusions in the United States.

AT&T's human resource plans evolve around creating change—influencing the leadership and managerial changes required to succeed in the marketplace. These plans illustrate a top-down corporatewide strategic thrust for managing human resources in order to enhance business competitiveness.

Bob Allen, the CEO, believes that AT&T, the most entrenched corporate culture in America, must finally change and change for good. People have talked about this need ever since divestiture, but too little had happened. "To compete in fast-changing markets—for that is where divestiture has taken all AT&T's businesses—the phone company of old had to learn to get aggressive, to take changes, and above all, to move quickly" (Kupfer, 1989).

Accordingly, AT&T adopted these priorities for the 1990s:

• Accelerate leadership development, to focus on AT&T's changing business realities and action.
• Forge new partnership with unions, to seek creative opportunities that will lead to quality improvements.
• Build a far more diverse workplace, for business as well as moral reasons; make employee diversity a competitive advantage.
• Focus on the human dimensions of quality.

• Deepen international experience; develop respect for offshore human assets.

• Provide more flexible compensation packages and different benefits for a changing work force.

• Improve core human resource services, improving cost-effectiveness through re-engineering.

AT&T's mission calls for the company to enhance shareholder value, be a technology leader, and improve service. These human resource priorities respond to the company's need to "slim down and learn to scrap." In the 1990s, the company will be pushing for major changes in the way the transformed "Ma Bell" performs.

The U.S. Postal Service

Another illustration is the human resource strategy developed by the Postal Service. According to Anthony Frank, postmaster general, "The demands of the 90s require changes in the manner in which we move the mail, in the way we deal with our customers, and most critically, in the way we treat our employees." Culture change, participative management, employee involvement, career awareness, subordinate feedback, peer review, and identification of a new corporate value system are all priorities in the Postal Service that were not visible ten years ago. "Culture change has begun to take hold in our workplace," Frank said.

The Postal Service Human Resources Group adopted three strategies as it entered the 1990s. As such, they are directional plans for the staff group, but respond to the needs of the overall organization. The three strategies are:

• Improve the work environment.
• Improve service to internal customers.
• Improve the functional effectiveness of human resources.

Major emphasis is on changing the culture of the postal work environment. This is reflected in a heightened degree of participation and involvement of employees, managers, labor unions, and management associations. Employee Involvement/Quality of Work Life processes, continuing since 1982, promote an environment in which employees come to work fully committed to the organization's success. "Work teams and quality circles are truly becoming part of the mainstream."

John Hancock

John Hancock Mutual Life Insurance Company, the nation's eighth-largest insurance firm, has among its human resource strategies one that illustrates a more operational focus: "Making John Hancock a more responsive and rewarding place to work."

Hancock has steadily diversified its financial products and services. Its mission is to be "a prominent and financially strong provider of a broad range of products and services promoting financial and physical well-being to individuals and organizations."

The strategic emphasis is on being customer-driven, with a heightened focus on markets and customers, providing competitive product value to customers, and attention to improving company strengths and resources needed for successful competitive performance. Of course, emphasis continues on financial quality—to generate the financial resources necessary to support future growth.

Hancock's strategy to help its employees with their family commitments addresses concerns for developing the talent and work environment that supports superior performance and customer service. This aligns with the company's strategic focus on expense containment, customer satisfaction, and quality.

Because the company's large white-collar work force is drawn from the metropolitan Boston employment area, attracting and retaining quality employees is considered vital to the business. Women make up 62% of the Home Office population; 50% of the employees are married. Employee surveys indicated a need for increased sensitivity to child care and elder care. Thus recruiting and retaining married women with children in the Boston labor market was perceived to require special attention to the needs of families.

Accordingly, Hancock emphasizes family care as an important strategic thrust in managing its people. "The John Hancock is real life, real answers to its customers," explained Hancock Executive Vice President David D'Alessandro. "If our employees have real family care issues, it is important for us to recognize these needs and provide some ideal answers. To the extent that we can put programs in place that address real family care issues, employees will be more productive."

"John Hancock will endeavor to provide an environment and policies that are supportive to our employees achieving their own necessary balance between work and family issues." Family care relates to the care of children, aging parents, disabled spouses, sick family members—all of which cross into an employee's work life. Programs include the following:

• Employees are given the opportunity to tailor their schedules to meet their home responsibilities.
• A child and elder care referral and information service provides family care support at critical times for employees.
• Flexible spending accounts allow employees to use pretax dollars for child or elder care expenses.
• Unpaid leaves of absence (up to one year with company subsidized benefits) allow employees to care for family members.
• Sick days may also be used to care for ill family members.
• "Kids-to-go" provides backup child care through a community social service agency.

• An on-site child care center provides services for employees in downtown Boston.
• "WarmLine" telephone service allows employees to call home to check on their children.

As a result, Hancock has been cited by Catalyst, *Working Mother* magazine, and others as one of the best companies to work for in America.

Kaiser Permanente

Finally, Kaiser Permanente of Southern California, a health care provider, develops and maintains human resource plans to guide and support its expansion. This planning is operational in character, but focuses on future requirements and plans. In the region, there are now nine full-service (acute care) medical centers; nine or more additional centers will be opened by the year 2000.

The planning process for each facility has a seven-year horizon. An economic analysis and a demographic analysis of the areas to be served guide planning of the mix of patient care services (e.g., inpatient/outpatient), facility design, location, etc. Once the configuration of the new facility is projected, planners make a first estimate of staffing requirements. The individuals conducting this planning represent economics and human resource disciplines.

Human resource planning begins twenty-four to thirty months in advance of each facility opening. A staffing team—consisting of human resource staff, line managers, and others—estimates internal and external availability of required skills.

As a result of this planning, it became evident that the required nonphysician talent is not readily available and is underskilled. Accordingly, plans are being addressed for augmenting educational systems with Kaiser Permanente schools, actively funding education in hard-to-fill areas, building alliances with teaching hospitals (e.g., providing clinical sites), and establishing a high school/community college (four-year) license program.

The human resource staff function prepares specific staffing plans for each facility, including transfers from other facilities and external recruiting. The plans for each facility are contingent on the labor market assessment and are reviewed and updated regularly. Recruiting and retention are so difficult in some locations that a special panel (task force) has recently convened to develop a recruiting and retention strategy for hard-to-staff facilities. Wider recruiting efforts and improved retention of talent will be emphasized.

Recommendations resulting from the planning process are presented to the top-level regional Kaiser management, to obtain concurrence for action and to resolve issues and alternatives raised. Also, assigned teams of senior managers are ultimately responsible for opening the medical centers according to the plans (on time and within budget).

Coordination is sought among the various planning efforts: facilities, staffing, and recruiting/retention. In addition, a new position at the Central Office, vice president of human resource planning, is being considered to coordinate efforts across all regions.

These case examples illustrate the breadth and variety of human resource strategies. In each case, the approach fit the pattern and time frame of the company's business planning and was aligned with the process.

STRATEGIC MANAGEMENT CONTEXT

Human resource strategies, as part of overall business strategy, are formulated and implemented within the same overall context as other functional plans. Company marketing strategies, financial strategies, information strategies, and technology strategies are all formulated and implemented within the same framework.

As illustrated in Exhibit 3-1, there are three phases in strategic management:

- Environmental assessment, the subject of Chapter 2
- Strategy development, in which the strategic direction is reviewed or defined, objectives and programs/activities are planned, and resources are allocated to them
- Strategy implementation, in which the levers of managing change are applied so as to ensure the desired business outcomes

The first two phases are typically called *strategy formulation* or *strategic planning*; the third, *strategy implementation*. However, in practice, these phases blend together and are actually conducted concurrently (Quinn, 1980b).

Formulating Strategy

Business planning examines relevant external and internal factors in the business environment in relation to the current situation. Conclusions are then reached on business definition, mission and vision, strategic objectives, performance targets, and action plans.

EXHIBIT 3-1   THE STRATEGIC MANAGEMENT PROCESS

Environmental Assessment	Strategy Development	Strategy Implementation
Scan external and internal environment	Review/revise mission, vision	Align expectations, organization, people, and performance management
Assess strengths, weaknesses, opportunities, and threats (SWOTs)	Set strategic objectives	
	Develop action plans/ programs	Apply systems and technology
Define core competence, competitive advantage	Allocate resources	Evaluate effectiveness
Define strategic issues		

Although textbooks and planning guides make planning processes look simple, explicit, and systematic, they are not always so in practice. In companies today, there are different planning processes—various ways that managers define future needs and plan actions to meet them.

As shown in Exhibit 3-2, planning processes have several levels of focus. Here's how it works in the classic strategic planning process, once an environmental assessment is completed:

• Management defines or affirms the mission, vision, and values of the business, setting the strategic direction of the organization.
• This is translated into strategic objectives and broad courses of action, including programs, projects, and processes that will achieve them.
• This provides the context for defining operating plans and objectives (by operating unit or function) and the allocation of resources through a budgeting and capital decision process.
• Units, teams, and individuals define their activity plans, with specific performance objectives.

The plans, or strategies, become more focused on specific actions as they cascade through organizational levels. Corporate strategic plans are appropriately broad and conceptual; they require translation into operating plans and individual performance plans to be implemented.

It is this integration, or linkage among levels of strategy formulation, which ensures that action plans respond to defined issues at each level and result in commitments to action. All levels of planning should fit together coherently.

What is the appropriate time frame for strategies? In some companies, strategies take a five- or ten-year view. In companies with rapid market, technology, or industry change, strategies may be limited to one or two years. The long term is defined as the planning horizon beyond the immediate, known,

EXHIBIT 3-2 ELEMENTS OF STRATEGY FORMULATION

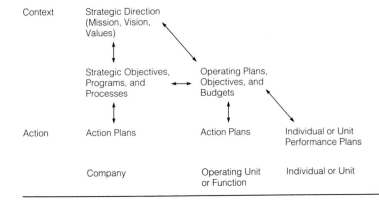

controllable period for a business (it may be one week or ten years, for example). The near term is the immediate action period—in most companies one year, although many revise their priorities, action plans, and budgets quarterly or monthly.

The Value of Strategic Planning

Strategic planning emerged in the 1950s as an outgrowth of programming and budgeting systems used to manage complex projects in government and business organizations. General Electric and other companies led in the development of strategic planning as a way to guide the management of change in complex organizations (Webster, Reif, & Bracker, 1989).

As companies grew larger, more diverse, and more complex in the 1960s and 1970s, strategic planning was widely adopted as a more systematic approach to managing various business units. It also helped management look beyond the near-term planning and budgeting horizon. Strategic planning represented a broader framework for planning, organizing, and controlling growth-oriented companies—beyond financial planning (which was well established).

Formal planning has a number of benefits. Foremost, it provides a discipline that periodically forces managers to take a careful look ahead. It requires explicit communications on goals, strategic issues, and allocation of resources. It lengthens the time horizon of decisions, such as those concerning investments, and stimulates longer-term thinking and analysis. It provides a framework and information base about the future against which managers can calibrate their near-term decisions and actions (Certo & Peter, 1988; Quinn, Mintzberg, & James, 1988).

In the 1980s, many companies realized that strategic planning is flawed unless it entails:

- Full commitment from top management; it is not a staff exercise
- Sufficient emphasis on data analysis
- Integration of longer-range planning with short-term planning and budgeting
- Follow-through attention to implementation

Strategic planning has become recognized as a means of disciplining planning activities and applying critical thinking to business situations. The payoff is longer-range, change-oriented thinking that guides management's near-term actions.

Some companies have fallen victim to overemphasis on the form, rather than the substance, of the planning process and, as a result, have cut back their attention to strategic planning. Sometimes it has been an exercise that has not substantially influenced near-term actions.

Harvard Professor Michael Porter believes that "strategic planning in most companies has not contributed to strategic *thinking*. The answer, however, is not to abandon planning. The need for strategic thinking has never been greater. Instead, strategic planning needs to be rethought and recast. While some companies have taken the first steps in doing so, few have transformed strategic planning into the vital management discipline it needs to be'' (Porter, 1988).

Planning in Actual Practice

Although strategic planning is often described and implemented as as top-down process, in practice it is multi-directional, especially if it is based on an "outside in" assessment of external (environmental/competitive) threats and opportunities.

Planning may start at the top, with overall strategic direction and objectives established by senior management and strategic objectives and directional plans developed based on environmental assessment. Unit managers are then asked to respond with proposed operating plans and objectives. Typically, there is an iterative review process in which plans are modified until the various unit plans fit into a larger whole. In the process, the overall company strategic objectives and programs themselves may be redefined.

In many companies, the top-down strategic direction is more fluff than substance. It may be the result of a periodic burst of strategic planning energy, laying out a plan that is used as a framework for five years or until a new "strategy study" is conducted. Or, it may be an ongoing set of assumptions about mission, philosophy, and goals that is reviewed (often perfunctorily) each year in the course of the actual planning process but is largely unchanged. The strategic direction is revisited, but does not change because there is insufficient analysis or thinking to support changes.

Some companies start in the middle: they focus on operating plans and then use strategic plans as a context for rationalizing them in broader terms. The strategic plans are the "front section" of what is essentially an operational plan. In fact, the budgets and action plans are where attention is placed. Financial planning and budgeting are the de facto strategy.

Many companies place emphasis on bottom-up planning, in which proposed priorities—action plans and objectives, as well as budget requests—come from the individual or unit level and roll upward. When companies use this highly participative but shorter-range planning, the reasons cited are:

- Rapid change and uncertainty
- Divisionalization and decentralization
- Pressing near-term business challenges—immediately evident threats and opportunities
- Direct involvement of employees with customers and other external parties, giving them direct knowledge of environmental threats and opportunities
- Desire to empower employees as part of an overall employee involvement or total quality effort
- Constraints on management time and planning resources resulting from leaner staffing and budgets

Emergent Strategies

To take this a step further, strategies may actually develop from the pattern of actions taken. Actions are often planned to respond independently to particular strategic objectives or unit operating plans and objectives. Team and individual performance plans and objectives are often set without regard to an overall planning context; for example, a manager and employee may set performance objectives based on their perceptions of appropriate priorities—a common application of management by objectives.

As a result, managers are expected to achieve different sets of objectives, which may be conflicting or, at best, place demands on the same limited time and resources. Actions called for by long-range objectives, such as the development of broader customer relationships, may conflict with near-term objectives, for example, sales or profit attainment. Incentives and recognitions may reward achievement of one set of objectives over another. Unit and individual plans may influence budgets and actions and, in turn, operating and strategic plans and objectives. The vision, if there is one, ultimately emerges from what we set as our near-term action priorities.

Strategic plans often evolve from specific decisions rather than from sweeping future-oriented planning. Planning expert James Brian Quinn described this approach as "logical incrementalism." He observed that executives usually deal with elements of strategies (e.g., structure, diversification, or governmental relations) rather than broad, systematic, formal strategic plans (Quinn, 1978).

This does not mean that emergent strategies are unplanned. Rather, they blend the benefits of the formal planning approach with the realization of behavioral realities in organizations—the power and politics of decisions and plans, the effects of negotiations and coalitions in establishing and achieving objectives, and the effects of precipitating events as they occur. It is not "muddling through," but a way in which managers consciously deal with an untidy world in planning.

McGill Professor Henry Mintzberg suggests that companies may be better off "allowing their strategies to develop gradually, through the organization's actions and experiences. Smart strategists appreciate that they cannot always be smart enough to think through everything in advance" (Mintzberg, 1987). Mintzberg sees these benefits from emergent strategies:

- Valuable strategies can develop from the strangest places; emergent strategies allow strategic learning.
- Everyone in an organization can be a strategist; emergent strategies encourage grass-roots management.
- Emergent strategies allow quantum leaps; they don't require building on past strategies and thinking.
- Allowing strategies to emerge gives an organization time to rest—to balance change and stability.

To manage the development of emergent strategies, process management skills are more important than deliberate, explicit strategic planning skills. Managers need to be learners, analyzers of patterns in thinking as well as strategic thinkers who can bring a creative vision to the organization (Mintzberg, 1987; Quinn Mintzberg, & James, 1988).

Flexible Planning

In reality, companies want (and get) both explicit and emergent strategies. Even Mintzberg acknowledges that both are used together in formulating strategies. Too much reliance on explicit planning drives out the creativity, innovation, and potential gains of widespread involvement in strategy development. Too much reliance on process risks loss of relevance to top management priorities and the results of explicit, rigorous environmental assessment.

In the flexible organization, increasingly today's norm, plans are developed more simply, informally, and collegially. In the spirit of quickness, nimbleness, efficiency, and simplicity, companies are seeking to cut away the bureaucratic trappings of planning and get to the results swiftly (see Exhibit 3-3).

The focus is on the future, looking at the changes that will most affect the business; and the assumption is that changes will continue to be fast and furious. Existing plans are viewed as historical documents; flexible planning starts anew. Environmental assessment is considered important, because of the competitive and external perspective, but the search and screening for issues are pragmatic, with data analysis focused where it matters most.

EXHIBIT 3-3 CONTRASTS BETWEEN INSTITUTIONAL AND FLEXIBLE PLANNING

Institutional	Flexible
Emphasis on linear, incremental planning; reliance on analysis of the past as the basis in defining future issues and priorities ("conventional wisdom" prevails)	Emphasis on futures analysis; looking at discontinuities and new conditions
Environmental changes assumed to be slow, evolutionary, predictable; hence longer-term planning horizon	Changes assumed to be rapid, even turbulent; imperative to anticipate and manage, not merely react to change
Tendency to review, revise, and refine existing plans (e.g., rolling five-year plan)	Tendency to "start from scratch"; create a new plan frequently
Highly systematic, formal, documented, step-by-step planning process; multiple-level "roll up" and review of plans	Data-based, but flexible, interactive, and iterative process; issues defined and addressed where they matter
Focus on the plan as a product—as a commitment to action	Focus on the process as a stimulus to strategic thinking and initiative
Staff-driven, line involved	Line-driven, staff involved

Flexible planning is not a staff-driven, systematic process as it is in more traditional, institutional organizations. It is, rather, a line management activity, involving people at all levels of an organization, with necessary staff guidance and support.

Stages of Business Development

An influence on strategy formulation is the concept of the life cycle. A popularly held view is that all products and businesses must eventually die (Anderson & Zeithaml, 1984). Products are created, develop, mature, decline, and die. Similarly, industries are perceived to have biological life stages: early development, rapid growth and takeoff, competitive shakeout and consolidation, early maturity, saturation, and decline and decay. According to this view, a business that has a portfolio of products in given industries is destined to mature and ultimately die.

The determinism implicit in such a life cycle of products and businesses is reflected in strategic plans which characterize a business as a portfolio of products, each with a defined future life. Business units may be characterized as growth, harvest, or investment opportunities. Strategies aim to manage each according to its stage: investing, "milking" (the cash cows), or disposing of business segments.

As a result, organizations are viewed as destined to follow predictable stages, progressing from start-up entrepreneurism to maturity. At each stage of development, there are different management needs and, therefore, different human resource issues. Numerous studies of organizational life cycles have shown that there are different management needs and, therefore, different human resource issues at each stage of development (Kimberly, Miles, & Associates, 1980; Meshoulam & Baird, 1984).

Stage I (initiation) is characterized by start-up, entrepreneurism, and founder management. To manage human resources, the organization needs systems for basic record keeping, employment, and compensation.

Stage II (functional growth) is characterized by technical specialization, growth in functional areas, expanded product lines and markets, and increased formality in organization structure and management process. Human resource management requires finding the right people to sustain the growth and training them to perform emerging tasks.

Stage III (controlled growth) calls for more rational, professional management in the face of scarce resources, new acquisitions, and diversified product lines.

Stage IV (functional integration) brings diversification, decentralization, product groups or divisions, and project management. The focus is on decentralization, coordination, and integration within functions. The company needs effective planning systems and methods for integrating its various activities. Human resource management focuses on coordinating and integrating growing activities in training, compensation, recruiting, and policy application.

Stage V (strategic integration) calls for collaborative teamwork, with increased flexibility, adaptability, and cross-functional integration. Strategic management aids team action and high sensitivity to changes impacting the business.

No simple indicators tell which stage a company is in; companies may even operate in multiple stages simultaneously. By applying flexible strategic planning, however, the opportunities and challenges inherent in such stages, if they are relevant, can be addressed.

The determinism implied in product, business, and organizational life cycles has been questioned sharply, however, as businesses can rejuvenate by pursuing new products or redefining the use of mature products. Industries evolve because forces are in motion that create incentives or pressures for change. It is not destiny but management action that results in change. For example, Sony's Walkman redefined the life stage of a product generally assumed to be mature: the radio (Anderson & Zeithaml, 1984; Chakravarthy, 1984; Porter, 1980).

Underlying such life cycles are driving forces from the environment which may be addressed. The challenge of business strategy, and human resource strategy which affects its implementation so greatly, is to allow organizations to survive and prosper—to understand and manage the forces affecting their long-term success.

FORMULATING HUMAN RESOURCE STRATEGIES

Within this context, how do companies formulate human resource strategies? Human resource strategies are functional strategies, like any other—financial, information, marketing, procurement. Any functional planning effort follows the pattern described above, complete with its variations. In many companies, long-term functional planning (for human resources, finance, information systems, technology, etc.) is a mandated element of the long-range business planning process.

Human resource strategies are different, however, in that they are intertwined with all other strategies; management of people is not a distinct function but the means by which all business strategies are implemented. If anything, human resource planning ought to be an integral part of all other strategy formulation. Where it is separate, it needs to be closely aligned.

Two-Way Planning Process

Like other business strategies, human resource strategies are shaped through both top-down and bottom-up processes in an organization. As shown in Exhibit 3-4, a top-down process provides the strategic context necessary for team and unit planning.

Through a focused company environmental assessment, it provides information on possible future trends and issues affecting the business and influencing the shaping of plans and objectives. People close to the operating business may

---

EXHIBIT 3-4 TWO-WAY HUMAN RESOURCE PLANNING

	Top-Down Planning	**Bottom-Up Planning**
PURPOSE	Provide strategic context	Plan specific actions
APPROACH	Typically flows from corporate to divisions	Typically rolls up from divisions, with corporate review
TIME HORIZON	Long-range	Short-range
ENVIRONMENTAL ANALYSIS	Part of or parallel to environmental assessment for business strategy	Identification of issues in the context of strategic trends and issues
IMPLICATIONS ANALYSIS	Assessment of HR implications of plans by managers and human resource staff	Assessment of HR implications of plans by managers and human resource staff
INTEGRAL PLANNING	Part of business planning process or separate human resource process to address people-related issues	Analysis, forecasting, planning on specific issues or subjects as appropriate
EVALUATION AND CONTROL		Monitoring and reporting of progress in resolving issues

This exhibit is based in part on ideas developed by Lee Dyer (1986) in *Human Resource Planning Practices,* Random House, New York.

---

not readily take such a broad future view. It requires looking outside the company to external competitive practices, economic and social trends, and possible future conditions that may some day have an impact on the business.

Such analysis is therefore typically top-down input, usually provided by corporate management (with staff support and leadership). Or it may be the result of a special task force or strategic planning project team. It may also be guided by external consultants, who bring the knowledge of the external factors and can take an objective view of the company's prospective challenges.

Because the goal is to promote awareness of long-term trends and issues and promote strategic thinking, it is particularly helpful to review and discuss the human resource implication of plans among managers and human resource staff.

A plan is strategic in character, as defined earlier, if it is focused on important issues raised in an environmental assessment. In today's competitive organization, it is important that employees at all levels be attuned to external forces and changes and to the strategic direction being taken to address them. In this sense, any plan—individual, work group, or operating unit—can be strategic. In fact, every level of plan needs to be strategic. Hence, this book discusses human resource strategy as the preferred form of human resource planning in today's flexible outside-in company.

The strategy and action plans at one level of management provide the context for strategy and action plans at the next lower level of management. This means-end chain forms the linkage among strategies necessary to align the entire organization with its overall strategy.

In a bottom-up approach, planning of human resource actions is a cumulative process. Instead of broad strategies being broken down into progressively greater detail, detailed strategies are aggregated and synthesized into meaningful umbrella strategies. Each business unit or department is asked to identify the human resource issues of concern, taking into consideration the guidance of the long-term planning inputs. They are also asked to develop specific analyses, forecasts, and assessments regarding these issues—considering scope, impact, and alternative options for resolving them. Specific action plans are selected and adopted. Both human resource staff and managers should participate in this effort.

Because there is a commitment to action at this level, there are additional steps in short-range planning. There is follow-up evaluation and control, provided by periodic monitoring and reporting of progress of implementation—relative to the issues (not just performing the actions).

Curiously, as illustrated in Exhibit 3-2, broad company human resource strategies may sometimes be acted upon directly by senior management without an operating plan translation. For example, corporate executives often communicate directly with all employees through broadcast or videotape media to implement a desired change in attitude, or at least understanding of the CEO's views and intent. The popular corporate management university or training roadshow is another example of a "skip level" implementation action.

Incidentally, one reason these direct actions sometimes fail is because they are not perceived as supportive or consistent with other initiatives that are being delegated through the organization for action. And employees are more likely to believe their trusted immediate supervisor than a videotaped executive they have not met. On the other hand, some CEOs, such as Jack Welch at GE, feel that the direct contact is vital to get the message through the change-resistant levels of middle management.

In human resource planning, companies frequently emphasize a top-down approach, a bottom-up approach, or a combination of the two. Case studies published by the Human Resource Planning Society in 1986 illustrate these different approaches (Dyer, 1986). Through that research, Lee Dyer noted various possible points in the business planning process where human resource planning may link (Dyer, 1984). The following discussion of three possible linkages builds on his findings.

An Aligned Process

As illustrated in Exhibit 3-5, the formulation of a human resource strategy may be parallel to the business strategy formulation process. At each step, it interacts with strategy formulation, drawing from it and contributing to it as it progresses. In this way, the human resource strategy does not complicate business strategy formulation, but rather ensures that human resource issues are given full attention.

In the environmental assessment phase, a human resource environmental assessment is conducted—separately from but parallel, concurrent, and

---

EXHIBIT 3-5 DEVELOPING AND IMPLEMENTING HUMAN RESOURCE STRATEGY

Environmental Assessment	Strategy Development	Strategy Implementation
INTEGRATED PROCESS: 　Human resources considered as part of environmental assessment	Business strategy covers all functional areas, including human resources	↑
ALIGNED PROCESS: 　Parallel and interactive environmental assessment; human resource issues influence overall results	Human resource strategy developed together with business strategy	Management of human resources: alignment of organization, capabilities, performance management
SEPARATE PROCESS: 　Environmental assessment focuses on human resources; past business strategy reviewed for inputs on human resource issues	Human resource strategy developed as a separate functional plan (by staff unit, companywide, or business unit)	↓

---

interactive with the business strategy. Some results of a human resource environmental scan are pertinent to business strategic planning and are applied to it. For example, in one company, certain changes in demographic patterns examined for work force availability purposes were relevant to formulating marketing plans and manufacturing site location plans for a new product line. In a chemicals company, an anticipated shortage of engineering graduates slowed the planned pace of capacity expansion.

In the aligned process, a human resource strategy is developed together with the business strategy. They may be presented together and discussed together, but they are distinct outcomes of aligned, parallel processes. By developing and considering them in tandem, there is a likelihood that they will influence each other and be adopted as a cohesive or at least adhesive whole.

In a world where human resource plans are still often considered to be staff-driven operational and implementation plans, an aligned process of this nature is a big step forward.

Separate Process

The next best alternative approach, and the most commonly implemented approach today, is the development of a distinct human resource plan. It is prepared separately and considered separately from the overall business strategy. It may be formulated concurrently with strategic planning, before strategic planning (as input to it), or following strategic planning (to examine its implications).

The environmental assessment is wholly independent of such efforts undertaken as part of overall strategy formulation. The assessment focuses on human resource issues and, to the extent possible, looks for business-relatedness of the information obtained. Since the assessment is outside the strategic planning process, consideration of business strategy depends on a review of the current and past business strategy documents, as well as interviews and focus group discussions within the company.

Human resource strategy is developed separately and is usually packaged and presented as a distinctly functional human resource plan. There may be such human resource strategies at multiple levels of an organization, designed to prompt management and human resource staff thinking and operational planning.

The disadvantage of a separate process is that it perpetuates the notion of human resources as a staff-driven, functionally specialized concern. Also, the value of the strategy is influenced by the sufficiency of business-related information.

The clear advantage is that, in the absence of alternatives, a human resource strategy is actually created and may be used to guide program, policy, and practice decisions and actions. Sadly, there are also companies that lack a sufficiently rigorous business strategy formulation activity to align with, and hence this is the only alternative: where there is no business strategy, go ahead anyway.

Sometimes, human resource planning involves separate processes focused on special issues or subjects that are considered tangential to business strategy or best handled separately for other reasons (time for sufficient attention, confidentiality, different managers involved, etc.). For example, planning for management succession and organization has received substantial attention in many companies, but typically as a process separate from strategic planning. This process is examined in Chapter 9.

Affirmative action planning is required for any company that is a contractor for the federal government. Accordingly, most companies conduct the necessary analysis, set targets, and develop action plans that will influence recruitment, education and training, internal placement and promotion, and other human resource activities.

Also, in many companies, major thrusts have been adopted to achieve desired changes, focusing on a particular theme—for example, planning for total quality, service quality, or productivity improvement. Companies may be seeking to "transform" the culture or otherwise emphasize specific dimensions of change considered particularly important for organizational success. These are often formulated and implemented independently of other human resource plans, other functional plans, or business strategy. Of course, such special thrusts are usually consistent with strategic direction and are referenced or called for in other strategies.

Human Resource Staff Department Strategy

In an additional variation on the separate process, the human resource staff in many companies prepare strategies and action plans and present them as a separate *functional* or *departmental plan* to senior management. These are initiated, developed, and used for the benefit of the staff, helping them to clarify their purpose and objectives, the process for operating, their involvement in management efforts, and the resources required.

Functional staff planning is a useful adjunct to the process of formulating broadly based human resource strategy. It is more than a mere staff unit operating plan in that it is based on its own complete strategy formulation process. However, when it substitutes for business-focused human resource strategy, it limits the potential contribution of the function and its partnership with management in addressing the organization's strategic challenges.

Some human resource functions approach their planning as a service provider, focusing on the expectations and needs of the line organizations as their clients or customers. This is helpful for improvement of staff service functions. However, it is insufficient as a basis for guiding the organization toward implementing responses to significant changes in the ways people are managed in support of business strategies. In short, it is useful but myopic.

Integrated Process

Surprise of surprises, the preferred approach for developing human resource strategy is for it to be an integral part of the business strategy—at each level of an organization. If it is truly important, along with other functional strategies, and more important than some, then human resource strategy should be inherent in the strategy formulation process.

Traditionally, business plans called for consideration of future organization structure, future head-count levels, estimated future payroll and benefit costs, and possibly other issues of importance, such as labor contract negotiation terms.

To be integrated, the changes in the environment are examined with regard to human resource issues as well as other business-related issues. The same people do assessment of all topics. An automobile company, for example, charged a team of operating managers from its various locations to develop a global human resource strategy as one of the focal areas examined in the development of the company's long-term strategy. It conducted a thorough environmental assessment, in collaboration with other strategic planning teams, and developed an agenda that became part of the business agenda.

In companies or business units where senior management recognizes human resource issues as important to the achievement of business objectives, such planning is often integrated. In strategy review discussions, questions are likely to address human resource topics in addition to financial, product and marketing, or other areas.

The integrated process does not mean that individual performance, staffing, development, or organization issues or problems are addressed. These are downstream matters that should not be part of strategic planning, yet sometimes creep into the process. The focus should be on external and internal changes, people-related business issues, strategies, objectives, resource allocation, and action plans.

ACTION PLANS AND RESOURCES

There is a growing bias toward action; companies are planning specific management actions as part of strategy formulation. They translate issues into action plans, with multiple-year programs and priorities, defined accountabilities, and measures of results. They assign clear responsibility, timing, and the resources required to implement the strategy.

Also, companies consider how the strategy will be executed—how all parties will be informed and involved in implementing the strategies. (One executive was recently given the position title of "director, strategy formulation and strategy translation" for a division, to emphasize the importance of implementation.) Companies are giving increasing consideration to the alternative actions that may be taken—human resource programs or practices that are applicable to perceived needs. For example, succession planning and related initiatives to recruit or develop management talent for the future are increasingly focused on the development actions that will be implemented.

Action Plans

Action plans address how the strategies will be communicated and executed. More attention is being given to how the plans will be implemented by managers—and the communication, training, performance objectives, incentives, and other tools required. Action plans also address needs for modifying human resource processes and operations of the human resource staff function to lead and support the implementation.

Most companies evaluate the results of human resource strategy implementation in terms of the actual completion of planned programs, projects, or other actions. This is consistent with the typical process of translating broad plans into specific operational plans, objectives, and activities. Accomplishment of the operational objectives is the measure of results attained.

In addition, many companies are now defining measures of achievement in terms of the ultimate impact on the issues defined. This requires definition of the specific measures to be used—the evidence required to determine the impact of the actions on the issue (e.g., turnover rates, personnel cost ratios, employee attitude indexes, productivity improvement, service quality, or skill development). These measures are stated quantitatively and, whenever possible, in financial terms.

Target levels of impact are typically defined for each measure (e.g., improvement in the turnover rate, reduction of costs, improvement of service). The timing and accountability for these results are specified, as for other management performance objectives. The evaluation process is often most effective when it is integrated with the normal business planning and review process. In a hotel company, for example, each business division reports performance against specific objectives in improving employee retention ("becoming a preferred employer"). The objectives and results are incorporated into the company's annual strategic review process.

Resource Allocation

A final aspect of strategy development needs to be mentioned: resource allocation. Budgeting is an important consideration, as human resource management continues to be treated as an expense. While companies may occasionally build an executive education center, a health care facility, or a new human resource information system, the capital expenditures are not the critical resources for human resource strategy implementation.

In addition to objectives, measures, activities, and timing, action plans need to specify the costs that will be incurred. Typically, individuals, teams, and units identify the expenses (and capital expenditures, if any) that are required.

Costs include employee salaries, related indirect costs, office expenses, and expenses for travel, meetings, and projects. Additional costs include contracted consultant or vendor expenses, specific expenses relating to the action plans (e.g., program development costs, search fees), and substantive costs inherent in the strategies (e.g., benefit costs, relocation costs, training costs).

These estimates, or proposed expenses, are reviewed as part of the action plans at each organizational level. They are typically classified by type, according to accounting practice, and are aggregated as unit expense budgets. As they are reviewed, of course, these estimates are challenged and revised. Although companies seek to contain expenses, action plans that address important strategies may be given greater funding. It may seem rare, but sometimes more resources are given an action plan in order to accelerate and enhance its implementation.

Human resource costs are typically viewed as indirect or overhead costs. As such, they are always subject to close scrutiny. Historically, overhead costs were termed a *burden*, suggesting an even lower estimation of the value added to business effectiveness. As human resource strategies are developed and adopted as important business thrusts, the costs are perceived on par with direct costs. Being indirect does not in any way mean that the costs create lower benefit.

In a pharmaceutical company, for example, the costs of producing and distributing products to customers are as "direct" as costs can be. However, the competitiveness of the business depends on results from research and new-product development, sales and marketing, and effective regulatory relationships (gaining product approvals and protecting existing products). Costs relating to management of human resources in these areas must be considered central to strategy implementation, even though they remain "indirect" expenses.

Impact of Budgets

Budgets are vital to management because they provide a detailed means for planning, controlling, and monitoring the use of financial resources. They are a tool that managers have become accustomed to, and devote significant time and attention to in developing. Budgets are also often used as an overt indicator of managerial performance, whether in a cost center or a profit and loss business unit.

Budgets allow managers to review overall resource requirements and allocate resources to the most promising action plans. A number of strategies may be defined as important, but because of finite resources, some will be funded and some will not. It is this negotiation process, based on the relative merits of different proposals in light of strategic objectives, which results in a sound plan for resource allocation.

However, there are pitfalls in the use of budgeting. In typical institutional organizations, management lives and dies by the budget. ("If it isn't in the budget, it can't be done.") Budgets are prepared as an annual ritual and dictate how action plans will be implemented during the year ahead. Often, the budget becomes management's main tool to gauge and manage performance.

In rapidly changing conditions, the drawback is that "making the numbers" becomes an overriding goal, instead of achieving the objectives that were determined to be strategically important. The budget may block the shifting of resources, the spending of more than was anticipated, or the changing of action plans during the budget period. The budget sometimes becomes an end in itself. It focuses management attention inward, rather than outward (to customer satisfaction, market performance, quality, etc.). "When you're controlled by a budget, you're not controlling the business" (Stewart, 1990).

In a flexible organization, budgets are important as management tools for allocating resources. Budgeting is a management process, intended to help provide the resources needed as priorities and action programs change. It is not an accountant's tool for controlling spending or constraining managers from taking action. Budgets should relate directly to strategies, operational plans, and performance plans.

Budgets need to be rooted in reality. First, there is uncertainty in the business environment, hence budgets must be flexible and adapt to changes as they occur. Second, because resources are finite, managers are tempted to treat budgeting as a game, in which some win and some lose resources. As a result, in budgeting "gamesmanship," managers overstate expenses and understate revenues or otherwise distort their budgets in order to win more resources. Gamesmanship is encouraged, too, by management incentive compensation that is narrowly based on "meeting the budget" (Bart, 1988).

Business and human resource strategies look toward long-term enhancement of the business. Often, short-term budgeting impedes the necessary spending for implementation of action programs that support these long-range priorities. Sometimes, too, executives cut spending on programs and activities that do not have an immediate-term payoff (e.g., training and development). This reflects an assumption that shareholders and investors favor short-term financial performance over sustained long-term development of a business.

In the 1990s and beyond, companies are challenged to take strategies having long-term payoffs seriously and to allocate the needed resources to them.

Companies such as Coca-Cola, IBM, Wal-Mart, Merck, Disney, Amoco, RJR Nabisco, and AT&T are recognized for their long-term management perspective. Their stock prices also reflect, in large part, the long-term prospects of the companies, rather than short-term returns (Hector, 1988). Companies can manage long term. Allocating sufficient resources to human resource strategies is a test of their will to do so.

IMPLEMENTATION

Tom Peters has said that "execution is everything." An excellent strategy is worthless unless it is implemented. As shown in Exhibit 3-1, strategy implementation requires alignment of employee expectations, organization design, staffing and development of capabilities, and performance management with the strategies. This is the subject of the remaining chapters of this book.

In addition, systems and technology as well as financial and other resources (other than human resources) are required, of course, as dictated by the strategies. However, our focus is on the management of human resources as the primary means of implementing strategies in the 1990s and beyond, where speed, service, quality, and cost are primary competitive considerations.

Implementation of human resource strategy is not a secondary priority for management. It is a primary responsibility, which gives a company a primary source of competitive advantage. Again, however, it is not just good strategy formulation that matters; it is also excellence in implementation.

Implementing Strategies for Organizational Change

Human resource strategies may be specific and narrowly focused on functional subjects, such as staffing or management succession. Or they may be broadly conceived and applied, as directional plans guiding major organizational change. While human resource planning has developed from origins emphasizing the former focus, the greatest opportunities for impact lie in the latter.

Because many companies are going through broad business transformation, they have broad strategies calling for structural changes, staff reductions and redeployment, massive investments in educating and retraining talent, and changes in systems aimed at reshaping culture.

When human resource strategies are used to help lead broad-based change, they need to be broader than focused action plans. They need to be sufficiently complex to address the challenges they address, but also adaptable to changing conditions and priorities. As noted, they may never be perfectly explicit, complete, or clear; they may emerge incrementally, as precipitating events, key decisions, and commitments for change unfold.

First, they need to address the issues that are important to achieving real and lasting change. Issues are often interrelated and even conflict. For example, a focus on quality improvement requires a focus on teamwork and a collaborative organization, staff development, and development of a high employee commitment. These efforts may be impeded by necessary restructuring and staff reductions. Morale was understandably shaky at AT&T among survivors of repeated organizational changes and two major rounds of job reductions totaling 18% of the work force.

Second, human resource strategies need to involve multiple actions—the right actions for the issues. And the elements of the strategy may change as conditions change and lessons are learned along the way. There are both explicit and implicit elements of an implementation plan. Explicit elements are those that have a full, open, and precise expression. They are the levers that management has to effect change. Implicit elements are those that emerge informally, as a result of the attitudes and behavior of people in the organization. They are typically tacit, not expressed openly or referenced forthrightly. All elements are essential for effective change.

Key Elements of Change

Many books written on the process of managing large-scale strategic organizational change address these elements in one way or another. Each author defines a model or list of the particular elements that need to be addressed.

• Ralph Kilmann defined five "tracks" to organizational success: culture, management skills, team building, a structure that fits the strategy, and reward systems. Each track addresses a different, yet interrelated, aspect of organizational life that must receive proper attention if the organization is to achieve its goals, solve problems rather than simply patch them up, and create lasting change (Kilmann, 1984).

• Dave Ulrich believes that competitive advantage is gained through superior organizational capability, which consists of four critical elements. First, the people in the organization need a "shared mindset"—common ways of thinking about goals and the means to reach them. The other elements are leadership (individuals at all levels with vision), management and human resource practices, and the capacity for change resulting from individuals being empowered and able to influence others (Ulrich, 1990b).

• David Nadler views an organization as a transformational process involving four primary components: the basic work to be done (tasks), the characteristics of the individuals in the organization, the formal organizational arrangements (structures, processes, and methods), and the informal organization (emerging arrangements including structure, processes, and relationships). He emphasizes the need for fit (congruence) among these elements (Nadler, 1989).

• Noel Tichy argues that three sets of managerial tools need to be used in strategic management. In formulating mission and strategy, there is the formal process; the political influence and coalitional behavior; and the influence of values, philosophy, or culture. Organizational structure and human resource management practices also have technical, political, and cultural systems. He, too, argues for alignment among the elements (Tichy, 1983, 1986).

• Finally, there is the 7-S model developed by consultants McKinsey & Company: strategy, structure, staffing, skills, style, systems, and shared values. This model pointed the way to the insightful work of Tom Peters and Bob Waterman (Peters & Waterman, 1982).

A reading of these perspectives suggests that different authors address many of the same elements for implementation of change. Also, all of these authors observe that there must be both internal congruence or fit among the factors (a systems view) and external congruence or strategic fit.

For example, a major oil company depicted its process for corporate renewal as a five-point star (see Exhibit 3-6). One point on the star represents the defined business strategy. The other four represent its implementation through structure, processes, people, and rewards. The notion of a coordinated multiple-factor implementation process seems to crop up everywhere, and makes a lot of sense to those who must bring it to fruition.

The Management of Human Resources

As discussed in Chapter 1, the process of managing people in an organization encompasses all of the variables that have been typically included in "change

---

EXHIBIT 3-6 MAJOR OIL COMPANY "CORPORATE RENEWAL PROCESS"

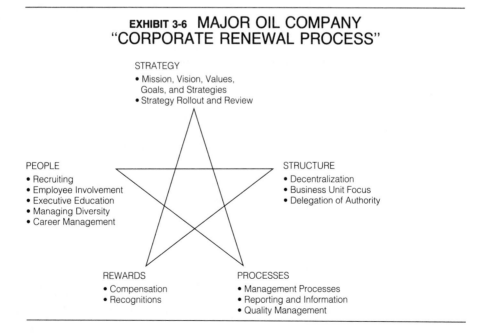

STRATEGY
• Mission, Vision, Values, Goals, and Strategies
• Strategy Rollout and Review

PEOPLE
• Recruiting
• Employee Involvement
• Executive Education
• Managing Diversity
• Career Management

STRUCTURE
• Decentralization
• Business Unit Focus
• Delegation of Authority

REWARDS
• Compensation
• Recognitions

PROCESSES
• Management Processes
• Reporting and Information
• Quality Management

models." Those presented in Exhibit 1-1, which constitute the structure of this book, are primary management levers for implementing strategic change:

- Aligning expectations: bringing employees into a full understanding of and commitment to the intended business strategy
- Building the organization: designing the organization, planning staffing needs, and strategic staffing
- Developing capabilities: developing employee capabilities and management talent
- Managing performance: enabling high performance, evaluating performance, and sharing successes

There is no need for specific change management models to guide implementation of different change strategies. Rather, the basic factors of managing human resources are pertinent in any implementation effort. Managers need to understand the need for a complete, balanced, and consistent view of the forces they have available to them to achieve the desired results.

Through management of these explicit elements of strategy implementation, the implicit (informal) elements are managed as well:

- Shared values and expectations: the cultural "binders" of an organization, such as trust, openness, customer focus, and the willingness to change
- Informal relationships: the personal relationships, liaisons, coalitions, and informal teams through which people work and act
- Information and influence networks: the patterns of contact by which people give and receive information and thereby influence relationships and actions
- Teamwork, cooperation, and conflict: the informal collaboration among people in performing tasks together
- Career expectations and plans: the anticipation of continued progress toward achieving personal objectives
- Commitment and motivation: the willingness of people to stay with the organization and contribute energetically to the achievement of shared objectives
- Continual learning: an attitude and behavior of ongoing discovery, innovation, growth, and development at work
- Performance orientation: an attitude and behavior of accomplishment, of self-direction and incentive, and of continual improvement

While these implicit factors represent the informal culture of the organization, they are very much part of the overall scope of strategy implementation. Managers who neglect them find that they have difficulty achieving the desired outcomes.

These elements of strategy implementation, both explicit and implicit, are presented in Exhibit 3-7 and are discussed more fully in the next chapter.

EXHIBIT 3-7 ELEMENTS OF STRATEGY IMPLEMENTATION:
MANAGEMENT OF HUMAN RESOURCES

	Explicit	**Implicit**
ALIGNING EXPECTATIONS	Vision, mission, values, strategy	Shared values and expectations
BUILDING THE ORGANIZATION	Structure	Informal relationships, information and influence networks
	Work design/tasks, empowerment	Teamwork, cooperation, and competition
	Staffing	Career expectations and plans
DEVELOPING CAPABILITIES	Training and development	Commitment and motivation/continual learning
MANAGING PERFORMANCE	Performance system/rewards	Performance orientation

---

Evaluation and Control

An emphasis on evaluation of results, rather than on the activities and day-to-day operating efficiencies, keeps the focus on the original issues that were defined as important. To implement human resource strategies in the nineties requires a focus on the end results—the resolution of issues, not merely the means. Measurement of results in terms of issues, however, requires a more diligent and comprehensive process of defining issues and developing management action plans. A strategic approach to human resource planning is thus becoming a more demanding task for management.

Every strategic planning book and model includes a box labeled "Evaluation and Control." It is the final word of strategy formulation and implementation. It is an important aspect, because too often companies plan and implement actions that are never evaluated. There is no assurance that the right issues were addressed, the right strategy was adopted, the resources were used appropriately, or the desired results were obtained.

Yet by the time actions are rolling out, management attention is on the next wave of activity and investment. There is little interest or patience in the evaluation of the process. Furthermore, there are few techniques that are helpful short of performance measurement and audits.

Evaluation and control in the flexible organization are inherent in the process. Just as total quality requires that a task be done right the first time, every time, and that employees check and affirm the quality of their own work, so strategy implementation requires that managers ensure its quality:

• Is the environmental assessment sufficiently thorough, objective, and properly conducted? If so, the results are credible.

• Is the process of defining and screening issues thorough, criterion-based, and suited to the company? If so, the issues are credible.

• Is the strategy formulation process sufficiently iterative, thoughtful, data-based, coordinated, and focused on the important issues? If so, the resulting objectives, programs, and plans are credible.
• Do the action plans, the resources allocated, and the measured perfor-mance results relate closely to the strategic objectives, programs, and plans? If so, the results are credible.

The final step is merely to measure performance results, which occurs as part of the performance management process. In fact, many of the above steps should be addressed carefully in implementing strategies. In the next chapter, some of these points are discussed.

While audits and special studies of the effectiveness of strategic manage-ment may be of interest to managers, or may be mandated by outside directors or regulatory bodies, they are not the preferred way to ensure that the process is conceived and applied effectively.

SUMMARY

Human resource strategies are critically important to organizational success in today's highly charged competitive environment. Human resource strategies guide development of a more flexible, adaptive organization. They are plans addressing opportunities to gain and sustain competitiveness through the man-agement of people. The capacity to implement business strategies requires implementation of human resource strategies focusing on people-related issues.

Some human resource strategies are focused on specific unit or individual action plans; others are broader, more integrative programs for managing strategic change. Like business strategies, they are integrated, multi-faceted, long-term agendas for changing the competitive character of a company.

Human resource plans are strategies when they help management anticipate and manage increasingly rapid, even tumultuous change. They are the means of aligning the management of human resources with the strategic context of the business. Hence, there may be human resource strategies at each level of a business: corporate, business unit, team, or individual. In a flexible organiza-tion, everyone needs to focus on issues and manage their work in concert with the strategies of the business.

Human resource strategies evolve from a business focus (customers, prod-ucts, competitors) gradually toward specific actions and programs, typically defined and implemented in terms of specific human resource functions (train-ing, recruitment, rewards, etc.). Similarly, the breadth of planning evolves from the conceptual and longer-range toward the transactional and immediate.

The process suggests a sequence, or series of steps, but in reality, planning entails defining issues and considering solutions concurrently. The outcome is a strategy that reflects the highest priorities for action. Too often, managers seize on actions they believe will yield positive results, without considering their strategic context. The purpose of human resource strategy is to provide this context, helping to ensure that the actions will, in fact, resolve the issues considered to be important.

The quality of a strategy is enhanced by more thorough, objective, and rigorous data collection and analysis. Accordingly, the more diligent the work in formulating a plan, the more likely the result will be considered relevant, well-reasoned, and grounded in fact.

The planning approach defines human resource strategy in the context of the organization's overall strategic management process. In this way, individual development, recruitment, compensation, and other activities become integral parts of a dynamic process for managing strategic change. Training programs, for example, are no longer warranted if they are not shown to be pertinent to changing skill or knowledge needs. College recruitment is tailored to satisfy specific needs.

The implementation of business strategies in the 1990s and beyond is achieved largely through the management of human resources. Hence the implementation process outlined in the following chapters, representing both explicit and implicit elements, is crucial to the future competitiveness of a business.

E. FOCUS ON MANAGING: MERGERS AND ACQUISITIONS

Many companies seek growth through mergers and acquisitions. The benefits they seek include economies of scale, market penetration, new products, enhanced systems or management capabilities, and diversification. Yet many mergers fall short of expectations. The performance of acquired companies often deteriorates significantly after acquisition as a result of ineffective management of the integration process.

For purposes of this discussion, both mergers and acquisitions represent the combination of two organizations, entailing some degree of integration. Where the two come together as peers, rather than one being dominant, the resulting organization typically represents a new combination, hopefully adopting the best of both companies.

This suggests that human resource strategies are important for mergers and acquisitions to be effectively managed. Focus needs to be on several aspects of the process:

- Consideration of human resource factors in merger evaluation and planning
- Preparation for merger implementation
- Postmerger management

Premerger Planning

A successful merger involves the right purposes, partners, price, plan, and process. The process begins with a preliminary agreement and letter of intent between the companies' top executives, as an outcome of a search for suitable candidates. Next, the companies conduct a process of due diligence analysis, which examines the quality of the business, asset value, and financial merits relative to the merger objectives.

In the financial area, human resource factors are typically considered. The compatibility of labor relations contracts is one example. In many union-free companies, the acquisition of businesses having labor agreements that are considered restrictive or costly may not be desired and may be avoided. Similarly, unfunded pension or other employee benefit plan liabilities may kill a deal. In some instances, grossly different (inequitable) incentive programs, pay levels, employee loan arrangements, or other practices may not be reconcilable.

As part of this process, or parallel to it, the companies may examine the business fit (evaluate how well the organizations and people will match) and identify issues that will need to be addressed. This includes evaluation of management and other employee capabilities (e.g., sales force or technical quality) and the relative strengths and shortfalls of the two organizations—how they might fit together and what benefits may be gained through the combination. The fit of values and practices is examined, to determine whether it is compatible and how differences may be accommodated.

This premerger period is typically brief, and the due diligence analysis may have only a short period for completion. The human resource factors need to be considered concurrently with the financial factors, not sequentially. As soon as there is an indication of a prospective deal, the total analysis process should be initiated. Both companies are typically concerned with confidentiality and with minimizing disruption and rumor or miscommunication.

In some instances, a qualitative human resource factor may be a fatal flaw. Companies that appear to be well managed may be thin in talent, or senior executives holding a company together may not be staying with the new company. Shortfalls or surpluses of talent may entail overwhelming costs to correct. Differences in values and attitudes (i.e., culture) may be determined to be too difficult to reconcile. Customer service, quality, and product management, as well as information and support systems, may be deemed inadequate.

Issues that are identified but not considered fatal to merger plans need to be recognized in the negotiation process and addressed as part of the implementation plan.

Implementation Preparation

Human resource issues become centrally important once an intended combination is announced and plans are being developed.

Of overriding concern is effective communications to employees in the affected organizations. Often more information is available in the press and in the financial community than is explicitly shared with employees. It is important that employees "hear it first" or on the heels of public communication.

When management hears news of the merger "on the street," the information should be passed on to employees, along with any explanatory comments, to keep them informed and to minimize the development of disruptive rumor.

Specific plans need to be developed to address:

• Retention of talent during the transition
• Maintenance of productivity and customer relations
• Selection of talent for positions affected by the combination; developing integrated succession plans and candidate slates for specific assignments
• Integration of compensation, benefits, recruitment, and other human resource processes and policies
• Adaptation and integration of cultures in support of the organization's objectives

Often the integration process is planned and coordinated by teams or task forces of managers assigned to specific areas for attention. Each team sets objectives, work plans, and schedules for accomplishing necessary tasks. As work progresses, each tracks and reports accomplishments and significant issues requiring attention.

As in premerger planning, the time constraints on implementation planning are also typically great. Events move quickly and management tends to hold cards close to the vest. It is important, then, for managers involved in implementation planning to address the key issues quickly and effectively.

Postmerger Management

Once a combination is completed, the task of putting it together begins. Here, decision making and implementation actions become predominant tasks. The design of jobs and organizations, the selection and assignment of individuals, the integration of systems and programs, and other integration steps are vital.

When an acquisition is a company in a similar line of business, it is more likely that management will seek to integrate the two companies and to do it quickly. When a company is in a different line of business, it is more likely that management will take a "hands off" stance, at least for a while.

Also, the process of managing expectations and communications moves into high gear. In the first several months after a merger, attention needs to be given to the concerns and apprehensions of affected employees, getting them to talk about changes and helping them develop new working relationships. The major employee concerns are:

• Loss of identity and purpose as their company changes or dissolves
• Loss of information and anxiety about changes that will occur but are uncertain
• Survival and protection from adverse effects of changes they cannot control

- Loss of valued coworkers
- Repercussions on their families as a result of the uncertainty, anxiety, frustration, anger, and heightened competitiveness

Such employee concerns are allayed by effective communications and involvement in managing changes. More broadly, however, effective management of staffing changes, the merging of cultures, reward systems, and organizational changes has the most substantive positive effects (Marks & Cutcliffe, 1988; Schweiger, Ivancevich, & Power, 1987).

In some situations, concerted efforts to manage stress may be needed. This may include individual counseling, surveying and feedback of attitudes during the transition, and group counseling or training on stress management for managers (Schweiger & Ivancevich, 1985).

F. FOCUS ON MANAGING: INTERNATIONAL HUMAN RESOURCES

Because business activity is increasingly global, companies are viewing the management of their human resources on an international basis. Among multinational corporations, a majority of revenues come from outside their home countries. And future revenue and profit opportunities for many lie internationally. Furthermore, the complexity of conducting business today impels companies to think globally. Companies are establishing joint ventures, alliances, and innovative business partnerships to capitalize on expanding opportunities worldwide.

The human resource strategy implications of global management are largely a matter of degree. The same basic processes and practices apply, but the variable of conducting business multi-nationally adds another level of complexity. For example, domestic firms seek to broaden managers through rotation among developmental assignments; the same applies for developing managers for global business, but the assignments are far more difficult to plan and implement. Although compensation and benefit practices have more commonalities than differences among different countries, the myriad of differences (many dictated by legal requirements as well as local customs) complicate the management of such reward systems globally.

As in a domestic company, decisions need to be made concerning integration and differentiation: when do practices and process in fact need to be different to fit business strategies and environments? Features of international human resource management that need to be considered lie in several areas, discussed briefly below (Butler, Ferris, & Napier, 1991; Dowling, 1988; Dowling & Schuler, 1990; Evans, Doz, & Laurent, 1990).

International human resource management involves a greater number and variety of functional activities, since it deals with different taxation and regulatory environments, international relocation and orientation of employees, and language and cultural differences. As companies seek to gain distinctive competence by managing globally in innovative and cost-effective ways, there are opportunities for human resource innovations as well. Companies are addressing global diversity, organizational design innovations, cross-cultural teamwork, values clarification, and skill development among their global management initiatives.

International management also involves a broader perspective in designing human resource programs, because of the variety of national groups among employees who may participate and the circumstances of countries in which they are assigned. Differences in benefit plan expectations, legal requirements, and cost implications require a broad understanding of country environments. In the Pacific, for example, labor is available at low wage rates, but experienced managers are scarce.

To manage talent globally, a company needs to have a greater interest and involvement in the selection, training, and effective management of professional employees. For international assignments, employees expect their company to provide assistance on housing, education, living allowances, language skills, culture orientation, and management of personal affairs (e.g., personal finances, taxes, property at home). They expect the company to plan for continued career development and, ultimately, repatriation. Development of managers who are effective in the global business environment is a particular challenge, since these individuals are concentrated on specific assignments and need guidance in building the experience base and perspective to think globally while acting locally.

By far, the majority of management attention is on international staffing. It is the most immediate, visible, and imperative area for activity. Through human resource strategy, companies may focus these staffing activities and make them more a matter of routine (for a global company) than a matter of dealing with difficult problems (for a domestic company doing business internationally). Furthermore, once these processes are re-engineered, management may turn attention to other less immediate, but farther-reaching, issues and opportunities.

Challenges for the 1990s and beyond include:

• Managing new organizational arrangements more effectively, including joint ventures, alliances, and project-based organizations
• Redefining managerial competencies required for effective management in a truly global business environment and determining more effective ways to develop global managers
• Balancing the needs of global and local management practices, allowing adaptation to truly different situational requirements while sustaining global business perspective and integration (avoiding the whipsawing that results from the argument that every international situation requires a different solution)
• Adopting perspectives and approaches from local country businesses and cultures, and treating the United States as merely one region of the global business (overcoming the U.S. home country bias)

• Finding new ways to enhance worldwide communication for purposes of speedy customer response, technology transfer, involvement of employees at widespread locations, and development of a shared mindset across the company

International human resource management is not a special function to be defined and performed. It is, rather, a dimension of human resource strategy formulation and implementation; it is a level of complexity that is challenging management in all companies that seek to do business globally.

G. FOCUS ON MANAGING: LABOR RELATIONS

In the 1980s, labor unions experienced strong employer challenges, resulting in concessions in contracts, reduced strength or decertification, and shrinking membership. Companies have sought competitive flexibility by containing wage rates, staffing with fewer employees, and averting union organizing efforts. At the same time, labor union relations are taking a more moderate tone; because management clearly has the advantage of power, it need not flaunt it.

Only 16.4% of all American workers belong to unions, down by half since World War II. France is the only industrial nation less unionized. Organizing unions is difficult because companies have become more effective in helping supervisors communicate with employees. Companies also wield threats of closures, often considered valid because of already high cost structures and stiff competition. Recruiting new members is costly for unions, limiting the scale of their efforts (Schiffman, 1991).

In 1989, Nissan turned away the United Auto Workers at the plant in Smyrna, Tennessee. The company based its campaign on treating workers fairly. "We involve them in decisions that affect their lives, and we believe that allowed the employees to believe the union could do nothing for them," said Gail Neuman, Nissan's general counsel and vice president of human resources (Schiffman, 1991). Nissan used 120 video monitors in the plant to communicate with workers. While staying union-free, the plant saw reduced turnover, increased productivity, and fewer accidents and errors.

As unions have weakened, companies are concerned with staying competitive with increasingly nonunion rivals. Where companies are union-free, they intend to stay that way; where they have unions, they intend to determine the terms of agreements. This has led to aggressively opposed organizing campaigns, aggressive decertification efforts, and aggressive efforts to preserve union-free status. In the 1990s, there will be forceful campaigns, but more positive relations are likely than the strong campaigns of the past decade (e.g., Eastern Airlines, Greyhound Lines).

Unions, which developed and evolved in response to changing labor-management environments, are tackling their challenges. In the absence of winning economic gains for members, unions are expanding their services to attract new members and retain their roles and influence. They offer employee assistance programs to prevent alcohol and drug abuse and are including family counseling and social services. Mortgages, credit cards, portable health insurance, auto insurance, and college loans are among the services that may be extended. Unions may find new roles as a sort of social organization or agency for workers.

In America, most union growth is in the public sector, where laws are more favorable and opposition is less severe. By one estimate, half of all union members will be in the public sector by the year 2000 (Holusha, 1990). Also, there is less pressure to cut jobs in the public sector. Public sector growth leads the union push among services workers, the fastest-growing segment of the work force. Private sector initiatives have focused upon retailing, food service, and office workers, with mixed outcomes.

Management has the option of embracing unions in cooperative endeavors, maintaining an arm's-length relationship, or adapting to the task and situation. Some companies have actively engaged unions in pursuing cost reduction, quality improvement, flexible staffing, and other strategies. Unions may smooth efforts to redesign jobs, introduce new technology, or adopt productivity-related pay programs (e.g., gainsharing).

Similarly, as advocates for employees, unions may seek to become involved in planning and implementing company actions affecting divestitures, close-downs, new operations, and other changes; or they may remain independent, to avoid loss of influence with members. At companies such as General Motors, unions have sought to collaborate with management in bringing about changes needed to maintain external business competitiveness.

While unions may be possible contributors to competitive advantage, managers typically perceive them as an intervening force complicating management. Because of the clear dualism in approaches to industrial relations (cooperative and adversary relationships), it is not yet clear that unions play a role in formulating or implementing business strategies (Butler, Ferris, & Napier, 1991).

For multi-national corporations, labor unions may constrain management flexibility when competitive actions are needed. Local country labor and political environments vary widely; in some situations, unions are regarded as key parties in management decisions (Dowling & Schuler, 1990). The presence of strong, influential unions may result in labor cost structures (higher wage levels) that are disadvantageous in certain markets. Unions may also constrain employment flexibility, including staffing reductions, job assignments, and hiring decisions (especially in Japan, Australia, and Western Europe). Most significantly, the myriad of union relations patterns and practices hinders management efforts to develop an integrated global management process. The focus on different situations draws attention and resources away from focused competitive actions.

H. FOCUS ON MANAGING: INFORMATION TECHNOLOGY

Companies are seeking to use information technology to help reduce the time and resources required for human resource management. They are re-engineering processes to reduce the number of activities and steps involved, and then applying information systems to automate them as much as possible. At the same time, by helping managers and employees use information systems directly, human resource staff gain time to address strategic issues and to pursue improvements in processes.

The automation of human resource processes is occurring at an optimal time—when information technology is poised to provide new and efficient ways to support management needs. Personal computers, information networks, local data bases (including use of large-capacity hard disks and CD-ROM), expert systems, and user-friendly applications software (e.g., icon interfaces) are among the numerous examples.

Information systems costs are typically 20% or more of a human resource staff function's total expenses. Increasing this expenditure allows reduction in staffing, travel, and other larger expenses. In addition, management and employee time and expenses may be reduced.

Existing systems have had several difficulties, which are being overcome through new applications. Often, line managers have not had direct access to systems, even to data on their own employees. Likewise, human resource staff often need to rely on computer specialists for special reporting and analysis; reporting is typically difficult. Changes in systems are often incremental, resulting in a jerry-built combination of mainframe and personal computer systems, multiple data bases and applications systems, and complexities in processes of updating and retrieving information.

Applications today are focused in the areas of compensation, benefits, and employee relations. The primary application is for routine record keeping in support of employment terms and conditions. More advanced applications lie in analysis and reporting of trends and issues, computer-based training, and automated employee surveys. Technology has the greatest impact on administration—and promises, through re-engineering, to greatly simplify processes (A. Walker, 1992).

Emerging applications are in these areas:

• Employee networking: for communications, involvement in quality improvement, continuous attitude surveys, and self-directed development (e.g., job posting, career planning)
• Training and development: skill assessment and training needs identification, and individual and team-based training (supplemented with on-the-job and classroom activities)
• Strategic staffing: identification of skill requirements, forecasting of requirements, and planning for recruitment and internal mobility (vacancy planning)

• Job analysis and design: computer-based job analysis and evaluation, and analysis of activities to guide restructuring

• Flexible compensation and benefits: tailored programs within an overall framework, with continuous monitoring of activities; expert systems to handle enrollments and information requests; and tracking of service vendor performance

• Legal compliance: tracking and reporting on chemical substances, health and safety, EEO, and other requirements

For economic reasons, companies typically make incremental changes to existing systems. In the 1990s, however, many are reexamining needs in light of future strategies and are designing new architecture for information systems for human resource needs. Many systems, introduced decades ago, were mainframe-oriented and inflexible. Today, relational data-base management systems provide the flexibility needed to accommodate varied and changing user requirements and connectivity (e.g., telephone, PCs). In the past, systems were built from scratch or adapted from a few semicustom products. Today, many software products are available amid a continuing torrent of innovations.

The emphasis is shifting, therefore, from HRIS (human resource information systems) toward effective use of information technology for human resource management. HRIS consultant Al Walker indicates that system design projects today typically start with an executive view of strategic requirements and desired ways for using systems to reshape human resource functions (A. Walker, 1992).

At the same time, the mainframe system is far from dead, as companies seek to retain consistency and control over information in an increasingly decentralized environment. The price of autonomy, a CEO once said to me, is information. Recentralization, often in conjunction with consolidated human resource services staffs, helps management achieve desired cost-efficiencies without loss of effectiveness.

Chevron, for example, is creating an integrated on-line HRIS which will support the company's strategic direction and management of human resources (Stright, 1991). The Chevron HRIS will improve management of organization planning, employee development, benefits administration, labor relations, compensation planning and administration, and human resources administration. Special applications will include:

• Organization planning: a data base on all existing and planned positions, their status and attributes, their incumbents, and skill mismatches

• Employment: management of requisitions in relation to job posting, applicant tracking, and candidate assessment

• Succession planning: identifying positions and requirements, and tracking multiple successors and their development

• Retirement counseling: on-line, real-time service to employees on retirement options and benefits

The major challenge in the 1990s will be to develop fully integrated, fully implemented systems that meet management needs. Piecemeal approaches will prove too costly and will fail to yield the competitive advantages that companies seek through such investments. Built around a core data base of employee and position information, these systems will serve specific locations or applications. Consultant Ren Nardoni (Nardoni Associates, Inc.) recommends rational combinations of PC-based systems with downloads and linkages to core data-base systems. These are the ideal solutions to ensure that basic data on employees are captured and entered once but used by multiple downstream systems.

Changes in systems will be continuous as technology develops and as management applications needs evolve. Investments will rise, but with the clear expectation of managing human resources more efficiently and serving employees and managers more effectively.

CHAPTER 4

ALIGNING EMPLOYEE EXPECTATIONS WITH STRATEGY

I'm damned pessimistic about the ability of huge companies to ever do anything that's new.

Tom Peters, interview in *USA Today,* June 7, 1990

Whatever strategies a company adopts, including human resource strategies, are useful only if they are implemented. Many managers have effectively aligned the expectations of the people in their organizations with new strategic directions and the new behaviors required to implement them. Many other managers lack either the incentive or the capability to effectively manage the process necessary to implement needed change. As a result, the failure of strategies is typically not one of inaccuracy, but of inactivity.

Strategies, first of all, must be communicated. Managers, employees, and others involved in implementing strategies need to understand the reasons for change, what changes are planned, and their expected effects. This includes communication of the mission, vision, and values of the organization, verbally and also symbolically, through actions and implicit signs. Furthermore, these elements of a strategic plan and specific objectives need to be communicated at all levels—to unit, team, and individual.

This communication process becomes more specific and tangible as managers translate strategies into performance expectations, typically as key result areas (KRAs) and objectives for groups, teams, and individuals. Also, managers help align employee expectations about the future through their efforts to change the organizational culture—the set of values, beliefs, and norms of behavior shared by people in the organization.

This chapter addresses the ways in which managers influence employee expectations as a first step in implementing business and human resource strategies:

- How management can shape employee expectations
- How strategies are communicated to build a expectation, even an excitement, about prospective changes

• How strategies are translated into operational terms, so that they may be acted upon

• How the underlying organizational culture may be modified to support strategy implementation

SHAPING EMPLOYEE EXPECTATIONS

If, at its essence, managing is getting things done through other people, then it is a basic task of managers to prepare employees for changes necessitated by business strategies. Among employee attitudes and perceptions that influence their behavior at work are their anticipations regarding the future. Managers cannot assume that employees welcome change, or are even ready for it to occur. They must, instead, help employees recognize the need for change, understand what is required, evaluate and accept the implications of change, and take needed actions.

Implementing Change

The process of managing change is the crux of aligning employee expectations with strategy. Where there is a strong prevailing culture, people are skeptical of the need for change and resist it. A series of steps should be followed in managing implementation of change, as illustrated in Exhibit 4-1. In each step, employees ask questions that need to be answered effectively.

First, employees ask "Why should we change?" Management needs to establish a shared recognition of the need for change. This awareness may be provided in large part by communication of the mission, vision, values, and strategy. Additional information on competitive conditions, consumer needs and expectations, and other external factors requiring the change also helps shape recognition of new needs. It is also useful to help employees understand the business and economic consequences of not making the change. This is typically done through management communications of various forms, including face-to-face discussions.

Next, employees want to know "What is the plan?" Management needs to help employees understand the required changes, in terms of more specific implementation plans, objectives, steps, and goals. Participation in the development of the plan is very helpful, as well as experimentation within units of the organization with the kinds of changes planned.

The question "How will it affect me?" reflects the anxiety about adverse consequences coming with change. Management needs to discuss, as openly and as candidly as possible, the positive and the adverse effects of change. Employees also want to know how much latitude they will have in adapting to the change: Is it voluntary? Can it be deferred? Do they have a voice in deciding changes? Many plans are not implemented because they are subverted, postponed, sidestepped, or ignored.

Employees want to know "What is expected of me?" Here management

---

EXHIBIT 4-1 STEPS IN IMPLEMENTING CHANGE

Step	Employee Questions Asked	Management Lever
Recognition of the need for change	Why should we change? • External conditions • Customer needs • Company challenges	Communicate vision, strategy
Understanding of required changes	What is the plan? • Desired end state • What will be different • Transition steps and goals • Experimentation	Communicate vision, strategy, and implementation plans
Evaluation and acceptance	How will it affect me? • Benefits • Negatives • Latitude	Discuss the need, plan, and effects Strong leadership
Action	What do you expect of me? • New relationships • Teamwork and cooperation • New activities/tasks • New learning/education • New focus in performance	Change structure, work design, staffing and development, performance system/rewards
Feedback	How is the change progressing? • What is going on • How I am doing	Communicate actions, activities, results

---

needs to specify and demonstrate clearly the changes that will be implemented and how employees will need to change their behavior. In the absence of clear direction, for example, people will reshape their own work—doing those things they think appropriate or that they have done in the past. The cascading of the plan to each unit and individual helps meet this need. Changes in the management systems—such as training, staffing, and rewards—help shape these expectations as well, if they are effectively attuned to the change agenda.

Employees want to know "How is the change progressing?" Too often, there is considerable energy and communication early in the implementation process, and then months later, business falls into a new routine. It is important to keep employees informed of changes, even if in an informal manner, and to provide regular feedback on the contribution they are making to the process. Even in objectives-based approaches, managers too often fail to review performance against the objectives and to communicate accomplishments to employees.

This process of aligning expectations with strategy is described more simply by Dr. Dale Dunn, a human resource manager at ARCO Oil and Gas. He cites five "A"s that individuals need to create an attitude of readiness for change.

These are, corresponding to the above steps, awareness, analysis, assimilation, action, and actualization. There are no shortcuts if changes are to be effectively implemented.

Such steps and cautions may seem self-apparent. However, managers in company after company launch new initiatives and refocus activities to implement strategies without following through in a meaningful way with the people who are responsible for bringing about the changes.

Each step is best implemented through a two-way communication process, with active employee participation at the appropriate level. Some companies involve employees intensively in the process, through discussion groups, interviews, planning activities, focus groups, and other means to allow them to think through each question (and typically come up with excellent responses). Reinforcement by management—in terms of external communications (press statements, for example), treatment of senior executives, recognitions and punishments given during the course of change, and other visible actions—is important. Management may need to "overcommunicate" during the process, repeating communications and discussions in order to make sure that people are fully answering their questions.

Management Levers

Management has three primary levers for aligning employee expectations with strategy. These are discussed in this chapter. They provide an important thrust for considering the other actions involved in the management of human resources, which are discussed in subsequent chapters.

Communicating the strategic direction is always a logical starting point. However, it is not merely a "one-shot" exercise. It requires ongoing communication of the mission, vision, values, and specific strategic directions of the business as they evolve. As shown in Exhibit 4-2, this effort helps employees recognize the need for change and helps them understand the changes required. However, this initial communication has little direct influence on their evaluation, acceptance, or action.

By translating strategies into performance objectives, management gives employees some tangible, specific information they can deal with. The less ambiguous this translation, the more helpful the effort is for employees and the more useful the lever for management. Performance planning has a potentially broad effect on employee expectations. When integrated with performance evaluation, it provides the feedback that employees expect and desire. Of course, customer feedback and direct observation of the results achieved may be more powerful than formal managerial performance evaluations.

Finally, a wide range of management actions helps reshape an organizational culture. It is not by rhetoric but by a multitude of demonstrated actions that the values, beliefs, and norms guiding behavior are changed. The way managers manage human resources has the primary influence on the behavior that reflects the culture. Management efforts to reshape the culture, therefore, have

---

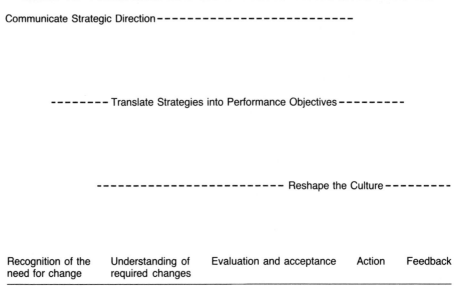

EXHIBIT 4-2 ALIGNING EXPECTATIONS WITH STRATEGIES

Communicate Strategic Direction ─

─ ─ ─ ─ ─ ─ ─ ─ Translate Strategies into Performance Objectives ─ ─ ─ ─ ─ ─ ─ ─ ─

─ Reshape the Culture ─ ─ ─ ─ ─ ─ ─ ─

Recognition of the need for change	Understanding of required changes	Evaluation and acceptance	Action	Feedback

---

major influence on the employees' understanding of required changes, evaluation and acceptance of change, and action.

COMMUNICATING STRATEGIC DIRECTION

The most important tool management has for implementing change is the strategy itself. In a rapidly changing business environment, employees welcome a sense of direction and purpose. An articulated strategy meets this need, both in its content and in its symbolic intent. The strategy itself may provide information on the mission, vision, and future priorities of the organization. It is inherently educational. More important, it engenders excitement, it builds fervor, and it energizes an organization.

The strategy provides a beacon which may guide everyone in the organization toward a common purpose. "It empowers individual employees and forms the basis of a planned culture. All practices, policies, and symbols of a high-performance, high-commitment organization are congruent and point in the same direction" (Sherwood, 1988). The strategy defines both "where we are" and "where we're going"—a commitment to continual progress toward a defined end state. As such, it also allows people to assess how well they are doing—their progress along the way.

Strategic planning, observed Rosabeth Moss Kanter, provides a "deliberate and conscious articulation of a direction. Strong leaders articulate direction and save the organization from change via 'drift'. They create a vision of a possible future that allows themselves and others to see more clearly the steps to take, building on present capacities and strengths" (Kanter, 1982).

Given the opportunity, people will rally to a cause they understand to be right and in their best interest. Within an organization, a considerable degree of existing support among employees gives managers latitude in shaping and adopting new directions for the business. Says DuPont CEO Edgar Woolard, "Employees have been underestimated. You have to start with the premise that people at all levels want to contribute and make the business a success" (Dumaine, 1990).

Whether a specific, focused plan or a broad agenda for change, strategies point to new opportunities for people in an organization. New strategic directions represent both positive and negative possibilities for people. In communicating new directions, managers obviously accentuate the positives, demonstrating the need for change and the anticipated benefits of change. But communications need to be realistic and allow individuals to believe that they can work their way through change for mutual benefit.

Communication Gaps

In recent years, a gap has developed between employees and management, particularly senior management. According to employee surveys in hundreds of companies, hourly employees, professionals, and supervisors increasingly mistrust senior management intentions. The trust gap is widening.

For example, employees see a growing difference between the pay and perquisites of senior management and their own. "Just when top management want everyone to begin swaying to a faster, more productive beat, employees are loath to dance" (Farnham, 1989). The gap is a result of different viewpoints.

Employees are not fully tuned in to the vision, values, and objectives espoused by managment. Conversely, senior management is not tuned in to what employees really think and want. The lines of communication are fraying, and with them, the bonds of trust and mutual respect.

Companies often fail to explain business priorities and business changes. Policy changes are not always articulated with their rationale. The rationale for management actions is often unclear. Employees are frequently the last to know about events they think they need to know. And employees are often not adequately recognized for their contributions. Of course, upward communication is typically faulted. Only 45% of large employers make regular use of employee opinion surveys, an obvious way to carry employee views upward (Farnham, 1989).

Mission: A Clear Purpose

A mission, or business purpose, defines the reason for a firm's existence. It also indicates the primary products, services, or lines of business the company is in. It should be short, clear, unambiguous, and memorable. Ideally, it is compelling, evoking a bone-deep emotional attachment that connects with personal interests (Harrison, 1987).

Mission statements are typically brief but far-reaching:

Help people transform the way they work, learn, and communicate by providing exceptional personal computing products and innovative customer services. (Apple Computer)

To be the leading restaurant chain in the world by satisfying customers' demands for quality quick service eating occasions with a chicken-dominant menu. (KFC)

To improve the financial well-being of individuals, business owners and employers, through providing trusted, competent advice to reduce the complexity of financial operations and by delivering a selected range of financial products and services principally through a face-to-face distribution network. (Manulife Financial)

Bringing refreshment to a thirsty world is a unique opportunity for our Company and for all of our Coca-Cola associates . . . to create shareholder value. Ours is the only production and distribution business system capable of realizing that opportunity on a global scale. And we are committed to realizing it. (Coca-Cola Company)

Mission statements rarely change, as they are explanations of "the business we are in" or "why we are in business." They provide the highest abstraction of strategy for employees, customers, and other constituents to consider.

Vision: A Future Scenario

A vision translates the mission into a future scenario for the organization. It defines what the company intends to become in the future (after it changes). Amoco Corporation, a leading oil company, says:

Amoco will be a global enterprise, recognized throughout the world as preeminent by employees, customers, competitors, investors and the public. We will be the standard by which other businesses measure their performance. Our hallmarks will be the innovation, initiative and teamwork of our people, and our ability to anticipate and effectively respond to change, and to create opportunity.

The scenario lays out specific characteristics that will distinguish the company in the future and define its success. It may include:

- Size: revenues, employees, profitability, assets
- Market impact: what markets and products, market share, position relative to competitors
- Identity: how the company will be perceived by customers, competitors, communities, and the public at large
- Management: how the company will be structured and managed in the future

A vision allows individuals to see what the future situation could be like, to imagine the experience of working in a different set of circumstances. It gives greater clarity for people who have a hard time envisioning the future and, as a result, are fearful of it. A vision of the business five or ten years hence is a way to build consensus and support for basic changes in organization, staffing, and focusing of services. Based on analysis of trends and alternative assumptions, a positive vision is something people can debate, react to, and understand.

Values and Beliefs

A company's values are also critical to communicating strategy. These are the underlying and relatively constant commitments to constituents—the set of beliefs, principles, or philosophy by which the company operates. They provide clear standards against which the company may be judged. Behavior may not always match the values, but they exist as a goal toward which everyone strives.

Values may be as simple as IBM's set of principles: "respect for the individual, the best customer service in the world, and the pursuit of excellence." For other organizations, there may be several levels of detail, starting with basic beliefs and then defining these in terms of behaviors, commitments, or actions.

Companies emphasize different themes in their communications. For example, Weyerhaeuser Forest Products Company emphasizes its dedication to "total quality" in its statements of vision, values, and business priorities and goals. In its business mission statement and statement of beliefs, Apple emphasizes innovation, teamwork, and performance achievement.

S. C. Johnson Wax, a century-old private company, emphasizes its high standards and consistent long-term growth (see Exhibit 4-3). "*This We Believe*

EXHIBIT 4-3 S. C. JOHNSON WAX: "THIS WE BELIEVE"

Employees

We believe that the fundamental vitality and strength of our worldwide company lies in our people

Consumers and users

We believe in earning the enduring goodwill of consumers and users of our products and services

General public

We believe in being a responsible leader within the free market economy

Neighbors and hosts

We believe in contributing to the well-being of the countries and communities where we conduct business

World community

We believe in improving international understanding

Source: S. C. Johnson Wax, used with permission.

states beliefs in relation to the five groups of people to whom we are responsible and whose trust we have to earn. These beliefs are real and we will strive to live up to them. Our commitment to them is evident in our actions to date." In a booklet, each belief is explained in detail.

Companies blend these three types of statements (mission, vision, and values) and use these terms interchangeably. For some, the mission statement encompasses a vision. For others, values constitute a broad philosophy for managing. The result may not be confusing at all, but beneficial as a meaningful, direct communication to employees.

Statements are made in terms of commitments, or promises. For example, Promus Companies (named for "promise," in Latin)—operators of Harrah's, Embassy Suites, Hampton Inn, and Homewood Suites—developed a vision based on "people pledged to excellence": promises to customers, employees, franchisees, shareholders, and communities. "Fulfilling our promises will make us the premier hospitality company in the world." Mission, vision, and values are wrapped into one powerful statement. Excerpts from Promus Companies' promises are presented in Exhibit 4-4.

Some companies keep the corporate communication at a minimum and focus on distinctive features of divisions. For example, National Westminster Bank,

---

EXHIBIT 4-4   PROMUS COMPANIES: PEOPLE PLEDGED TO EXCELLENCE

We promise:

Excellent service to every casino and hotel customer every time. Our promise is unconditional and backed by our satisfaction guarantee.

High quality products and outstanding services at prices that create exceptional value for our customers.

To continually improve the quality and value of existing products and services.

To be good listeners to both customers and competitors; in order to develop innovative new products and services to meet the changing needs of tomorrow's customers.

To continually reduce our costs and improve productivity to create outstanding value for our customers.

To attract and retain the best people by providing each employee the opportunity to develop to their full potential.

A growing company, with a bias toward action and the encouragement of risk-taking by being willing to let people fail and learn.

A climate of open, two-way communication based on mutual respect for each individual, and trust and integrity in all our relationships.

To foster teamwork and cooperation, and to minimize layers of supervision so that each employee is allowed greater responsibility for the fulfillment of our promises.

To create growing hotel systems with superior competitive advantage in well-defined market segments delivering long-term brand superiority and outstanding financial returns.

To be the industry leader in financial performance as measured by return on equity, growth in cash flow and earnings, and return on invested capital.

Source: Promus Companies, 1990.

USA, focuses on its core businesses: consumer, middle market, corporate, and international. While Marriott has an overall philosophy, its businesses have distinct missions and management approaches. In fact, its Courtyard Division defines four values as the "cornerstones for success": promote respect for the individual, provide care for the guest, pursue excellence, and produce value for the corporation.

Developing Deeper Understanding

There is a risk in communicating "a little." Managers and employees lack enough knowledge of the business to be able to judge whether the stated direction is reasonable or appropriate. Too often, companies suffer the "Plexiglas syndrome." As described by David Nadler, head of Delta Consulting Group, executives rush to put the strategy into Plexiglas on walls or desks, without providing the amplification or follow-through necessary for credibility. The plan may appear poorly conceived, and implementation may be poorly planned, or even at odds with the current reality. As a result, people are skeptical.

What is preferred is a common mindset, a way of thinking that is shared by members of an organization (Ulrich, 1990b). When people think similarly, unity of purpose and activity follow, and individuals work together toward a common goal. As discussed above, a mindset may be shared regarding the company mission, vision, values, and competitive business context. This is the predominant approach for shaping expectations, although an alarming number of companies still maintain strategies as confidential and do not take the time or effort to openly communicate them with employees.

In other ways, a shared mindset may be developed. It may form around the way "things are done around here" or should be done. Thus, the focus of expectations is on the means, not the ends: how decisions are made, how people are oriented and trained, how people are treated, etc. It may also form around expectations of outsiders—most importantly customers, but also business partners, suppliers, or others. In this way, employees focus their expectations on serving customers or meeting other stakeholder interests.

A deeper understanding of the business may be developed by communicating the competitive business conditions that give rise to the strategy. People are capable of learning about and caring about the competitive effectiveness of the business. There is no reason they cannot or should not be part of the company's solution to its competitive problems.

Sometimes senior executives are acutely aware of the competitive need for change, but others who were not part of the planning process were not exposed to the issues of concern. This can be compensated for by sharing competitive information with employees: information on competitor practices, customer satisfaction survey results, product performance in the marketplace (sales, share, trends), or outsider views of the company (e.g., Wall Street, distributors). In a sense, managers may "diffuse dissatisfaction throughout the organization" as a way to align expectations with strategy (Specter, 1989).

This approach involves employees directly in the process of developing strategy-related information. Competitive assessment projects can be conducted by teams, including employees at all levels. Banks even have their tellers "shop" at competitor branches to assess their service quality. Restaurants reimburse staff for meals at competitor establishments for the same purpose. Companies applying the total quality process routinely do competitive benchmarking, survey customer expectations/standards, and solicit and evaluate feedback. Thus employees are direct participants in the process of defining the "pain."

It is important to recognize that the direction is not always clear. Regardless of the efforts to align employee expectations, the strategy has to be in place to align with. For example, as AT&T was launching its major changes, Charles L. Brown, former chairman of the board, said, "I think we can do the internal job without fear of failure, once we're given some decent understanding of what is expected of us. But the complexity of trying to change ourselves, when we don't know what the future rules are going to be, injects a degree of uncertainty that creates a lot of anxiety" (D. Nadler, 1982).

Managers must do the best they can to shape expectations, but must also recognize that it is a slow and evolving process. "Blueprints and forecasts are important tools and should be provided as much and as frequently as possible. But they are only approximations, and they may be modified dramatically as events unfold. And they are fundamentally different from the emotional appeal—the appeal to human imagination, human faith, and sometimes human greed—that needs to be made to get people on board" (Kanter, 1983).

Involving Employees in Communicating Strategies

Communications on strategy are best when they involve two-way interaction. Research and experience show that face-to-face communications are generally preferable to one-way communications. Interactive discussions may supplement printed material, speeches, videotaped presentations, etc. There are many ways to create opportunities for discussion, through team meetings, training events, planning sessions, and one-on-one meetings.

Employees need to learn about planned changes from credible sources. Whether this means that an organization needs to have one or a few truly respected and inspiring leaders is not certain. At the very least, the managers who present a view of the future should be individuals known as trustworthy, knowledgeable, and energetic. Employees generally prefer to hear information from managers they know, rather than from distant leaders.

A few years ago, Tandem Computers, a California computer manufacturer, staged some 600 hours of meetings over several months to explain its strategy to employees. Televised discussions with the various senior executives (marketing, finance, manufacturing) were beamed to U.S. locations, with telephone hookups for questions.

Other companies use off-site meetings, retreats, and junkets as forums for discussion of strategy. "We talk strategy wherever and whenever we meet," said a CEO of a company trying to "turn on" its employees and charge up growth and competitive edge. Another organization stresses personal involvement as it "deploys" its strategies. On-site visits, interactive meetings, and discussions address the whats, whys, and hows. The company measures success in terms of employee ability to translate strategy to "my daily work."

Some managers go a step farther. They involve employees in the total process of defining the mission and vision. Design teams explore opportunities for change (often including development of the strategic business plan), assess and choose alternatives, and prepare the plans for implementing actions. In this radically bottom-up approach, senior executives are merely sponsors (facilitating strategy development, not dictating it). The idea is that change should be systemic and that commitment will result naturally from a plan that everyone helped create (Sherwood, 1988). "When we treat the mission-building task as a technical or pragmatic exercise, we do not pay enough attention to building that sense of community and mutual support required for real organizational change" (Harrison, 1987).

TRANSLATING STRATEGY INTO OBJECTIVES

People can't do things "in general." Broad strategic directions need to be translated into performance expectations at the unit, group, team, and individual levels of an organization. Well-defined objectives provide the foundation for managing the organization, people, and performance in a business.

For decades, Peter Drucker has argued that management by objectives is the only practical way to run a business. "Objectives are the foundation for designing both the structure of the business and the work of individual units and individual managers." Drucker believes that objectives are important because the measurements available for most aspects of managing are still largely haphazard. We don't know what we "ought to achieve" (e.g., appropriate profitability levels), so we set reasonable targets, or objectives, based on what we do know (Drucker, 1973).

Through a total quality management process, employees at all levels may be involved in defining performance requirements, based on analysis of customer requirements. Customers may be external or may be other individuals or units within the company. Through this process, performance objectives are not imposed by management, but shaped through an ongoing process of assessment, feedback, redefinition, and continual improvement.

Performance objectives should derive from the strategy of a business—the mission, vision, and overall business objectives. They should be action commitments, through which the mission is to be carried out, and the standards by which performance is to be measured. In a practical sense, the objectives that managers set (collectively and individually) represent the actual strategy of the company. In some companies, broad objectives are called goals. They are typically more directional and less specific.

Objectives operationalize strategy in another important way. They specify accountability for results and guide decisions regarding allocation of resources. Capital, expenses, assets, material, human effort—all resources should be concentrated on the right areas. Because resouces are scarce, they need to be placed where they will achieve the greatest yield.

Links to the Planning Process

As discussed in Chapter 3, performance expectations stem from three aspects of the overall planning process in a company:

- Strategic objectives, programs, and processes
- Operating plans and goals
- Individual or unit performance plans

Ideally, all three of these levels in the business planning process are closely interrelated. All performance objectives are consistent and synchronized as a common set of objectives at each level of the organization: division or group, unit, team, and individual.

Managing strategically requires managers to drive performance from the strategic direction and, in turn, from operating plans and objectives. It is clearly a top-down, management-driven process aimed at bringing about the desired behavior and organizational change need for competitive performance. It is intentional, dynamic, directive, and change-oriented.

For performance management, specific objectives and measures are established jointly by individuals and their managers. However, they should be set within a clearly defined context of business priorities. To an extent, a "shared mindset" is sufficient as a context for setting objectives, but this depends on how aligned everyone is with the true needs of the business.

Conversely, some people argue that the business plans are a weak foundation on which to build performance plans. Plans in many companies are weak because they are not rigorously developed. Why? Because they are not used to shape performance. The negative cycle results in deterioration and neglect of planning and strategic thinking.

Human resource objectives, at any level of planning, should be among the functional objectives in a manager's plan. At each organizational level, objectives relating to organization structure, work design and management, staffing and development, and performance are potentially critical to achieving the business plan. Hence they should be addressed directly in the plan.

This needs to be mentioned only because some companies still view strategic and operating plans (and budgets) as primarily financial, marketing, production, or otherwise functionally oriented. However, the human resource factors, acknowledged to be the key elements of a change strategy (see Exhibit 3-4), are not peripheral or supporting. As many companies have demonstrated, the implementation of human resource strategy is pivotal to gaining and sustaining competitive advantage.

Focusing on Results

The translation of strategy into objectives is in terms of results to be achieved. From decades of managing by objectives, companies have learned that:

- The clearer idea you have of what you are trying to accomplish, the greater are your chances of accomplishment.
- Simply by having objectives, people tend (or try) to perform at that level.
- It's not what you do, but what you get done that counts.
- Progress can be measured only in terms of what one is trying to move toward.

Most people are results-oriented, and when given the opportunity (and support) to perform, they will voluntarily do so in a manner consistent with their objectives and those of their organization.

A company's objectives should be defined in terms of results. While the strategic direction may be broad, key priorities can be established in a way that allows specific targets and measures. In fact, of the myriad of priorities that an organization may have, only a few are critical—make a significant difference in performance. "Setting priorities encourages managers to emphasize the 20% that will make the difference and, in a sense, to let the other 80% (which will at best contribute 20% of the impact) take care of itself."

This is why organizations define priorities and goals. A well-managed company committed to total quality has business goals and priorities that provide an excellent basis for setting specific performance objectives (see Exhibit 4-5). These goals reflect both operational and strategic concerns.

EXHIBIT 4-5 EXAMPLES OF BUSINESS PRIORITIES AND GOALS

Customer satisfaction

- Fully meet our commitments to customers, both external and internal
- Increase the value-added services provided with each product sale, according to business plans
- Achieve a six sigma quality standard in all products
- Reduce order-to-delivery cycle time to 16 weeks

Organization effectiveness

- Implement total quality management at all levels, company wide
- Attain an 80% rating on employee opinion survey results in all units, world wide
- Reduce work days lost and workers' compensation costs by 25%

Financial performance

- Achieve financial measures in the top quartile in our industry comparison group
- Achieve a net 22% cash flow return on assets
- Become the low-cost provider of products and services in our industry

---

A national restaurant chain developed key result areas (KRAs) for a restaurant manager. They translate the strategy and objectives of the organization into concrete performance areas:

- Food quality
- Employee relations, training, and development
- Management training and development
- Clean, well-maintained stores
- Customer service
- Controllable costs
- Sales

The first four result areas are considered directly controllable by unit managers and contribute to performance in the other three result areas. In addition, management training and development as well as employee relations, training, and development are considered important KRAs because they support the rapidly growing chain's needs for talent in a tight labor market.

Common performance measures for each KRA are defined, and objectives (performance levels relative to the measures) are set, as applicable to each unit. The unit management team, consisting of three to five managers, is awarded bonuses for achievement of the specific objectives.

Key result areas are often used as categories in which specific objectives and measures of a manager and others are defined. For example, key result areas for a hotel general manager are presented in Exhibit 4-6. For each KRA, specific observable measures are listed, which provide a basis for evaluating the achieved results. How can one person effectively address all of these areas? A general manager is responsible for the overall performance of the property, as reflected in these key areas. Accomplishment of the results involves the performance of the entire management team at the property.

The concept of key result areas was pioneered by Peter Drucker and has been used widely as a bridge between broad strategies and specific performance objectives. He identified these areas as important for defining "key results": profitability, market standing (share), asset utilization (ROI), productivity (efficiency), research and development (innovation), organization development and human resource management, and social/corporate responsibility.

Similar processes are used in other companies for defining expectations of performance relative to the overall strategy. For example, Procter & Gamble focuses strategy within each department on each individual as a "personal accountability plan." This includes tactics, objectives, success measures, and stop items.

This cascading process of objective setting contrasts sharply with bottom-up performance objective setting, where there is no clear and direct linkage with strategies. It contrasts even more sharply with management practices that lack specific results-oriented objectives—where objectives are defined in terms of activities and duties, or where there are no objectives at all. In high-perform-

---

EXHIBIT 4-6 KEY RESULT AREAS: HOTEL GENERAL MANAGER

Revenue
- Average daily use
- Customer count
- Group sales, catering

Cost management
- Payroll
- Food and beverage
- Room supplies and housekeeping

Guest service
- Satisfaction scores
- Repeat business results

Human resources
- Employee retention/turnover
- Productivity
- Training and development

Asset purchases
- Refurbishment commitments
- Capital improvements

Engineering
- Maintenance
- Utility/energy savings

---

ing, flexible organizations, performance objectives, either for individuals or teams, are vital to align behavior with strategy.

CHANGING THE CULTURE

Expectations are not shaped only by communicating an intended vision and strategy for change or by establishing performance objectives, however relevant they may be. Change is threatening to people accustomed to stability and continuity. Strategies imply change, and so some people resist them.

Hence more must be done by a company seeking to implement a significant agenda of change—strategies that represent significant shifts in the business. Management must change the organization structure, work design, staffing and development, and performance systems and rewards, all in a synchronized way to influence expectations and, therefore, behavior. Management must also directly influence the values, beliefs, and norms that knit an organization together—the culture people live and act within. Much has been said of corporate culture, and a lot of it is true, especially the part about it being essential to change and hard to change.

Implicit and Explicit Culture

Culture is the very essence of an organization, the psychological qualities that reveal agreement, implicit or explicit, on how decisions and problems are approached (Kilmann, Saxton, & Serpa, 1986). It is the "pattern of basic assumptions that a group has invented, discovered, or developed in learning to cope with its problems of external adaptation and internal integration, and that have worked well enough to be considered valued, and therefore, to be taught to new members as the correct way to perceive, think and feel in relation to those problems" (Schein, 1984).

In practical terms, corporate culture is for most companies simply "the way we do things around here." It is a summary of the way all of the conditions and factors affecting change fit together, or don't fit, as the case may be.

Culture is a powerful competitive weapon. When people share common values and beliefs, and live by common norms of behavior, they can achieve outstanding results. Organizations such as Disney, Apple Computer, IBM, and others with strong cultures believe that they have a distinct advantage in implementing their strategies.

Similarly, culture is a constraint or an obstacle to desired change when it is not aligned with the strategy. When there are many different sets of values and different norms for behavior, there is a lack of integration that undermines strategic focus, implementation of business plans, consistent service to customers, and teamwork. Change itself needs to be a value that is part of the culture, as opposed to preservation of an existing or past culture.

The challenge to management is to shape the culture (however gradually), to strengthen it, and to bring it into line with the necessary strategic direction. The usual aim is to make the defined management culture the dominant culture and to develop a single, common, shared set of values, beliefs, and expectations that guide behavior. "The most effective way to change behavior is to put people into a new organizational context, which imposes new roles, responsibilities, and relationships on them. This creates a situation that, in a sense, forces new attitudes and behaviors on people" (Beer, Eisenstat, & Spector, 1990).

The explicit and implicit cultures need to be integrated, or at least made consistent. Otherwise the organization will end up with two separate cultures: the explicit culture, emphasized by management, and the implicit culture, reflected in the behavior of people in the organization.

There is a continuing, dynamic tension between explicit and implicit elements. Resolution typically requires redefinition of both. In a public utility, for example, long-service employees resisted management exhortations and concerted efforts to reduce administrative and service costs. Why? They believed strongly that service to the customer was of fundamental importance. Change required a new understanding and definition of customer service, which included cost as well as effectiveness.

Managing Cultural Change

Most important, when management acts to focus explicit structure, work design, staffing and development, and performance system/rewards on desired changes, the combined impact can be tremendous. Through management action, the culture can be changed to support the business strategy. This book emphasizes the use of these management levers in implementing strategy (see Exhibit 4-7). Management communication of the company mission, vision, values, and strategic objectives is only the first step in this process.

Top executives must promulgate a vision; however, a brilliant vision statement won't budge a culture unless it is backed up by action. The management system has to be put into place, and then management has to live by it. Culture is not something managers set out to change directly; rather, it is an outcome of consistent, positive management action, every day and in every way.

Too often good strategic ideas and directions are translated too narrowly into plans. There are many examples, including quality of work life, participative management, quality circles, and service excellence. Even broadly conceived total quality management efforts risk faltering because they are being implemented as programs, rather than as broad, deep, multi-faceted activities.

Rosabeth Moss Kanter, author of several excellent books on managing change, observed that "the problem is not the association of an idea with a program, but rather the existence of too few programs expressing the idea. Changes take hold when they are reflected in multiple concrete manifestations throughout the organization. . . . It is when the structures surrounding a change also change to support it that we say a change is 'institutionalized'—

EXHIBIT 4-7 ELEMENTS THAT SHAPE "THE WAY WE DO THINGS AROUND HERE"

	Management Levers (Explicit Elements)	Behavioral Forces (Implicit Elements)
ALIGNING EXPECTATIONS	Vision, mission, values, strategy ⟷	Shared values and expectations
BUILDING THE ORGANIZATION	Structure ⟷	Informal relationships, information and influence networks
	Work design/tasks, empowerment ⟷	Teamwork, cooperation, and competition
	Staffing ⟷	Career expectations and plans
DEVELOPING CAPABILITIES	Training and development ⟷	Commitment and motivation/ continual learning
MANAGING PERFORMANCE	Performance system/ rewards ⟷	Performance orientation

that it is now part of legitimate and ongoing practice, infused with value and supported by other aspects of the system" (Kanter, 1983).

In a flexible organization, management practices take into account the behavioral forces, so that they may be effective. As will be discussed in the subsequent chapters:

• Organization structure accommodates and nurtures informal relationships and networks that provide for effective information flow and influence.
• Work design provides empowerment for employees to act, and thereby accommodates and nurtures teamwork, cooperation, and competition.
• Staffing and development build commitment and motivation, and foster continual learning.
• Performance systems and rewards accommodate and nurture an appropriate orientation toward tasks, objectives, and rewards.

The approach, in short, includes implicit elements in the overall design, in order to develop an overall company culture that fits the changing future needs of the business.

In the flexible organization, neither the explicit nor the implicit elements are more important. The energetic, self-directed, motivated teamwork; the quick response; the creativity and innovation; and the sheer power that is unleashed by a turned-on work force—all require great respect (and care) for the implicit elements of a culture. Both implicit and explicit elements are essential, hence the creative tension that must be managed.

In companies such as Apple Computer, Digital, Nordstrom, and a myriad of organizations regarded as high-performance and high-commitment, employees do what they believe needs to be done to serve the customers, to create innovative products, and to solve problems. Even in the more explicitly managed, formally structured companies, this is the case, although the "system" tends to be more visible and gets more credit.

In different parts of a company, there may actually be different cultures, which may be conflicting and result in creative tension. Any large company that operates in different business environments has a need for somewhat different cultures, and this should be appreciated as appropriate. Honda, for example, encourages each of its three main divisions to act like an independent company. The R&D division, for example, has its own president and a deep culture of innovation and eagerness for change. Honda believes that evolving, competing cultures help the divisions and the entire company to be more responsive to rapidly changing conditions. Divisions are encouraged, however, to learn from one another's experience.

BP America (British Petroleum in the United States) restructured, scrapping a third of the headquarters staff and most central committees. A new long-term strategy includes creation of a new tiered corporate culture, guided by an internal "corporate culture group." The corporate culture will be barely visible, with only the usual commitments to quality of service and environmental responsibility. Each of BP's four operating divisions will develop its own culture. This may result in tension, but it may also be constructive. According to Richard Pascale, a consultant to BP and a Stanford University professor, "The smartest companies use conflict to stay ahead."

Through their own direct behavior, managers can shape the culture by directly influencing the implicit elements of the organization. They can demonstrate how the decisions they make are reflective of and consistent with the new values that are called for. Also, through the very process of managing change, managers can influence shared values and norms, by addressing the concerns and self-interests of employees confronted with potential threats inherent in planned change.

Behavioral Change Approaches

Change is most effectively implemented by working the explicit levers available to managers. Management can control organization, staffing, and performance and reward systems, and thereby influence the implicit aspects of change. When companies adopt strategies for change, these are the things that can most readily be affected.

Activities performed in an organization are influenced by the manner in which managers effect change. Leadership, communications, and day-to-day interpersonal relationships are potent variables affecting organizational performance. What people perceive as expected or desired behavior will serve as guides to their behavior, regardless of defined job or organizational designs.

During the 1960s and 1970s, a body of techniques was developed and applied in a wide variety of organizations to bring about improved performance and working relationships through behavioral intervention. Even without changing organization structures or job activities, changes could be effected in the way individuals *perceive* their roles and relationships and their expected behaviors. Organization development, in its pure form, is concerned primarily with the process of organization changes, and not so much with the content factors such as the activities or tasks, technology, or formal structures of the organization.

Many managers (and consultants) focus on the implicit side of organization—the right side of Exhibit 4-7. They plan and implement organizational changes using applications of behavioral sciences. Such an "organization development" process typically focuses on modifying interpersonal behavior, group behavior, and interactions among groups. The approaches used originated and flowered in the 1960s and 1970s, when behavioral science was seen as the key to responding to heightened employee interests and expressed needs.

Over the years, behavioral interventions have focused on such areas as:

• Team building: improving interaction among group members in setting goals, working together, and getting work done
• Quality of work life: developing a work environment conducive to the satisfaction of individual needs
• Task redesign: implementing changes in jobs to improve performance and work satisfaction, and to reduce turnover and absenteeism

• Management style and practices: improving individual skills and effectiveness in managing people

• Organizational climate: improving the conditions of work, affecting satisfaction and performance

The methods typically include extensive involvement of employees, through collection, analysis, and feedback of data, using such means as surveys, action research, focus groups, or participative change processes. Actions are taken through a planned change process, often involving pilot projects (which try out change) and experiments (which test alternative types of interventions) (Beckhard & Harris, 1987; Moorhead and Griffon, 1989).

Such approaches are a valuable supplement to the management of the explicit elements of organization. Such methods are effectively used in the context of implementing organization changes, in developing employees and managers, and in managing performance, as will be discussed in later chapters. Behavioral approaches are preferred (or the only course of action) when there is no clear management direction for strategic change or where the aim of organizational change is to improve the functioning of the organization within a continuing strategic context. Quality of work life initiatives, job redesign programs, participative management, career management, and other efforts focus on the perceived needs of employees. To be effective on a small scale, they do not require a context of management-driven strategic change.

Sometimes, however, the outcomes of behavioral intervention work against the intentions of management, rather than supporting them. In fact, the explicit elements of the organization are sometimes considered barriers to achieving the aims set by employees in an organization development effort. In today's business environment, the pace of change is so rapid, the competitive challenges are so great, and the need to implement focused strategies is so acute that companies are concentrating on managing change through the explicit, managed elements of organization (from the left side of Exhibit 4-7 rather than from right to left).

It is not sufficient to rely on behavioral interventions to bring about strategic change in an organization. Without a focus on strategy, it is difficult to ensure that behavioral change "interventions" are in tune with strategic priorities. Expectations of employees need to be shaped by management, in relation to the company mission, vision, values, and strategic objectives. As discussed in this chapter, the way the organization is built and the way performance is managed are the key levers for implementing strategies.

LEADERSHIP

The role of managers as leaders is key to implementing strategic change. A leader's role is to set an organization's direction, communicate this to the work force, motivate employees, and take a long-range perspective. A leader adapts the organization to changing competitive circumstances.

Managers can play a key role in shaping expectations for change. In recent years, much attention has been given to the difference between managers (as mere managers of continuity) and managers as leaders—"changemasters" or "pathfinders" (Bennis, 1985; Kanter, 1983; Kouzes & Posner, 1987; Leavitt, 1986; Tichy & Devanna, 1986). While these are subtle differences among these definitions of leadership, there is significant agreement among them on the critical role of managers in bringing about a more competitive corporate culture.

Roles in Aligning Expectations

The need for leadership in managing strategic change is illustrated in the case of Levi Strauss & Co., the makers of jeans and casual apparel. The company went through a "revitalization" in the mid-1980s as it adapted to changes in the markets for its products. A leveraged buyout of the company resulted in stronger, more focused leadership and an updating of the company's values to reflect contemporary circumstances. Exhibit 4-8 presents an outcome of this redefinition—a profile of the type of leadership desired to pursue the company's shared aspirations.

Effective managers personally establish the relationship of mutual trust and confidence with employees. A manager, as a coach, makes a personal and professional investment in the success and well-being of each individual. In rapidly changing organizations, employees place high value on relationships with people they respect and trust, including managers, team members, and other stakeholders (e.g., customers, vendors, investors). When managers show that they genuinely care, people are encouraged to put more effort and commitment into their work.

The manager acts as a vital communications link between senior management and employees. As organizations reduce management levels and the number of middle managers, managers are becoming increasingly important as "linking pins" of the organization. "Working managers," who spend 25% or less of their time with their people, can hardly be effective in this role. Where managers do act as the primary, visible, positive contact for employees with the rest of the organization, they build a sense of identity, involvement, trust, and confidence that contributes directly to performance motivation and employee retention.

There are many companies that exemplify this caring attitude among managers. Herman Miller, an office furniture manufacturer, credits much of its success to treating employees right. At the heart of the management system are "covenantal relationships" between management and all employees. The company seeks to "share values, ideals, goals, respect for each person, and the process of our work together." Managers are firm in decision making, but also sympathetic to employee concerns. Some managers do not pick up the beat, and eventually leave the company. To be successful, the CEO says, "you have to know how to dance" (Labich, 1989b).

EXHIBIT 4-8 LEVI STRAUSS & CO.

Mission statement

The mission of Levi Strauss & Co. is to sustain profitable and responsible commercial success by marketing jeans and selected casual apparel under the Levi's® brand.

We must balance goals of superior profitability and return on investment, leadership market positions, and superior products and service. We will conduct our business ethically and demonstrate leadership in satisfying our responsibilities to our communities and to society. Our work environment will be safe and productive and characterized by fair treatment, teamwork, open communications, personal accountability and opportunities for growth and development.

Aspiration statement

We all want a Company that our people are proud of and committed to, where all employees have an opportunity to contribute, learn, grow and advance based on merit, not politics or background. We want our people to feel respected, treated fairly, listened to and involved. Above all, we want satisfaction from accomplishments and friendships, balanced personal and professional lives, and to have fun in our endeavors.

When we describe the kind of LS&CO. we want in the future what we are talking about is building on the foundation we have inherited: affirming the best of our Company's traditions, closing gaps that may exist between principles and practices and updating some of our values to reflect contemporary circumstances.

What Type of Leadership is Necessary to Make our Aspirations a Reality?

New Behaviors: Leadership that exemplifies directness, openness to influence, commitment to the success of others, willingness to acknowledge our own contributions to problems, personal accountability, teamwork and trust. Not only must we model these behaviors but we must coach others to adopt them.

Diversity: Leadership that values a diverse workforce (age, sex, ethnic group, etc.) at all levels of the organization, diversity in experience, and a diversity in perspectives. We have committed to taking full advantage of the rich backgrounds and abilities of all our people and to promote a greater diversity in positions of influence. Differing points of view will be sought; diversity will be valued and honesty rewarded, not suppressed.

Recognition: Leadership that provides greater recognition—both financial and psychic—for individuals and teams that contribute to our success. Recognition must be given to all who contribute: those who create and innovate and also those who continually support the day-to-day business requirements.

Ethical Management Practices: Leadership that epitomizes the stated standards of ethical behavior. We must provide clarity about our expectations and must enforce these standards through the corporation.

Communications: Leadership that is clear about Company, unit, and individual goals and performance. People must know what is expected of them and receive timely, honest feedback on their performance and career aspirations.

Empowerment: Leadership that increases the authority and responsibility of those closest to our products and customers. By actively pushing responsibility, trust and recognition into the organization we can harness and release the capabilities of all our people.

Source: Levi Strauss & Co., used with permission.

Some studies have shown that many managers dedicate themselves to building up the self-worth of the employees. "These managers tell the truth, share power, praise good performance, and in other ways take practical action to show they care about their employees. These managers replace political maneuvering with genuine support for risk, innovation and growth. Their employees, free to put forth their best efforts, thrive in this environment and are able to create worthy products and services" (Ludeman, 1989).

Managers play a key role in shaping expectations and implementing change, yet they often fail to perform fully this potential role as leaders. Many of the ways that companies change their culture and shape expectations for change are focused on actions of individual managers, as leaders. Managers need to:

• Understand and appreciate where the company has been, and not underestimate the importance of long-accepted values, traditions, and ways of doing things

• Encourage employees who are bucking the old culture and who have better ideas for the future

• Find maverick units in the company that are "doing it right"—with good morale, low costs, high quality, innovation—and hold them up as models for others to learn from

• Encourage and empower employees to develop changes, including new ways to accomplish their tasks, and cultural change will follow

• Communicate and live by a vision, using it as a context for communicating decisions and actions, and update it when necessary

• Celebrate the successes—recognize people for accomplishments, the right behaviors, teamwork, and innovation

All of these activities require personal initiative by managers. They do not just happen because policies or systems are in place.

Leadership Qualities

"We've had managers at GE who couldn't change, who kept telling us to leave them alone. They wanted to sit back, to keep things the way they were," said Jack Welch, CEO of General Electric. "We still don't understand why so many people are incapable of facing reality, of being candid with themselves and others. What determines your destiny is not the hand you're dealt; it's how you play the hand. And the best way to play your hand is to face reality—see the world as it is and act accordingly" (Tichy & Charan, 1989).

There are leadership qualities that may be sought in selecting managers and developed in preparing managers for future responsibilities. Leaders are distinctive in that they:

• Challenge the status quo: they are curious, courageous, and outspoken, and act to change the way things are done.

- Inspire a shared vision: they articulate mission and values, set the right objectives, and behave in a manner consistent with them.
- Help others to take action: they provide guidance and resources, and work toward empowering others to act on their own.
- Cope with ambiguity, uncertainty, and complexity: they act comfortably within a changing, flexible organization.
- Genuinely care about people: they are sensitive to people, listen to them, share their concerns, and keep them motivated.
- Are self-aware: they know their strengths and limitations and have a degree of humility that prompts continual learning.

Leaders are needed at all levels of a company. The more flexible, networked, and global the organization is, the greater the need for change-oriented leadership. Here, their job is more one of changing rather than running the business. They foster collaborative relationships and develop new patterns of influence that help reshape the culture to fit the demands for performance. Implementing strategy in the 1990s and beyond may depend on finding leaders to inspire and motivate employees throughout an organization's network and in different countries in which it operates.

Most managers have modest talents as charismatic visionaries or transformational leaders. But many achieve significant results by doing what they do to initiate, implement, and sustain changes that support the business mission. While some leaders are better than others, few are of the superstar quality of Jan Carlzon, who transformed SAS into a service culture, or Jack Welch, who repositioned General Electric as a flexible "growth machine." Most are normal life-size humans who try hard to shape employee expectations and move things forward.

In fact, companies may find that the pressure on individuals to be strong leaders is eased by relying on "leadership teams." A team may include top leaders and top managers. It provides an obvious tension that can actually help sustain changes, once initiated. Compaq, the computer company, prospered with the guidance of such a leadership team.

SUMMARY

Human resource strategies are plans for changing the way things are done in an organization. They are changes developed and initiated by management in support of business strategies, which in turn are externally driven. While some human resource strategies may emerge bottom-up through an organization, most are explicit and directional.

Accordingly, an important step in their implementation is the alignment of employee expectations with the company mission, vision, values, and strategic objectives. This is addressed in part through communications on the strategic direction of the business. This helps employees recognize the need for change and understand the changes required.

However, more than communications is required to help employees evaluate, accept, and act on strategy-focused changes. A powerful means of alignment is the translation of strategies into unit, team, and individual performance objectives. Focusing on key result areas and specific performance objectives and measures has a powerful influence on employee behavior. With clear performance plans, employees may gain direct feedback on the results they achieve and how they contribute to broader business performance. This process has been used for decades by companies, sometimes not so effectively, but it remains the best way to help employees commit themselves to meaningful performance plans that are relevant to the success of the business.

More subtly, management may take actions to reshape the culture: the shared norms, values, and beliefs that drive employee behavior. Culture is influenced explicitly through the process of managing human resources. The behavioral forces driving the implicit, or informal, culture will yield to a carefully managed process of explicit change.

None of these means for aligning expectations with strategy are new. And none alone will achieve the desired results. Where companies have succeeded in managing broad strategic change, including cultural change, managers have effectively used all of the levers available to them. Picking only one or two, or implementing efforts sequentially, fails to attain the mass impact required to overwhelm the status quo and direct the attention and energies of employees to the business agenda.

I. FOCUS ON MANAGING: TOTAL SERVICE QUALITY

Quality is found in virtually every company's plans for improving competitiveness. As President George Bush has stated, "The improvement of quality in products and the improvement of quality in service—these are national priorities as never before."

Companies are committed to the goal of satisfying the customer in every way—before, during, and after the sale. Company efforts usually include wide-ranging, long-term programs aimed at providing error-free products and services. Quality improvement ultimately reduces costs, increases revenues and customer loyalty, and creates profits.

Originating with a focus on improving product quality, total quality management has broadened to include services. Quality management began with statistical process control, just-in-time inventory management, cycle time reduction, and other manufacturing techniques. Today, the emphasis is on total quality, with service considered an important value-added feature of a product. In addition, businesses that sell services are expanding rapidly, with substantial economic activity.

Service quality depends primarily on people, although technology is a valuable resource. Therefore, human resource strategies need to guide and support quality management. Above all, involvement of employees in shaping and implementing the quality process is critical.

Focusing on Customer Needs

Quality today is not what management defines it to be, but rather what the customer perceives. Effective companies today make a science out of finding out what customers really want and then meeting their needs. In the process, employees need to have direct contact with customers, to understand and help to define customer expectations which shape performance standards.

Dave Ulrich calls for a step beyond customer satisfaction. He believes that companies can achieve customer commitment in the long term through hundreds of small actions that build loyalty and devotion (Ulrich, 1989). Such bonds require that management actively bring customers into decisions regarding organization, hiring, staff deployment, appraisals, rewards, and other human resource practices which affect customer satisfaction.

IBM's market-driven quality aims not merely to satisfy customers but also to delight them. In 1991, IBM set a goal of limiting defects to fewer than 3.4 per million units—not just product defects but defective service transactions, both internally and externally (Rose, 1991). IBM believes that it will succeed in the highly competitive computer technology and services marketplace through customer responsiveness, competitive products and services, efficiency, and market-driven quality.

Employee Involvement in Improving Quality

Every employee needs to feel responsible for quality—for satisfying customers. To do this, employees need to understand the needs of customers and how the business meets these needs. They need to be actively engaged in assessing the current situation and identifying ways to serve customers better, more quickly, and at lower cost.

In most companies, quality training is a prerequisite for total quality management. Training builds a common mindset for service quality among employees and provides a common set of concepts. It also provides needed skills for analyzing and acting on improvement opportunities, strengthening team effectiveness, and managing customer relationships. Unfortunately, some companies invest obsessively in training and then falter in implementing other essential elements of the process. They get stalled in the starting gate.

Teamwork is essential for cooperation, innovation, and improvement. In one company, quality improvement teams are formed with employees who naturally work together. Their activities are prompted and their results reviewed by steering teams functioning at corporate, group, and location/function levels. Other companies rely on natural work teams and the management hierarchy to implement quality initiatives. Experience indicates that with greater reliance on self-managed teams, more change occurs.

Many companies find that structural and staffing changes are required to achieve quality objectives. New skills may need to be recruited, entailing new selection processes. Jobs are redesigned and organization structures flattened and matrixed to encourage teamwork. Processes for decision making and communications, eminently important for serving customers quickly and accurately, are re-engineered. Even management roles change as coaching and empowerment replace direction.

With new performance standards and the introduction of new ways of performing, changes are typically needed in performance measurement processes. The methods need to be flexible and suited to the customer situations. Measurements are a key to higher service quality. "What you cannot concretely measure, you cannot effectively track, alter, and improve" (Maital, 1991). Often inputs on service quality are solicited from peers and customers, external as well as internal.

Rewards also change. Where appropriate, financial rewards such as bonuses and variable pay focus on team performance rather than individual efforts. Increasingly, employee recognitions for quality results are preferred over financial rewards. If employees identify closely with customers, feedback on the impact of service is the most potent reward of all. It is the recognition of making a difference.

Doing the Basics Extraordinarily Well

At Hughes Aircraft, total quality management is characterized by "an organization of quality trained and motivated employees, working in an environment where managers encourage creativity, initiative, and trust and where each individual's contributions are actively sought to upgrade quality."

"Total quality means 'doing it right the first time,' not correcting it after the fact; delegating decisions to lower levels of the organization, not requiring approvals from on high; and controlling processes through prior analysis and careful design, not through inspection, checking, and continual oversight" (Garvin, 1989). Such shifts are difficult in a manufacturing company, but they are even more complex where services are involved.

There are no human resource management practices uniquely used for total quality management. They are common practices applied to an uncommon, exciting challenge. In the pursuit of continual improvement of product and service excellence, companies rediscover the value of many management practices that have not been fully appreciated or used.

PART TWO

BUILDING THE ORGANIZATION

CHAPTER 5

DESIGNING THE
ORGANIZATION

Perfect balance in a business exists only on the organization chart. A living business is always in a state of imbalance, growing here and shrinking there, overdoing one thing and neglecting another.

Peter F. Drucker

Flexible organizations are decentralized, networked, team-oriented, customer-driven, flat, and lean. Furthermore, they are constantly changing as employees and managers, empowered to seek opportunities for improvement, introduce new ways of working together to achieve business results. The flexible organization is in flux, anticipating and adapting to changes in relationships with its customers, vendors, distributors, and other business partners.

At its simplest, an organization is a group of people working together to achieve common goals. Management sets the direction of an organization by defining its purpose, establishing the goals to meet that purpose, and formulating strategies to achieve the goals. Organization design affects the relationships among activities, information flows, and decision making within which work gets done. Structure provides order and coordination for the activities of employees in achieving organizational goals.

The top manager or "chief executive officer" of any business unit—whether corporate, divisional, or location—needs to be confident that the organization structure fits its strategies. Effective organization involves more than structure; it requires people with the right capabilities, the right tasks (work activities and processes), and the right culture (values, use of power, informal arrangements, etc.) (D. Nadler & Tushman, 1988).

This chapter addresses the ways in which companies plan and implement changes in organization structure:

• What factors or criteria should guide organization design
• How an organization may be aligned through differentiation and integration to perform competitively
• How management spans and levels are designed in flexible organizations

- How roles and responsibilities of management at each organizational level may be clarified
- How informal networks, power, and influence are accommodated in organization design
- How an organization can support evolving global business activities, innovation and entrepreneurship, and the need for internal balance

ORGANIZATION DESIGN CRITERIA

The "right" organization structure is the one that best fits the needs of a situation and that has, at the same time, a sense of internal balance and order. It is not enough to be an ad hoc organization, adaptive to significant external forces. It is also necessary to maintain a degree of consistency within the organization, an integration of the various functions and processes that allow people to know how to act (Mintzberg, 1991).

Because each situation has many needs, some of which are conflicting, a search to identify the contingencies and objectively define the "right" structure under each would be an unduly complex exercise. Instead, managers identify the factors that are most important and proceed to modify the organization to fit them more closely. Tom Peters observed that in the more sophisticated organizations, "reorganization is no more than a means of enhancing organizational effectiveness over the short to medium term in response to changing internal and external pressures" (Peters, 1979).

For example, a consumer products company set the following criteria as guides for determining the optimal organization:

- Support rapid international business growth.
- Have the capacity to absorb and achieve 15% to 20% annual growth.
- Be flexible and adaptable to different market conditions.
- Promote entrepreneurial spirit and, at the same time, maintain accountability; reflect a balance between managerial autonomy and synergies.
- Encourage and foster innovation, new product development, and acquisitions in areas related to the existing business.
- Allow enough slack and flexibility for the development of talent; provide opportunities for management talent in the company before recruiting externally.

Such factors, defined through management analysis and discussions, provide a framework for designing organizational changes.

Factors Relating to Strategy

The appropriate organizational design in a company or business unit depends in large part on the business strategy. The factors which drive the business, or the key levers for managing the development of the business, also drive organization structure.

Rapid growth is a primary force for organizational change. Internal growth, reflected in revenues and volumes, results from expanded activity in current markets, entry into new markets, or the introduction or extension of products and services provided. Growth also results from external acquisition of businesses, as business entities or as product lines, additional capacity, or assets. The direction and nature of growth influence the shape of organization structure. As noted previously, slower-changing organizations can be more institutionally managed; fast-growth organizations need to be flexibly managed—and structured.

Diversity of products and services, resulting from growth, influences organization. Companies with single products, or closely related products, may be organized functionally. As products and services become more diverse, there is a need to focus management on different business groups, resulting in a divisional structure.

The results of growth and diversity are size and complexity. A large company can establish independent product-focused businesses, but a small business with a wide line of products has to find other ways to balance focus and integration. More organizational options are open to the larger, more complex organization.

Also relevant is the extent of current, or intended, international business activity. Companies that are trying to manage globally, or multi-nationally, require a different structure than those that focus on a domestic market or merely export goods and services. Multi-national organizations need to accommodate diverse markets, economies, cultures, and distances.

Internal Management Factors

The intended sources of competitive advantage also drive organization. Structure can influence how a company will seek to achieve low costs, provide superior capabilities (speed, quality, innovation, etc.), or attain superior employee commitment. If customer service and quick market response are primary, the structure should be aligned with key market requirements (e.g., primary customers, market segments, geographic market areas). On the other hand, a low-cost operation may suggest a more centralized structure focused on products or functions.

Some companies consider the requirements for information to be a significant driver of organization. Different kinds of work have different information requirements. The independence (or interdependence) of activities, the predictability (or unpredictability) of activities, and the effects of external forces on activities—all influence information requirements. The flow and use of information need to match the requirements of the jobs (Lorsch, 1977). The organization may be structured to facilitate the needed flow of information, by combining and linking activities according to their information requirements.

A related factor is decision making. Where in an organization are pricing decisions made? How about purchasing decisions, hiring decisions, production volume decisions? If an organization wants rapid decision making, it seeks to "empower" employees so that decisions are made at the lowest possible level. If, on the other hand, the organization wants slow but deliberate decisions, with maximum consistency and control, it centralizes decisions or guides decisions through defined "delegations of authority" limiting decision making.

Major changes in a company's management also drive organization. A CEO or other senior executive may wish to reshape the organization as a way to influence the management process, or merely to signal new thinking and behavior. External threats, such as takeover attempts or major initiatives by competitors, also influence changes. When companies change their financial structure, increasing debt substantially, conditions change which typically lead to organizational changes.

Some companies seeking to promote an environment of flexibility implement organizational changes for the sake of constructive self-improvement. In the process of restructuring, management encourages people to rethink their roles, responsibilities, and relationships. Change often promotes improvement in operations. Organizational changes are made simply to promote new thinking and behavior changes. For example, one company reorganizes only for a good business reason: "If the organization hasn't changed in two years, that's a good business reason." At the same time, too frequent changes can be disruptive. At Apple Computer, there were four major reorganizations within two years. This was perceived by many employees as unduly disruptive.

Flexible Organization

Companies that are both complex and rapidly changing typically seek to be flexible. Flexible organizations are characterized by dual or multiple reporting relationships, lateral relationships, increased teamwork, and empowered employees making decisions interdependently. These characteristics can make them difficult to manage. A flexible structure can drive traditionally oriented managers crazy.

A flexible organization is a network of relationships. Within the network there is a formal hierarchy, but work gets done because individuals cooperate in teams and work directly with each other. Flexible structures are flat, lean, and changing. They are always in transition. When people change jobs, the structure changes and the informal networks change as well. Staff and line are partners, working jointly toward achieving objectives. And teams are a vital force—whether focused as a work unit, or as temporary project or coordinating linkages across units or functions. Information flows freely in a flexible organization among employees, aided by direct access to information systems.

It is said there are no flexible organizations, only flexible people. If so, a flexible structure is one that merely does not impede behavior that leads to desired results. Digital Equipment Corporation has been referred to as one of the best "nonmanaged companies in America." The structure was sufficiently loose and flexible so that its professionals and managers could shape their organizations and tasks in the ways they considered most suitable.

In contrast, traditional institutional organization structures are hierarchical, with single lines of authority and accountability. While a minimum number of levels is desired, the need for control and risk avoidance requires management oversight. Spans of management (the number of direct positions reporting to a manager) may be narrow for the same reason. Information flows vertically, with interactions among units intended to "go through channels," relying on key managers as the coordination points. Staff functions exist to assist, monitor, and control: "Line manages, staff advises." Also, managerial work is separated as distinct from other work, treating it as if it were a specialized function (Dougherty, 1989).

Contrasts between flexible organizations and slower-changing institutional organizations are presented in Exhibit 5-1. Of course, these are extreme comparisons; actual organizations show great variation on such characteristics.

Entrepreneurial organizations act small. Whether independent enterprises or ventures within a larger organization, the structures are simple and lean. The managers are the hubs of wheels, working closely with employees to get the work done. Management is on a first-name basis, open, and "shirt-sleeves." There is a mutual respect among managers and employees; in fact, strong values and culture help keep it that way. Spans of management are wide, relationships are fluid, and levels and accountabilities are not particularly relevant. There is a minimum of procedure, policy, or protocol. One of the "turn-ons" about a garage is the absence of such "bureaucracy."

Usually providing only one or a few products or services, an entrepreneurial organization does not have many alternative structures. Only as the business grows and becomes more complex does structure become important. These are organizations built around people.

EXHIBIT 5-1 INSTITUTIONAL AND FLEXIBLE ORGANIZATION FACTORS

	Institutional	Flexible
STRUCTURE	Hierarchical	Network
COMMUNICATION AND INTERACTION	Vertical	Vertical and lateral
MODE	Formal, plus informal	Informal, plus formal
DIRECTION OF WORK	Immediate manager	Self, teams
DECISION MAKING	Focused at the top, defined authorities	Focused at the bottom, empowerment at the appropriate level
STAFF	Independent—advisory, audit, control, assist	Partnership
COMMITMENT	Loyalty to organization and career	Involvement with work, team, customer
CHANGE ATTITUDE	Stability, authority, control, risk avoidance	Anticipation, adaptation to change, innovation

These factors lead to the consideration of specific dimensions of organization design. Of course, a company may include multiple situations and thus require a mixed form of organization. If there are strategic situations requiring institutional, flexible, and entrepreneurial forms, all within the same company, the organization has little choice but to manage flexibly. This is the only organization that can accommodate the others.

EXTERNAL ALIGNMENT

A primary concern is how to group activities. An organization should align activities with its customers, markets, or processes. Companies typically divide themselves into chunks according to some logical differentiation. At the same time, they seek to find ways to glue these chunks together as a logical, coherent enterprise.

A flexible organization is always in a state of creative tension. It needs to give enough autonomy to its units to allow them to be aligned with its external environment—particularly its customers and market segments. It also needs to maintain enough integration to enhance competitive advantage through efficiencies, expertise, synergies, and other value added.

Differentiation

Divisions of a company are typically by function, by product, or by market segment (geographic, demographic, customer size or type, etc.). These divisions may represent relatively autonomous business units, responsible for all functions supporting a line of business. They may, furthermore, be profit centers, having responsibility for business profits.

Divisionalization allows a large organization to get "close to its customer" and to break the organization into smaller units that can be more easily managed and focused. The key is to determine the differences that make the most sense—that will yield the best results for the customer and gain competitive advantage.

Small companies with little product diversity (e.g., "garages") are best managed as functional organizations. As they grow and become more diverse, they may opt for either a functional or a multi-divisional organization, with appropriate staff coordination. Larger organizations with diverse products are best structured along product lines, ultimately with divisional profit centers and staff only at the lowest levels (Nathanson & Cassano, 1982).

There is, of course, a cost connected with differentiation.

> Differentiation means that members of each unit will see problems that involve them with other units primarily from their own point of view. It is not surprising, then, that differentiation produces conflict. The sales manager wants to move up scheduling an order from a big customer. The plan manager is opposed because such an interruption will lead to higher manufacturing costs. Resolving such conflicts is the stuff of which management is made. (Lorsch, 1977)

Integration

However a company may be structured in terms of groups or divisions, there is a need for integration among them. Integration refers simply to the quality of the necessary relationships among the units of the organization if the organization's overall goals are to be achieved. The more differentiation, the more varied the viewpoints of the units involved in decisions and, therefore, the more difficult it is to achieve integration (Lorsch, 1977; D. Nadler, 1989).

Organizational units are necessarily interdependent in one way or another.

• At a minimum, they are separate businesses, but are part of the same company family with at least financial interdependence (e.g., different product divisions in a diversified company).
• Units may require sequential interdependence (e.g., units each adding value in a production sequence).
• They may be reciprocal, interacting with each other (e.g., R&D, engineering, manufacturing, marketing, and sales).

This interdependence is a business necessity and should be recognized and formally addressed, either through structure or through other integrating mechanisms (Kotter, Schlesinger, & Sathe, 1979). Some of the ways that integration may be achieved are:

• Goals and plans: commitment of independent units to shared goals and plans, including client specifications for products and services; the units perceive an interdependence to achieve the desired results. Sometimes understanding of a common plan is all that is required.
• Integrating roles: special staff positions may provide coordination where it is particularly difficult and important; product managers, project managers, or "expediters" help facilitate performance involving multiple units.
• Committees and task forces: meetings, cross-unit teams, temporary task forces, and similar devices facilitate integration and give people exposure that helps build lasting relationships.
• Broadly experienced people: managers who have worked in different aspects of the business are likely to facilitate integration and, more broadly, a culture of cooperation and collaboration.

Within a functional structure, research, manufacturing, marketing, information systems, or other functions may operate almost independently. Too often, the necessary integration does not exist; or devices such as committees, task forces, or project teams are viewed as window dressing or impediments to independent action. Each function goes its separate way, and coordination occurs only where management connects—at the top of the structure. As a result, adaptability and effectiveness in a rapidly changing marketplace are impaired.

Needed coordination among decentralized units may be achieved through more subtle means than decision authority. In a divisional organization, the need for integration is addressed also through information systems, financial systems and data, accounting and control systems, focused planning and objective setting, and compensation systems. For example, customer order processing involves functions ranging from sales and customer contact to distribution (and indirectly, manufacturing to replace stocks) to finance/accounting.

Consistent application of planning and control processes helps coordination, but assumes a need for consistency of actions and results. This may be traded off by management in favor of flexibility and initiative. Differentiation may be more important to competitiveness than consistency (Lawler, 1989).

Hierarchy and Matrix

Hierarchy may be relied on as an integrating device; for example, higher-level managers provide integration for the interdependent units that report to them. Similarly, standardized systems and processes (policies, procedures, approval requirements, reporting requirements) can help ensure integration, or at least consistency of behavior. However, both hierarchical authority and control systems may conflict with the emphasis on more personal, informal lateral relationships fostered by the other approaches described.

Some companies have maintained hierarchy while formally acknowledging the need for coordination on another dimension. By formally establishing dual reporting relationships, companies set up a matrix organization. In this way, managers report through two structures of differentiation. For example, managers in a product group may also report to their respective functional organizations (Davis & Lawrence, 1977).

> The matrix forces decision making to be a constant process of interchange and trade-off, not only between the overall system and its specialized components and interest groups, but also between and among the specialists in the interest groups themselves. As such, the matrix is a far cry from the organizations most managers have read about and idealized. Clean lines of authority, unambiguous resource allocation to each problem or goal, clear boundaries separating jobs, divisions, organizations, and loyalties are all part of that simpler life that we need to forsake in a dynamic world of overlapping and contradictory interests and goals. (Sayles, 1976)

Example: Market Focus

A company providing contract food services to hospitals, nursing homes, businesses, and educational institutions grew rapidly through development of new accounts and through acquisition of several regional competitors. The company was structured by type of customer, reflecting differences in contract terms, different needs (e.g., nutrition/dietitians in health, retail/cash services in business and education), and the expertise of the key managers (see Exhibit 5-2). Primary competitors were organized similarly, although they had national coverage.

EXHIBIT 5-2 FOOD SERVICES: CURRENT ORGANIZATION

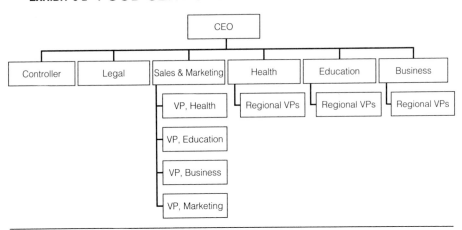

As a result of the expansion, the company felt that several strategic challenges needed to be addressed:

• How to increase sales/market share in the geographic and business markets served

• How to realize the goals of superior management, employees, food quality, and service in a diverse operating environment

• How to provide improved coordination of management activities across lines of business and geographically

A restructuring of the organization established management accountability for all business results in three large geographic areas (see Exhibit 5-3). These group executives, as general managers, were charged with formulating and implementing marketing and operations plans for all lines of business in their areas. With minimal realignment of regional or district management, each group focused on addressing its market opportunities and improving its business results. No additional staff were required by the shift; in fact, some efficiencies were realized, and individuals perceived that they had gained increased management authority and responsibility.

To provide a line of business focus, the most experienced managers in each line of business formed a strategy committee, to set priorities and objectives and to determine the company support required. Staff services, once decentralized but located together, were consolidated in a staff services unit to enhance their responsiveness to needs and to allow them to be supported adequately.

The resulting organization prompted increased interaction and cooperation among managers, planning and decision making at levels below the CEO, and

EXHIBIT 5-3 FOOD SERVICES: NEW ORGANIZATION

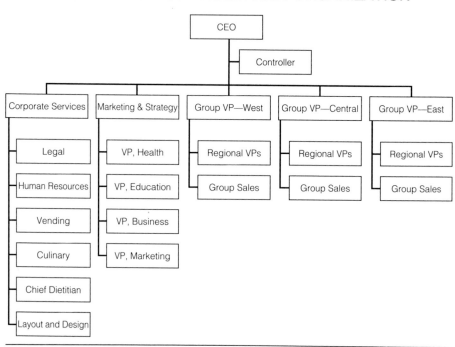

assessment of market opportunities. Many key managers took on somewhat different roles and responsibilities, and as a result, the company is positioned for continued expansion and improved performance.

MANAGEMENT STRUCTURE

The design of an organization reflects and affects the roles managers play. In organizations with many levels and narrow spans of management, managers tend to be closely involved in decision making at lower levels. At AT&T before the breakup, senior managers making major decisions were as many as ten levels away from employees who dealt with customers, regulators, or competitors (Marcus, 1991). Today, the competitive necessity of a customer focus and rapid decision making requires organizations to have flatter management structures.

For example, Toyota Motor Co. eliminated two layers of its organization, reassigning about 1,000 managers. The company now has seven levels between the chief executive and the production floor. This contrasts with seventeen at Ford and twenty-two at General Motors. Cost cutting was not the aim; quick decision making was (Marcus, 1991).

The span of management is the number of people reporting to a manager.

Management levels refer to the number of reporting levels in an organization, from the individual contributor to the top executive. These considerations are important because they define the size of work groups and how flat the organization is. They also affect management and employee communications.

Flexible organizations have a minimum number of levels (one rule is no more than six to eight levels from the top to the bottom of a large organization). Fewer layers of management can mean fewer approvals and quicker decision making. It means senior management and lower-level employees have closer contact with and higher visibility to one another.

Management Spans and Levels

Sir Ian Hamilton, a British general, concluded from the history of military organization that spans should range from three to six. This range has been the practice for decades in companies, with the rationale that managers can effectively be informed, be involved, and cope with uncertainty when the scope of their responsibility is limited.

A control-oriented institutional organization typically has many levels and spans that are often narrow, including one-on-one or one-on-two management reporting relationships. This has the advantages of providing checks and balances on decision making, involving more managers in decision making, and providing more steps for management career advancement.

However, deep organizations have difficulty making quick decisions and tend to generate duplicate or unneeded work. Organizations that seek to respond rapidly to customers need to be flatter.

As a result, flexible organizations tend to have wide spans. Executives routinely manage six to ten managers without difficulty. At General Electric, some executives have spans in the low twenties. Wider spans prompt managers to delegate authority because they do not have time to be involved in details. Increasing the span helps management cope with the growing size of an organization by reducing the number of levels and giving subordinates greater autonomy to act, with less close supervision (Galbraith, 1977).

Spans of management vary widely with the nature of the work. They are typically narrower at higher organizational levels, where positions are unique and managers work as decision teams. At other levels, the optimal management span depends on coordination requirements, including the degree of specialization, similarity of tasks, the types of information required, experience and preferences of the individuals involved, and the need for access to the manager (Mintzberg, 1979).

The number of levels depends on the size of the organization and the intended emphasis in management roles and responsibilities. Many companies focus on controlling the spans of management. Assuming that the organization is staffed correctly, the number of levels is minimized. Conversely, as organizations are flattened, with layers removed, the number of direct reports may be increased.

Asea Brown Boveri (ABB), an electrical equipment company in Europe, has a CEO and only twelve top executives in the Zurich headquarters (six Swedes, three Swiss, and three Germans). The company controls 4,000 profit centers in 140 countries through local managers. There are never more than five people between the CEO and the shop floor. Headquarter staffs in the business units are thin, often with fewer than 100 people, in some cases down from 1,000 or more before units were acquired by ABB.

Clarifying Management Roles

Conceptually, there are three primary levels of management in any company: senior management, middle management, and first-level management. If there are more than three levels, they are variations on these (which is why they may be easily consolidated to create a flatter organization). The levels and roles at each are presented in Exhibit 5-4.

However, managers tend to do what they have done in the past, what they are good at, what they enjoy, what they are rewarded for, and what they think is expected of them. What they do may not be what they should do to execute the strategy, build an effective organization, and manage performance. It is essential, therefore, to clarify at each level exactly what is expected.

Senior management includes top management (chief executive officer, chief operating officer or president) and primary group executives. The work of senior management is managing the overall enterprise toward key objectives, and defining and charting new directions. Today's senior executives

> ask more questions than they seek answers, and derive energy and efficiency from struggling with a constant flow of choices and dilemmas. Ultimately their job is to construe the world for themselves and others so that collective action and meaning is possible. They do this primarily through creating a captivating context for change, promoting a sense of commitment and ownership in others, and carefully shifting attention between stability and innovation in their organizations. (Jonas, Fry, & Srivastva, 1990)

Middle management includes business unit and functional executives who are charged with translating these strategic directions into operational management terms. Their work is to translate strategic objectives into operational performance objectives and plans for each unit and help their units achieve these objectives by providing the needed resources, information flow, talent, and technical expertise.

Middle managers are concerned with operating their businesses, balancing the need of the subenterprise with the needs of the company as a whole. In the information based, flexible organization, there are typically fewer management levels and wider spans, resulting in increased strains on managers. Many feel overworked, overstressed, and underpowered. Responsibilities are increased, and important business decisions have to be made quickly. At the same time,

---

EXHIBIT 5-4 THREE PRIMARY LEVELS OF MANAGEMENT

Senior Management
- Define mission, values, and vision
- Set strategic objectives and initiate significant shifts in the direction of the enterprise
- Monitor corporate and group results
- Obtain and broadly allocate capital resources
- Maintain relations with key external parties, including shareholders, key customers, public
- Ensure availability of senior management talent
- Determine the overall management organization structure
- Provide the philosophy and example on "how we manage"

Middle Management
- Set operational performance objectives for each unit
- Allocate resources needed for performance
- Exchange information with other management levels and units
- Participate in key customer relations and account decisions
- Develop key management and professional talent

First-Level Management
- Set employee performance activities, objectives, standards
- Provide training, coaching, resources to support performance
- Give employees feedback on performance
- Provide recognitions, rewards, and incentives
- Ensure that business practices are consistent with desired values
- Maintain contact with key customers

---

middle managers find that they often lack enough authority to truly manage independently and, at the same time, feel vulnerable to further middle management staff reductions. The essential role—becoming one of information processor, translator, and facilitator—is difficult for many managers.

First-level managers are expected to bring about improvements in performance, productivity, quality, and work force motivation and retention through direct day-to-day contact with employees. The work of first-level management is essentially "contact sports"—interacting with employees to clarify performance expectations, supporting performance, giving feedback on performance, and providing recognitions and rewards.

The role of the first-line manager, or supervisor, is one of the most demanding and challenging jobs in any organization. A supervisor is not merely a lead performer in a work group, as has often been the case, or a directive management boss. The job involves day-to-day interaction, coaching, leading, nudging, encouraging, training, etc. As work groups become increasingly heterogeneous, the first-level manager's job becomes more difficult and important. Interpersonal management skills are critical.

Buried in an organizational web, this person must be adroit at administering a unit and perceiving which, among all the daily tasks delegated downward, are the most important to accomplish. Through such administrative competence, he or she must be able to link the unit's accomplishments to the functioning of other organizational subunits. (Sasser & Leonard, 1980)

Few management jobs reflect these pure distinctions. For one thing, managers at higher levels love to perform lower-level roles. As managers advance, they continue to do what they did in the past and did best. Middle managers meddle in supervisory matters and want to stay close to details and day-to-day decisions. Senior executives, who thrived as middle and first-level managers, continue to be involved in those roles, forgoing attention to the broader, more vague, and less comfortable strategic management tasks. In many cases, senior executives go directly from individual contributor roles in finance, law, engineering, or research to top management responsibilities without fully experiencing the tasks of managing.

Organization structure and clarity of job activities and expectations help managers do the "right work" at the "right level." Flatter structures and less overlap among levels, units, and jobs help managers focus. GE has sought to "load up" middle managers with work by increasing their spans and reducing levels. CEO Jack Welch assumes that they will sort out and perform the truly important tasks. Also, management development helps. Most important, open discussion and continual change help managers concentrate on the most appropriate activities.

INFORMAL ORGANIZATION

In a flexible organization, the way that people actually do their work is as important as, if not more important than, the explicit, formal organization design.

For decades we have recognized that there is an informal or "shadow" organization at work in any company. It was once viewed as disruptive or even subversive, and management sought to emphasize formal job definition, authorities, and "channels." Increasingly, however, managers have embraced the dual organizational forms and have recognized that it is difficult and unnecessary to distinguish between the two.

Organization as a Network

Decades ago, Georg Simmel, a sociologist, characterized organizations as a pattern of interlocking circles. In reality, he observed, people interact with different individuals who, in turn, have their own interaction patterns. Today, one organization analysis tool charts such patterns of interaction as a way to understand the actual, informal way things get done. The idea is to design the formal organization to match the informal network, or to modify it in support of the organization's agenda.

With the advancement of information and communications technology, organizations will be increasingly structured around their communications networks. Span of communication will gradually replace span of management. Managers will be able to obtain information quickly and directly from the field (and throughout the organization) electronically and will have the capability to analyze it quickly and efficiently. The organization structure will not impede communication; managers will be more directly within the network.

One advantage of acting as a network is that an organization is more open and more sensitive to external trends. It can then be prepared for change and move more quickly to address changing external conditions.

> If management is to respond to constraints and changing environmental contingencies, and if there are multiple and conflicting interests involved, then an effective organization design would prevent management from insulating itself from the environment or from the consequences of its own mistakes. To accomplish this, information would have to be widely shared and power less institutionalized. (Pfeffer & Salancik, 1977)

Companies in a wide variety of industries are finding that their networks go beyond their own boundaries. Strategic relationships are becoming commonplace with suppliers, distributors and dealers, customers, joint venture partners, and even competitors. "Lean, agile, post-entrepreneurial companies can stretch in three ways. They can *pool* resources with others, *ally* to exploit an opportunity, or *link* systems in a partnership. In short, they can become better 'PALs' with other organizations" (Kanter, 1989).

Relationships with outside vendors are expanding, as in the steel and aluminum industries. Automobile companies are including their vendors and dealers in their networks, requiring participation in quality management and other processes as if they were divisions. Many companies are bringing contractors inside their facilities to operate mail services, food services, security, and office services. Some even "lease employees," letting a partner company handle all employee administration matters.

As part of a network, a company can expand and cut back the services provided by its contractors (and thereby control costs and service quality). To avoid keeping staff on the payroll, companies go to the outside to handle cyclical activity or for specialized expertise. This is reflected in the continuing growth in the use of management consultants in many fields.

American firms, particularly small ones, have allied with other firms for specific purposes. However, today, alliances have taken on larger scale and diversity, such that they are regarded as common. International partnerships and alliances are associated with competitive strength; they are established for strategic, rather than tactical, reasons (Porter, 1986). By 1987, Ford Motor Company had more than forty major coalitions with outside commercial entities. IBM, once a company that sought to be self-sufficient and independent, has in recent years established formal partnerships with many companies, including some potential competitors, as "value added resellers" (Kanter, 1989).

On a smaller scale, Tom Peters has described his own business, The Peters Group, as essentially a "hollow" organization. This is a company that has very few employees and very little capacity other than to pull together and manage the resources and energies of others. "Even my own tiny company," he said, "is enmeshed in (and busy creating) a spider web of shifting, complex relationships with a host of tiny and huge outsiders. One of our five independent firms, TPG Communications, is hollowed to the point that just four full-time employees produce $4 million in revenue, which translates into sales per person seven times higher than at IBM" (Peters, 1990). Peters observes that this kind of structure, a nonstructure by traditional standards, is becoming the norm in business.

Companies with "blurred boundaries" give up some of their independence in return for stronger ties which, they believe, will give them competitive advantage. They remain legally independent companies and retain their separate culture and management processes, but they share with others in important decisions.

Power and Influence

It is often said that people can make any organization work if they want it to. Certainly, there is no structure that is "people-proof." Put differently, people are the key to making any organization work effectively. The talents, interests, attitudes, and goodwill of employees are critical for an effective organization. The values they hold and share together mold a culture. The use of influence and power in processing information and in making decisions is critical.

While traditional organizations rely on top-down use of management authority, the flexible organization rests on responsibility shared by all employees. The flow of information must be both from the bottom up and from the top down. A company needs to have employees understand and accept strategic goals and contribute their utmost to meet competitive challenges. Each individual and each unit must accept responsibility for fulfilling their roles in the organization—setting and achieving objectives, maintaining work relationships and communications, and continually improving the process. Employees need to be decision makers, equipped with the understanding and ability to genuinely affect company performance. Flat structures and information sharing create high-performance environments.

Peter Drucker observed that an organization should be like an orchestra. "In an orchestra," he said, "the score is given to both players and conductor. In business, the score is being written as it is being played. To know what the score is, everyone in the information-based organization has to manage by objectives that are agreed upon in advance and clearly understood." This requires self-control and high self-discipline. It requires that the "most junior instruments play as if the performance of the whole depended on how each one of these instruments renders its small supporting part." In turn, it allows fast decisions and response to changes. "It permits both great flexibility and considerable diversity" (Drucker, 1985b).

Of course, this view assumes that people will act rationally—focusing on relevant objectives and appropriate behaviors. But there are often conflicting demands, competition for power and control, and unclear strategies and objectives. Information is often limited, and planning is not all it could or should be. Employees are not uniformly interested in what is going on. Managers are not uniformly able to work effectively with people. People often tend to resist, rather than embrace, changes. As a result, people don't always do the "right thing." Power, values, and people may impede, rather than support, the ends of an organization.

Hence organizations are viewed as coalitions, "in which parties with various interests come together in partly cooperative, partly conflicting efforts. An organization is like a market for influence and control, in which social power is transacted" (Pfeffer & Salancik, 1977). It is difficult to manage in such an environment, and more difficult to organize because of these tendencies. Both the strength and the challenge is that people act with diverse interests, preferences, and ideas.

Consideration of human elements may be built into the process of organization design. These questions may be addressed:

- How will existing people fit into the design?
- How will the design affect power relations among different groups?
- How will the design fit with people's values and beliefs?
- How will the design affect the tone and operating style of the organization?

There is no simple way to answer these questions in the course of *planning* organizational changes. They require largely subjective judgments, which are best made with the participation of the people involved. The process of designing organizational changes may be open and inclusive, rather than secretive and exclusive. In this way, the behavioral impact is more fully considered (D. Nadler, 1989).

It is natural, and inevitable, for the key people to be consulted in designing an organization. While the design may not be perfect, or entirely rational, it is more likely to work when the people who will live with it help shape it and buy into it. How widely people need to be involved is a debatable point, but the human element needs to be considered in the process (Stebbins & Shani, 1989).

The human factor may also be addressed in the process of *implementing* organizational changes, as discussed throughout this book. This includes the formulation and implementation of plans for staffing, developing employees, supporting performance, evaluating performance, and rewarding performance.

FINDING THE RIGHT BALANCE

In a flexible organization, managers constantly seek ways to balance dual needs. With regard to organization design, managers face several important dualities. The most common concern is maintaining balance between decentralization and centralization—how much autonomy to delegate to business units and how much control to maintain over them through central management. Related to this concern is a need for balance between a global perspective and approach to managing and a local business focus.

Within a company, managers seek to balance the need for coherence, consistency, and uniformity associated with "maintaining order" with the need to foster innovation and creative change through entrepreneurship (encouraging and managing chaos). Also, managers seek to maintain the right balance between line management and staff leadership and services.

In each of these areas, there is a creative tension to be maintained. Managers seek to build and maintain a natural balancing process that is essential to an adaptive, changing business. In a flexible organization, this role is especially important.

Decentralization and Centralization

In early forms of organization, all decisions were made centrally by one or a few managers. All other employees were merely implementers. As organizations grow larger and more complex, decision making must be delegated to allow for work to be performed on a timely basis. The question must continually be faced: Where should decisions be made in the organization?

Centralization allows management to control decisions that affect business performance. In many companies, decisions regarding capital expenditures, company financing, major contracts for purchases or sales, pricing, joint ventures and alliances, and other significant matters are referred up the hierarchy. Delegated decision authority is limited by rigid guidelines (e.g., spending authority, approval to hire). Specialized advice and counsel from staff may be considered in such decisions. Central decision making may be more efficient if there are economies of scale or expertise (e.g., investment banking relationships).

Centralization also avoids redundancies in staffing, to the extent that different organization units might duplicate efforts, functions, and personnel. Centralization may require fewer resources. At least that is one rationale used by managers who favor centralization. Of course, advocates of decentralization typically argue about lower costs as well. Both sides may be correct, of course, because costs depend on the circumstances, not on the form of structure.

However, centralized management is usually slower, more cumbersome in larger organizations, and less responsive to local unit or customer needs. The absence of involvement by employees across the company is demotivating and sacrifices the value that employees might add to the quality of the outcomes.

McDonald's is known and respected for its disciplined management control systems, clear values and standards, and personnel systems, all meshing to result in exceptional organizational performance. It is a highly consistent and coherent organization structure. Yet in recent years, McDonald's has recognized its fixation on the hamburger, limiting its profitability and growth. Autonomous franchisees are credited with such new products as McD.L.T. and Egg McMuffin. The need for innovation became evident, and the company now boasts a vice president for individuality to help "make the company feel small."

In recent years, the trend has been relentlessly toward decentralization. Here, decisions are made at the lowest possible level in the organization. (One CEO called it "the lowest level of competence," but we don't mean that.) The ultimate in decentralization occurs when individuals or work teams control the decisions affecting their work. Typically, decentralization entails managing an organization through multiple levels and units, each with a wide latitude for action within its established plan, objectives, and budget.

Decentralization is favored in flexible organizations because it allows individuals and units to be highly responsive to changes occurring in local situations. It allows companies to be "close to the customer" and able to react quickly to emerging threats or opportunities. It allows the people closest to problems the latitude to solve them. It is also the form of organization which best suits the attitudes and talents of the current generations of workers.

Big companies have led the trend to decentralize. AT&T restructured six major businesses into nineteen or more smaller units. The purpose was to encourage risk taking, improve focus on individual markets, reduce internal turf wars, and deemphasize management by committee. CEO Jack Welch has sought to remove "big company encumbrances" at General Electric by cutting management layers between factory floor and corporate management from nine to as few as four.

Decentralization can be carried too far, of course. Once an organization has multiple units, operating autonomously to the extreme, opportunities become evident for improved integration through consolidation of certain activities. In the 1990s and beyond, we will likely see a "refocusing" of many activities in companies to gain improved coordination, efficiency, and expertise.

Hewlett-Packard Company (HP), for example, has long prized its decentralization. Large-size units and bureaucracy are considered grave threats to the entrepreneurial spirit at HP. By policy, whenever a division exceeded 1,200 employees, a new division was created. At one point, the company had fifty units with profit, planning, and support responsibilities. This worked well when each unit was dedicated to a distinct market segment; but HP has found itself designing and manufacturing computers. Here, excessive decentralization was counterproductive. The company is now seeking new ways to stay entrepreneurial while maintaining systems thinking and linkages (Pascale, 1990).

The swing of the pendulum need not be wide. In fact, actions to centralize or decentralize should be determined on specific merits, not broad philosophy. An organization may make some decisions (such as capital decisions) centrally and others (such as customer contract terms) locally. In a flexible organization, the balancing is not simple and involves a myriad of judgments.

Also, organization structure provides a way to achieve only temporary balance between autonomy and control—and that may be enough to expect of it as conditions evolve and change. "No structural solutions, least of all overdetermined structures like matrix, can ever resolve the healthy, inherent tension between centralization and decentralization. That resolution must be actively managed over time" (Peters, 1979).

By viewing an organization as a network, managers can have the best of both centralization and decentralization. Managers at headquarters can monitor progress and set overall objectives, while operating units or divisions can analyze their own situations and make informed decisions. Levels of management in between are needed to the extent that they add value to the decisions being made. It is ironic that managers set about designing and building a flexible organization using institutional tools and terminology (such as hierarchy, authority, delegation, and control).

Global and Local Focus

The development toward global markets, global products, and a global strategy implies a need for global organization, or at least geographic diversification. Global organization allows companies to weather downturns and risks in particular markets and to develop synergies on a worldwide basis. A global focus requires adjustments in all internal and external activities. There is little about organization that is unique to global enterprises; it's just that the efforts take on a higher complexity and difficulty. It is hard to be sensitive to local conditions and also conform to expectations of the corporation as a whole.

For example, 3M is organized worldwide by product groups. But to take advantage of significant business opportunities in Europe, 3M needed to adapt. Thus it uses a team approach for coordinating across organizations worldwide. A European Management Action Team (EMAT) evaluates and acts on opportunities on a Pan-European or regional basis, making decisions on product and service offerings, and provides direction on planning and budgeting. It is also the communication channel from Europe to and from the U.S. divisions. The team, which meets at least three times a year, includes members representing the countries, manufacturing and marketing organizations, technical and controllers' organizations, and the applicable U.S.-based product division. The approach provides the global coordination without yielding the advantages of the overall company product organization focus.

Phillips, a staid multi-national institution in lighting and electronics markets around the world, only recently recognized a need to adapt its organization. It is seeking to encourage different points of view, develop a more flexible power structure, and meld diverse perspectives relating to regions, products, and functions into a single approach for solving complicated problems.

The company has both worldwide product groups and a geographic structure of national organizations. Where products are complex or customers are specialized, sales is part of the product groups. Where local orientation is key, the national sales organizations operate, but with coordination along the product axis. Also, smaller entrepreneurial business units have been established to react rapidly to new technological and market developments. Product teams are also used to help a product group develop new products.

The company's challenges grew when it acquired Magnavox, parts of GTE Sylvania, the lighting division of Westinghouse, and the leading lighting company in France. It is now the largest manufacturer of lighting in the world. Joint ventures with AT&T (for switching and transmission systems), DuPont (for audio and videotape production), and Sony (for the digital compact disc) all influence the way the company is organized and managed. These partnerships require their own organizational patterns and arrangements—with limited interference from the top in daily operations.

Global Alliances

A partnership is one of the quickest and cheapest ways to develop a global strategy. It is also one of the toughest and riskiest. Some alliances fail. Others end up in a takeover by one partner or the other. McKinsey & Co., the management consulting firm, found in a study of 150 failed international alliances that three-quarters had been taken over by Japanese partners. "The partner that learns fastest comes to dominate the relationship and can then rewrite its terms. Thus an alliance becomes a new form of competition. The Japanese excel at learning from others, while Americans and Europeans are not so good at it" (Main, 1990).

As economic power has concentrated in Europe, Japan, and the United States, the notion of "centers of competence" has developed. These are centers where economic, educational, scientific, and cultural resources interact to provide a fertile environment for innovation. Silicon Valley, in California, has been a center for microelectronics innovation. Japan has been a center for manufacturing innovation. Any important multi-national company must be present in the centers of competence related to its business in order to prepare for its future. Or, if not present, a company needs alliances to gain the knowledge and resources that are important.

Global alliances require a company to take time to know, trust, and select a compatible partner. It is advisable to select one with complementary, rather than directly competitive, products and markets. Patience for the deal and for achieving results from the alliance is important (and difficult for restless, short-term-minded American partners). It is important to learn all you can about a partner's technology and management, without unnecessarily yielding your important secrets.

There are different kinds of cooperative relationships, including projects, licensing, and ventures. Each has different staffing, compensation, training and development, and other human resource requirements (Butler, Ferris, & Napier, 1991; Lorange, 1986).

- A project-based alliance is usually finite in duration and managed as a temporary organization. This requires recruitment and assignment of talent on a fixed-term basis, with the expectation of returning to their "home" organizations.
- Licensing allows one partner the benefits of an alliance, but allows the

other to manage it through its existing organization, under its own practices, and with its own staff.

• Ventures with permanent complementary roles or with joint ownership require development of organizational arrangements tailored to the situation. Staff may be recruited from either partner or externally, on a long-term dedicated basis.

Strategic alliances are not fail-safe. A partner weakened by its own difficulties may find itself at the mercy of the stronger. Other alliances fail because the partners expected too much from them. U.S. Sprint, the alliance between United Telecom and G.T.E., was envisioned by both companies as a way to build a strong competitor to AT&T out of two fledgling ventures in long-distance service. It did not turn out as positively as hoped. Alliances benefit from specific skills or markets that may be provided by partners, but they may still lack other key competencies needed for their own independent competitive success.

Entrepreneurship and Coherence

Managers must also balance the need for innovation and entrepreneurship within a company with the need to keep the organization design coherent. There remains a tendency in companies to stifle innovation and change. Larger, more institutional operations in a company, often the big-income generators, often draw much of a company's resources. Practices and thinking associated with larger, more complex organizations may overwhelm smaller, entrepreneurial operations. A flexible organization needs to be able to accommodate the needs for innovation (Drucker, 1985a; Kanter, 1989; Peters & Waterman, 1982; Pinchot, 1985).

Managers are entrepreneurial when they search purposefully for changes, respond to them, and exploit them as opportunities. They see changes as the norm and look at them as opportunities for successful innovation. Managers then help others bring these innovations into reality; they are able to manage innovation for business purposes. The objective is to have entrepreneurism widely spread through an organization, not focused in a few protected pockets (Drucker, 1985).

Successful innovators in large companies are sometimes called *intrapreneurs*, but the distinction should be unnecessary. Managers should be able to develop and act on fruitful ideas within a flexible organization just as easily as an independent start-up businessperson. They get ideas for products that their companies could make and then act on their ideas as if they had formed their own companies (Pinchot, 1985).

Innovation is changing the products or services provided by a company, resulting in increased value and satisfaction to the customer. We often think of pure product development, resulting from research, development, or production innovation. But the way products or services are delivered can also add value. It is simply a matter of turning ideas for improvements into action. Innovation is the means by which managers, as entrepreneurs, exploit change as an opportunity for a business. It is a way of behaving and performing which can be learned and practiced (Drucker, 1985).

Often, new product development was left to staff groups, such as R&D, or was achieved through acquisition. Then the innovations were turned over to the mainstream to manage. Entrepreneurs were viewed as strange types of individuals, outside the mainstream of the business and somehow unacceptable. Efforts to protect pockets of innovation or entrepreneurism often failed, because the culture simply did not support or tolerate them (Kanter, 1983).

Flexible companies find that they don't do "business as usual." Instead, they:

- Recognize the importance of innovative behavior among people and are willing to accept and support it
- Are willing to look the other way when organization charts and established procedures are disregarded
- Are open to new ideas, whenever and wherever they emerge
- Realize that failures are inherent in the pursuit of opportunity

Above all, innovative companies are alert to change and make sure they respond to it. This requires a more adaptable, more openly communicating, more consensual, and more loosely controlled organization. It requires managing chaos within guidelines (Butler et al., 1991; Little, 1985; Quinn, 1985; Slevin & Covin, 1990).

Line and Staff

Organizations require a balance of line and staff. The line is responsible for the primary tasks of the organization; they are the ones who design, produce, sell, and deliver the products and services. Staff units typically include finance, information systems, legal, human resources, and planning. Staff add value to this core process by providing particular skills and expertise, or facilitative processes and perspectives.

Staffs have grown since the 1940s in response to demands for specialized services, adoption of new computer systems, coordination across diverse business units, and relief for line managers from tasks better delegated to staff. Their emerging importance accompanied the movement toward decentralization and the need to manage risk, information flow, and coordination.

In flexible organizations, staff activities are important for these same purposes. However, the desire to be lean and mean puts a focus on staff groups. The idea, of course, is to cut fat, not muscle. Judgment is required to know whether staff can be eliminated without long-term harm. Value that is not added is opportunity lost—not an easily measured factor relative to the clearly evident reduction in expense and perceived bureaucracy.

Staff services are often viewed as overhead or indirect cost (in earlier times blatantly known as *burden*). Because staff services are separate from the core process, they tend to be oriented more to their specialities than to the mainstream business. Worse yet, they are often perceived as obstructionist, defensive, competitive, and empire building. No wonder, then, that managers target them when the cost-reduction knife comes out.

The focus should be on appropriate staff roles. General Electric CEO Jack Welch believes that staff should take on the role of "facilitator, adviser, and partner," and not be "monitors, checkers, kibitzers, and approvers."

The focus should also be on the appropriate location of staff. Peters and Waterman observed that most excellent companies "have comparatively few people at the corporate level, and that what staff there is tends to be out in the field solving problems rather than in the home office checking on things." They found that McDonald's, Intel, Wal-Mart, and other companies operate with very little staff.

In a decentralized, flexible organization, managers should be encouraged to develop the staff expertise and services needed to succeed competitively. But in a large company, a significant mass of staff across a company yields opportunities to share resources, particularly in perceived service areas such as human resources (training, recruiting, etc.), information systems (design, user support, and processing), planning (external scanning, benchmarking, analysis support, building company linkages, etc.), and office services (e.g., printing, facilities management).

Through shared corporate services (sometimes called the *corporate center*), staff can provide useful tasks at a lower cost. Also, some services, such as finance and law, are typically viewed primarily as functions serving the corporation as the primary client, protecting the assets of the company and interacting with external parties (Moore, 1987; Pare, 1989).

The relationship of staff to line functions is becoming more collegial, with the emphasis on advice and service. As one executive put it, there are no more "gotchas": in his company, staff members who were once judged on their ability to point out line deficiencies must now work with operating managers on projects before they are submitted for senior management review. Such change do not come easily. Many companies are pushing activities that were once traditionally handled by staffs down into line organizations. Line managers are assuming more direct responsibility for such functions as planning, budgeting, human resources, and information systems. Staffs work directly with line managers, providing initiative, prompt response to requests, and needed support.

SUMMARY

Can an organization ever be too lean, too flat, or too flexible? The flattening and loosening up of organization structures have the primary purpose of enhancing competitiveness by increasing speed, reducing cost, and increasing quality.

Like all good things, however, there may be a point of diminishing returns. An organization may, at some point, need more management levels, more staffing, and more centralized staff services. More levels may provide more perspective in high-risk decisions (and perhaps slow down the pace of action), improve integration of scattered management units represented through wide spans, and provide bite-sized steps in developing managers. More staffing may allow an organization to develop its talent—its intellectual capital or distinctive competencies which are considered increasingly important. Staffing slack may also allow people time to manage or may ease job-related stress and give more time and attention to matters of quality, innovation, and performance improvement.

Signs of recentralization have cropped up in companies that "overdecentralized" and found that focused expenditures have high paybacks for all. The pendulum will inevitably swing further from "Peterian" and "Porterian" emphasis on contingency management, where organizations seek to respond to situational opportunities, back to an emphasis on integration and consistency.

Knowing the right factors to guide organization design and maintaining the right balance in design choices are critical. The most salient factors are those specified in business strategies, which dictate how work will be allocated among positions, groups, and organizational units. Alignment calls for the right balance of integration and differentiation. Internally, the roles of management, spans and levels of management, the need for centralized management, attention to global and local concerns, and balance between line and staff are all organization design considerations.

Organization is a key element in the process of managing human resources. Once expectations relating to business and human resource strategy are shaped, the organization structure defines the work to be performed.

CHAPTER 6

DEFINING
STAFFING NEEDS

There are no right or wrong staffing strategies, merely choices and consequences

Douglas T. Hall and Jim Goodale

To plan effectively for its staffing needs, a flexible company has a clear idea of what its needs actually are and what they will be in the future. It should be aware of how its employees are currently deployed, how well their talents are being applied, and how the available talent supply matches up with projected future requirements. This understanding requires an appreciation of changing conditions and anticipated future events affecting both the supply of talent and the demands of talent imposed by business plans.

Defining staffing needs allows managers to guide staffing activities toward appropriate, realistic objectives. Forecasting can be simple, direct, and logical. It need not be complex or require masses of historical data. The results should help managers recruit, select, redeploy, and decruit talent effectively—in advance of needs. Strategic staffing then allows managers to have the right talent in place, just in time.

This process is a central aspect of implementing human resource strategy, as it provides the estimates of staffing required to achieve the organization's objectives. It guides recruiting and other staffing activities. It helps management ensure that the talent will be in place to meet the organization's needs in the next year and beyond.

This chapter addresses ways in which management may define future staffing needs, including:

- Issues typically addressed in the process of defining staffing needs
- How management can project its future staffing requirements (demand)
- How management can project future staffing availability (supply) in an organization
- Techniques for forecasting availability to support these planning efforts

STAFFING ISSUES

Forecasting and related analysis of staffing needs involve the process of analysis and questioning. Forecasting guides management thinking about future staffing needs and how they will be met.

Fundamental questions address the future numbers, levels, and organizational deployment of talent:

• What will be our needs resulting from expansion, contraction, or business changes?

• What staff will we have available during the future planning period (after attrition, promotions, etc.)?

• How may we adjust or influence movement within the organization to help us meet our needs (transfers, promotions, redeployment)?

• What will our recruitment needs be next year? After that?

These questions may be addressed through standard human resource forecasting techniques, as discussed in this chapter.

Influencing future staffing is the mix and utilization of current staff; the organization needs to identify ways that the current staffing base may be utilized more effectively. Addressing these issues helps management ensure the optimal use of talents and avoid unnecessary future additions to staff. The organization needs to explore the following issues:

• Are we properly staffed? Where are we overstaffed? Understaffed?

• How can we better utilize our employees?

• How could we function efficiently with fewer people?

• Are we likely to be caught short in any skills area?

• What should be our work force diversity objectives, and how can we meet them?

• Do we have the right mix of employees relative to costs (high level/low level, technical and professional, clerical, managerial)?

These issues require study, with specific data collected and analysis relating to specific circumstances conducted. In human resource planning, the questions need to be carefully framed and addressed so that the answers are meaningful.

Forecasting Staffing Needs

Forecasting is a process of estimating available supply and demand for talent. It is usually based on the best available information provided by the managers responsible for operations in each unit of the organization. Mathematical forecasting models may be used as supplements to management-based judgments regarding future needs.

Future staffing needs are easily defined in organizations where requirements change slowly, if ever. In the past, many organizations were quite stable and changed slowly, such as the "old" AT&T, electric and gas utilities, insurance companies, financial institutions, airlines, railroads, and many manufacturing companies. Also, governmental and military organizations have generally been relatively stable, permitting reasonably accurate forecasts to be based on past staffing patterns and trends.

Planning for staffing needs is more difficult when conditions are changing rapidly, but this is also when planning is of greatest value to management. For example, where new technologies or operating processes are being introduced, management needs to act swiftly to address changing staffing needs. Similarly, rapidly expanding enterprises and situations of new management directions and priorities create a high need for adequate staffing. Where labor markets are tight, planning for staffing is important because companies need to focus their recruitment efforts.

Larger organizations face the difficult task of allocating talent to diverse business activities, shifting personnel among locations and divisions to meet changing requirements and to develop individuals' full potential. The importance of planning for effective staffing and for development and utilization of talent is greatly increased under these conditions.

Here, forecasting is most useful when it takes the form of simulation—examination of future needs based on different sets of assumptions. The result is not a prediction but rather the determined outcome of prescribed circumstances: "What would happen if certain assumptions came true." And the value of forecasting in changing environments is to provide a guide to action, not an accurate or true picture of the future.

To forecast the demand for talent and to match this demand with supply we need:

• Knowledge of our objectives for the future and what various business indicators will be (revenues, outputs, volumes, etc.)
• An organization plan
• Knowledge of work activities and requirements
• Appreciation of technological and productivity changes

Because we do not know precisely what future business requirements, organizational changes, economic conditions, productivity, and technological changes will be, forecasts are not often on the mark. And they are not expected to be. We are less concerned with the need for accurate forecasts than with the need for enlightened thinking as a basis for planning staffing actions.

A company may develop several scenarios of future staffing needs, based on different demand assumptions. Each may be used in developing projections. For example, a company with a strategy that called for a series of acquisitions developed a plan with different levels of "success" in these acquisitions, creating different levels of demand for management and professional talent. Another company may develop different scenarios based on different growth rates, believed to be contingent on economic conditions.

The point of forecasting is to provide information that is understandable and useful to managers. The single end result desired is a table of projected staffing requirements. Projected demand and supply never match perfectly. Hence through the forecasting process, demand must be adjusted (e.g., require fewer employees) or supply must be adjusted (e.g., specify accelerated transitions or increased recruitment) until the plan is balanced.

Steps in Forecasting

There are several steps in the process of developing staffing plans. These are illustrated in Exhibit 6-1 and are discussed in this chapter. While emphasis may be given to particular steps because of a situation, all are necessary in providing a foundation for the staffing actions—recruiting, selection, internal deployment, or decruitment.

Forecasting begins with an understanding of the external and organizational conditions affecting future staffing needs. Human resource strategies, future organization design, and the business and external strategic context in which they were developed all influence future staffing requirements and availability.

In some companies, special in-depth studies are needed to provide this foundation for planning staffing needs. Companies often conduct studies of changing conditions affecting human resource needs, such as causes and patterns of employee turnover, effects of organizational structuring and job design changes, available labor supply (including availability of minorities and women in the applicable work force), legal and regulatory constraints and pending legislation, or technological changes affecting staffing requirements.

The second step is to project future staffing requirements—the *demand* for talent. This requires examination of the impact of factors *driving* work load and, in turn, staffing needs. These factors include business indicators (projects, volumes, sales, etc.) and changing customer service or quality requirements. A variety of forecasting techniques is available.

Also influencing future requirements are opportunities for improving the levels, mix, and utilization of staffing. Here, analysis of potential "rightsizing" and restructuring of activities may result in reduced or refocused staffing requirements in the future. Staffing is usually controlled in business organizations through organization structure, job definition, the number of authorized

EXHIBIT 6-1   DEFINING STAFFING PLANS

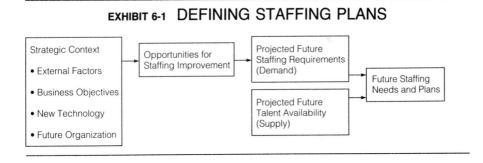

positions, and expense budgeting. An organization may not be optimally staffed at the current time, but planning prompts examination of demand, as it is currently defined and may be redefined for the future.

Next comes the projection of talent availability. Through analysis of the current supply of talent (inventory), past patterns of change in this supply (such as mobility and attrition), and logical assumptions regarding future changes, managers can project the future availability of talent in an organization. This forecasting is typically done in the context of projected future requirements—as a concurrent analysis of future talent supply, matching or balancing this projected supply with projected demand. The results represent needs for human resources and indicate necessary staffing actions, including recruiting.

The analysis of projected staffing availability within a projected demand scenario is not conceptually tidy. It would seem logical to develop separate demand and supply forecasts and then, as a separate step, compare and integrate the two. However, the defining of staffing needs is made easier by using forecasting models now available through personal computer applications, in which the separate third step is unnecessary and redundant.

How much managerial judgment and how much science are to be applied in the process? The techniques of forecasting staffing needs range from the highly subjective and rudimentary to the highly quantitative and complex. For most companies, the simplest models are most practical and quite adequate for most human resource planning applications. In some organizations, however, more complex forecasting models are needed (for example, personnel planning in the military or airline staff scheduling). The techniques used should be those which are best suited to an organization's circumstances, requirements, data availability, and managerial style.

PROJECTING FUTURE STAFFING DEMAND

Various methods are available for determining the relationships between human resource requirements and determinant variables or drivers. These include "base plus" forecasts, bottom-up forecasts, judgmental forecasts, ratio and trend analysis, regression analysis, and deterministic relationships based on "drivers." Other techniques—such as the Delphi techniques, econometric models, or time series analysis—may be applicable, but are not commonly used and will therefore not be discussed here.

Updating Current Requirements

The most common approach to forecasting is to begin with the current base of staffing and define any incremental changes—additions, shifts, or deletions of positions. The current organization, with its authorized levels and mix of staffing, is a logical place to begin the analysis of staffing requirements. Even organizations that are flexible and constantly changing define their current "demand" as "approved staffing" and not merely the current employee population.

Many organizations use a formal position allocation and control procedure to regulate additions to staff and modifications in jobs and organization structure. Here, executives (or a committee or staff unit) review proposed new positions or organizational changes, including expansion of staff. Whenever a position becomes vacant, it may be reviewed to consider whether it is really necessary and whether it is properly structured. This approach, assuming a "zero change" strategy in planning for human resource needs, calls for justification by unit managers proposing new positions or replacements of staff.

A similar but somewhat less restrictive procedure involves a necessary approval or authorization of new positions, organization changes, and hires. A human resource information system (HRIS) can provide an automatic indication of whether positions were included in budgetary plans and thus authorized.

Budgetary procedures often define precisely the positions authorized currently and for the near-term future, as well as the associated costs. If staff costs are budgeted only in gross dollar terms, without detailed staffing data, supplementary information may be required to provide this detail, position by position. Some organizations control staffing very strictly by assigning a number or code to each position. Authorization must be included under the budgeting process in order for staff to be added. This procedure also minimizes the staffing variability caused by use of temporary hires, "double-occupancy staffing" (essentially two people in the same job while one is in training, awaiting transfer, etc.), and "upward drift" in the grading (compensation level) of positions each time they are filled. Budgetary authorizations may specify exactly what staffing is needed and how it differs from previous staffing requirements.

Rather than controlling staffing by organization units, some organizations consider occupational grouping. Ratios of clerical and support staff positions to professional and managerial positions may serve as a guide for staffing. In some companies, such as IBM, authorizations for employment of engineers or other specialists may depend on the current availability of employees, organization-wide, in these occupational groups.

Bottom-Up Forecasts

To define future requirements, someone must make a decision. Mathematical analysis of data may be useful, but ultimately, the determination of "how should we be staffed" is a management judgment that will guide future action.

Accordingly, the basic approach commonly followed is a bottom-up estimation process, usually linked to a budget and position control procedure such as described above. In many instances, these "enlightened guesses" are not formal plans but represent actual authorizations for new positions, changes in job titles or content, recruitment and hiring, and positions left unfilled.

The manager in a local unit is the best-informed person to make judgments regarding staffing requirements necessary to achieve that unit's objectives. The quality of judgments depends on the manager's estimates and is enhanced by the use of the information developed through forecasting.

The "ask and find out" method of forecasting is often adequate for an organization's needs, particularly where operations are stable and staffing requirements are not variable. It involves gathering judgmental estimates from unit managers and aggregating them into an overall forecast. Adjustments may then be made based on successive management reviews and analysis as the aggregate forecast is prepared. Once completed and approved, the forecast is disaggregated (broken apart) and returned to the managers as authorized staffing plans.

This approach represents a formal, systematic planning process, but one which still relies heavily on the subjective judgment and knowledge of the unit managers. The "asking" in the forecast should include estimates of:

- New positions needed
- Positions to be dropped or left unfilled
- Changes in existing positions
- Double staffing, overtime expected, etc.
- Slack expected (due to orientation of new employees or lag periods between projects, etc.)
- Fluctuations in work load during the planning period
- Budgetary impact (costs) of changes
- Changes, if any, in overhead, contracted labor, and supervision

These adjustments are applied to the current staffing table, yielding a forecast of future staffing for each unit. This table provides a forecast and a benchmark for future planning by level and type of job within the unit.

Applying Drivers to Define Demand

Certain factors drive activities or work load and, therefore, determine staffing requirements. As such, they are directly related to the essential nature of the business. The same variables are used in business and operational planning (for example, goods produced, accounts opened or served, miles flown). Sales (in dollars) may not be a useful factor because it is indirect; it reflects price changes (inflation), foreign exchange rates, and other factors.

Drivers of staffing include:

- Changes in outputs produced (revenues, units or volumes produced or sold, projects completed, transactions, etc.)
- Changes in services provided (quantity, quality, timing, etc.)
- Changes in customer relationships (size, longevity, quality)
- New capital investment (equipment, facilities, technology, etc.)

Staffing requirements may be determined by directly applying the "drivers," as discussed above. Expansion, new acquisitions, new equipment, organizational restructuring, or other factors may directly define future staffing requirements. A project organization, such as a research and development function, defines staffing needs based on specific project plans, each with a defined work plan and resource requirements.

In a production and engineering division of a pharmaceutical company, for example, a team of staff and operating managers reviewed the various drivers affecting future staffing needs and developed a forecast as input to a "one plus two" year divisional business plan. The impact of each factor was discussed by the team; and where additional input, differences of opinion, or analysis was required, this was performed between team meetings.

In service functions—such as information systems, human resources, public affairs, or administrative services—the drivers of demand are service requirements. These are often defined by the providers themselves, but are increasingly determined jointly with the users. In this way, the work load required is dependent on variables that may be examined and directly managed, such as level or amount of service, speed or timeliness of service, and cost of service. Total quality management requires that internal service providers treat their users as customers. In this way, the requirements are subject to planning beforehand.

This is the preferred technique among companies today, as it is overt, rational, and deliberate. The direct cause-effect impact of business drivers on staffing needs is clear to managers and may be adjusted based on their judgment. It also allows for the rapid adaptation of the planning "model," in that the drivers may be reviewed, reassessed, and edited whenever a plan is updated. It also links human resource planning directly to operational and capital planning.

Applying Ratios and Regression Analysis

Simple ratios and trends are useful in short-term planning periods and in circumstances where operations are static, change is slow, activities are "normal," and past ratios tend to have a strong influence over future staffing. For example, companies have long added sales positions based on ratios of customers, market size/potential, or sales volume per sales representative.

Allowance needs to be made for possible productivity gains as volumes increase. Production of 30% more widgets may not necessarily require 30% more employees. Thus estimates or targets for improvement in productivity need to be included as variables in forecasting staffing requirements. Work study measurements may help define what these ratios have been and suggest what they might be (as staffing standards). However, simple ratios are more often applicable to operative and clerical positions than to managerial, professional, and technical (exempt salaried) positions.

Regression (correlation) analysis is a widely used family of techniques for measuring the degree of relationship between two variables. Multiple regression has the capacity of identifying patterns among many variables simultaneously. This technique is widely used in human resource forecasting where it is believed that future staffing requirements are correlated with some measurable indicators of output, revenues, etc. When we can quantify the relationship between staffing and other factors, we have a basis for accurate forecasting.

Regression results do not necessarily represent desired or optimal future staffing levels. Rather, they represent levels which are based on historical policies and actions in the aggregate. As such, the analysis is most applicable where staffing needs vary directly with other measurable factors such as production, sales, and unit costs. Simple relationships are often difficult to isolate, however, and many planners have searched in vain for staffing determinants. Multi-variate analysis has not been applied widely in human resource planning and has the disadvantage of being an abstract planning technique—a "black box" in which managers cannot easily discern the rationale for future staffing needs.

The technique provides a useful supplementary base of information to aid in making managerial judgments about future needs. Its real value may be in its usefulness in identifying alternative staffing levels as possible staffing objectives rather than in the precision of its quantitative forecasts. Regression analysis may alert management to the human resource implications of production, sales, and other operating plans.

Improving Staff Utilization

Under conditions of rapid change, it is important to continually pursue opportunities for improvement in staffing, rather than perpetuating past practices. Special efforts are needed to promote innovative thinking about staffing and staff utilization. Improvement in staff costs, staffing levels and mix, and effective utilization of employee talents is vital.

The number of people on the payroll may not directly reflect the capabilities being applied to achievement of organizational objectives. To manage costs and provide employees with more challenging work assignments, managers need to examine ways to utilize people more fully.

To examine talent utilization, it is necessary to focus on the work activities, not on the people. To reduce staffing requirements, work activities need to be reduced, eliminated, or performed more efficiently. These questions may be addressed:

- How may work be streamlined or simplified?
- How may work be restructured or reassigned to provide a more effective use of talent?
- What activities may be eliminated, consolidated, automated, or contracted out?
- What work can be performed more efficiently (at a lower cost) by others?
- How may skills be applied more effectively?
- What skills need to be added or emphasized to improve utilization?

These broad questions are addressed through analysis of activities performed—the utilization of time by employees. Managers may have direct knowledge and opinions regarding these opportunities. In addition, data may be collected and analyzed on actual on-the-job activities using activity profile questionnaires or team analyses. This indicates what people really do and how they perceive opportunities for improved utilization.

Once data are collected and tabulated, areas of "organizational slack" may be identified—time and skills that are not being appropriately applied for achievement of critical business objectives. Typically, overhead activities (e.g., staff work, coordination and administration activities, personnel work, information reporting, or planning) are common target areas because the work is more flexible and can be contracted by redefining the services provided (level, speed, cost). All steps in work processes are examined for improvement opportunities—process re-engineering.

From an organizational viewpoint, the aggregate time allocations required to perform necessary tasks may result in fewer overall positions required; the available supply of talent may be more effectively allocated to the work required and thus reduce the overall demand for employees. For example, a group of engineers may allocate 20% of its time to clerical, drafting, and other support activities which could be reassigned to clerical positions. This would free up time for higher-skill engineering work and reduce the pressure for recruitment of scarce engineering talent.

By examining changing work requirements, skills mix may also be analyzed. Job requirements are typically defined in terms of experience, skills, knowledge, and educational needs. In any group, there may be employees who are overqualified or underqualified in relation to the actual job requirements. If we can match more precisely the skills of people with the skills required by the work actually performed, we may utilize the higher-talent individuals better on more demanding jobs, motivate employees by challenging them more fully, and thus reduce the overall demand for talent and related payroll costs.

There is also the question of whether an employee is underutilized in a position or is overqualified for the position. Should employees be promoted before they are fully qualified for a position (stretching them and allowing mastery of a job once on the job), or should they be advanced only after becoming fully qualified through training? The utilization of skills is an important variable influencing the availability of talent and thus forecasted requirements.

A human resource planning process used in a pharmaceutical company guides managers through a logical sequence of questions:

• What are the business indicators (e.g., production volume, sales, projects, external demands) that affect your work load or the demand for your services? Explain.

• What changes in these indicators or new indicators do you anticipate that may affect your need for staffing? Explain.

• What actions have you taken in the past year to improve utilization of current staff? Explain the effect of these actions on future staffing needs.

• What actions do you intend to take in the next year to improve utilization of current staff? How will these actions affect your staffing needs?

• Please attach a current organization chart that includes all regular employees and any leased employees or contractors who perform work for you. Explain any organizational changes that you anticipate in the next year.

- What will be the net effect of all the above changes on your staffing needs for next year (adding, consolidating, changing, eliminating positions, etc.)? Include in your net effect regular, temporary, and contracted employees.

Managers are also asked to identify activities that are duplicated in other areas of the company—activities that could be consolidated with resulting reduction of work and associated staffing.

The process is initiated at the first management level, where managers examine inputs from their employees (using activity profile questionnaires) and other pertinent information on staffing drivers and changes, planned organization changes, and net staffing changes. They then address the above human resource planning questions.

These first-level departmental human resource plans are reviewed at the next level, where each manager prepares an integrated human resource plan for the division. These divisional plans roll up as unit plans, and ultimately become part of an overall company plan. Issues that are raised in the plans are addressed at the appropriate management level. For example, department managers address redeployment and job design issues within their organizations, while duplications with other departments are addressed through discussions with other department managers or by the division manager.

By limiting staff additions and careful management of attrition, the pharmaceutical company in our example achieved containment and gradual reduction of head count. The process focused on improved utilization of staff as a way to avoid budget-driven head count reductions. The company sought to emphasize actions to reduce work, to streamline activities, and to redeploy current employees to match this redefined work. In this way, the company avoided staffing reduction programs (e.g., layoffs, open-window retirements) and retained a tradition of employment security, which is believed to foster high loyalty and work motivation. External hiring was limited to cases where special skills were required.

A feature of the process is the attention given to contractors and temporary employees. Many flexible organizations have "shadow" staffing—resources who are not regular employees or a part of head count. When head count alone is the focus of planning and control, companies may shift work outside, without considering the cost-effectiveness of the action. Looking at the drivers of the overall work allows consideration of the need for all resources. Plans may therefore cover head count, regular employee costs, the use of temporaries and the costs involved, and the use of contractors and the costs involved. Work is work, expense is expense, and heads are heads, regardless of where they are located.

PROJECTING TALENT AVAILABILITY

Projecting the future availability of talent requires examination of the flows of employees within an organization over specific periods of time. Employees move up, over, and out of an organization as they move through the structure.

EXHIBIT 6-2 EMPLOYEE MOVEMENT IN AN ORGANIZATION

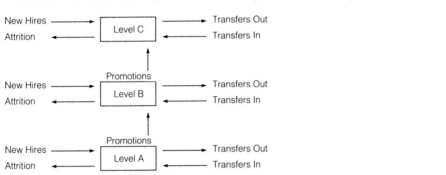

These flows are simple and logical, and may be examined easily through use of forecasting models. This flow of talent is illustrated in Exhibit 6-2.

It is fundamental for companies to forecast changes in their talent supply—losses resulting from turnover and availability changes due to transfers and promotions. Such forecasting should be within the same time frame and follow the same structural logic as the forecasting of staffing demand. Yet few managers take the time to do this analysis and use the results in projecting future staffing needs because they lack the ready tools, information base, or staff support.

Inventory

A prerequisite to forecasting future talent supply and demand is an inventory of the talent available in the organization. Most managers feel that they already have a pretty good idea of the talent they have and what they can do. But this knowledge is not always current and complete. Nor is the information in a form that can be assembled and used as a basis for forecasting future needs.

An inventory is necessary to provide a snapshot, both quantitatively and qualitatively, of the human resources in an organization. It provides a benchmark for planning future requirements, surfaces potential problems and issues relating to future staffing, and suggests reasonable assumptions regarding future attrition and mobility.

Companies typically maintain basic employee data as part of a payroll system or a broader human resource information system. For purposes of forecasting, the following data elements are helpful in formulating plans to meet anticipated needs:

- Position data (position title, code, organizational unit, salary grade or level, etc.)
- Service data (service with the company, time in position)
- Demographic data (age, sex, EEO code, level of educational attainment, etc.)

- Appraisal data (performance rating, readiness for promotion, etc.)
- Job history (previous assignments, moves among organizational units)

In today's flexible organizations, it is sometimes hard to define even current staffing. For planning purposes, the inventory needs to be specific, including:

- Temporary employees (or part-time employees) made permanent
- Permanent employees made temporary, part time, or granted special status (for example, leaves of absence, special assignments)

The usual approach is to plan needs on the basis of full-time employees, either regular employees or contractors. However, with increased use of flexible work arrangements, some companies do planning on the basis of full-time equivalents (FTEs). The inventory, then, must reflect the fact that some employees are part time, filling positions that are part time or shared.

Turnover

A primary reason for change in the supply of talent in an organization is attrition. Employees leave for various reasons: voluntary termination (to take other jobs, to return to school, etc.), involuntary termination (elimination of work/reduction of staff, or termination because of poor performance, discipline, etc.), and other reasons (e.g., retirements, deaths, disabilities).

Turnover is normally reported as a ratio of the number of separations during a period to the average number of employees on the payroll during the period, expressed as a percentage. It includes all permanent separation, whether voluntary or involuntary, but does not usually include employees placed on temporary or indefinite layoff or granted leaves of absence.

Overall turnover rates reported by companies range from 10% or less annually to 100% or higher. Turnover rates vary, of course, by industry, by occupational and job category, with length of service, and so on. The costs of turnover are substantial to any company and include separation costs, replacement costs, and training costs. For a computer programmer, the turnover cost has been estimated at $20,000. The cost is far higher for professionals and managers requiring search fees, relocation, and other costs. There is also the loss of productivity during the transition (Blakeslee, 1985; Mercer, 1989).

To control turnover it is necessary to identify the factors associated with high turnover rates and correct them. Various causes have been cited by companies and through research, most commonly promotional opportunities, pay opportunities, satisfaction with supervision or coworkers, satisfaction with the work itself (e.g., repetitiveness, autonomy, responsibility), and personal factors (age, short job tenure, individual anxiety and instability). Causes are best assessed on a situational basis (Jenkins, 1988; Mobley, 1982; Watts & White, 1988).

Voluntary turnover is typically forecasted based on past turnover rates, subjectively adjusted to reflect management knowledge of changing conditions such as pay rates and economic conditions. Trends in turnover rates may be examined for particular locations or occupational groups/job categories to project turnover. The rates projected forward are used as inputs (parameters) in forecasting talent availability in future periods.

Involuntary turnover usually follows a determined pattern, the result of management actions. There are typically few employees terminated "for cause" in a given population each year. Reductions in staff are special events that may be judgmentally anticipated, if management plans are known.

Losses from death, disability, and retirements are usually estimated by reviewing the demographic characteristics of specific employee groups (e.g., age distribution, length of service) and losses experienced in recent years. Where large numbers of employees are involved, these losses may be addressed actuarially, using tables that are based on past experience and used in funding pension plans and determining insured risks. These are simple "annual loss probability" tables based on employee age and sex (although sex is not used as a differentiating variable where "unisex" tables are applied).

Internal Movement

Internal movement needs to be examined in forecasting talent availability in order to define how employees move into, over, up, and out of an organization. When segmented by levels, occupational groupings, or organizational units, it is possible to examine this flow and project future flows, or movement paths.

One approach to forecasting internal movement is to ask each unit manager to indicate past paths of promotions into, out of, and within the unit—or likely future paths (including new paths suggesting alternative sources of talent). This would include identifying the preferred entry-level positions for hiring from the external labor market.

With an inventory of current staffing and information on past hires, movement, and attrition, the next step in human resource forecasting is to project future inventory changes. This entails adjusting the current staffing table to reflect estimated future staffing changes: promotions, transfers, and demotions within a unit, additions from other units, and losses of talent to other units.

These estimated changes may be applied to current staffing to create a reasonably accurate one-year forecast of available supply. The same estimates may be projected two, three, or more years into the future, but the results are less reliable because conditions are less certain. The basic approach is to adjust current staffing data as follows:

- Define current head count, less turnover for the period.
- If there are no hires or promotions, what would be the net needs relative to demand?
- Define the demand for talent, to be met through a combination of internal movement, based on paths, and external hiring.

In this pragmatic approach, the number of people hired or moved is directly determined by the requirements defined by management. This is the approach most commonly used in forecasting among companies today.

TRADITIONAL APPROACHES FOR FORECASTING AND PLANNING

Presented in Exhibit 6-3 is a format developed and used in an oil production company. The format concisely summarizes (1) staffing requirements, (2) key ratios and indicators, and (3) planned staffing sources. It is a general structure for presenting the results of the forecasting effort, whether anchored in intuitive management judgments or quantitative analysis.

Modeling techniques have been applied in analyzing or simulating human resource flows and needs. Models assist in examining the flow of talent through an organization as a system and comparing it with projected demand for talent. Models serve primarily as a description and simulation tool for managers in human resource planning. In one major company, for example, modeling efforts provided managers with "best estimates" of future demand and supply of talent for a number of years. Standard statistical techniques are used in such modeling (Bartholomew, 1982; Makridakis, Wheelright, & McGee, 1978; Willis, 1987).

Today, models are used primarily to simulate prospective staffing configurations—to generate several alternative scenarios. Managers may review these and select the forecasts they consider most realistic and practical for their planning needs. Simulation techniques make it possible to evaluate the relative importance of the factors that influence an organization's human resource needs and availability. Modeling enables managers to explore aspects of systems they cannot easily observe directly, such as the patterns of movement of employees among different sets of jobs in an organization over time and reactions of internal work force supply to changes in management policies and employment decisions.

Through modeling, managers may examine the implications of past policies and organizational conditions on future supply and demand of talent. Furthermore, the effects of changes in policies, staffing and development actions, and organizational changes may be examined and considered in formulating human resource plans. Modeling, then, represents a powerful tool and a valuable source of feedback in this difficult management task.

Two fundamental types of models are often used: a supply push model and a demand pull model. The former uses rates of movement among units and levels to project future movement. The latter relies on analysis of movement among levels created by vacancies, representing a "renewal" or pull effect. These are briefly described below.

Supply Push Models

In this method, the movement of employees through an organization is projected using a bottom-up approach. Employees are assumed to move (are "pushed") out of their current jobs into others (through promotions, lateral moves) or out of the organization (through terminations). Their movement is dictated by rates that may be based on past experience or on assumptions (judgment).

A basic matrix structures the model. Typically this is a two-dimensional matrix where columns are defined as projects, functions, or organizational units, and rows indicate levels (salary grades or organizational levels). From the inventory, the actual numbers of current employees are assigned to each cell of the matrix. This matrix should be the same as that used in forecasting demand for staffing, as discussed above.

If we look at the probabilities of employees moving from one "cell" to another or out of the organization altogether, we will have generated a matrix or table of "transition rates" or probabilities. This gives us the dynamics of flow in the system from one time to another, the basis for a forecast. If we adjust the probabilities based on managerial judgment of how movement will change, we move toward having a flexible simulation model. Here projections are based on assumptions instead of past system behavior. In fact, in some models, each and any transition rate may be changed, allowing forecasts based on very specific assumptions.

Applying the transition probabilities to the matrix, the process tells us whether employees will remain in a given state or move to each of other possible states at some future time. In simple terms, for each cell of the matrix, the model calculates the number of employees who will:

- Leave the organization for any reason
- Be promoted to a job in another cell
- Make lateral or downward moves
- Move into the job from another cell
- Be hired into the cell from outside the company

The model would perform this sequence of addition and subtraction for each cell of the matrix, thus defining the number of employees who will end up in each cell at the end of the planning period (e.g., one year).

A true Markov process contains certain mathematical properties, such as strict independence of the states (job categories), constant transition probabilities, and an infinite (or at least large) number of forecasting cycles. Because most human resource planning applications are for a few periods and the classifications may be somewhat arbitrarily drawn, it is more accurate to refer to such models as merely probabilistic or simulation models ("supply push" models).

Once all calculations are completed and the projected future inventory of talent is completed for all cells, the result can be compared with the "demand" for talent—the projected future requirements for each cell and the resulting surpluses or shortfalls identified. Today, all supply push models include this feature. In most cases, supply will not match demand and the number of new hires, terminations, and movements will have to be adjusted accordingly. The

EXHIBIT 6-3   SUMMARY OF STAFFING REQUIREMENTS AND SOURCES

A. MANPOWER REQUIREMENTS

Covering Period _____ to _____

Prepared by _____
Date _____

Major Job Categories and Classifications	1 Current Manpower A/O ____	2 Planned Manpower A/O ____	3 Net Change ±	Anticipated Losses to Each Job Category						10 Total Needs for This Period
				4 Transfers	5 Promotions	6 Resignations	7 Retirements	8 Discharge	9 Other	
1. Executives and Managers										
2. First-Level Supervisors										
3.										
4.										
5.										
6.										
7.										
8.										
9.										
Total Employees										

B. KEY RATIOS AND INDICATORS

	Current	Planned
Revenue/Employee		
Net Income/Employee		
Direct Labor/Indirect Labor		
Management/Employees		
Total Payroll Cost		
Average Salary		
Other Key Indicators (Specify)		

C. PLANNED STAFFING SOURCES

	Total Needs from Col. 10 Above	Promotion of Current Employees of This Organiz.	Promotion of Current Employees of Other Organiz.	Employees to Be Hired and Trained Prior to Promotion	Employees to Be Hired for Immediate Assignment
1. Executives and Managers					
2. First-Level Supervisors					
3.					
4.					
5.					
6.					
7.					
8.					
9.					
Total Employees					

173

process typically continues several cycles until the preferred staffing strategy is identified.

Demand Pull Models

A variation on this technique is the demand pull model. If promotions are made only to fill jobs that become vacant and recruitment is constant, the movement of people responds directly to vacancies created. In a demand pull model, flows of staff are viewed as triggered by vacancies. These vacancies, when filled from lower levels of the organization according to user-defined decision rules, *pull* personnel up through the system.

The result is a chain effect as a person moves to fill a vacancy, creating a vacancy at another level. Movement occurs only if an actual opening is being filled; these openings are created, in turn, when employees leave a position as a result of promotion, transition, or termination. The analysis begins at the senior level in an organization. Here there can be no promotions, so openings are created only through transfers, terminations, or the creation of new positions (expansion). Of course, as has often been the case in companies, the number of management positions and openings may actually diminish (through flattening of levels and elimination of positions).

These "renewal" models have not been as widely applied as other models, but they are increasing in use because they allow a manager to determine movement. In models based on historical movement patterns (supply push), movement and hiring are dependent on historical rates. One of the earliest applications was by Harrison White, who developed a series of such models for analyzing mobility and measuring vacancy chains. His application of the models to a fifty-year history of mobility of clergy in three national churches demonstrated that individual careers are not independent of the careers of others in an organization (White, 1970).

This type of model is particularly useful in forecasting promotion opportunities. It is important in setting affirmative action plan objectives that are realistic and achievable relative to actual opportunities to provide promotions and transfers. It also helps identify areas where blockages are greatest, so that remedial actions may be taken to increase the movement of talent in slow-growth and change situations.

Optimization Models

Some models do more than manipulate data to forecast future staffing patterns. Some forecast not what is likely to happen, but rather what is necessary to happen if certain objectives are to be achieved. The optimal (or "best") future staffing patterns might mean minimized costs, minimized turnover among employees, target proportions of women and minorities in certain groups, achievement of a specified talent mix, or other objectives. The tools described above are often incorporated in optimization models, but such techniques as linear programming are also used. Optimization models are more commonly used in large organizations with considerable management concern for future staffing, such as governmental or military organizations (Niehaus, 1979).

Linear programming (LP) provides a specific solution which is "best" according to measurable criteria. It is useful for considering staffing needs at a particular point in time and within given constraints. Deviations from the plan can be examined through the model in terms of their impact on the actual end results. Essentially, an LP model determines the level of staffing required to meet organizational objectives when a number of specified constraints are defined. Linear programming is a mathematical technique for determining the optimum solution under a set of given constraints, represented as mathematical expressions. It is applicable when expressions are proportional to the measure of the activities and all relationships are in the form of linear inequalities.

Because relationships are not always linear, *nonlinear programming* is sometimes used. This may involve convex, concave, or quadratic programming. Another variation on the technique is *dynamic programming*, which is similar but involves a series of optimization decisions or solutions, one at every stage of a multi-stage problem. At any one stage, several decisions may appear to be of equal merit; only when the effect of all stages on the overall goal is determined is the optimal solution reached.

A refinement of a linear programming model is a goal programming model, a variation of a demand pull model in that it is not based on historical rates. This approach uses Markov analysis and linear programming in combination. It is applicable where several constraints affect staffing (for example, budgetary and promotion policies) and where the problem extends over several time periods.

Goal programming as a work force planning technique was pioneered by a group of researchers under the auspices of the Office of Civilian Personnel in the Navy Department. A series of studies has provided models useful in planning recruitment, promotions, and transfers, and affirmative action planning (Niehaus, 1979).

Goal programming models permit more comprehensive analysis of the behavior of human resource systems. In addition, they permit the development of goals that are realistic and attainable. The modeling tests alternative goals by examining the discrepancies between forecasted results and identified targets, and thereby suggests optimum goals that are attainable. For this reason, goal programming represents a powerful advancement in modeling technology for human resource planning as well as for planning equal employment opportunities and affirmative action.

Included in the system can be such factors as external availability of talent, personnel movement, and budgetary and other policy constraints, for example, required time on a job (Niehaus, 1979). While most goal programming applications have been in governmental and military organizations, a few companies have used them in affirmative action planning and other applications.

Mathematical models are particularly useful when integrated with bottom-up judgmental forecasts. An approach of TRW's Systems Group, for example, used marketing projections and project plans to determine staffing needs from the top down. At the same time, estimates by the managers on the various projects planned and under way were obtained. For each unit, direct labor, overhead (utilities, materials, services, etc.), and staffing needs were determined. These data were integrated, resulting in a dynamic plan for overall staffing levels and mix, recruitment, assignment, and development.

In one large company, an annual forecast is made based on bottom-up departmental forecasts by titles and pay grades. These data, in the form of desired year-end populations for the next six years, are then applied to a companywide model which forecasts all types of work force activity. From this model are determined the actions necessary to reach desired populations. Embedded in the model is a supply push model. The actions are translated into assessment, promotions, development, and other necessary program plans. In this approach, the forecast by managers is the starting point, not the analysis of data through the model. The model itself involves hundreds of assumptions regarding future personnel movement and company needs; these are improved in quality through the integration of judgmental forecasts.

SUMMARY

Defining an organization's future staffing needs and plans is at the heart of human resource planning and, if aligned with people-related business issues, is of strategic importance.

The logic of forecasting and planning for staffing supply and demand is simple: estimate future staffing requirements, estimate future staffing availability, compare the two, and define net needs. In organizations with high stability, little change in work demands, and little movement of people, the process is, indeed, simple.

However, in today's flexible organizations, the factors driving future staffing needs and supply are variables. The process of defining future needs, then, is one of developing scenarios based on different assumptions about changes. Managers may then select among these alternatives as a basis for action.

Basic modeling techniques have advanced and have been made easier through the use of personal computers, but the most important aspects of forecasting are the future assumptions. Identifying, analyzing, and applying the factors that drive future demand for talent require management judgment and an understanding of the business strategic context that gives rise to most drivers of work load. Similarly, while the logic of supply and demand is distinct, today's models analyze the flows of talent and calculate the net needs (comparing supply with demand) in a single operation. It may not be conceptually tidy, but it works.

In the middle of the process, there is a step that used to receive only lip service but is crucial today to the process: companies aggressively seek out ways to improve the utilization of talent. In a process of continual improvement, work load is always subject to review: "Can the work be eliminated, reduced in scope, automated, delegated, or combined with other work?'' Streamlining of jobs, flattening and restructuring of organizations, and rapid changes in work requirements make the demand for staffing a moving target. There is a vital link between future staffing needs and the strategic context for future staffing.

As organizations become more flexible, with changes occurring rapidly, managers are often tempted not to plan for staffing at all, but rather to act situationally. To align the management of human resources with strategy, this temptation must be resisted. When conditions change rapidly, careful analysis and planning of future staffing are all the more important as a guide to strategic staffing, the subject of the next chapter.

CHAPTER 7

STRATEGIC STAFFING

Through planning, management strives to have the right number and the right kinds of people, at the right places, at the right time, doing things which result in both the organization and the individual receiving maximum long-run benefit.

Eric W. Vetter

Staffing plays an increasingly vital yet difficult role in the process of implementing strategy. Strategic staffing is the process of implementing a plan of action to secure the needed talent through recruitment, selection, promotion, and transfers (Hall, 1986).

Companies have always had staffing; so what makes staffing strategic? In the face of rapidly changing needs for talent and changing demography and labor supply, companies must recruit more aggressively and effectively, improve their selection and retention of talent, and manage internal deployment more effectively. This is a basic management responsibility—one that is becoming more important and requires new, improved approaches.

This chapter examines the approaches management may follow in staffing an organization to support its strategies. It discusses:

• How staffing practices can result in just-in-time staffing to meet changing needs
• How multiple approaches may be used to match employees with job assignments
• How career opportunities may be managed in a flexible organization
• How strategic staffing supports employee career development

JUST-IN-TIME TALENT

The ideal result of strategic staffing is *just-in-time talent,* a term used in the quality management process, suggesting that we should have the people we need just when we need them. According to consultant Bob Eichinger, ''When any key position opens within the organization, a replacement is ready and available the next day, promoted from within the organization from a pool of talent that was hired at entry and has experienced zero turnover, and this replacement performs better than the prior incumbent and after some time period is available for increased responsibility if needed.''

The desire for just-in-time talent was expressed by the CEO of a large diversified company, but with a different approach. He hired replacements for nine division senior executives from outside the company within two years. ''Why should I invest in developing managers when there are so many other companies out there doing it for me?''

Staffing needs are met either through external recruiting or through redeployment of talent already in the organization. Staffing surpluses relative to needs are addressed either by reassigning employees to other jobs (and providing them with retraining when necessary) or by moving them out of the company (''decruitment'').

Companies seek to have the required talent—with just the right skills, knowledge, abilities, and experience—to meet their needs. They seek to maintain sufficient (but not excessive) inventory and the right flow of talent, just as they seek to maintain sufficient physical inventory of raw material and components for manufacturing. Companies operating as lean and flexible organizations seek to be staffed ''right,'' neither overstaffed nor understaffed.

Staffing decisions also shape an organization. The culture and character of a company are influenced by the choice of executives, the determination of jobs as critical for the organization, and the identification of characteristics needed by people who fill jobs. Similarly, the systems used in staffing may also affect an organization—the emphasis on analysis and planning, the balance of external and internal staffing, the way new employees are oriented and socialized, and the movement of employees through promotion, transfer, and demotion (Butler, 1991).

The challenge of strategic staffing requires careful choice and use of approaches for recruiting, deployment, and decruitment of talent.

Recruiting

Companies have normally been able to recruit the talent they need; jobs rarely go unfilled. However, positions may remain unfilled longer than management may wish, resulting in adverse effects on organizational performance. Or they may be filled with individuals who are not of the desired quality or do not have the desired qualifications. Companies also seek to recruit individuals in such a way that those hired will stay with the company, minimizing future turnover. Accordingly, companies find it helpful to plan strategies for attracting a sufficient flow of desirable applicants, defining and applying relevant recruiting requirements and job qualifications, applying useful selection methods, and helping new employees ''join up'' and become effective contributors.

Recruiting individuals from outside a company is important because it:

• Brings in talent with new ideas, different experiences, and a diversity of skills and education required to implement needed change

• Helps bring a cultural diversity into the work force and representation of minorities in various job categories
• Continually sets a quality standard to help guide internal training and development and selection/retention decisions
• Brings in younger, less experienced (and less costly) talent into a pipeline for longer-term development

Any human resource textbook or reference details the usual sources for recruiting, including the experienced labor market, schools and institutes, colleges and universities, the government and military. The methods of identifying prospects are also described: advertising, referrals, employment agencies and search consultants, etc. While the mix of sources and approaches used may vary, there are finite alternatives (Farish, 1989).

Complications arise in recruiting when these sources fail to yield an adequate flow of candidates considered to be qualified. Shortcomings are not necessarily due to the sources or to the methods used for tapping them, but rather to changing labor market circumstances. There is sometimes a tendency to question the utility of particular sources that seem to have dried up.

As discussed earlier, demographic patterns and educational patterns will influence the availability of talent in the 1990s and beyond. Cycles will exist in particular occupational segments, industries, and geographic areas. Competition for talent will be intense in areas of shortages.

For example, in the late 1980s, John Hancock faced a severe market shortage of talent for entry-level and low-level positions. "Hancock simply could not fill the roughly 1,000 full-time, part-time, and temporary jobs that become available each year at the Boston headquarters" (Fraser, 1989). Hancock responded by expanding community outreach efforts to attract every possible job applicant, by broadening corporate training programs to prepare otherwise marginal candidates to function on the job, and by enhancing productivity to make the best use of each available worker. For the longer term, the company became more actively involved in improving the educational system of Boston, the primary source of talent.

Related to the problem of availability is the matter of retention. Churning of recruits increases recruiting demands and also impairs a company's recruiting effectiveness. Hence an important consideration in planning a recruiting process is the development of sources which demonstrate good retention after employment (low turnover) and the avoidance of sources which demonstrate higher turnover. Too often, companies get into a routine (for example, at colleges and universities or through search firms) which sustains a recruiting problem. A different approach is called for, based on a refocused strategy.

The use of employment agencies or search firms is a concern also because of the expense involved. While these external agencies provide a valuable service in identifying and screening prospective candidates, the costs are high. And the criteria used by the search firms may not be wholly consistent with those of the employer, if for no other reason than that the agency's primary criterion of success is typically placement, not subsequent performance or retention. As a result, some corporations have placed stringent controls over the use of agencies as a recruiting source, including centralized direction over all managerial-level searches. Some large companies may be using several different agencies for different positions; efficiencies may be gained by coordinating these sourcing activities.

Effective recruiting requires consideration of wider issues than merely the techniques applied. Knowledge of market conditions, competitor requirements, and excessive recruiting demands imposed by poor retention of hires are essential factors.

Screening and Selection

Recruiting is a step in the process of screening and selecting employees. The manner in which prospects are identified, solicited, and drawn into the employment process is clearly a procedure which influences the characteristics of resulting staff. In turn, the procedure is also subject to unfair or discriminatory practices. Specification of opportunities to prospects has the potential effect of encouraging or discouraging some applicants.

Selection implies a focused choice among alternative candidates for employment based on some established criteria. Accordingly, it is not enough to know how many individuals are to be recruited. It is important also to know the skills, knowledge, experience, and attributes required for effective performance.

For more than half a century, industrial and organizational psychologists have been devising, studying, and applying techniques for employee selection. Their traditional role is to provide information to be considered in making decisions. To this end, they develop and test hypotheses about applicant characteristics that can be used to predict employee performance and show how to assess them. Presumably, where valid tests are available, the employment decision is itself made more valid—a presumption rarely checked since the decision process itself is rarely studied.

The selection process used by managers is judgmental. But judgment may be enhanced by the use of selection tests. Tests, in professional and legal usage, refer to all steps in the selection process: recruiting of prospective applicants, application forms, interviews, paper-and-pencil tests, work-sample tests, physical examinations, etc. Typically the selection process represents a series of tests, acting as successive hurdles. The systematic use of various types of tests, shown to be related to performance, is believed to be a valuable supplement to managerial judgment.

Today, formal screening and selection processes are used variably by companies. Most companies specify the experience, education, knowledge, skills, or abilities sought in candidates, relative to position descriptions and requirements. However, some use these criteria as broad guidelines in screening and interviewing candidates. Some use formal testing (e.g., paper-and-pencil tests, exercises) or structured interviews to evaluate individual capabilities relative to requirements. A few apply formal scoring to evaluations at each "successive hurdle" and strive to develop a selection process that is valid and reliable.

The employment interview is the most common and yet the most difficult test in the selection process to specify. Its measures are drawn from judgments and perceptions of interviewers. For interviews to be more job-related and to be defended as such, the judgments inherent in the interviewing procedure should be anchored to the criteria defined. Structured interviews are one way to establish a framework for decision making. Training of interviewers is another (Byham, 1978; Gatewood & Ledvinka, 1976).

The use of paper-and-pencil testing, however, remains controversial, largely because of the apparent intrusion into personal affairs—invasion of privacy and the risk of excluding, without cause, individuals who are actually qualified. Many employment tests are believed to favor white males and to discriminate against females and minorities. Drug testing, increasingly adopted by companies seeking to become or remain drug-free, is also being challenged. While employment testing will continue to develop (it is a billion-dollar industry), its use by companies will depend on management attitudes and assumptions regarding the merits and disadvantages of testing, and on company staffing strategies (Arvey, 1979; Martin, 1990).

Peter Drucker observed that "of all the decisions an executive makes, none are as important as the decisions about people because they determine the performance capacity of the organization. Therefore, I'd better make these decisions well" (Drucker, 1985b). Drucker defined five basic principles as important steps in making effective staffing decisions:

- Think through the assignment and what it requires.
- Look at a number of potentially qualified people.
- Think hard about how to look at these candidates; do they have the right strengths for the assignment or weaknesses that may rule them out?
- Discuss each of the candidates with several people who have worked with them, whenever this is possible.
- Make sure the person understands the job.

Redeployment

The most readily accessible and best-known talent pool to meet changing needs is the existing complement of employees. Many companies prefer to look within rather than outside as part of their staffing strategy:

- The talent within is already known, both its strengths and its weaknesses.
- Looking within fosters a policy of providing opportunities for advancement to employees.
- Internal candidates are more likely to stay with the company, and advancement opportunities further reinforce this retention.
- Retraining costs are invested in individuals who have already been trained in related tasks and who are known to be solid performers.

Jerome Rosow, president of the Work in America Institute, says, "If you think of people as a piece of capital equipment—well, you don't junk equipment on a minute's notice. You have it in reserve. Companies should look at human resources the same way." Such companies as Hewlett-Packard, IBM, Pacific Bell, and Xerox are recognized for retraining and redeploying their employees.

Development of employees is the most fruitful way for companies to ensure the supply of talent needed to meet future needs. Companies invest in training, job assignments, on-the-job tasks and coaching, and other developmental experiences in talent with the expectation of broadened, deepened, and improved capabilities. As will be discussed in the next two chapters, development is best managed when it is based on defined needs, in advance of actions. This requires development planning, conducted in relation to identified staffing needs and to individual performance.

In a sense, redeployment of current talent requires the same elements as external recruitment: sourcing, screening and selection, and placement. Specific systems for identifying talent for vacancies within an organization are discussed in the next chapter. A company can observe the performance and development of individuals and, hence, have information accumulated by management that is not available on outside recruits.

There is a need to manage the rate of movement—the flow of talent through an organization. Too rapid movement results in disruption to the organization, inability to learn and master jobs, and limited performance results. Too slow movement results in blockages, frustrations among employees regarding development and opportunities for advancement, and stagnation in development and performance. A flexible practice of redeploying and retraining talent is a valuable supplement to promotions in maintaining the desired flow of talent.

Decruitment

In institutional organizations, employees join on a career basis and stay until normal retirement. In today's fast-changing, more flexible organizations, most new hires sever their ties long before retirement, seeking opportunities elsewhere. The process of managing the way people leave an organization may be called *decruitment*, the opposite of recruitment.

Decruitment is important to the implementation of strategic staffing because it:

• Allows management to act proactively, influencing who leaves and when, and allowing for redeployment of talent or recruitment of new talent that may better match changing needs
• Eases the negative or disruptive effects of any reductions in force due to restructuring or business contraction
• Influences voluntary turnover, whether the individual quits or retires

Retirements continue to be important because the eligible individuals are usually long-service and higher-cost employees. Also, they sometimes have knowledge and skills that are critical to maintaining operations and cannot readily be replaced in a tight labor market. Under the protection of the Age Discrimination in Employment Act, retirements must be voluntary; there can be no enforced mandatory retirement at any age. Hence predicting when employees will opt to retire and planning for the necessary staffing to replace them are important and difficult tasks.

Reductions in force, or downsizing, are necessitated by sudden changes in staffing needs. Ideally, staffing is adjusted continually and gradually, avoiding the need for sudden reductions. However, when they are necessary, they become a de facto part of a staffing strategy. Companies have developed and applied procedures for identifying necessary cuts and for managing the process of downsizing under these circumstances. Increasingly, outplacement services are provided to aid employees in the transition to employment in other companies (Sweet, 1989; Tomasko, 1987)

Experiences at several General Electric facilities show ways that companies can help displaced workers find new jobs. Most workers affected by closing of facilities found new jobs or acquired new skills through GE's comprehensive outplacement services. "Whenever we make a business decision that will result in a plant closing or other work force reduction, we look closely at the human resources plan associated with that decision" (Wagel, 1988a). GE provides six months' notice before a layoff and an income extension program. A Reemployment Center provides a two-week workshop on résumé preparation and interview training. Classes are provided for specific skills sought by other employers and for personal needs, such as budget planning. Family, financial, and professional counseling is also provided (Wagel, 1988).

To avoid charges of wrongful termination and to make downsizing a positive experience, some companies are offering "voluntary severance" programs. For example, Arizona Public Service Company (APS), an electric utility in Phoenix, eliminated 1,197 positions. Overall, 747 people accepted the severance package, 72 more than APS had targeted, and 450 vacant positions were eliminated. The company had about 4,100 full-time employees. Staffing at the company's triple-reactor nuclear power plant was not included in the job reductions. Leslie Brockhurst, APS personnel vice president, concluded that "most people were able to say they were treated fairly."

IBM reduced its staffing by nearly 40,000 employees in a five-year period (from 404,000 in 1986) through gradual job reduction programs. To keep costs down, it instituted a series of early retirement programs "known in IBM-speak as voluntary transition payments" (Carroll and Hoope, 1991). IBM also changed its pension plan to encourage retirement after thirty years, as a way of smoothing out its reductions in employment and avoiding the hefty payments it makes under the early retirement programs. In addition, IBM reduced staffing through the sale of product lines and through management-initiated separations (firing people for cause). Through these actions, IBM has effected changes while preserving its full employment policy.

Some terminations are initiated by management for reasons of inadequate performance or other just cause (e.g., improper conduct, malfeasance). While management may assume an absolute right to terminate whomever it pleases, known in common law as "employment at will," limits are being defined under suits for wrongful termination. Companies should follow established procedures which provide for consistent performance evaluation, feedback, and progressive discipline (Ledvinka & Scarpello, 1991).

Due process and fair-play thinking should occur before such terminations take place. Management should be clear and direct about its standards for performance and provide instruction, training, and support to the marginal performer who is motivated to improve. Management should also be sensitive to what the terminated employee has at stake and do what it can to leave the person feeling whole (Culbert & McDonough, 1990).

When employees leave, most companies conduct exit interviews. Done correctly, these interviews benefit both the employer and the employee. The employee gets a sense of closure, can say good-bye, and then moves on to the next adventure. Exit interviews usually make individuals feel more kindly disposed to their former company. The employer also hopes to learn more about what's causing voluntary turnover (Kiechel, 1990b).

STAFFING ALTERNATIVES

Managers have less time and resources to devote to the assessment, tracking, and planned movement of talent. With pressures for performance, rapid changes in needs, restructuring, and employee turnover, managers are using different approaches to meet different needs. Accordingly, flexible approaches for staffing and for guiding career development are used.

Formal systems for matching employees with assignments are being used more selectively. Managers seek to staff openings with forward career development planning in mind. By practical necessity, companies focus their efforts on employee groups that are considered particularly important:

• Management talent, including incumbents, succession candidates, and high-potential future managers
• International talent, that is, employees with assignments, or those being prepared for assignments, in different countries or with multi-national business responsibilities
• Women and minority employees who may benefit from special development support, monitoring, and accelerated moves
• Specific talent groups, such as technical specialists, research talent, or sales personnel

At the same time, more informal, "open market" approaches are being used to allow employees to bid for positions and to enable managers to act quickly in filling them. Employees are encouraged to be self-reliant in defining their career development plans and in pursuing developmental assignments. Managers provide tools for self-directed career development planning, guidance regarding development plans (linked with current performance planning and appraisal), and day-to-day coaching and mentoring.

In the more formal approach, management addresses its defined staffing needs through a directed "demand pull" strategy. In the more informal, flexible approach, companies are responding to the needs and desires of the larger employee population (a "supply push" strategy) in a manner consistent with the flows discussed in Chapter 6.

Facing rapid change, companies are adopting flexible approaches to staffing. They use the staffing process that best suits their immediate needs: succession planning, targeted development, focused internal search, job posting, or informal staffing. Each process has its advantages and disadvantages, which are presented in Exhibit 7-1. In practice, companies use a combination of these approaches.

To meet their staffing needs quickly and expediently, managers tend to respond to those needs as they develop. Here, career paths and career development do not play a significant role in staffing decisions. However, where companies are committed to providing job security (career employment) and promotion from within, managers use staffing approaches which emphasize development. In this way, a pool of talent is developed in advance of needs and employees are given an incentive to pursue learning and growth.

Staffing systems, however short-term-focused, may be development-oriented. Flexible companies take actions that address their staffing and development needs, especially forward planning for critical needs. Even in rapidly changing conditions, all employers should plan ahead for recruiting, promotions, training and development, and other career management actions. To be passive is to fail to manage a critical business resource. Yet the costs and time required are often viewed as impediments to proactive career management.

Training and other off-the-job development activities are valuable, but challenging job assignments are the most useful development experience. When managers fill position vacancies, they should have career development in mind. Candidates readily available, even if qualified, should not automatically be assigned to positions when others might gain development experience in the assignment. Where positions are blocked, moves or swaps may be negotiated to provide career opportunities.

All managers should be talent agents. They are stewards for the talent placed in their charge and should be accountable for managing employee career development. At IBM, for example, managers are expected to help subordinates prepare for and obtain their next assignment, within widely known guidelines. Their performance as managers includes this function. Yet many managers elsewhere feel that this is not part of their role, are uncomfortable (and untrained) in guiding career planning, and openly resist mandates to counsel individuals on career matters. It is tough enough to have to appraise performance, managers say, without having to deal with career issues.

Companies need to maintain policies, guidelines, systems, and practices that are perceived by employees to be fair. To build employee loyalty and trust, managers will need to be consistent in their actions.

EXHIBIT 7-1 ALTERNATIVE APPROACHES FOR MATCHING EMPLOYEES AND JOBS

Approach	Advantages	Disadvantages
Informal staffing	Often the quickest, easiest for managers Candidates are known Opportunities provided first within unit	Qualified, interested employees may not be considered Fosters "old boy network" Reactive, developmental, depends on managers Job requirements, individual qualifications may not be fully considered
Job posting	Managers consider a wide range of candidates from the overall organization Better candidates may be identified Supports EEO/AA objectives, promotes sense of fairness Employees can participate actively, voluntarily	May be unwieldy and slow Employees expect feedback Credibility difficult to sustain Requires job definition, use of selection criteria Skills difficult to define for many positions
Focused internal search	Search may be wide or narrow Candidates may be considered across organization Individuals may provide current information Can support diversity objectives	Inventories or data base difficult to maintain Identified candidates may not be interested or available Difficult to maintain consistent practices Process may be reactive, not developmental
Targeted development	Mobility options considered in advance of needs Training or development may be provided in advance and considered in making assignments Employees participate in the process	Requires time and effort from managers Requires a sense of options, forecasted needs and skill requirements May be unwieldy in filling positions quickly; sometimes employees assigned for development reasons are not the most qualified
Succession planning	Orderly succession is planned; management thinking is stimulated about future needs Flexibility can be planned, talent pools identified Development plans are specific and focused Implementation of actions can be monitored	Process requires time and effort Often does not determine actual assignment decisions Can be applied to limited numbers of positions and individuals

From a legal perspective, also, fairness and consistency are important. Selection and promotion decisions are continuing to be subject to judicial scrutiny. Employees expect companies to have "due process" for handling grievances regarding unfair treatment. Since companies act quickly and unilaterally in many employment decisions, guarantees are needed that fair and equitable systems are in place and are applied evenly. Companies are responding by adopting more flexible approaches for matching individuals with job assignments. Described below are the primary approaches being used.

Targeted Development and Succession Planning

Proactive career development typically involves targeted development, or the more focused process as applied to managers, of succession planning. Over the past several decades, companies have sought to develop and apply these processes, which provide planning and individual development in advance of vacancies.

Through targeted development, companies fill openings with employees who have been prepared for possible future assignments, as a result of development planning focused on career path steps. Through succession planning, companies fill management openings with individuals identified and prepared as candidates for one or more specific management positions. These approaches are closely interrelated.

Targeted development and succession planning, while desirable, are not used as widely as they might be. Managers feel that changes are too rapid to plan very far ahead; they do not have time to allow for management education, developmental assignments, and so on. Companies report that fewer than half of all management appointments involve individuals named as candidates in succession and development plans. Because of lean staffing and the high costs, companies are typically reluctant to rotate individuals for developmental purposes.

This emphasis on filling positions as they become vacant, without forward planning, has also resulted in an emphasis on external recruiting in many companies. It is often easier for managers to turn outside for individuals who appear, at least on paper, to be a better fit with new position requirements than to consider internal candidates. External search in some companies is more expedient than a thorough internal search. Also, the desire for new skills, industry experience, and a "fresh perspective" tilts the scale toward external hires in many situations. Of course, the downside of external recruiting is that the outside candidates are not as well known to management and therefore entail a risk of not performing well or of leaving the company. Also, outside hires block career opportunities for employees and may adversely affect their morale.

Management succession and development is an important focus of human resource planning. Because of its significant and visible impact on the future development of the business, it is an area of senior management interest and attention. Executives also personally identify with management succession and development concerns; they are both participants and managers in the process. Accordingly, they understand the need for forward planning of development for key individuals (such as themselves) and for their prospective successors (London, 1985; McCall, Lombardo, & Morrison, 1988).

Less Formal Approaches Are Used

Today, many companies feel that they cannot effectively plan ahead for all employees, even if they ever did. Development planning with specific targets is increasingly difficult. As a result, informal staffing is common. Openings, even in management positions, are filled on an ad hoc basis, relying on a search for the best-suited candidates available. There is pressure to sustain performance, to keep the organization moving, and to keep jobs filled.

Some companies fill openings with employees identified through a focused internal search process using records (usually computerized) on education, training, experience, and skills. Such a process works best for "tangible" attributes, such as technical skills and knowledge, product knowledge and experience, and language skills. Searches may rely on past job history, looking to certain positions as fruitful sources of talent. However, searches rarely involve development or use of logical career paths, either in identifying candidates or in guiding future development.

Self-nomination or job-posting processes are still widely used (sometimes by policy mandate). Through job posting, managers fill openings from slates of candidates developed with inputs from employees responding voluntarily to announced openings. Individuals may be aware of past movement from position to position and of apparent career paths. They nominate themselves based on their perception of their qualifications for the position, their interest in it, and their perception of realistic opportunities.

However, managers often handle positions "off line"; ready candidates are selected even while the formal search process is under way. The use of posting is more "judgmental," managers say. Its intent is usually to limit management's burden in the internal staffing process, not to increase it by implying career options that may not become realized. Rarely do job posting and informal processes involve forward planning. In fact, most companies are careful not to promise career movement options to employees; they seek, rather, to use posting to support an open internal labor market.

The last recourse for managers (although, in practice, the first for many) is informal staffing—filling openings with employees they know, relying on data gathered informally from employees and other managers. If there are career paths used here, they rely on the personal experience knowledge, or intuition of the managers participating in the process.

As managers adopt these "open market" approaches, the more formal staffing systems they are bypassing become less effective. For example, the misuse of job posting by managers is a common employee complaint. Employees and managers widely note that development planning processes, whether linked to performance appraisal or a separate process, are rarely meaningful;

and development actions do not usually follow. Succession planning systems are being reexamined, streamlined, and updated to fit the conditions of more rapid change. Managers are not accountable or rewarded for the way they address staffing and development needs in support of effective career management.

International Staffing Practices

As companies strive to manage globally, they establish processes to identify, assign, develop, and compensate individuals for assignments in different countries. Expatriate programs have provided special arrangements for individuals on international assignments. As companies seek to staff local country operations with local country nationals or third country nationals, the planning for international staffing broadens and becomes more complex.

Today, companies that manage globally need managers who understand the global implications of the business and who can operate effectively in different environments. These organizations are also seeking to develop local expertise and build host country talent—to improve sensitivity to local markets and also to contain the high costs of international talent assignments.

Nevertheless, the career paths defined for professionals and managers on international assignments are also tentative. A large moving company reported that of four employees transferred overseas by a company, only three are moved back. A large multi-national company found that even fewer managers return to assignments in the U.S. organization after assignments overseas. They may move on to other companies or, upon their return, simply not be offered positions that are perceived to be at the same pay level or provide the same challenge as their overseas assignments.

Repatriation or continued progression to other international assignments is difficult to plan, given the uncertainty of staffing needs and openings. Career planning for individuals on international assignments is particularly difficult because they are out of the mainstream of the business and out of touch with the managers who are making domestic staffing decisions. It is important, therefore, for companies to provide focused planning for employees on international assignments—career development for this group with a special need.

To be sure, some companies are managing talent effectively on a global basis. Citicorp, IBM, Coca-Cola, and other multi-nationals are highly regarded for their focused attention to their talent on a worldwide basis. They do, in fact, define career paths among the logical options open to individuals and track movement according to length of assignment guidelines. Even in these companies, however, the career paths are more tentative, and staffing practices are more flexible than in the past.

Special Group Focus

Longer-range career planning is also used when it is necessary to ensure the desired flow of certain types of talent into an organization. While the overall talent flow is difficult to manage, companies do conduct efforts focused on specific talent groups.

Companies focus planning on women and minorities, in support of affirmative action plans and objectives. To help talented individuals move into higher-level professional and managerial positions, companies identify target assignments (in the context of paths or a grid of options) and specify development plans. Regular reviews of progress for these groups are typically conducted, often in conjunction with succession reviews.

For example, many large companies, including Quaker Oats Corporation, have established "glass ceiling" programs. These are special planning and development programs aimed at assisting talented females in professional and lower-managerial levels to prepare for and advance to senior management assignments. Research has indicated that a perceived barrier to advancement exists which is overcome through such a proactive development effort.

Similarly, companies often focus on employee groups with critical skills (e.g., project managers, software specialists, technical specialists, top sales talent). Such planning and reviews may involve tracking the progress of managerial or technical career paths designed to motivate and retain these employees.

MANAGING CAREER MOBILITY

In the midst of organizational ferment, employees need job assignments that provide the opportunities to learn needed skills and capabilities. Traditionally, this was accomplished through well-defined and established lines of career progression, or career paths, which were typically vertical. Rapid changes in job content, organization structure, and talent requirements result in shorter-term career planning and step-by-step progression.

Even in today's flexible organizations, information on career opportunities is needed to:

• Guide the movement of talent among assignments and manage assignments as a developmental resource
• Define the skills, knowledge, and abilities in specific positions or types of positions, and the ways employees may develop these in incremental steps, through assignments or job content changes
• Facilitate movement among functions or units and foster understanding and cooperation across lines (necessary for team effectiveness)

For employees, career paths serve a useful function. Employees think in terms of steady, sequential progress; managers think in terms of talent "pipelines." Even under changing conditions, there is a need for career management, for a sense of the opportunities available. A "road map" of career alternatives is a useful reference for charting paths, even when the roads and paths keep shifting.

Defining Career Opportunities

Employees move through patterned sequences of positions or roles, usually related to work content, during their working lives. This is the essence of a career path. As such, a career path does not need to be described in writing in order to exist. It is a fact. Everyone has one.

For purposes of career development and other applications within an organization, career paths are most useful when they are formally defined and documented. Then, career paths become objective descriptions of sequential work experiences, as opposed to subjective feelings about career progress, personal development, status, or satisfaction. For example, an individual may view increasing responsibilities or changing work assignments within a single job as career development, but this subjective view does not constitute a career path, as defined above.

Most employees want to know about the career opportunities available in an organization to help them set realistic career objectives and plan practical steps for their personal career development. Career development workshops, self-directed materials, and career counseling are often available. However, information on career paths, including progression possibilities and the associated qualifications required, is not generally available.

Managers, too, want career paths to be defined, so that an adequate number of individuals may be identified and prepared to fill future vacancies. Because employees want to know what opportunities are available to them, career paths and effective career development are positive features that help attract and retain employees, increasingly important in tight labor markets.

Also, for the development of senior management talent, career paths are useful as guidelines for career development assignments across functional and organizational lines. Increasingly, senior executives are the product of varied job experiences, including assignments in different units, functions, and countries. Accordingly, many companies have attempted to define career paths for these purposes.

Career Paths Are Changing

Companies have sought to move individuals along defined career paths, in order to develop the capabilities necessary to staff various levels and types of jobs. Accordingly, career paths have traditionally emphasized upward mobility within a single organization unit or functional area of work (e.g., sales, accounting, engineering). In many organizations, paths have meant step-by-step progression geared to years of service. If an individual deviated from the prescribed lock-step pattern and timing, he or she faltered.

Such career paths (or ladders) are developed in the following manner:

• Examination of the paths followed by individuals in the past to the top "rungs of the ladders"

• Identification of entry points in the career path, traditionally at the bottom, and exit points along the way
• Definition of requirements for entry to positions, usually in terms of educational level, specialized skills, experience, and years of service
• Identification of the important job experiences leading to the top rung and benchmark timing for reaching each rung

This process describes a generalized or idealized route for advancement within a unit or function. It makes paths explicit.

A typical career path within the sales function, for example, might include five steps: salesperson, account supervisor, sales supervisor, district manager, regional manager. Each step in the progression is largely paced by years of service—a tenure considered necessary to master each level of responsibility. Such a simple functional path may be modified to include other options that provide valuable experience in developing district and regional managers. Assignments in finance, marketing research, or production, for example, are also valuable in sales management. Along these paths, high-talent individuals may progress at a faster rate than the norm.

Traditional career paths imply a necessity of moving up—of climbing career ladders and the corporate hierarchy. Lateral moves, downward moves, or staying at a given level are not perceived as attractive options. The bias toward promotions as the only meaningful career direction is clearly built into this perspective.

Career paths are often influenced by pay and recognition. Employees seek job advancement in part because of the recognition and status associated with it, and for the increased compensation typically related to it. Hence organizations have ladders within common job families (e.g., Technician I, II, and III). Technical ladders or paths provide recognition (e.g., more distinguished titles such as Research Fellow) and higher pay, even while the content of work performed does not change significantly. Here experience, skill level, and loyalty are rewarded by paths.

While the development of career paths has an attractive logic, companies find that rapid change makes this effort difficult. Because of rapid organizational changes, career paths are typically in flux. They change as organization structure, job content, and skill requirements change. Most organizations are constantly restructuring and redefining requirements. They are becoming flatter and leaner, with most jobs shifting their content with every change. Specific efforts are made to eliminate unneeded work and to streamline management processes. As a result, different work is called for in jobs, and there are often fewer positions and fewer levels of positions.

Career Grids Replace Paths

The management response to rapidly changing conditions is to be more flexible. Companies are adopting alternative ways to guide career development.

They are charting career moves more cautiously and are limiting in-depth planning to specific employee groups of highest management concern. Movement among positions is becoming slower; employees are encouraged to find challenge and satisfaction through improvement of current responsibilities— "more interesting work."

To this end, some companies have adopted a way to define career opportunities without explicit paths. By defining a grid of positions in an organization, an employee may identify alternative career movements as paths. Traditional vertical paths within functions or units are suggested in columns, but the juxtaposition of other vertical paths provides a way of identifying a multitude of lateral, diagonal, and even downward career progression alternatives. The possibilities are limited only by the vacancies that actually occur and by an individual's qualifications relative to the position requirements.

Exhibit 7-2 presents such a grid, adapted and excerpted from a career planning grid used in a commercial bank. The numbers indicate the positions existing for each title listed. Related forecasts provide the estimated number of vacancies anticipated for each title based on turnover, mobility, and projected growth in the bank. The levels are broad and are not linked directly to salary levels. The intent is to avoid confusing the career planning activity with compensation considerations.

Using the grid allows employees and managers to consider alternatives to the usual "up the ladder" career progression. A commission lending officer in the retail banking division, for example, could most easily move to any of the other titles in Level A within the division. The second most likely progression would be to Level B positions within the division. Other alternatives might be positions in Level A or B in other divisions.

For each position title, a brief profile of position activities and qualifications is provided. Thus the employee and the manager have available a sort of catalog of job options to consider in career planning and in career development activities. Qualifications are stated in terms of skills, experience, and knowledge required, interpreted from the statements of activities performed (e.g., "ability to . . . "). Appropriate kinds of job experience, educational specialization, and other indicators of these capabilities may be indicated, but educational degrees, years of service, age, personality characteristics, and other such factors not clearly job-related are not included.

On the basis of such information, a company can identify alternative career mobility options for employees progressing from common entry-level positions. These paths reflect both the actual ones followed in the past and possible paths based on logical analysis.

Realistic options are anchored in the facts of the situation. From the employee viewpoint, they:

• Represent real progression possibilities, whether lateral or upward, without implied "normal" rates of progress or forced technical specialization

• Are flexible and responsive to changes in job content, work priorities, organization patterns, and management needs

EXHIBIT 7-2 CAREER PLANNING GRID FOR MAJOR DIVISIONS OF A BANK

Level	Retail Banking (Title/No. of Positions)	Corporate Banking (Title/No. of Positions)	International (Title/No. of Positions)	Operations (Title/No. of Positions)
D	District manager 12 Branch manager A 6 District lending manager 4	Department manager 8 Senior account manager 9	Regional manager 4	
C	Branch manager B 38 Lending manager A 4 Branch operations manager A 5 Branch manager C 66	Institution manager 6 Senior account manager 21		Section manager 6
B	Commission lending manager 11 Branch operations manager 12 Branch manager D 40 Branch operations manager B 19 District trainer 11	Account manager 11 Associate institutional manager 12 Associate account manager 4	Area manager 5 Liaison representative 4 Area specialist 9	Senior programmer 5 Service representative 4 Analytical programmer 25 Operations supervisor 9
A	Branch operations manager B 11 Commission lending officer 27 Operations specialist 12 Retail lending officer 69 Operations supervisor 9	Account administrator 16	Account representative 8	Industrial engineer 5 Operations analyst 12 Associate programmer 19 Technical writer 4 Buyer 3 Procedures analyst 2

Source: Adapted and excerpted from an actual grid of all multiple incumbent positions in a commercial bank.

• Specify acquirable skills, knowledge, and other attributes required to perform the work in each position along the paths
• Take into consideration the qualities of individuals or of others influencing the way work is performed (e.g., team members)

A company may help guide employee career planning in this manner by analyzing positions and grouping them on the basis of their actual work content and competency requirements. This may rely on existing job descriptions or on newly collected information from incumbents and managers. Objectivity is enhanced by collecting data directly from incumbents through questionnaires, interviews, direct observation of work activities, or focus group discussions.

As a result, the career paths represent logical and possible sequences of positions that could be held. The paths, therefore, are rational definitions of progression alternatives, based on analysis of what people actually do in an organization. They provide a basis for career management actions and for guiding individual career planning. Companies concerned with job-related selection practices find that career paths assist forward planning and decision making regarding promotion, transfer, and other actions.

The Information System Division (ISD) at General Mills developed a "career progression network," a detailed and integrated system defining mobility options. The network is based on hierarchical ratings of the technical and nontechnical skills and knowledge required for successful performance of tasks in each position within ISD. It provides employees with a starting point for realistic career planning and development (Hoban, 1987). Exhibit 7-3 presents career mobility options into and out of a specific unit manager position (EUC center manager).

SUMMARY

When business performance calls for managers and employees to accelerate speed, lower costs, raise quality, and improve customer service, having the right talent is essential. Many managers honestly plan for a lean, mean organization and then find it chronically understaffed. Performance, morale, and credibility of planning all suffer.

In an institutional organization, staffing is a lifetime affair. Employees are recruited young and stay until retirement. Managers patiently and systematically move people along as others retire or as needs gradually change.

In today's flexible organization, managers need "just-in-time staffing"—the right people right there when they are needed. This requires a more flexible approach to staffing and alignment of the approach with changing human resource strategies. Managers use multiple staffing approaches to choose among employees or external talent and match them with jobs. Increasingly, more participative and informal approaches are used—to allow swifter choices and a more fair and open staffing process. The organization is, in a sense, a labor market in which employees pursue career opportunities as they develop.

EXHIBIT 7-3 EXAMPLE OF A CAREER MOBILITY OPTIONS CHART

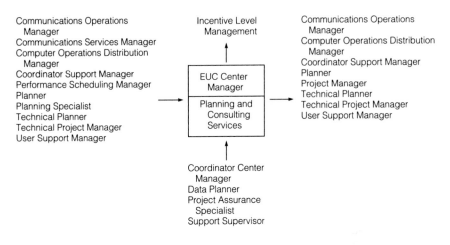

Communications Operations
   Manager
Communications Services Manager
Computer Operations Distribution
   Manager
Coordinator Support Manager
Performance Scheduling Manager
Planner
Planning Specialist
Technical Planner
Technical Project Manager
User Support Manager

Incentive Level
Management

EUC Center
Manager

Planning and
Consulting
Services

Coordinator Center
   Manager
Data Planner
Project Assurance
   Specialist
Support Supervisor

Communications Operations
   Manager
Computer Operations Distribution
   Manager
Coordinator Support Manager
Planner
Project Manager
Technical Planner
Technical Project Manager
User Support Manager

General Competencies

1. Business awareness
2. Identifying and solving
   problems
3. Speaking and writing
4. Organizing
5. Planning
6. Assertiveness/Conflict
   resolution
7. Coaching/Motivating
8. Consideration/Social
   skills
9. Delegating
10. Leadership
11. Adaptability
12. Keeping up-to-date

Technical Competencies

1. Computing systems
   (software)
2. Computing systems
   (hardware)
3. Systems programming
4. Communications
5. Analysis and design
6. Application programming
7. Data architecture

Characteristics

1. Risk taking
2. Creativity
3. Professional appearance
   and image

Reprinted with permission of MDA Consulting Group, Inc., Minneapolis, from "Creating a Hierarchical Career Progression Network," by Kevin J. Nilan, Sally Walls, Sandra L. Davis, and Mary E. Lund, *Personnel Administrator* (June 1987), p. 178.

At the same time, formal planning allows critical talent to be aligned with strategies. Succession planning for managers, targeted development planning for managers and professionals, planning for international staffing, and focused planning for women and minorities are vital as management levers. Through these processes and through all staffing decisions, managers ensure that staffing actions fit the company's needs and the employees' best interests.

PART THREE

DEVELOPING CAPABILITIES

DEVELOPING EMPLOYEE CAPABILITIES

Sustaining Levi Strauss & Co. as a profitable, vital and improving organization requires the continuous development of all employees. Accountability for and participation in this development is shared among employee, manager, and the company.

Executive Management Committee, Levi Strauss & Co.

Employee development is becoming a critical factor differentiating the more successful from the less successful companies. Motorola, Toyota, and other technology-oriented manufacturers have become industry leaders at least in part because of aggressive, comprehensive employee training. Banks have stressed relationship management skills; service companies gain and retain customers by emphasizing service quality training.

This chapter addresses the ways in which companies develop their employees: It focuses on:

- How career development opportunities are provided in flexible organizations
- How individual development planning is used as a way to emphasize employee self-reliance
- How training and education are planned and implemented in flexible organizations
- How organizational learning is used as a focus for development

Companies provide support for all employees in developing their careers because they have an important stake in furthering employee loyalty and retention, particularly as talent becomes scarce and is more competitively sought. Managers strive to help employees perform effectively and to give them an environment for personal growth and satisfaction. In the 1990s and beyond, companies will invest more, not less, in efforts to retain, train, and develop talent. For most employees, the onus for development rests with themselves, with management providing resources, a supportive environment, and encouragement.

CAREER DEVELOPMENT IN FLEXIBLE ORGANIZATIONS

Rapid changes in the way work is performed require adoption of new skills and capabilities at all employee levels. Future changes called for in business strategies require training and development for improvement of current performance and also in anticipation of future needs.

Managers, as part of their responsibilities, need to identify needed skills and actively manage employee learning for the long-range future in relation to explicit corporate and business strategies. Management is concerned with performance (to meet short-term needs) and adaptability (to meet long-term needs). Meanwhile, employees are concerned with their feelings and attitudes relating to their work (their short-term needs) and their sense of career identity and progress (their long-term needs). Developing employee talent requires attention to all four of these outcomes (Hall, 1984).

Changing Career Expectations

Necessary staffing changes, reorganizations, and the slower progression experienced in the 1980s and early 1990s have reshaped employees' perceptions of their career development. Many employees are skeptical of their companies' capacity or willingness to provide career opportunities.

According to Karl Price, of the consulting firm TPF&C, survey results from client companies show these employee perceptions:

- Opportunity to reach full potential (55%)
- Organization provides good career opportunities (50%)
- Promotions are handled fairly (48%)
- Chance of being promoted (46%)

Survey data collected by another consulting firm found that only 40% of employees rate their company as above average in advancement opportunity.

If employees are not getting their desired career opportunities, they change their expectations and behaviors. In the face of uncertain opportunities and increased competition for fewer positions, employees look at career opportunities more flexibly.

Baby Boomers and Busters

The bulge of "baby boomer" workers has resulted in stiff competition for fewer advancement opportunities and an awareness that psychological success may be achieved through ways other than job advancement. And the "baby busters," the far smaller group following them, are avoiding the competitive track. Their attitudes profoundly influence the shape of careers in the 1990s.

In 1955, *Fortune* reporters interviewed 25-year-old "junior organization men" in *Fortune* 500 companies and found them quietly confident of a secure and prosperous future within their organizations. A similar survey in 1980 found the baby boomers ("yuppies") arrogant and impatient; they believed that business offered "the fastest means of gratifying their frankly materialistic requirements." In 1990, they found baby buster 25-year-olds to be individuals who can say no—who aren't lured into workaholism by money, title, security, or ladder climbing. *Fortune* calls them "yiffies," for young, individualistic, freedom-minded, and few (Deutschmann, 1990).

As baby boomers hit "career gridlock," their attitudes toward work are mellowing. In the 1990s and beyond, this group faces fewer promotion opportunities and the likelihood of career plateauing. Researchers Douglas T. Hall and Judith Richter offer this profile:

• A strong concern for basic values: They question why they are seeking success and what the personal meaning of success is to them.

• A sense of freedom to act on values: They act in accordance with their values (they "do it").

• A focus on self: A healthy narcissism helps them find their work in life and express self-identity.

• Need for autonomy and questioning authority: They are distinctively impatient with formal hierarchical authority—and, as a result, are often hostile, cynical, and difficult to manage.

• Less concern with advancement: They have lessened their desire to become part of management—and when they are, they are not motivated to act like traditional managers.

• Crafting (in-place career development): They are oriented to high quality in the current job; they want to perform well.

• Entrepreneurship: They find the option of self-employment attractive.

• Concern for work/family balance: They have a total life perspective, including parenting.

Their recommendations for company career development practices in response to these characteristics are presented in Exhibit 8-1 (Hall & Richter, 1990).

The baby busters, born after 1965, are seeking to recast the rules of business according to their own demands. They say no to promotions, to relocations, and to increased responsibility. They want satisfaction from their jobs, but refuse to make personal sacrifices for the sake of the corporation. "Other interests—leisure, family, lifestyle, the pursuit of experience—are as important as work. It's hard to figure out what they think is most important. They don't seem to have much sense of themselves as a distinct generation, and they certainly aren't impassioned about political or social issues. Nobody would describe them as a bunch of activists" (Deutschmann, 1990).

For example, two young lawyers, married to each other, were both employed as associates in a highly respected law firm. With dual careers and dual incomes, they "had it all." After less than two years in the arduous legal routine, they opted to resign, cash in their assets, and travel the world for a year or longer. They casually assumed that they could always get jobs along the way and ultimately return to the "treadmill" when, and if, they need to. A company needs to keep the career opportunities sufficiently stimulating and

---

EXHIBIT 8-1 SUMMARY OF BABY BOOM CHARACTERISTICS AND RECOMMENDED ORGANIZATIONAL ACTIONS

Profile of Baby Boom Characteristics	Recommended Organizational Action
1. Concern for basic values	1. a. Replace promotional culture with psychological success culture b. Examine, change corporate career criteria c. Focus on corporate ethics
2. Freedom to act on values	2. a. Support protean career paths b. More lateral mobility c. De-couple rewards and the linear career path
3. Focus on self	3. Build on-going development into the job through: • Self-development • Life-long learning
4. Need for autonomy	4. More flexible careers
5. Less concern with advancement	5. More diversity in career paths More change: • within present job • within present function • within present location • across function and locations
6. Crafting	6. Reward quality performance, not potential
7. Entrepreneurship	7. a. Create internal enterpreneurial assignments b. Encourage employee career exploration (internally and externally)
8. Concern for work/home balance	8. a. More organizational sensitivity to home life b. Training for managing the work-home interface c. Inclusion of spouse in career discussions d. Career assistance for employee spouse e. Flexible benefits to help meet family needs (e.g., child care, elder care, care for sick children) f. More flexible work arrangements

---

Reprinted with permission from "Career Gridlock: Baby Boomers Hit the Wall," by Douglas T. Hall and Judith Richter, *Academy of Management Executive* (1990), Vol. 4, No. 3, p. 19.

varied to retain the interests of such talent. Hard work with high pay is not the only option available. In fact, some professional service firms are adopting alternative career patterns which allow different interests and lifestyles.

Just as baby boomers are reducing their commitments and expectations, all people move through a normal cycle of maturation. Research suggests that there are different stages in careers and that different activities, skills, and relationships are required to be effective in each stage (see Exhibit 8-2). While there are varied definitions and interpretations of the life cycle, they help explain the inevitability of changing attitudes, as individual needs and circumstances change (Greenhaus, 1987; Hall, 1976; D. Levinson, 1978). The stage an employee is in influences his or her career expectations and plans.

EXHIBIT 8-2 STAGES OF CAREER DEVELOPMENT

EXPLORATION	Developing ideas about the choice of career—the field of occupational choice, not a specific job (typically early 20s)
TRIAL AND ESTABLISHMENT	Getting settled in jobs through which they can support themselves and their families, use their abilities, and express their interests. Conflicts between work and family pressures develop (ages 25–44)
MAINTENANCE	Maintaining an established position in the face of competition from others; keeping up on new developments or adapting to new tasks and activities (ages 45–64)
DISENGAGEMENT	Letting up as they get older, tapering off before retirement to avoid the shock of a sudden withdrawal from work (65 and on)

As employees mature, they are progressively more concerned with getting and staying established, and with balancing work with family and other personal interests. As baby boomers move into their fifties and sixties, the concerns associated with disengagement will emerge, resulting in new demands for flexible retirement, part-time work, protection from age discrimination, and retirement pay and benefits.

It is important to help employees understand their changing needs and chart development plans and objectives that are realistic, given the opportunities open to them.

New Views of Career Paths

By and large, employees define their career paths—their future career opportunities—in terms of their own experience, needs and desires, management actions, and the example set by their peers. Paths that they believe are open to them are shaped as a blend of fact, fiction, and desire.

Many employees today are adopting new views of career paths:

- Lateral moves are becoming more routine and even desirable.
- Jobs last longer; responsibilities evolve with no title change.
- Success means inner fulfillment and money, not promotions.
- The work itself is important, along with opportunity to influence the shape of work, management practices, and the organization.
- Work lasts until the job is done, however long it takes; even while tuning out, many are workaholics.

The key issue for many people today is getting satisfaction in their work and feeling that they are making a contribution. It's a feeling employees have always sought, but earlier generations were more willing to suppress this desire in return for job security, job advancement, and rewards. "For all of their careerism, many baby-boomers, steeped in the heritage of the sixties, are decidedly ambivalent about compromising personal goals in pursuit of a job somewhere up there'' (Kirkpatrick, 1990).

Individuals are shaping their own definitions of the ideal career. Some seek the fast track, with rapid advancement and increased responsibility—even with the high demands involved. Others seek a track that allows modified work commitments to accommodate family responsibilities. Still others are passive, expecting companies to set the pace of careers.

Clearly, employees are more alert than ever to new options open to them. They are more willing than ever to change companies—and have ready access to information on opportunities in other companies through their aggressive recruitment efforts. In fact, many employees consider it easier to move ahead by moving out than by staying. With the projected shortage of talent in the 1990s, this behavior may be even more common, and companies will be in a perpetual scramble to recruit and retain talent.

Employees are also taking advantage of the options to get off the traditional career path. Many more people are working part time or as contract workers, or work with multiple companies. This enhances a sense of self-reliance and independence, and provides greater flexibility in lifestyle. The downsizing of companies is resulting in more use of talent at all levels as contractors and contingent employees.

Concern for Plateauing

Already, because of their advancement in companies and the shrinking opportunities for promotion, many employees are finding their careers stagnating or "plateauing" at increasingly early ages. There is more competition for a diminishing number of higher-level positions for managers.

A plateau is the point in a career when the likelihood of further promotion is very low. "Although people are reluctant to admit to themselves, or to colleagues, family, and friends, that they have achieved the highest level of their careers, most managers have subordinates who are plateaued" (Slocum, Cron, Hansen, & Rawlings, 1985).

Plateauing is a management concern because some employees, who are valued high performers and perceive that they are plateaued, may leave to pursue opportunities elsewhere. This necessitates costly, time-consuming recruiting and training of replacements in a tight labor market. Also, employees who see their jobs as mundane and dead-end do not produce the highest-quality work.

"A big company that operates hierarchically may tell its employees 'initiate, be an entrepreneur,''' said Judith Bardwick, author of *The Plateauing Trap*. "But that can't happen if everyone is looking upward. Instead what's created is passivity and play-acting. People are discovering that there are fewer ranks to strive for and less to work towards—they're leaving their companies to use their skills elsewhere, often with consulting firms, or more likely, small companies. It will be disastrous if companies don't change their culture to shift away from the traditional emphasis on promotion" (Bardwick, 1986).

Management can ameliorate the effects of fewer advancement opportunities in several ways. Lateral moves may be encouraged. Duties and performance responsibilities may be frequently changed, keeping jobs in flux—and hence more interesting and challenging. Alternative career paths—involving non-management, specialist, or individual contributor roles—may be emphasized. The normal pace of job progression may be slowed, and this norm communicated so as to lower employee expectations (e.g., at IBM, moves that used to come at five or six years now come at seven to eight years).

However, employee perceptions of plateauing are changed only by changing the career structure, not just the career stage. According to Judith Bardwick, "If white-collar employees are not pressuring themselves for promotion, they begin wondering what they are doing with their careers." Recognition and status—long tied to job level, title, promotion, and compensation levels—need to be tied instead to performance, expertise, entrepreneurism, and teamwork. As organizations become more flexible, these shifts are often implemented, reducing the effects of slower and fewer promotions.

Also, greater emphasis may be given to training and development for plateaued employees. By encouraging development of skills for multiple jobs, resulting in generalists, companies develop more flexible staffing and more effective team members, necessary to achieve total quality objectives. Career recognitions and compensation may reflect, in part, this broader capability and experience (rather than advancement). Formal job rotation programs and fluid job design allow management to take advantage of these expanded talents. Also, plateaued employees may be involved in developing others, as instructors in training programs, as mentors, and as leaders of special project or task teams.

Self-Reliance Is Key to Today's Careers

Because of the uncertainties in organizational and personal life, career paths exist largely in retrospect. Individuals look back and see where they have been, and how they have progressed—that is what constitutes a career in today's flexible environment. Few look ahead and chart the sequence of positions or roles they will hold in a company or in their working lives.

Even if companies provide explicit information on logical career paths, individuals may not find this to be particularly relevant. In a rapidly changing world, an open labor market, and an era of balancing personal priorities, employees often see career options far differently than their employers do.

Company career paths are useful as a set of data on career options. But other options are available. As noted, job assignments open up in a company on an ad hoc basis, often not following formal career paths. Flexible arrangements for working provide new opportunities that are not contemplated in paths or formal career development systems. External options create a myriad of paths that may be shaped as individuals take different jobs, whether full time or part time, or become entrepreneurs.

Self-reliance is becoming more important in career development. In past decades, companies played a far more prominent role in defining career options and determining individual career progress. The idea that a career lies primarily within a company is becoming a myth. In a lifetime, an individual may be employed by half a dozen companies or more and adopt three or more different "careers," involving different skill sets.

INDIVIDUAL DEVELOPMENT PLANNING

The organization, the manager, and the employee—each has responsibilities in the process of career development. The organization provides the business context, the information, and the systems necessary for learning and growth opportunities to exist. The manager provides communications and encouragement for development, helping the employee focus on a realistic plan. The individual employee actively formulates development objectives and follows through on their achievement.

Exhibit 8-3 presents an outline of career development responsibilities provided as guidelines to managers at S. C. Johnson Wax. The desired outcome is a "realistic development strategy which clearly defines the actions the employee commits to take in pursuit of his or her goals." The manager can provide valuable input in terms of honest feedback relative to the individual's capabilities, information about the organization's needs and future direction, and ideas and suggestions for training and use of company resources.

Development Planning Elements

As part of the performance appraisal process, or as a separate process, employees may establish specific needs for training and development. They relate to:

- Specific needs for improving performance on the current job
- Needs for preparing the individual for targeted future assignments
- Needs for allowing the individual to consider longer-term career plans, including retirement or alternative career choices (for example, moving into a different functional area)

These needs emerge from self-assessment and from discussions between individuals and their managers. A preferred technique calls for the individual to identify his or her own needs, followed by a formal discussion. The outcome is an agreed-upon development action plan.

Some companies provide resources to aid individual employee self-assessment and career development planning. Career development resources provided at Burroughs Wellcome Co. are described in Exhibit 8-4. Use of such resources is voluntary and usually at the employee's initiative. Companies often increase the emphasis on such resources when employee surveys indicate that career planning is a high concern or when management perceives that career development will enhance retention, mobility, or development of needed talent in a tight labor market. For some companies, it is offered simply to maintain parity with similar practices of other employers.

EXHIBIT 8-3 CAREER DEVELOPMENT RESPONSIBILITIES

Effective career development requires that the organization, the manager, and the employee accept their responsibilities. The manager's role is vital to the process.

Employee	Manager	Organization
Take responsibility for career development	Support employees in their career development responsibilities, including communicating employee career information to others as needed	Communicate business mission, objectives, and strategies so that realistic career development can occur
Help to establish and meet objectives and performance requirements on current job		Provide information on career requirements, organizational options and opportunities, and developmental systems
Engage in realistic self-assessment	Establish and communicate job requirements and responsibilities	
Obtain and use feedback or career options and realistic potential	Provide open and honest ongoing performance feedback and coaching	Design and implement an effective supervisor–subordinate career development discussion process
Communicate career interests and discuss developmental needs with manager	Provide organizational career information and realistic feedback on employee career aspirations	Train managers to coach, evaluate, and conduct employee career discussions
Actively follow through on developmental plans on an ongoing basis	Conduct career development discussions with subordinate as appropriate	Provide employees with the resources necessary for development, to include on-the-job experiences, training, and education
	Encourage and support implementation of the employee's developmental plans	Ensure integration of career development components into a comprehensive system
		Evaluate and recognize managers for their role/success in employee career development

Reprinted with permission of S. C. Johnson Wax from *Career Development Process: Managers' Communication Package.* Copyright © 1989, S. C. Johnson & Son, Inc. Prepared with the help of Dr. Thomas G. Gutteridge, management development consultant, Carbondale, Illinois.

Self-assessment workbooks, questionnaires, or computer software are often used. Or these may be combined and offered as a career planning workshop for interested employees. Such tools include use of career planning checklists and standardized tests (e.g., interest inventories, aptitude testing, leadership style indicators). These help the employees better understand their capabilities and interests. In a workshop setting (or assessment center), employees may discover their strengths, weaknesses, and interests through interactions with others and through exercises that draw out their perceptions (London & Strumpf, 1982; Walker, 1980).

A career development program at DuPont's Pioneering Research Laboratory for Textile Fibers provides all of these elements. Its aim is to make development planning a "legitimate activity for individuals so they can maximize personal effectiveness and job satisfaction and improve communication between employees and supervisors" (Nusbaum, 1986). A similar program, but

---

EXHIBIT 8-4 CAREER DEVELOPMENT RESOURCES AT BURROUGHS WELLCOME CO.

Career Resource Center

Media library with assessment tools, computerized programs, skills inventories, career planning exercises, books, magazines, and audio/video programs to help employees develop career plans

Career Planning Software

A self-assessment tool that matches employee values, interests, preferences, and skills to specific Burroughs Wellcome positions through a job database; it also helps employees develop career goals and action plans and write resumes

Career Planning Workshop

Allows employees to learn from others while developing realistic career plans and familiarizing themselves with resources available

Career Development Workshop for Managers

Helps managers establish their own career goals and plans and understand their role in supporting employee career planning

Job Sourcebook

A reference containing organization charts, mission statements, and objectives for each company unit, as well as demographic data and information on trends affecting career choices

Career Guides

Staff members from Human Resources and Corporate Training and Development serve as career advisors. They are acquainted with career development resources and help employees plan their initial steps in career development

Career Counselor

Counseling involves one-on-one sessions, on-site, with a professional career counselor, who assists with self-assessment, goal setting, and planning. Confidentiality and privacy are assured.

Source: Burroughs Wellcome Co., used with permission.

providing six half-day sessions for managers, is used at KLA Instruments Corporation at Santa Clara, California. The first three sessions focus on assessment of leadership and management skills and identifying areas where growth is needed. The last three focus on necessary actions, helping employees focus on achievement goals. This program aims to help plateaued managers find meaningful and stimulating work opportunities without promotions (Wagel, 1988b).

An insurance company has used a detailed "development aid" for its employees. The grid calls for identification of development needs in five areas: administrative skills, communications, situational skills (for example, managing time, problem solving), technical job knowledge, and experience. For each need identified, development activities are outlined as ways to gain new skills, knowledge, or experience. These activities are then listed down the left side of a grid; timing for completion is indicated for each by months listed on the horizontal axis of the grid. The activities are thus scheduled for completion during the year ahead.

Pacific Bell Training Services developed a software system for maintaining career development information including job listings, opportunity forecasts, wage schedules, required skills for jobs, and development resources. It is updated through word processing packages or text editors. The system also provides information on educational opportunities, corporate directions, and promotional trends.

It is important for individuals to consider the opportunities open to them—opportunities for growth and performance improvement in the current job and opportunities for different assignments. This can result from review of career information, as described above, and from discussion with the manager.

In addition to identifying perceived development needs, both for the current job and for the future, a development plan should identify development activities. These are specific actions planned, with completion date, resources required, and responsibility. The most common type of activity is participation in training or education programs, largely because they are tangible, visible, and logical. Other types of activities may involve on-the-job development, such as self-study, special projects or additional responsibilities, or initiatives for development involving coaching by the manager or others.

A plan need not be elaborate; but it should be realistic, and it should represent a commitment to action. IBM has a development planning form which may be initiated and completed by an employee at any time during the year, reviewed/discussed with the manager, and filed for follow-up action and review.

Managers as Coaches and Mentors

To help employees develop, managers need to act as coaches or counselors. They need to listen, draw out employees' goals, and help them identify their interests, values, and skills.

In addition, managers need to be appraisers (as will be discussed in Chapter 9), defining and implementing effective performance standards, giving useful feedback that will help improve performance, and helping employees clarify the opportunities and limits that exist.

Finally, the manager provides advice—helping to define options and assess the organization's future directions, while helping the employee shape development plans to fit in with the company's future. The manager may also refer employees to others for information, advice, and development resources.

Managers are sometimes trained specifically on coaching and counseling skills. To help managers fulfill these roles, Johnson Wax provides a two-day training program called "Partners in Career Management." Other companies require development planning for managers themselves, giving them personal knowledge of the process and its value (Gilley & Moore, 1986).

One variation on coaching is mentoring. This involves a relationship between a senior and a junior colleague, viewed by the junior colleague as making a positive contribution to his or her development (Kram, 1984). Such contributions may be career enhancement or personal support. The mentor provides teaching, counseling, psychological support, protection, and, at times, promoting or sponsoring. Such a relationship is typically long-term, extending for several years or for a phase of a person's career. Mentor relationships emerge informally in life, but may be established formally in an organization to ensure steady development progress for high-potential individuals. Women and minorities may particularly benefit from the attention and support provided (Jacoby, 1989; Zey, 1984).

TRAINING AND EDUCATION

Training and education are central elements in the process of developing employees. Training in its myriad forms is provided to help employees learn job-related skills and obtain knowledge that will help them improve their performance and further the organization's goals. Education is provided to equip employees to expand their capacity to learn and to perform in the future.

Training and education is the principal vehicle for developing skills and abilities of employees other than through job assignments. It is also important as a way to implement strategy because it influences employee values, attitudes, and practices; it is a primary communications vehicle controlled by management.

Defining Training Needs

The principal challenge in training and education is knowing what is needed. Too often training is planned in the form of "programs" and is announced to prospective participants. Human resource planning calls for the tailoring of programs to fit needs, not the marketing of programs within a company. Yet many training and development staff professionals seem concerned with refining programs and then "selling" them within the company. External vendors of programs abet the condition, promoting programs that have been packaged or that may be tailored for use within a company.

Ideally, training and education needs emerge on a continuing basis from individual development plans, as discussed above. Managers review their employees' identified needs each year and define the training and educational support required to supplement on-the-job development. Alternatively, training staff may directly review individual development plans and define program requirements. This is more commonly done for management levels; needs at other levels are defined more as common, or generic, requirements.

Training may be tailored to address the specific tasks required in performing a job. Here analysis of tasks is a necessary approach for defining training needs. Various methods are available, ranging from simple review of job descriptions to use of detailed task inventories, interviews, or direct observation (Wexley & Latham, 1981).

An alternative approach is to conduct needs analysis surveys. Whether by interviews with managers or by use of a survey questionnaire, a needs analysis study can identify the topics perceived as requiring attention in an organization. Such surveys may be open-ended, soliciting viewpoints and suggestions regarding training and development, or they may be structured, asking for ranking of topics as to relative needs. Surveys may address general needs or specific functional, product, or job-related needs.

A pitfall in surveying needs, however, is ending up polling interests in various topics, not bona fide needs. A survey may simply end up being an endorsement of various programs already offered or of topics selected in the course of developing and conducting the survey, thus failing to yield definition of changing needs. It is important to focus on the needs of the business which drive performance requirements (current and future) and, in turn, training and education needs.

In one company, training activities are planned three years in the future, based on analysis of the training implications of business issues in each organization. The planning process includes:

• Interviews with managers in each unit to identify critical business issues and changes, the employee population they affect (and total number of employees), the nature of the impact, the priority, and the timing

• Assessment of skill and knowledge topics required by these employees, applicable training techniques, and the training activity required

• Determination of a specific training plan and the staffing, facilities, and budget required

The advantage of this approach is that it directly addresses the training implications of current management concerns and objectives. It is a strategy-driven approach that reflects management priorities. As such, training and education becomes a valuable tool for implementing business strategies.

Companies have eliminated many of their "nice to know" programs and courses, and have concentrated on those closely connected to the needs of the company. According to one training director, "Management has become satisfied that we only do the essential—that we're contributing to the bottom line."

Some companies cut back on training during adverse business conditions and rebuild when business improves. Some opt to "buy talent" rather than develop it, at least for a time. Yet short-term savings may be offset by longer-term costs, as some companies have discovered. Employees become outdated, lose their habit of learning, feel that they are not valued—and leave. Training resources are lost and costly to rebuild. Some companies believe that training is just what should be done when business is slow, and people have the time for and interest in learning.

Innovations in Training and Education

Companies spend considerable amounts of time and money in training and education programs to help employees contribute to achieving desired business results. They design courses and develop new educational techniques, conduct programs, and carefully monitor the results. In the 1980s, companies spent an estimated $60 billion each year on corporate training and education, as much as

dedicated program basis. The trend is to focus on priorities of the business, tailoring programs and participation to changing needs. Larger companies are increasingly developing their own management programs, customized to fit their needs (Bolt, 1985).

At Hewlett-Packard, for example, a corporate training department consists of eighty people. It provides employee education, management development, and executive development. The largest unit maintains a corporate television network. Through this group, the company transmits via satellite to more than sixty company facilities around the world. The use of television focuses on new-product training for sales, service, and support, but is also used for engineering education. In addition, the department is responsible for developing applications of computer technology for instruction purposes (Lusterman, 1985).

IBM uses satellite education as well, but has also developed an advanced technology classroom. Instructors call up visual materials, through a personal computer, in a myriad of forms—computer-generated slides, videos, and role-playing. A keypad at each desk enables students to respond to questions; a tabulation of responses helps the instructor know whether the material is getting across. Technology-based presentations are more interactive, use more varied forms of presentation, and rely less on the skill of the instructor. As a result, they have been shown to increase learning, and students say that they prefer them (Galagan, 1989).

Most companies also rely on individual learning. Courses of self-study are being used more widely because they may be done at the pace, location, and timing individuals prefer. Readings and exercises remain the most common approach. However, use of new technology, such as interactive videodisc/personal computer combinations, is being adopted. Individual learning does not apply to all topics, but when used appropriately, it is typically quicker and more cost-effective than classroom training (Galagan, 1989; Sims, 1990).

As companies seek to contain staffing levels and costs, reliance is increasing on external resources for training design, curriculum and materials development, and delivery. The use of "packaged" programs developed and even conducted by training vendors (consultants or suppliers) continues to increase, and many vendors will adapt their programs to company needs. At Xerox, for example, much of the design and development work is contracted out, but actual instruction is done by employees—not necessarily training professionals but employees tapped for special assignment. Companies use outside resources in various tasks. The choice is no longer "make or buy"; companies maintain involvement and control in the areas they feel are most important and cost-effective, and contract out work as well.

Evaluating Training and Education Results

Many companies specify expected results before training activities are undertaken. For technical and skill training, objectives may be set for improved performance back on the job, in terms of quality, rework, waste reduction, speed, or cost. Measurements may be taken before and after training to determine behavioral changes and improved results. However, alert supervisors who send their people for training can directly assess whether the training is beneficial.

In companies where team performance is emphasized, such evaluations may be on a group basis. If all employees (and managers) in a work group participate in training, the results may be assessed for the group, in terms of productivity, quality, absenteeism, attitudes, or other factors.

Management development programs and other training and education with less tangible learning objectives are more difficult to evaluate. Typically, evaluation relies on the reactions and suggestions of participants. Participants may also be asked several months after completing the programs to report on the value of the experience and offer further suggestions. Of course, performance improvement, as assessed by managers and peers, provides an input, but is not easily tied to the training experience.

Evaluation depends on the objectives of a program and the intended level of impact. Because many other factors are involved in addition to training, the effects of training are more difficult to isolate and measure as the learning is applied. Training has the strongest impact on developing awareness, and lesser impact on the subsequent aspects of learning and applying skills and knowledge (see Exhibit 8-6). Deeper levels of learning require other forms of development, particularly on the job. The measures should be developed and applied which best fit the level of impact that may be addressed.

ORGANIZATIONAL LEARNING

The aim of individual development is to help people be effective learners. "We should think of learning as the expansion of one's capacity—to create, to procuce results" (Senge, 1990a). In this way, the objectives are more broadly defined—not merely the development of knowledge, skills, or abilities, or the influencing of attitudes, but the development of capacity.

EXHIBIT 8-6 LEVELS OF INDIVIDUAL DEVELOPMENT

AWARENESS

UNDERSTANDING

KNOWLEDGE AND SKILLS

ACCEPTANCE

APPLICATION

INSTITUTIONALIZATION

The learning organization is an ideal for the 1990s. In it, management invests continually in employees and empowers them to learn, grow, and contribute. Employees respond with a new sort of loyalty—a reciprocal commitment to learn, grow, and contribute. An overriding, shared sense of vision and purpose is necessary in such an organization, to focus the energies of all.

A learning organization takes the idea of continuous improvement seriously. Employees are constantly seeking ways to improve the way they perform their jobs and the quality of resulting products and services. Learning allows employees to try out new ideas, and occasionally make mistakes. Learning requires stepping back from day-to-day operations and reexamining how work is done.

The idea of organizational learning has been addressed thoughtfully by Peter Senge, author of *The Fifth Discipline* (Senge, 1990b). In his work at M.I.T. and with companies, he has applied systems thinking to the challenge of developing the potential capabilities of people in an organization. As illustrated in Exhibit 8-7 and discussed below, he focuses on five disciplines of organizational learning. If they are effectively applied, organizations will gain a potent new source of competitive advantage.

Personal Mastery

Individual learning is the starting point for organizational learning. Individuals need a discipline for personal growth and learning which allows them to continually expand their creative contribution. Personal mastery, as a discipline, means that people achieve a "special level of proficiency in every aspect of life—personal and professional" (Senge, 1990b).

This discipline has two aspects: a sense of vision and a sense of how reality relates to this vision. Individuals need to know what is important to them—to

EXHIBIT 8-7 FIVE DISCIPLINES OF ORGANIZATIONAL LEARNING

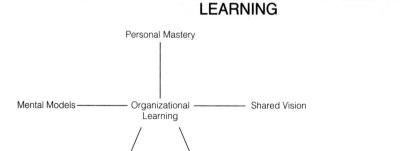

Source: Adapted from Senge, 1990.

have a sense of personal vision or destiny. They need to have some idea of where they are going, what they seek to accomplish, what they want to "be." Of course, people who are continually learning keep setting a higher vision and never arrive. Along with a vision, individuals need to have a realistic view of current circumstances and not be naive about what may be attained.

The gap between these two views results in creative tension which needs to be balanced—stretched, certainly, but kept within check. This means that people need to make choices as they learn and grow; they need to decide where to devote time and energies, which aims warrant personal commitment, and what "really matters." Personal mastery calls for a disciplined process of "continually focusing and refocusing on what one truly wants, on one's visions" (Senge, 1990).

People who lack a sense of purpose, of vision, or of discipline, or the will to pursue personal growth can make only limited contributions to their organizations. Management, then, needs to undo the constraints and provide a climate that fosters the quest for personal growth.

Mental Models

Individuals also need to be able to think in ways that open up learning and growth. Too often, people think and act based on assumptions that limit change. Employees often think functionally rather than around products, markets, and customers. Employees think in terms of past decisions, not possible alternatives. They too often think in local country (e.g., U.S.) terms, rather than in terms of other economies and cultures (global).

Within organizations, people often think in terms of existing hierarchy, job definition and authorities to act, power alliances, and established norms of behavior. As a result, the current and past situation shapes the decisions that are made. In a learning organization, these preconceptions are challenged and adapted to support change.

Often people fail to learn and grow, not because they are unable to do so but because of barriers that they perceive to exist. Chris Argyris, a Harvard professor, observed that people are reluctant to change existing reasoning patterns in their organizations; it is easier to follow past reasoning than to appear strange, or dangerous. People need to learn how to learn (Argyris, 1991).

In a learning organization, mental models are changed largely by confronting thinking with reality. Openness, trust, effective use of data, and rational inference and problem-solving processes are vital. Planning processes are an excellent vehicle for changing mental models, when used effectively. When they are not, they perpetuate old thinking and actions.

Shared Vision

The third dimension of organizational learning brings people together in establishing shared visions and in confronting realities. This requires that people talk and listen to each other, that they share personal visions, and that they reason together about what is desired and possible.

The aim in a learning organization is to forge a bond among people through a partnership focused on a common purpose. There needs to be developed an overriding sense of mission, vision, values, and destiny. As discussed earlier in this book, the shaping of expectations needs to be based on inputs from employees as well as from senior management. A vision cannot be imposed; it must be accepted. An organization requires commitment, not merely compliance.

When the current situation is perceived to be far apart from the desired situation, there is a tremendous task in defining the gaps and building a shared commitment to bridge them. It's easier to build a shared vision in an entrepreneurial garage than in an established institution like General Motors, where both the perceptions of the future and the gaps need to be redefined.

Team Learning

Team learning is the fourth dimension. In teams, individuals act as colleagues and work together openly to achieve a new level of knowledge and capability as an organization. This requires lowering defensive barriers and motivating employees to learn and act together rather than individually.

The lifeblood of a learning organization is information. Senior managers set strategic goals, chart new directions, and set performance objectives. Operating employees generate new ideas on ways to achieve these objectives; a lot of learning should be going on among the mass of employees, not just at the top. To link the top-down and bottom-up development of ideas and new directions, middle managers build networks and teams to exchange and process information. "Working in multifunctional teams," argues Ikujiro Nonaka, of Hitotsubashi University, "they integrate what's coming from above and below to develop products and processes, compressively—think of a turbocharger—accelerating the creation of information."

Senge stresses that team learning itself is a team skill. "A group of talented individual learners will not necessarily produce a learning team, any more than a group of talented athletes will produce a great sports team, (Senge, 1990)." And, as with sports teams, the way to learn is through practice.

Systems Thinking

Each of these four disciplines contributes to, and depends on, systems thinking. Not a new idea, systems thinking has been advocated and applied in the sciences, including the behavioral sciences, for decades. The fifth discipline calls for an understanding of the interrelatedness of behaviors.

Individuals and teams are part of a dynamic process, and thrive on interaction and feedback. The central notion of systems thinking is feedback—learning from experience and from others. And related to this is the interdependence of all elements of the organizational "system." Individuals alone cannot bring about the needed organizational learning; everyone shares responsibility.

Many barriers and dysfunctions in organizations impede learning. Hence systems thinking requires a high level of pragmatism—a continual recognition and rechecking of reality. Both integrative conceptualization (lateral thinking and synthesis) and reality testing and feedback are vital. Only in this way can people in an organization focus their energies and resources in areas that will gain leverage.

In a learning organization, everyone contributes. Everyone leads. Everyone chooses to learn or not to learn, to work as a team member or to act alone. The capacity of an organization to be competitive depends on all employees developing their capabilities together.

SUMMARY

In the 1990s, training and education will be increasingly important. The rapid advance of technology is resulting in accelerated obsolescence and the need for current skill and knowledge development. In addition, the rapid pace of business change—itself reflecting social, political, and economic change—will require adaptability among employees. According to Ray Stata, CEO of Analog Devices, "The rate at which organizations learn may become the only sustainable source of competitive advantage."

CHAPTER 9

DEVELOPING EFFECTIVE MANAGERS

I believe in putting the best possible talent around me. You've got to be able to spot it, you've got to be able to recruit it, you've got to be able to retain it, and you've got to be able to develop it.

Nolan Archibald, CEO, Black & Decker

As companies grow and change, the need for high-quality management talent increases. Emphasis on managing new products and services, technological advances, global business activities and alliances, and improvement of competitive performance—all create strains on managerial abilities and adaptability. The more rapid rate of change experienced in many organizations today, compared with a generation ago, compels special attention to the development of managerial talent.

This chapter addresses the ways in which companies develop their management resources. It focuses on:

• How organizations plan ahead for management succession and development

• How future management requirements are defined in the context of business change and future strategy

• How individual capabilities and development needs are evaluated relative to these requirements

• How individuals best develop their talents as managers

The previous chapter addressed approaches for the overall development of employees. This chapter examines the ways in which companies specifically develop *managers* for their future needs. While development of all employees is important, the planned development and succession of management talent is typically a special focus of company efforts. Management talent represents a critical resource, by virtue of the experience, skills, and knowledge required, as well as the significant potential impact that individuals and teams have on the execution of company strategy.

By *managers* we mean the individuals responsible for implementing strategies and achieving results through their organizations. Our focus is on developing managers who can act as effective leaders or pathfinders, as well as effective problem solvers and implementers (Leavitt, 1986; Tichy, 1986).

SUCCESSION AND DEVELOPMENT PLANNING

For decades, companies have conducted management replacement or succession planning and have guided high-talent managers toward job assignments and management training programs aimed at developing their capabilities. To meet future needs, planning for management development requires increased attention to the changing requirements for management in a company, more rigorous evaluation of individual capabilities and development needs relative to these requirements, and increased attention to the actual implementation of development action plans.

Effective planning for management talent involves a flexible, long-range view of future management succession and development. It calls for systematic planning for the broadening of high-talent individuals and involves assignments under different managers in different functions or units. It confronts directly the tendencies of managers to fill management positions informally. It is far easier for most managers to deal with a crisis—a problem that demands immediate, urgent resolution—than to anticipate possible future problems and to plan ahead to avoid them. It is also far easier to be a mentor and sponsor for your own selected successors than to work with other managers in a systematic process of evaluation, rotations, and career guidance for a pool of management candidates.

Accordingly, management succession and development planning is difficult to implement. A survey by Sibson & Company, consultants, showed that many companies do not have comprehensive processes for this purpose.

> They have failed to commit themselves at the most senior management levels to carefully examining the way they recruit, select, develop, and promote their future leaders. . . . Many companies have failed to gather the right leaders, in large part due to their inability to develop effective succession planning systems. The result has been a talent drain and subpar performance at the highest levels of their organizations at a time when critical business challenges are facing virtually all companies. (Sibson & Company, 1990)

The key factors in implementing the process are policies and systems that will make succession planning part of the ongoing management process, and attitude shifts in support of developmental objectives. Tools need to be practical and results-oriented, tailored to fit the style of management and characteristics of the organization. Some companies have worked at doing a good job in this area for many years (e.g., GE, GM, IBM, AT&T, Weyerhaeuser, and

Exxon); others have set clear objectives and have implemented an effective process in a short time.

Going beyond Replacement Planning

To meet their future needs for management talent, most companies provide management development for their executives and high-potential management candidates. Their specific objectives and the approaches they take to meet them vary widely.

In the 1990s and beyond, there will be many "baby boomer" managers available as candidates for advancement, with fewer opportunities. However, having the right set of skills and experience to fit a company's strategy requires careful recruitment and selection, or development of known candidates within the company. Because of the significant impact an executive has on an organization, companies prefer to develop candidates for key positions from within.

Over the past several decades, many companies have practiced replacement planning, a process of reviewing the availability of candidates to replace incumbent executives when they move on to other assignments or leave the company. Such replacement planning often included suggested executive development actions, usually in the form of executive education programs or seminars.

Replacement planning implies continuity of requirements; incumbents will be replaced by individuals with similar skills and capabilities. "A manager's first responsibility," it used to be said, "is to groom his or her successor." Managers would identify and prepare individuals to move through the levels of management necessary to take over responsibilities.

Today, however, development of managers is more complex because requirements are changing as business demands change. Accordingly, the process requires definition of changing needs, consideration of alternative succession candidates, and planning of assignments in the context of organizational changes. Also, development is much more situational than in the past. It is difficult to develop well-rounded managers when organizations are flatter, leaner, and performing under great competitive pressures. Succession planning is aimed at broadening managers and increasing organizational capabilities.

The contrasts between replacement planning and the more intensive succession planning are shown in Exhibit 9-1. The former concentrates on immediate needs and a "snapshot" assessment of the availability of qualified backups for key management positions. Succession planning, by contrast, is more concerned with longer-range needs and the cultivation of a supply of qualified talent to satisfy those needs. Succession planning entails a more intensive management review of job requirements and the dynamics of changing organizational needs, candidate information, development needs, and specific assignments and developmental actions for candidates. Replacement planning and succession planning are not opposing alternatives; succession planning is a logical and natural evolution of the rather simplistic charting of static requirements and supply.

EXHIBIT 9-1 CONTRASTS BETWEEN REPLACEMENT AND SUCCESSION PLANNING

Variable	Replacement Planning	Succession Planning
Time frame	0–12 months	12–36 months
Readiness	Best candidate available	Candidate with the best development potential
Commitment level	Designated preferred replacement candidate	Merely possibilities until vacancies occur
Focus of planning	Vertical lines of succession within units or functions	A pool of talent candidates with capability for any of several assignments
Development planning	Unusually informal, a status report on strengths and weaknesses	Specific plans and goals set for the individual
Flexibility	Limited by the structure of the plans, but in practice a great deal of flexibility	Plans conceived as flexible, intended to promote development and thinking about alternatives
Basis of plans	Each manager's best judgment based on observation and experience	Result of inputs and discussion among multiple managers
Evaluation	Observation of performance on the job over time; demonstrated competence; progress through the unit	Multiple evaluations by different managers on different assignments; testing and broadening early in careers

---

Companies are realizing that on-the-job experience is the key development activity. Planning and tracking individual progression through relevant developmental experiences are acknowledged today to be the key to building management capabilities. Ironically, this was the emphasis decades ago, although on an informal basis, before executive education was expanded. "Developing managerial competence occurs on the job," reported a 1964 Conference Board study report. "Recognizing this, many firms mold the work experiences of their managers by paying attention to sound organization planning, coaching by superiors, and the use of special assignments as a means for getting tasks done. Performance appraisal is used to stimulate and encourage managers to develop further. Off-the-job methods are used to supplement the growth that occurs at work" (Wikstrom, 1964).

What is relatively new, and the critical aspect of concern in human resource planning, is a more systematic process of defining future management requirements, assessing individual capabilities and development needs, and planning and implementing developmental actions. The process of management succession and development planning is becoming an important adjunct to strategic business planning. Decisions regarding organizational changes, international expansion, and new ventures and initiatives increasingly take into consideration the availability of management talent.

THE SUCCESSION PLANNING PROCESS

Various approaches are used for management development and succession. In large divisionalized companies, approaches range from highly informal (simple, confidential, personal) to highly centralized, formal, and documented systems, with extensive staff support to maintain the information and track implementation of plans. Most companies have processes that involve formal data collection and review, standard formats, and formal review processes (Rhodes & Walker, 1984).

All of these approaches involve the same basic activities, which are outlined below. All of them are line management processes, coordinated and supported by staff, as necessary. All involve preparation and review of data and plans by the responsible managers, as well as efforts by managers to implement these plans.

Key Activities

The following activities are considered necessary for the effective development of managerial talent in a large organization:

1 *Definition of succession requirements.* Future management staffing needs are reflected in business planning and organization planning. At senior management levels, this is often a highly subjective and sensitive activity, but nevertheless an important one in defining the "demand" for managerial talent. The qualitative requirements of future managerial positions are defined. A "position profile" may define the activities to be performed in a management position as it is expected to change in the future. This profile thereby provides criteria for assessment and development of prospective successors.

2 *Inventory of talent.* Biographical data on prospective managerial candidates and incumbents are considered, including career progress, experience, relevant education, and self-reported interests and preference regarding future career steps. Individual attitudes regarding relocation, dual-career situations, and specific career interests and aspirations are often highly relevant in realistic management succession planning.

3 *Assessment of capabilities and development needs.* Individual capabilities are evaluated against the established criteria. Performance in challenging positions is regarded as an important indicator of future performance and development potential as managers. Feedback of appraisal results to the individuals and constructive dialogue are important as input to development planning.

4 *Planning for succession.* The availability (bench strength) of candidates and their readiness for management assignments are considered in succession planning. This typically involves the use of summary listings, tables (by position and by individual), or organization charts indicating the individuals identified as succession candidates.

5 *Planning development actions.* The actions for training or development of each succession candidate are specified. Such actions may include a targeted job assignment, a temporary developmental assignment or project, a formal training program, or external activity. Progressively broader job experiences are planned, with evaluation of high-talent candidates under different supervising managers. "Fast-track" candidates are moved along these developmental paths at an accelerated pace.

6 *Implementation.* The individuals actually participate in planned training or education programs, and undertake planned on-the-job activities or other development experiences. Managers acting as mentors and coaches may help follow up on development plans. Also, formal monitoring and follow-up reports may be given to managers regarding implementation.

7 *External recruiting or other actions.* Plans are devised to meet identified shortages or surpluses for managerial staffing (for example, through recruiting, special assignments to meet gaps, terminations, restructuring of positions, changes in business plans requiring management staff).

The relationships among these activities composing the succession planning process are represented in Exhibit 9-2. The process is an integrated set of activities, and therefore, the outputs of one cycle contribute to inputs for the next. When effectively implemented, the process feeds upon itself, resulting in more and more comprehensive and objective plans and more fully developed managers each year.

Implicit is a commitment to an investment in the development of employees as managers and the intentional movement of individuals among job assignments for developmental purposes, even where short-term business necessity may dictate that an individual should stay put to maintain critical performance. In turn, a high degree of support from senior management and involvement in important succession decisions are important prerequisites of succession planning.

EXHIBIT 9-2 MANAGEMENT SUCCESSION AND DEVELOPMENT

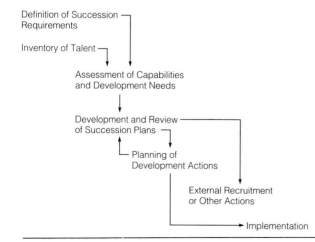

DEFINING MANAGERIAL REQUIREMENTS

A major advancement in management resource planning in the past several decades has been the improved definition and consideration of management requirements. In planning future management staffing needs, senior management considers the following questions:

• What capabilities will be required of future managers in the company (in general)?
• What capabilities will be required for specific business units or functions (e.g., international managers, finance, consumer products marketing)?
• What specific capabilities will be required on each key management position?

These three levels of requirements are illustrated in Exhibit 9-3. This focus provides a direct, practical linkage between the criteria used to evaluate and define development needs of individuals and the overall strategic requirements of a business.

Generally, the higher-level management positions require more focused definition of requirements (entry-level requirements are more general; key executive positions are position-specific). Also, requirements are usually considered cumulative, with each level of specificity building on the previous level. Accordingly, some companies have defined requirements as "management building blocks."

To be able to assess the development potential and needs of individuals as management candidates and to plan for developmental activities, a definition of requirements is needed. "Development for what?" is an important question. Because of the rapid changes influencing the demands on management, the factors used must be relevant to current and future requirements. It is important to define exactly what an organization expects of its future managers.

The value of succession and development planning is its flexibility in allowing a changing definition of the criteria for considering candidates. The requirements of the position may change, and thus the obvious immediate candidate may not be the best suited as a longer-term successor, or may not be properly prepared for the changing requirements.

Management Criteria

Companies have sought to promote those individuals who displayed certain qualities relating to managerial capability. Often these qualities represented personality traits largely beyond the reach of development programs ("Either you have it or you don't"). Education, job experience, specialization, and other factors such as height, age, and gender played roles as indicators of managerial competence.

Criteria used in assessment of managers and candidates have often emphasized personal qualities believed to be associated with (or predictive of) successful performance or advancement in management. Harry Levinson, a highly

---

EXHIBIT 9-3 DEFINING MANAGEMENT REQUIREMENTS

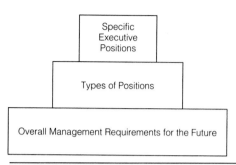

Specific
Executive
Positions

Types of Positions

Overall Management Requirements for the Future

---

respected psychologist consulting on management succession, used twenty dimensions of personality to select leaders. These dimensions included intelligence, judgment, authority, sensitivity, maturity, involvement, interdependence, articulateness, stamina, adaptability, sense of humor, perseverance, and integrity (H. Levinson, 1980).

A method of selecting criteria to be used involved examination of the characteristics and behaviors of current managers, both successful and less successful. Differentiating factors were incorporated into the assessment step of the process. Such criteria focused on the person, not the context of management. Also, the criteria were oriented to the present and past, not to future requirements.

Today, many companies have a model of their ideal manager, the "manager of the future." This manager is typically viewed as a person who will maintain order while also bringing about creative change. According to researcher Morgan McCall, "Managers are the glue that keeps systems from falling apart, from running down, from spinning out of control." Yet they are also expected to be creative and bring about change necessary for a company to adapt effectively to its environment.

Such models typically call for competence in a variety of areas of behavior. A pharmaceutical company developed and uses a series of management dimensions including planning and decision making, organization, communications, development of subordinates, interpersonal relations, external relations, interpersonal skills, leadership, and managing change. Exhibit 9-4 presents examples of management factors related to these dimensions. They are used in defining requirements and in evaluating and developing successors. Technical or functional requirements are not usually included in the model because they relate to specific positions or types of positions.

Leadership Competence

Requirements reflect distinctions between "managers" and "leaders." "The difference between managers and leaders is fundamental," observed Warren

---

EXHIBIT 9-4 **EXAMPLES OF MANAGEMENT FACTORS**

Planning and Decision Making

Financial planning/analysis: Gathering, analyzing, and using financial data effectively; drawing accurate conclusions from financial information; applying financial and/or accounting principles to management plans and problems; developing budgets to support the accomplishment of organizational goals at a realistic cost.

Strategic thinking: Taking the long-term, broad view of a situation; identifying the potential impacts on the business of external forces such as industry changes, competitor actions, legal, regulatory, and political changes, international trends, and technological changes that represent a business threat or opportunity; formulating and evaluating appropriate options.

Organization

Allocating/controlling resources: Ensuring that employees have necessary resources and authority needed to meet objectives; establishing only necessary controls; monitoring progress and outcomes against plans.

Personal organization/time management: Setting personal priorities and objectives in support of organization goals; allocating one's own time efficiently; processing paperwork and managing administrative requirements effectively; processing information without either overlooking important items or getting overly involved with details; sustaining high levels of energy in response to work demands.

Communications

Listening: The ability to hear and comprehend messages and information delivered by others.

Presentations: Developing and delivering prepared or spontaneous presentations that are appropriate to the audience and topic and that achieve the intended results.

Development of Subordinates

Developing others: Developing skills and competencies in others through identifying needs; providing challenging tasks and assignments; providing appropriate developmental situations; coaching, counseling, and acting as a mentor to both subordinates and others to enable them to take on broader or higher responsibilities.

Motivation: Creating an environment which encourages people to contribute, achieve, and develop their talents; fostering a sense of energy, enthusiasm, commitment, trust, and pursuit of excellence with employees.

Bennis. "The manager administers, the leader innovates. The manager maintains, the leader develops. The manger relies on systems, the leader relies on people. The manager counts on control, the leader counts on trust. The manager does things right, the leader does the right thing" (Bennis, 1985).

The rational, cool, problem-solving executive who succeeded in the sixties, seventies, and eighties is deemed no longer up to the challenges of today. "The new paragon is an executive who can envision a future for his organization and inspire colleagues to join him in building that future. Perhaps the most notable departure from managerial practice: The leader does not fear change, but instead embraces it and creates it. He knows that his most important job is probably to transform the way his company does business" (Main, 1988).

Over and over, studies point to the same set of capabilities as essential for managers to be effective. John Kotter, author of *The Leadership Factors* (1988), believes that the leader needed today has vision and also the ability to

---

EXHIBIT 9-4   *(Cont.)*

External Relations

Managing business relationships: Developing and maintaining constructive relationships with internal and external customers, suppliers, contractors, community representatives, and government officials; demonstrating customer orientation and focus in providing products or services.

Representing the company: Representing and communicating the company's viewpoint to outside organizations; acting as an agent of the company before government, political, community, or industry groups; understanding the impact of business activities on the community, the industry, and the public; working in ways that enhance the company image with these constituencies.

Interpersonal Skills

Interpersonal skills: Ability to interact effectively with people; ability to garner support of individuals at all organizational levels.

Managing conflict: Managing a diversity of viewpoints; managing tension, stress, and crises; bringing conflict or dissent into the open and using it productively to enhance the quality of decisions.

Leadership

Quality orientation: Demonstrating and encouraging a commitment to quality performance at all levels, both inside and outside the organization; demonstrating dissatisfaction with less than excellent performance.

Results achievement: Work results in goal accomplishment; accepting accountability for results, and working in ways that reflect a sense of urgency and commitment to productivity.

Managing Change

Adaptability: Demonstrating effectiveness in varying environments, tasks, and responsibilities; responding appropriately and confidently to the demands of work challenges when confronted with changes, ambiguity, adversity, or other pressures; providing sufficient flexibility to accommodate needed changes.

Risk taking: Able to analyze and select courses of action that involve risk when it is in the best interest of the company to do so.

---

build a network of people and resources to implement the strategy. A leader needs anticipatory skills, visioning skills, value-congruence skills, empowerment skills, and self-understanding skills. A line manager, writing in the *Harvard Business Review,* sees effective managers like wagon masters, with these roles: decision maker, listener and communicator, teacher, peacemaker, visionary, self-critic, team captain, and leader of people (Ninomiya, 1988).

A recent study examined what "real managers do" (Luthans, 1988). The study found that managers spend their time as follows:

- Communication (30%): exchanging information, paperwork
- Traditional management (30%): planning, decision making, controlling
- Networking (20%): interacting with others
- Human resource management (20%): motivating/reinforcing, disciplining, managing conflict, staffing, and training/development

For the most effective managers in the study, the biggest contributions came from communicating and human resource management activities. This affirms the importance given today to these "soft" aspects of managing.

In a different study of 165 middle managers in five companies, Rosabeth Moss Kanter found that the most enterprising, innovative, and entrepreneurial managers were not extraordinary individuals. However, they shared these characteristics: comfort with change, clarity of direction, thoroughness, participative management style, and persuasiveness, persistence, and discretion.

A study by the Center for Creative Leadership asked 400 executives who were considered effective in their companies to identify the key events in their careers and the lessons they had learned from them. Among the findings were sixteen fundamental skills and perspectives essential to management and executive success. These were grouped into three primary areas: vision, team building, and self-awareness. The focus was on the dimensions of development that these individuals perceived as important—not on their organizations' definition of requirements.

For the most part, the qualities sought in a leader are not new and different; they are the essence of the capable manager that companies are seeking to recruit, develop, and promote. Good managers are transformational leaders. "The game is over," Columbia University professor Leonard Sayles indicated. "No organization confronting this competitive world can afford plain-vanilla managers: managers who are merely caretakers of the status quo. Change is . . . everyday managerial life. Every manager I know who works in a dynamic organization spends each day coping with change" (Sayles, 1990). A manager needs to be a pathfinder, problem solver, *and* implementer.

Focused Criteria

Criteria may be adapted by managers for specific situations. Their knowledge of the requirements of the business, the management team and organization, and anticipated challenges for management suggests needs for specific types of experience, attributes, skills, or knowledge.

The requirements for effective staff leadership, for example, are a somewhat different set of capabilities than those for a line manager. One discussion identifies these dimensions as key: managing toward results, leading with confidence, working with management, serving customers, supervising staff professionals (Bellman, 1986).

Requirements may focus on the special capabilities required of managers whose roles are changing. For example, capabilities in managing technology are important for engineers and scientists who are becoming managers (Badawy, 1982).

Requirements for advancement among management positions also sometimes reflect general views of requirements, in terms of logical career progression. The kinds of experience required represent de facto requirements. An individual may be expected to move first from making an individual contribution (as a technical performer) to managing functional work or project work.

Then the progression moves to managing a business or profit center, to managing several businesses, and ultimately to leading an institution. It is easier to move an individual geographically, across product or even functional specializations, than to progress among these managerial stages.

Similarly, at IBM managers in various functions are guided through developmental assignments and broadening activities according to an overall functional plan. The company consistently and explicitly strives to give future managers the experiences that will give them needed exposure to and experience in different facets of IBM management. Development may entail both assignments and broadening activities focused on needs at each stage. Exhibit 9-5 presents such a guide for financial career planning. The information, similar to the career grid described in Chapter 7 (see Exhibit 7-3), involves a "demand pull" —management facilitating the planned development of individuals as candidates for these positions, rather than merely providing individuals with options.

International Focus

International business understanding and perspective are becoming important for all managers, as businesses become global. However, managers assigned to international management responsibilities have a specific (and intensely important) set of requirements: cross-cultural understanding and skills, economic and political understanding, abilities in managing joint ventures and alliances, and understanding of markets and competition. At a minimum, orientation for international assignments is needed. Many companies seek to prepare managers before sending them to overseas assignments (Blocklyn, 1989). According to Gerald Hornsby of Dow Chemical Company, "There was a time when we had real career expatriates. . . . Today we are identifying people willing to gain specific developmental experiences, sending them where their skills are needed, and bringing them back to jobs where they can use their new skills" (Deutsch, 1988).

In a broader sense, being a global manager means having a global mindset and vision. It means "knowing how to find the right country in which to build a plant, how to coordinate production schedules across borders, and how to absorb research wherever it occurs" (Kupfer, 1988). It means understanding the business in the global context—far more than merely cultural orientation. Finding executives with global management skills has become intensely competitive; developing executives with the right skills for international assignments is a growing priority (Tully, 1990).

For example, Colgate-Palmolive Company has a global marketing training program that seeks to develop managers so that they will work in a variety of international markets and learn the strategic leadership skills required for work in a global economy. Pepsi-Cola International, IBM, and other global companies view international managers as the source of global leaders.

Of course, the requirements depend on the stage of the company in its global evolution. The demands on managers increase as a company moves from being a domestic enterprise to an exporter, to an international or multi-national cor-

---

EXHIBIT 9-5 FINANCIAL CAREER EXPERIENCES AT IBM (LIMITED—TYPICAL M&D CAREER PATH)

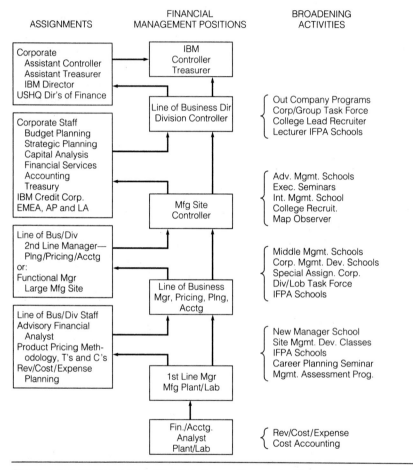

Source: International Business Machines Corporation, used with permission.

---

poration, to a truly "borderless" global enterprise (Rhinesmith, Williamson, Ehlen, & Maxwell, 1989). Even within companies, the evolution varies among divisions. Each of General Electric Company's fourteen key businesses is in a different stage of globalization. Plastics, aircraft engines, and turbine businesses place a high premium on overseas experience; other businesses do not (Deutsch, 1988).

Focus on Strategic Fit

Just as company global management requirements vary and evolve, so do other strategic requirements. Some companies have made a special effort to define management requirements that apply to specific business situations. General Electric has long sought to develop and match management talent with the requirements of its different business segments. When circumstances change, companies often look to recruit individuals who fit the new situation, implicitly defining new strategic requirements.

Different strategic situations affect human resource strategies. An institutional organization requires a more traditional manager, one who can maintain continuity, stability, and control. As as organization becomes more flexible, adapting to changing competitive conditions, it requires a more flexible manager, or "transformational leader." Entrepreneurial organizations—ventures or "garages"—require hands-on managers with a breadth of skills and high energy.

Various ways of considering the match between managers and strategies have been developed as a result of business strategy concepts. A direct tie to strategies is suggested by Michael Porter. He identifies different managerial characteristics required for key strategic choices: cost leadership, differentiation, or focus (Porter, 1980). These are sometimes addressed specifically in the criteria for management development.

Miles and Snow describe managers using the terms *defender, prospector,* and *analyzer.* Defender managers need expertise and focus on improvement of efficiency in narrow businesses. Prospectors are continually searching for opportunities and are creators of change for their competitive advantage. Here, managers are innovative, flexible, and creative leaders. Analyzers are characterized by stability, but they also react promptly to competitive changes. These managers are alert to change, and they evaluate options before acting (Miles & Snow, 1984).

Specific business situations may require managers with different capabilities. Start-ups, rapidly growing businesses, mature businesses, turnaround situations, and divestitures or liquidations represent the potential stages of an organization's life cycle. The management of acquisitions, managing redeployment or redirection of businesses, or managing in joint ventures requires special skills (Gerstein & Reisman, 1983; Kimberly & Miles, 1980). There is no simple catalog of such situations, but the definition of management requirements when a special situation develops is a useful tool in considering management succession and development.

Position Requirements

Future requirements should also reflect actual activities expected and the demands of key management positions for which individuals are considered prospective candidates, recognizing that as conditions change, such requirements also change. In turbulent times, such requirements are necessarily broad—focusing on the flexibility of managers to adapt to rapidly changing business demands.

Most large organizations have managerial position descriptions. These descriptions cover the basic function of the position (purpose, mission, objective), duties and responsibilities, accountabilities, reporting relationships, and limits of authority. They are written for organization purposes and are used as a basis for determining job worth for compensation. Such descriptions are helpful tools in defining what the positions require. However, managerial activities are not easily specified, since they adapt to changing business demands and to the abilities and interests of the incumbents. Position descriptions tend to look at jobs as static and finite when, in practice, they are dynamic.

A profile of a position provides a more complete perspective of the activities performed in the future. Job descriptions may be supplemented with a description of the managerial activities performed, or separate profiles of positions may describe changing activities and the implied requirements for succession and development.

In the pharmaceutical company mentioned previously, the list of management factors or dimensions is used as a template for all candidates, to evaluate individual capabilities and overall development needs. It is also used to define the specific requirements for each management position, resulting in a "position profile."

A position profile typically includes the following elements, usually in a formal, established printed format to ensure consistent and easy use:

Key activities:

- In what ways will the work of the position change in the future (two to five years)?
- What aspects of the work in the position are likely to be the most difficult, challenging, or demanding for a future successor?
- What will be the most important dimensions for considering successors (refer to list)?

Technical and functional competence:

- What experience within the specialty is required (or desirable) of a successor? Indicate the types of assignments or other experience a successor should have.
- What experience in other areas is required (or desirable) of a successor?
- What international experience is required (or desirable)?
- What education, training, or certification is required (or desirable)?
- How will the paths leading to the position be different in the future?

Management factors:

- Indicate the dimensions of management (see list) that will be most critical in evaluating and developing successors for the position during the coming five years.

Position profiles provide the criteria for evaluating individual capabilities and gaps that may be bridged through individual development actions. Accordingly, the requirements must reflect reality, both in terms of the way the position is currently structured and in terms of the changes anticipated in the work relating to business plans and future organizational changes. As an initial step, position requirements are typically defined to reflect current requirements and are then modified in successive cycles of succession planning to take into account the changes anticipated.

Organization and Staffing Requirements

To provide the context for succession and development planning, the definition of a company's management requirements should also include a projection or major organizational changes and management staffing needs.

An organization should plan ahead for changes in structure, new positions, and new ways of conducting business. The succession and development planning process is an excellent forum for periodically reviewing plans for changes, progress in their implementation, and follow-up assessment of how well they are working. Review of the organization also sets the stage for discussion of changing management requirements and the strengths and development needs of alternative succession candidates. In succession planning, each presenting manager reviews the current organization structure and discusses prospective changes that would affect management succession and development or recruitment.

This organization review also identifies specific new positions, changes in positions, or eliminated positions. New position profiles are discussed, at least for key positions or for any that will be filled in the next year. This information suggests changes in staffing requirements, quantitatively and qualitatively. In addition, there may be planned retirements or transfers to other organizations. In this way, a manager projects vacancies and needs for action.

INVENTORY OF TALENT

The process also addresses the supply side of planning. It requires identification of the current incumbents and the possible candidates. Candidates are usually nominated by the immediate or unit manager, and the inventory typically sweeps widely, including all viable management candidates rather than being exclusive at the outset.

Included among the candidates are in-line successors (essentially replacements "waiting" to move up), candidates elsewhere in the organization, and longer-term or "high-potential" candidates. Many companies make a specific effort to include all women and minorities who may have management potential, near-term and long-term.

Individual Profiles

In most companies, a biographical summary is prepared for each individual who is included in the process as an incumbent or prospective succession candidate. A standard format is typically used, although this is rarely required of divisions in a decentralized company—as long as the following information is provided:

- Current position information
- Previous positions in the company
- Other significant work experience (other companies, military, Peace Corps, etc.)
  - Education (including degrees and certifications)
  - Language skills (and relevant international exposure)
  - Education and training programs attended
  - Community or industry leadership responsibilities

In many instances, current or past ratings of performance are included. Salary grade and bonus eligibility may be included, but not actual compensation amounts.

Much of this information is usually found in the company's payroll system or in the human resource information system (HRIS). Hence the data may be extracted from existing files for purposes of management succession and development planning. For information that is not currently included in the system, files can be expanded to include the desired data (e.g., work history beyond the most recent five or ten years, significant other work experience, training programs attended).

Information provided by the individuals may also be included. This input is based on the most recent career discussion (date indicated). A chemicals company, for example, includes factors that may limit an employee's mobility, such as health, family circumstances, or spouse's employment/occupation. IBM includes the employee's expressed preference for future assignments and locations, including interest in staff/line positions in other IBM locations and divisions.

For career development, as discussed in Chapter 8, this inventory of information may be maintained on the HRIS. However, for succession planning, confidential information is included which most companies prefer to maintain separately. In fact, legal counsel often advises that management succession and development information and plans be considered privileged company information—like strategic plans—and hence not be included in the normal "personnel files." This also protects the information from inappropriate access and interpretation (avoiding litigation over management employment issues).

Accordingly, companies typically establish separate systems, maintained on personal computers. Numerous commercial products are available. One such system, SUCCESSION PLUS⁽™⁾, is a data-base management system tailored specifically to support succession and development planning as discussed in this chapter. The basic information available in a payroll system or HRIS may be downloaded electronically into the succession planning system and updated in the same way as desired. All other data are entered directly at the level where plans are formulated (e.g., divisions), using on-screen formats. The software system provides all the necessary reports for management review, plus a capability for creating any special reports desired. The information on the system may be consolidated, or "rolled up," to provide integrated plans for larger organizational entities or for corporate review.

Adequacy of Talent

The process requires that the talent be within the organization, ready to be developed and deployed against future needs. This means that management should evaluate the quality of the talent in the inventory relative to the talent available outside the organization.

One way to do this is to regularly examine the quality of the company's talent and compare it with that of competitors and with the talent available in the open market. Several ways that companies do this were described by Jim Peters, a succession planning consultant:

- Competitive benchmarking of talent: performing competitive benchmarking activities to identify the best-in-class companies for a specific type of talent
- Continuous improvement of talent: the consistent and sustained practice of identifying the bottom performing portion of a talent pool, outplacing them, and then replacing them through external sources
- Talent parade: an informal process of identifying, evaluating, and reviewing talent from outside the organization for some unknown or contingent future need (a networking strategy)
- Open slating: a formal process, typically using external search consultants, to identify and evaluate members of a given function or industry group in anticipation of a given company talent need

Such practices, while not common, represent ways to "open up" the organization to a wider comparison and, possibly, to higher standards (Peters, 1990).

While a company can develop its talent, it needs to ensure the selection and progression of people with the right talents—new managers, high potentials, as well as external hires—who have the interest, willingness, and ability to learn and grow, and who *also* have the basic intellectual capacity to do so effectively.

EVALUATING CAPABILITIES AND DEVELOPMENT NEEDS

The next element of the process is the evaluation of each individual's capabilities and development needs. This has several facets:

- The identification of possible future assignments (target positions) and the prospective timing (immediate, ready in one to three years, or three to five years)
- Primary strengths (abilities or skills that the person has demonstrated through his or her performance)
- Primary development needs (areas for improvement, related to the company's management factors or dimensions and the specific requirements of the target positions)

Development needs relating to the current assignment may be included, but are typically addressed in the context of the management performance appraisal. As noted, overall current performance level is usually considered in the evaluation process, as an indicator of future strengths and development needs.

Conducting Evaluations

Most evaluation (and feedback) to managers on their development is done by their immediate supervisor. ("In traditional practice, the boss evaluates and tells the subordinate the results.") In a constructive mode, the two discuss and consider the results and come to agreement on an evaluation and plan for action.

Most evaluation also tends to be conducted in the context of the performance appraisal (discussed in Chapter 10). As a result, current performance issues and even compensation issues complicate and overshadow the discussion. The evaluation of development needs should examine the individual's capabilities relative to *future* performance demands.

The most commonly applied techniques in evaluating the development needs and potential of management candidates involve consideration of individual qualities and circumstances. A specific position is usually considered as a prospective assignment for an individual, the capabilities of the individual for this assignment are considered relative to the position requirements, and the net gap is defined. If the gap is not too great, developmental actions may be taken to make the candidate better qualified.

Flexibly applied, assessments may differ from candidate to candidate. In the process, a manager typically considers the key elements: target assignments, capabilities represented in demonstrated past performance, and specific development needs. Documentation may be prepared and maintained in support of the assessment, but the judgments are inherently clinical.

The quality of managerial assessment is usually monitored, and enhanced, through a second-level review. The individual's second-level manager reviews the evaluation and raises questions, different views, or comments. This should lead to discussion between the managers, culminating in a shared view of development needs.

Of course, all the potential biases and difficulties of any top-down management appraisal are inherent in this process. Furthermore, the quality of appraisals is limited by a manager's knowledge of the requirements of other positions, including those outside the area or at a higher level.

360-Degree Evaluation and Feedback

Higher-level managers certainly have a major say in the evaluation, development, and succession of individuals. However, there is benefit in obtaining evaluations from others as well, including the individual's manager and other members of the work team: subordinates or other managers who are peers (who work with the person on a daily basis). Also, customers or clients can provide valuable inputs, as can other colleagues in the organization at the same level. As noted above, the person's second-level manager provides a tempering viewpoint in evaluation and a wider perspective of promotability options. Other higher-level managers may also have useful inputs based on their interaction with the manager in the course of their work.

In conducting downward evaluations, many managers solicit inputs from a variety of sources. However, the idea of 360-degree evaluation is that inputs from all of these sources are solicited in a rather formal way. This enhances the quality and usefulness of the evaluation and feedback for an individual manager. Robert Eichinger, a proponent of the technique, noted that "executive growth is in part due to receiving on-target, accurate, comprehensive, timely, and actionable feedback continuously throughout their careers and specifically at critical junctures of change and opportunity."

Individuals behave differently with different people; hence each evaluator has a different perspective of a manager's capabilities. Also, each source brings the benefit of a somewhat different vantage point—looking at different facets of a manager's capabilities.

The technique has a particular benefit over a manager's appraisal in that it fosters a developmental climate. Individuals are encouraged to solicit feedback and to reconcile different inputs as a basis for action. Generally, people like feedback; they don't particularly like evaluations. The use of feedback lowers defensiveness and allows the individual to "take charge" of the evaluation process, or at least participate in the development of evaluation results.

Any effort to solicit inputs on a 360-degree basis enhances managerial evaluations. Today, however, the process may be implemented formally, using questionnaires. Several excellent questionnaires are available commercially, including Benchmarks^sm, developed by the Center for Creative Leadership (CCL) using its sixteen research-based dimensions. Of course, the ideal approach is to use dimensions based on an effective manager model developed within a company as the basis for evaluation.

Self-Assessment

Asking individual managers to rate their own capabilities against established criteria and to identify development needs is valuable and yet widely neglected. For decades, we have said that responsibility for development rests with the individuals and that feedback from others is useful only if individuals accept it.

In a 360-degree evaluation, the individual is an active participant. In management evaluations, the individual may or may not be active, depending on the climate set by the appraising manager. Too often we think of evaluation as a passive experience for the individual, when it should not be at all. Hence companies have sought ways to involve the manager actively in the evaluation process. CCL's Benchmarks was originally developed as a self-assessment technique.

Syntex, a health care company with more than 1,000 managers worldwide, adopted a self-assessment process. Using CCL research results, the company developed a "Leadership Template." The tool involves two sets of cards, one listing thirty-four leadership qualities and the other listing ten factors that may lead to career derailment. Managers are asked to pick their greatest strengths as well as their possible derailment factors. Using a card sort technique, they are then asked to rank the cards in a forced distribution. "It forced me to acknowledge both my strengths and weaknesses," said one manager. "It helped focus attention on the few most important areas for development" (Fairhead & Hudson, 1989).

Psychological Assessment Techniques

Such an assessment procedure is troublesome to those who prefer a more controlled, systematic, or even mechanical approach. Some assessment specialists, particularly measurement psychologists, seek predictive tests and interviewing formats that distinguish high-talent managerial candidates from those less likely to succeed (Ghiselli, 1971; Guion, 1965). Mechanical approaches require the application of decision rules developed through selection validation studies; these rules may be applied to the information collected by trained individuals. This type of procedure reduces the subjective element in selection decisions. Unfortunately for advocates of such systems, the assessment task has been complicated (in most instances) by so much variation in the facts to be considered that judgment (clinical judgment) seems to be inevitably required.

Assessment inputs are also frequently provided by personnel staff specialists or by external assessors such as managerial psychologists. At best, one-on-one psychological testing can "predict performance in at least 85% of the cases." At the very least, it provides helpful input to managers in their development planning: testing can shed light on such questions as the person's overall intellectual ability (of which IQ is a part), basic skills (such as reading and math or more advanced technical skills), interests and inclinations (preferences for work variety or stability, technical or nontechnical work, etc.), and personality characteristics (e.g., reaction to pressure, flexibility, reaction to uncontrollable events) (Sahl, 1990).

One variation on psychological testing is the assessment center. Each manager participating in an assessment center is observed and evaluated by a team of managers (or other assessors). Candidates go through a series of exercises and in-depth interviews, as well as team projects, as a basis for demonstrating their managerial ability and potential. The team's evaluation results in a written assessment report on each candidate, including numerical ratings on a series of behavioral dimensions. The report is then used as an input to succession planning and management development decisions (Bray, 1976; Finkel, 1976; Moses & Byham, 1977). Assessment centers have been used in many companies, particularly for evaluating large numbers of individuals for common job categories (e.g., sales management).

Perhaps the most noteworthy application was at American Telephone and Telegraph, where a program was conducted for more than twenty-five years. This "management progress study" tracked the career progress of 274 employees who went through an assessment center program (Bray, Campbell, & Grant, 1974; Campbell, 1970). With the breakup of AT&T and the resulting changes in AT&T's management requirements, however, the process was discontinued.

An aim of this program and of some others is to determine predictive patterns that may suggest a valid mechanical process for assessing managerial potential. Bray has called the assessment center "the most elaborate, most expensive assessment method known to man" (Bray, 1976). At the same time, assessment centers remain highly clinical and subjective, relying on the judgments of a team of observers.

In a practical way, management resource reviews provide a check on objectivity in evaluation. In the process of reviewing the performance, career progress, and capabilities of identified high-talent employees, managers discuss specific individual qualities and developmental needs. At a minimum, these reviews provide a useful comparison of the managers' assessments. In some instances, the group may get deeply involved in judging the capabilities and development needs of individual succession candidates.

Assessments are most useful when applied to the planning of individual development activities and to decisions regarding succession prospects. They are most valuable, then, when they are keyed to specific managerial position requirements, rather than broad managerial qualities. Companies are eager to identify high-talent employees early and accurately, so that training and development efforts may be wisely invested.

Objectivity in assessing talent is encouraged in several ways. Companies use multiple assessment tools, and use them over a period of years. On-the-job performance continues to be a primary indicator of future performance of managers and can be directly observed or measured against objectives or standards (see Chapter 10). Also, the collection of assessments of individuals from more than one appraiser (as through 360-degree evaluation) is helpful. Training and the monitoring of assessment practices and results are, of course, basic ways of strengthening the assessment processes.

PLANNING DEVELOPMENT ACTIONS

The payoff of planning is assurance that the most capable managers are considered to fill key managerial positions. But more than that, planning directs training and development activities toward the specific needs for improving capabilities.

For each individual, specific development actions should be planned in response to the identified development needs. From a process perspective, the development action plans are typically integrated with the evaluation, as a single document or record. Managers often need assistance from staff or reference materials, however, in defining implementable development activities.

Developmental Experiences

Various approaches are used to develop managers. Management development occurs on the job, of course, but also in programs off the job, both in-company and external. Challenging job responsibilities—combined with coaching and performance appraisal and feedback—are a potent development tool and the focus of basic management development. Rotational assignments, special assignments, task force assignments, and transfers across functional or unit lines all provide additional developmental experiences. Off-the-job training and development resources include courses, seminars, professional meetings and conferences, interaction with consultants and other external representatives, management meetings, and committee or task force assignments (see Chapter 8).

Some examples of developmental activities drawn from or based upon company experience and research, are described in Exhibit 9-6. As an outgrowth of the CCL research, Mike Lombardo and Bob Eichinger identified eighty-eight assignments for developing managers "in place." Most of the experiences described in their study may be provided, to an extent, on the job. Others involve small strategic assignments or projects, coursework and coaching assignments (either for self or for others), and activities away from work (e.g., activities in professional, volunteer, community, or charitable organizations) (Lombardo and Eichinger, 1989).

These experiences include some which require changes in assignments and some that require special initiatives in the current assignment. In the slower-growth company environment of the 1990s and beyond, more emphasis will necessarily be placed on development within current assignments. When promotions or reassignments are made, they should be carefully planned to provide individuals with the development experiences they need, as well as to simply meet management's near-term staffing needs (Lindsey, Homes, & McCall, 1987).

In a 1984 survey by The Conference Board, 139 companies reporting generally successful results in developing executives were found to use these approaches (percentage of companies responding):

- Planned on-the-job development* (91%)
- Processes for guiding individual development* (86%)
- Planned use of in-house educational programs (80%)
- Planned changes in organization, compensation, or other management systems* (76%)

EXHIBIT 9-6 DEVELOPMENTAL EXPERIENCES

Work for the "Right" Boss

Having the individual report to a manager who can act as an advisor and who can develop specific skills in that individual. Normally, the "boss" has a reputation of excellence in the area in which the individual is to be developed. Alternatively, the individual could be assigned a mentor who would be responsible for developing required skills in that individual (although reporting relationships would not change).

Manage Difficult Subordinates

Ask the individual to manage a group of subordinates who are extraordinary. Such subordinates would include those who are especially bright, technically advanced, and extremely intelligent. Difficult subordinates may also include problem performers, those with high potential but low actual performance, and employees with attitude problems.

Take on a Larger-Scope Assignment

Placing an individual in a position that requires managing an increased amount of resources, including personnel, dollars, accounts, etc. Normally such a position is at a level above the employee's current position. Alternatively, the scope of the employee's current position could be increased by adding responsibilities and subordinates.

Switch Between Line and Staff

A switch either from a line management position to a staff job or from a staff job to a line management position. In many organizations, staff positions exist at the divisional level as well as at the corporate level.

Tackle a Difficult Problem

This activity normally involves analyzing a significant business problem, creating possible solutions, assessing or evaluating those solutions, and recommending a course of action. A definition of the resources needed to address the problem or to implement a solution is sometimes included.

Start Something from Scratch

Any effort that creates a plan of action and starts up a new function, product, service, or organization unit. Such start-from-scratch efforts usually entail planning, design and/or development, creation of recommendations, and execution.

Participate in or Lead a Task Force

Any group that is created to investigate options, analyze potential approaches, and/or make recommendations to management on particular courses of action. Task forces can be formed to address issues within or across departments.

Source: Adapted with permission from Michael M. Lombardo May, 1985, "Five Challenging Assignments," *Issues & Observations* (Greensboro, N.C.: Center for Creative Leadership, 1989).

- Planned use of outside education programs (71%)
- Planned changes in individual job assignments* (57%)

A smaller sample (21) of companies reporting generally unsuccessful results used the same approaches, but significantly less than those noted with an asterisk above. This suggests that balance is needed and that development experiences more closely aligned to the job are more potent (Shaeffer, 1984).

What makes an experience developmental? An experience should involve change and challenge. A developmental experience may provide the chance for success or failure (and an evident outcome); may require individual "take charge" leadership; may involve working with new people or a lot of people; may create additional personal pressure; and may require influencing people, activities, and factors without direct authority or control. It could involve high variety, be closely watched by others whose opinions count, require building a team or something from scratch, and provide a strategic or intellectual challenge (Lombardo and Eichinger, 1989).

Many managers find it more difficult to define appropriate development experiences for individuals than to identify development needs. Accordingly, some companies have developed reference guides to help managers consider alternative development activities. The pharmaceutical company that uses the management dimensions presented in Exhibit 9-4 has developed such a guide. For each management dimension, a variety of possible developmental activities are listed and described. In addition to training programs and suggested readings, activities representing different kinds of development experiences are included (Bechet and Brand, 1991).

Each developmental activity should have learning objectives. A learning objective describes the specific skill or ability that is to be developed through an experience, expressed in behavioral terms. The following are examples of learning objectives included in the guide:

All about the business: a basic knowledge of the business, including its goals, objectives, and operations; the ability to take a "bottom line" orientation and think within a business perspective

Basic management values: being able to understand, communicate, and demonstrate in action the basic management values of the organization; the ability to understand and work within the culture of the organization; the ability to develop and adopt a management style that is consistent with the overall values of the organization

Being tough when necessary: the ability to make difficult decisions and live with their consequences; the ability to make difficult judgments, especially those that may negatively impact an individual or unit; the ability to assess employee capabilities fairly and honestly and deliver candid feedback when required; the ability to develop and take disciplinary action when necessary

Building and using structure and control systems: developing and utilizing budgets, financial control systems, production control systems, organization charts and systems, and other structured methods for allocating and controlling resources; the ability to identify and resolve variances between actual and planned performance

Coping with ambiguity: the ability to cope with and work within situations and scenarios that are not well defined; dealing successfully with contingencies and "what if" analyses; the ability to plan courses of action even when outcomes are undefined or uncertain; the ability to structure and analyze problems for which the correct answer is not clear

Dealing with executives: the ability to relate to, interact with, and communicate with executives and others in an organization who are above one's own level; the ability to command and keep the confidence and respect of executives; the ability to present oneself in a businesslike manner

Handling political situations: being politically astute; the ability to anticipate and resolve conflicts; knowing when to "fight" actively in support of an effort and when to yield to pressure from others; effectively creating and using political networks and alliances within an organization in order to meet objectives; the ability to devise "win-win" solutions to difficult problems

Understanding the perspectives of others: the ability to draw out, listen to, and comprehend the viewpoints of others (both inside and outside the organization); the ability to hear what is being said without screening messages through personal experience

Such learning objectives help clarify for individuals what they are expected to gain from a developmental experience. Also, their managers may better evaluate the benefits of the experience (Bechet, 1991; Lombardo and Eichinger, 1989).

Management Training and Education

If on-the-job experience is so great, what do managers gain from courses or seminars? Curiously, it isn't all what it seems. The major benefits of training and education are not what's being "taught," but what's "learned." With regard to program content, managers learn what they do and don't know, how valued it is and why, some new terms and concepts, their own capabilities, and insights on how others apply it. With regard to process and interaction, managers compare notes with others on where they stand, gain and give feedback, clarify values and feelings, and learn how interested they are in learning more about the subject.

Some companies seem to regard training as a reward for performance or service. Attendance at programs is a perquisite or, at worst, a relief from routine. In some organizations, individuals seem to self-select for programs, with some attending many and others attending none. Participation in programs also builds confidence, according to one study. "Many executives reported to us that in coursework they discovered that they were as good as the next person, that they had unique talents to offer, and that their abilities were up to the task at hand. This boost to their self-esteem seemed to be the key lesson of experience from coursework, far outweighing whatever they learned from the content of the course," (McCall, Lombardo, and Morrison, 1988).

Companies are tailoring executive education to make it relevant to needs (Bolt, 1985). For example, TRW's two-week Advanced Management Program for division vice presidents focuses on the fit between business strategy and the organization. The first week concentrates on leadership and organization issues through the case study method. Then, during the three-month period before the second week of the program, participants examine their own division's structure, systems, and culture. They also prepare an Executive Development Profile on themselves, using a 360-degree evaluation of their leadership and management skills. In the second week, they build an agenda for change. Managers learn a lot about themselves and about their divisions, but also come away with an action plan.

To bridge the gap between the classroom and the job, General Electric uses action learning. Its business management course at Crotonville takes managers out of their traditional environments, teams them with peers, and challenges these groups to solve vexing problems facing GE businesses. Faculty help managers prepare for the project and evaluate the result; however, during the project, they're largely on their own. "We went to the businesses, interviewed the key players, developed real solutions, presented them, and got honest feedback. And along the way, our groups became teams." The benefits to GE go beyond the lessons learned; one group found the potential for $200 million in additional annual sales (Tichy & Charan, 1989).

The use of formal training and development programs for managers should be planned on the basis of organizational patterns and needs, focusing ultimately on each individual management candidate's strengths and weaknesses. Executive development programs no longer need to be created and individuals "sent." Rather, training and development activities may be specifically tailored to individual needs. Development planning provides the specific, evaluation-based process for determining these needs and plans, linked with realistic expectations of future organizational changes and managerial staffing requirements.

Guidelines for individual participation in programs usually call for a review of the particular programs in terms of their content, the level and representative mix of participants, and the reputation of the sponsoring organization. Checking word-of-mouth opinions of particular programs is helpful, as is a debriefing of executives after they have attended them. It is impractical to attempt to measure a participant's learning, but directed questioning may be able to sense more than merely attitudes. Participation in developmental programs is costly and should be viewed as an investment, with the same dollars-and-cents evaluation as every other corporate expenditure.

To make suitable selections, many companies use guides which describe the university executive development programs and highlight the subject areas covered. Such descriptions are prepared by the training and development staff or are taken from published sources. Some companies also provide guidelines for the types of courses or programs that are suited to different stages of managerial careers. In addition, human resource or executive resource staff may provide information on alternatives and guide choices.

In a company, it is important to design training and development programs in relation to development criteria—so that they will be in tune with each other. Too often, training and development programs are based on needs assessments and surveys of managers largely independent of management succession planning.

RESPONSIBILITY FOR DEVELOPING MANAGERS

Each manager in an organization should be responsible for the development of talent in his or her organization. While managers should not select or groom their own successors, they have a responsibility, or "stewardship," for talent. In a small organization, the responsibility is obvious and is shared by the senior managers. In a larger organization, the responsibilities need to be clarified and assigned by level, function, or unit.

As a practical matter, few managers can ably evaluate and plan for more than fifty individuals. In some companies, CEOs have attempted to review and influence development plans for several hundred managers and candidates; however, they rarely know enough about many of the individuals to add much value to the discussion and sometimes even impede development of talented candidates.

If an organization assigns responsibility for management development and succession at its various levels and units, a network of management inputs, planning, and activities needs to be established. Most companies seek to formalize the process of planning, reviewing, and implementing succession and development plans. The human resource staff may support these efforts, but the responsibility rests with managers.

Effective implementation of these plans requires that managers be held responsible for the completion of each activity. The individual should commit to the action plans. The immediate manager should commit to the action plans and set a specific date for completion. If resources are required, they should be noted. Also, the plan should ask:

- How will we know that the need has been addressed?
- How will we know how well the need has been addressed?

The quality of the answer is less important than having an answer. The purpose is to encourage the individual candidate and the manager to focus on achievement of specific goals.

Many companies actually collect these commitments and report back to managers on progress through a tracking system. The SUCCESSION PLUS(™) system mentioned previously automatically reports to managers on the status of the various development action plans they committed to.

It is important that senior managers hold managers accountable for actually acting on these plans, and reward or recognize those who are most effective. Budgets for education and training, decisions to reassign or relocate talent for development purposes, and on-the-job developmental experiences need to be established as clear management commitments.

Effectiveness in developing management talent is part of regular management performance. Managers' performance in this regard may affect their performance evaluations and compensation opportunities. In many companies, the development of subordinate managers is a factor considered in determining incentive compensation (bonus) awards. The emphasis given management development has been as much as 25% of the weight. If managers neglect this responsibility, their own future opportunities may be influenced adversely.

Finally, staff involvement helps ensure implementation of plans. Some staff support actually helps to get things done—arranging developmental experiences, designing and providing a management education program, etc. In a consulting role, however, staff may provide "divine intervention" as they assist managers in matching candidates to the right jobs, coach managers on key development problems, etc.

Shared Responsibilities

Review of succession plans and individual development plans emphasizes management responsibility and also establishes shared responsibilities, where appropriate and necessary. Whether at a local unit level, divisional or group level, or corporate management level, the discussion that occurs in reviews allows sharing, sifting, challenging, and interpreting of the data on needs and available talent.

Each organizational division has responsibility for its own employees (particularly in a decentralized management organization). But at some level, to be determined by management, there should be coordination among managers for management development activities. Responsibilities of divisional management include the use of procedures for recruiting, selection, placement, appraisal, and development of their employees either as prescribed by the company or as deemed appropriate to the business. Divisions are expected to analyze their own human resource needs, constraints, and opportunities as part of their business planning activity and to identify development actions planned for key individuals as part of these plans.

Succession and development planning is, therefore, a process that may be applied at any level of an organization. Plants or office units within a division may conduct planning, but the division (or other integrative organizational level) may act to pull these plans together and broaden them. Reassignments of high-talent individuals may cross unit lines, contradicting the more restrictive plans formed (whether formally or informally) by particular unit managers.

A similar integration occurs at the corporate level of an organization; here the process works best. Senior corporate management believes that there are needs of a corporate nature, warranting involvement of senior executives and senior divisional executives in the succession planning for "corporate positions." Typically, the chief executive officer and the president assume responsibility for management succession and development for division manager positions, for positions reporting directly to division managers (at least in larger

---

EXHIBIT 9-7 MANAGEMENT TALENT POOLS

CEO

Division Heads

Direct Reports

Next-Level Managers

---

divisions), and for other positions selected for organizational or business reasons.

There is a pool of talent identified as "corporate property," that is, individuals whose careers should be managed to serve the total corporation's needs, not merely those of a particular business unit. These individuals (often representing 1% or more of the salaried employees) are to be reviewed and discussed by a corporate-level interdivisional committee. Their job assignments are to be planned at this level, and not by immediate unit management alone.

This notion of "corporate talent" and "corporate positions" is a troublesome one for companies that merely plan for replacements. Yet it is a crucial response to the obstacles blocking the development of broadly experienced managerial talent. Exhibit 9-7 illustrates the way these levels of responsibility should overlap and shows the focus of responsibilities at each level.

In the succession and development process, the role of the human resource staff is to serve as a resource for the divisions and corporate management and to assist in their succession planning and in the implementation of developmental actions. Staff professionals may get directly into the act by facilitating assignments and participation by managers in developmental experiences or training programs. HR staff may develop, implement, and monitor the processes necessary for succession planning and may also be responsible for arranging interdivisional transfers in accordance with succession plans and corporate policies.

SUCCESSION REVIEW MEETINGS

The key to implementing the process is direct involvement by senior managers in reviewing the results as they unfold. Most companies conduct a review of succession and development plans at least annually. Some conduct quarterly reviews, often in conjunction with strategic plan review meetings.

When senior managers in a company meet to review succession and development plans, they:

• Identify critical management resource issues impacting on and resulting from business plans (e.g., organization changes, acquisitions, divestitures, new priorities)

• Review and discuss the availability of successors identified for key management positions (including near-term staffing needs requiring senior management approval for appointment)

• Review and discuss the development plans and the progress of individuals considered to be succession candidates for these key positions

• Specifically review the availability and progress of women and minorities who are candidates or who have management potential

• Consider ways to improve the process for identifying, evaluating, and developing high-potential talent as a corporatewide management talent pool

• Understand and support the business unit management resource plans and development activities, ensuring that they are adequate to meet business needs and priorities, and evaluate the results of these programs against corporate standards

• Facilitate movement across the organization, and discuss actions required on important management resource issues or themes of companywide concern

Level-by-Level Reviews

At the corporate level, the focus of discussion is on corporate needs and strategies, whereas in divisions it is on the resource requirements and action plans. In the corporate review, management considers changes in policies guiding management development as well as standards for evaluating candidates. Requirements for developing candidates for key corporate positions would be clarified as a basis for facilitating developmental assignments across divisions and functional lines.

The succession reviews conducted at the divisional and corporate levels remind managers to look at managerial development as a business need. A steel company executive noted that, as a result, "key openings should not be filled until consideration is given to all qualified people in the corporation, thus increasing the lateral movement of personnel and widening their experience. In the long run, this will provide more people in management who are capable of taking the broad view. To the individual, the approach provides challenging opportunity; to top management, it insures an increasing number of personnel alternatives—the key to change and progress."

There is an added benefit for managers in reviewing succession and development plans together: it is a developmental experience for those participating. One company president noted, "As we look ahead, I expect the work of the reviews to stimulate and encourage even more thought and effort at all levels, not merely to develop managers but to build a management that is resourceful and adaptable to change.'' If changing management development practices is so difficult, maybe that is a good place to influence management attitudes toward change, to help managers accept new ways of managing, and to work as part of a larger corporate management team.

The focus of the reviews and discussions is upon change. What organizational changes, new management positions, or changes in management positions are planned? The scope of the process typically covers no more than 30 to 50 key executive positions and 100 to 150 candidates at each level, although this may vary with the size of the organization. Are there any losses of key people (retirements, terminations) that have succession planning implications? What developmental assignments (transfers or promotions), including moves across lines, are proposed? Such changes may surface through review of divisional succession plans as well as through direct consideration of the corporate management structure. Succession planning is not a conceptual or academic exercise; it is an action-oriented management tool.

Also in the discussions, management may consider broad human resource needs indicated in the plans. Supply-demand imbalances, apparent common training needs, significant needs for external recruiting, patterns in performance appraisal results, affirmative action plan shortfalls, and other common patterns may indicate need for corporate actions or policies. The committee, then, may help be a sensor and guide for corporatewide human resource policies and practices. Management succession is a logical focus, but the development actions provide the results.

Many companies also conduct reviews for primary functions, across organizational units. Finance, information systems, and human resources are typically decentralized staff functions. Managers and professionals are assigned to the various organizational units, either on a solid- or dotted-line basis. The senior corporate functional executive usually feels responsible for the development and succession of talent across the function, but often lacks direct control over all staffing because of the decentralized structure. A succession and development review for each function provides the means for examining the talent across the company, prospective reassignments of functional talent, and development plans for individuals.

In some companies, these functional reviews are conducted as part of the overall succession reviews, providing an integrative perspective for the function across the company. In this way, the line managers whom these staff serve continue to play a direct role in the matrix management of the functional talent.

SUMMARY

Many thousands of hours of management time are devoted each year to the meticulous review of current managers' strengths and weaknesses, succession coverage for key management positions, and development action plans. It is a process that requires managers to step back and consider the development of management talent, long acknowledged to be a fundamental management responsibility. It is also a process that helps managers at successive levels of a company consider the depth and readiness of individuals to take on new responsibilities.

In spite of their efforts and good intentions, many managers find that the potential benefits of the process are not always realized. They find that:

• They recruit externally too often, frequently lack enough candidate choices for key assignments, have too many executives who are plateaued and nonpromotable, and lose too many talented managers to other companies.

• In spite of many efforts to improve them, development plans are pathetic; and not many plans are implemented.

• Managers shy away from candid discussions with subordinates about needed development.

• Progress is too slow for moving women and minorities into management positions.

In a flexible organization, such concerns are accentuated. Changes are rapid, needs are urgent, and high-talent managers are restless and eager to progress. Furthermore, managers feel that they have fewer opportunities to develop their succession candidates, as management positions and levels are fewer and attrition is low. Positions change and requirements change, but the need for development of capabilities, focused on the changing demands on managers, is high.

The basic process of management succession and development planning described in this chapter is being effectively applied by many companies. With the proper investment of time and effort, it yields high results. In the 1990s, I believe that companies are seeking, more than ever, to develop the managers they need to implement challenging business strategies—to be effective strategy implementers.

To align management development with strategy, a company needs to define the "manager of the future"—to establish the dimensions which are used for assessment, development planning, job assignment, and development activities. Furthermore, the application of the process needs to mesh with the way the company intends to manage in the future. Left to their own devices, few managers would probably do succession and development planning for others; hence it needs to be driven by senior management—used as a lever for achieving desired strategic change.

PART FOUR

MANAGING
PERFORMANCE

ENABLING HIGH PERFORMANCE

We are all born with intrinsic motivation, self-esteem, dignity, an eagerness to learn. Our present system of management crushes that all out.

W. Edwards Deming

Implementation of business strategies requires that employees be given the guidance, support, authority, and resources needed to accomplish action plans and performance objectives. Yet for many organizations, there is a tremendous gap between reality and the vision of the high-performance, high-commitment organization.

People in an organization are not often extraordinary in their talents. The purpose of an organization, observed Peter Drucker, is to "enable common men to do uncommon things." It is a task of management to organize, motivate, equip, and direct rather ordinary people to perform at their highest possible levels.

In the flexible organization—where goals, circumstances, organizational structure, staffing, and activities are constantly changing—managers play an especially important role in helping employees understand what is expected of them (establishing performance objectives), helping them meet these expectations successfully, evaluating performance and providing feedback, and providing meaningful recognition and rewards. These are integral elements of the overall framework for human resource strategy presented in Chapter 1 (Exhibit 1-1).

Any one of these factors may be a weak link, contributing to suboptimal organizational performance. A lack of clear objectives or expectations—or objectives that are not linked directly to relevant business objectives and plans—creates problems at the outset. As discussed in this chapter, managers may not be successful in enabling employees to perform effectively. Evaluation of performance as well as employee feedback may be lacking, even with a formal appraisal system. Finally, rewards and recognitions may not be sufficient or effective.

The factors also need to relate to each other and support each other. Where rewards are not closely related to the objectives or expectations of performance, they lack relevance in the cycle. Feedback and measures, too, need to be aligned with the objectives (even though objectives may change under fluid circumstances) and with rewards. When they work together, they provide a single, focused context for behavior.

As a result, the cycle can be a powerfully positive process, resulting in continual improvement of performance. The self-reinforcing process is inherent in every quality improvement process—setting new objectives or standards, achieving them, measuring them, and rewarding them. Or it can be a negative cycle, when objectives are poorly defined, support and feedback are lacking, and rewards are insufficient or irrelevant, successively reducing the likelihood of effective performance.

This chapter focuses on the ways in which managers can create conditions supporting effective employee performance. The next two chapters focus on the ways in which managers evaluate, reward, and recognize performance. Companies typically give greater attention to the latter two aspects of performance management, because they are usually institutionalized through systems and procedures.

Managers have increasingly recognized the need to enable employees to perform effectively, as well as the need to measure and reward performance. This requires direct, personal involvement by managers in creating and sustaining effective work design, empowering employees to act, providing the resources needed, and coaching employees.

Three key ways in which managers enable employees to perform effectively are discussed:

- How managers and employees design work for the highest motivation and utilization of talent
- How managers empower employees to manage their performance in support of business objectives
- How managers personally coach and support employees in managing their performance

The issue for management is not so much one of techniques for optimum performance, for many are available. It is, rather, a planning issue: What should be done and why?

An underlying focus in enabling performance is the management of quality. A company prospers by satisfying the needs of its customers, and thereby the needs of its shareholders, employees, and other stakeholders. Competitive effectiveness requires that management continually seek opportunities to improve individual, team, and organizational performance.

BEHAVIOR AND PERFORMANCE

Underlying the way we manage performance are certain assumptions about employee behavior, or "motivation." From a commonsense viewpoint, job

EXHIBIT 10-1 A BEHAVIORAL VIEW OF PERFORMANCE

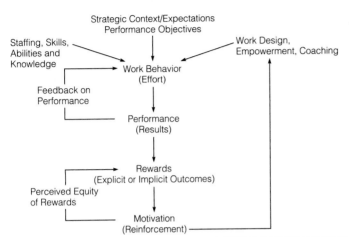

performance is obviously affected by how people respond to conditions influencing their work.

Conditions may be a constraint, in that strong employee dissatisfaction with the work or working conditions may impede performance. Hence we often concentrate on exceptions to performance—performance problems or deficiencies—rather than on the positive effects of increased satisfaction. In managerial, professional, and technical positions, signs of employee dissatisfaction—expressed in the form of turnover, absenteeism, and verbalized attitudes—are often more visible than performance problems. We assume, also, that satisfaction is a key factor in motivation. If motivated, most high-talent individuals have the capabilities necessary, so it is largely a matter of putting in the effort.

However, research studies over the years have shown little relationship between measures of job satisfaction and performance outputs. Highly satisfied workers may be poor performers; highly dissatisfied workers may be good performers. The relationship among these variables is compounded by a number of other variables.

Exhibit 10-1 identifies the primary determinants of individual behavior, performance, and motivation. The model is adapted from performance-motivation models developed by researchers (Moorhead & Griffin, 1989).

Certain variables which influence performance are controllable by management: work design (the tasks or activities to be performed, job content), organizational context (e.g., supervisory style, organization of the work, physical working conditions, commutation, hours of work, etc.), and performance objectives (presumably related to organizational objectives). All have a direct effect on the extent and nature of an individual's efforts devoted to a job.

Individual competence is also an important variable. Hard-working individuals without the necessary skills, abilities, or knowledge are not likely to achieve much on their jobs. Also, effort is a prerequisite for performance, which we may define as the accomplishment of certain defined tasks or objectives. Performance is a function of both effort and abilities (and there may be some trade-offs, as one compensates for the other).

Performance results in outcomes—productivity for the organization and personal rewards in the form of pay, benefits, job security, recognition from coworkers and superiors, and promotional opportunities for individual employees. Employees often measure their job satisfaction largely in terms of these rewards, which are the most tangible ones received from the job. Individuals may gain job satisfaction from a personal sense of accomplishment through work and also from feedback about their performance.

If performance is a function of effort and competence, it is important that the individuals believe that they are able to perform at the desired level (Nadler & Lawler, 1971). Effort depends on:

- Positive or negative feelings about the outcomes or rewards associated with performance
- Expectancy that effort will result in accomplishment of defined tasks
- Expectancy that accomplishment will obtain or avoid certain outcomes or rewards

This "expectancy theory" of performance motivation says that employees' perceptions and values are important determinants of the effort they will expend.

Motivation is merely the reinforcement of a positive effort-performance-rewards experience. Future effort and behavior are influenced by past outcomes. Motivation itself is meaningful only as a summary factor—"a label for the determinants of the choice to initiate effort on a certain task, the choice to expend a certain amount of effort, and the choice to persist in expending effort over a period of time" (Campbell & Pritchard, 1976). Hence the loop is closed.

WORK DESIGN

The objectives or goals of work are important, but the actual tasks undertaken by individuals are also important for effective performance. It is not enough to set targets for desired results and assume that these justify the means. The means, or activities, and the "how" of a job are equally important. The activities performed by individuals are identifiable, tangible, and controllable. An employee's most fundamental question is "What is my job?"

Accordingly, it is important for managers to help employees understand and define the structure and content of their work activities. How employees spend their time, what tasks are important enough to receive priority attention, which activities they consider primary sources of job satisfaction, and which activities help prepare individuals for future tasks and job assignments are all pertinent issues.

Job Design

Over the years, considerable research has been focused on job design and its potential contribution to enhanced employee motivation and performance (Berlinger, Glick, & Rodgers, 1988). The primary techniques involve changing the characteristics of tasks on the job. However, improvements in performance have been achieved in some instances by merely changing employees' *perceptions* of the work and thus their attitudes toward work and work relationships.

Jobs are formally defined in job descriptions. But these do not necessarily tell what a person *actually* does on a job. Managers think they know what their subordinates do, but when confronted with data, they are often surprised to find that their assumptions do not fit with reality. Managerial, professional, and technical employees have considerable influence over the actual activities they perform on their jobs, as long as the goals or objectives (or standards of performance) are satisfied. Thus there is often no established, single definition of the jobs—no agreement between the individuals and their managers about what the job involves. Regardless of how formal job descriptions are used, managers and employees need to develop a shared understanding of job activities as they evolve and change.

A large commercial bank, for example, conducted a study of the activities of its lending officers. Assigned to branch offices around the world, these individuals performed their jobs as they felt appropriate to achieve their targeted results. Through an analysis of the ways they reported they spent their time on their jobs, however, efforts were redirected toward those activities that made the greatest contribution to branch objectives (for example, obtaining new deposits or short-term corporate loans). The study relied on information provided by the officers themselves, through interviews and data-collection questionnaire. The officers were again involved in the review of the resulting data and interpretation of implications for possible improvements. The application of the findings required the reassignment of certain tasks, adjustments in staffing at both officer and support staff levels, and the setting of new performance objectives geared to the actual activities to be performed on the jobs.

Work design involves specification of the activities, methods, and relationships of jobs in order to satisfy performance requirements. And the motivational impact of job design is a central concern, often as great as the technological or productive impact. An aim of job design is to build increased challenge and autonomy into the work for the people who perform it—to empower employees to act. By creating job conditions that motivate employees internally, companies ensure that gains are made both in the productive effectiveness of the organization and in the personal satisfaction and well-being of employees.

Job design can stretch individual performance. Jobs can help individuals stretch and grow as human beings and increase their sense of competence and worth. This means that jobs can be designed in ways that will provide maximum motivational impact.

Motivational Impact of Job Design

Jobs have greater motivational value when they give individuals greater planning and control responsibilities over their work, as opposed to greater simplification and specialization in work. The concept of job enrichment, developed and applied primarily to clerical and production jobs, was widely acclaimed as an important technique for improving the quality of working life and, indirectly, individual performance and organizational productivity (Campion & Thayer, 1989).

According to a widely used framework for analyzing and designing jobs, employees respond positively to a job when they find it generally meaningful, valuable, and worthwhile; when they feel personally responsible for the results of the work; and when they continuously know how well they are performing (Hackman and Oldham, 1976). Five job characteristics, or "core dimensions" of job design, contribute to these conditions:

- Skill variety: different activities are required to carry out the work, involving different skills and talents.
- Task identity: workers complete a "whole" and identifiable piece of work—doing a job from beginning to end.
- Task significance: workers have substantial impact on other people, whether in the organization or externally.
- Autonomy: employees have substantial freedom, independence, and discretion in planning and performing the work.
- Feedback: work activities result in direct and clear information about the effectiveness of the worker's performance.

Job design typically entails building greater individual planning, decision making, and control into jobs. It is not merely a matter of changing the scope of a job by adding more activities to it or by eliminating activities. Job design may entail work simplification, minimizing relatively unsatisfying work activities which are felt to be repetitive, dull, or routine.

Employees want to perform activities that utilize their highest-level skills. By refocusing activities, employees may perform work that they find more challenging and which adds greater value. Jobs may be restructured, and people take on different tasks. Where individuals lack the needed skills, training may be required.

Changes in the ways people are assigned to jobs complement job design improvements. For example, job rotation can give work more variety without changing the particular jobs themselves. Flexible working schedules and modified workweeks may also improve work motivation and job satisfaction, while balancing commutation patterns. Many employees enjoy a degree of autonomy and flexibility regarding working schedules and the choice of tasks to be performed. In many companies, however, jobs and working conditions remain relatively inflexible, in the interest of consistency and common treatment.

Improving Utilization

Another important way to enable employees to perform effectively is to eliminate from their jobs the least productive tasks—relative to their talents, the costs entailed, and the value to the organization. By redesigning the work to continually strengthen and refocus activities on the most valuable tasks, managers help employees make the highest possible performance contribution.

Through periodic review of activities performed in jobs, managers help employees:

• Eliminate duplicate work within the work unit and across units (different jobs with essentially the same tasks)
• Eliminate unnecessary work (i.e., work that is not essential to the job or is not needed by others in performing their jobs)
• Automate tasks, where cost-effective
• Consolidate similar tasks performed in multiple jobs or units, to gain economies of time and resources
• Reallocate time and resources among activities, according to priorities
• Reassign tasks to others who may perform them more effectively, or at lower cost
• Contract work outside the company (consultants or vendors), where cost-effective
• Streamline the process of work or reduce it in scope, such as handling paperwork, approvals, or information flow
• Redefine service levels within the company (e.g., speed, cost, quality)

Similarly, as a result of utilization analysis, some individuals may be better assigned to different jobs—ones that more closely match their skills. Redeployment of talent gives the organization more flexibility and may open up opportunities to hire new talent with different skills. Keeping employees moving among different jobs also enables them to learn and adapt to change.

To identify and plan opportunities for improving staff utilization, managers need to know what people actually do in their jobs and they need to obtain their employees' perceptions of ways their jobs may be changed. Many companies use activity questionnaires to help managers identify ways to improve the utilization of talent under their stewardship. A profile used in a pharmaceutical company asks these questions:

• What are the most time-consuming parts of your job? Estimate the percentage of time required (include all activities that take at least 10% of your time), and rank the order of importance.
• If you suddenly had an extra day a week (20% more time) to devote to your job, on what major activities (existing and new) would you spend it?
• If you suddenly had one less day a week to devote to your job, what major activities that you now perform would you scale back or eliminate?
• What impediments add to the time needed to do your job (e.g., getting

approvals, lack of clerical support, lack of effective information systems, lack of clear priorities)?

• What activities in the job should be expanded, eliminated, or otherwise changed (see above list of possible changes)?

• Do others in the company perform activities that duplicate what you do or what your department does? What actions would remove these duplications?

• Do you currently perform any activities that are not formally part of your position description or performance plan? If yes, should they be continued?

• If you were to make one change in your job to increase its value to the company, what would it be?

The major value of the questionnaire lies in the analysis of inputs. Managers and employees often have different views of how time is spent and the importance of activities. Because time spent and importance do not normally relate to each other directly, managers gain insights into ways to shift time and effort to more important areas.

The questionnaire is designed as an interview. Often, managers use it as an interview guide with employees, to create a dialogue about work design and opportunities for improvement. It may even be used independently by employees or work teams to generate ideas for improvements.

In the pharmaceutical company, it was used at each management level, beginning with first-level managers, as a tool for involving employees in reviewing work activities. It drew positive reactions from employees who felt they were burdened with more work than they could perform. It was uniformly perceived to be a realistic and valuable tool for refocusing work, containing needs for additional staff, and avoiding staff reductions (Walker & Weingarth, 1991).

As a result of such analysis by managers and employees, work may be reassigned, jobs restructured, and working relationships redefined. Some work may be automated; some may be contracted outside the company (or brought back into the company). Above all, work may be simplified and priorities set more clearly.

The focus of utilization analysis is on the activities that constitute the job, not the current performance of the employee or the skills and development plans of the employee. It is vital to eliminate unneeded work and focus activities on the right priorities. It is important not to focus on the people themselves as the work is examined.

To match new requirements, some employees may need to be redeployed, retrained, and refocused in their work. Some may need to be replaced with talent that is better suited to the tasks (although this may involve redeployment rather than leaving the company). In this way, the organization and the focus of activities are directly related to performance.

Improving utilization brings to mind the concept of ''rightsizing.'' In a positive sense, rightsizing is a process by which a company reviews its organizational requirements, examines the effects and consequences of various re-structuring tactics, and devises a rational plan for eliminating unneeded work and excess employees. More simply, it has been defined as "making sure that organizations are the right size and shape." Rightsizing means having the right number of qualified employees performing essential work activities in the most effective and efficient manner. In most companies, however, rightsizing means downsizing, although staffing may be increased in some priority areas at the same time that reductions are made elsewhere. Rightsizing, therefore, focuses on the people as well as on the work and implies a reduction in overall employment.

EMPOWERMENT

Beyond work design, employees want to be given the resources necessary to act and the accountability for results. They want to feel that they count. Says Harvard Business School Professor J. Richard Hackman, "If you want me to care, then I want to be treated like an owner and have some real voice in where we're going" (Main, 1988). The concept evolved from the "employee involve-ment" emphasis of the 1980s, which brought employees more directly into decision making.

Empowerment, literally "the gaining of power," is a term that has been applied for more than a century to the strengthening of political influence, generally among people not involved in key decision making. It became popu-lar when the Students for a Democratic Society, in the 1960s, "condemned the 'Establishment' and sought 'empowerment' for 'helpless minorities outside the system.'" It grew from the slogan "Power to the people" (Safire, 1990).

Managers have several ways to empower employees to perform effectively. First, they ensure that employees have the resources they need, particularly information. They give individuals and teams the authority and responsibility to act and to manage themselves. Managers help build lateral relationships across the organization that facilitate problem solving and learning.

Work Teams

In flexible organizations, more authority and responsibility are delegated to employees, with less overall management involvement. Where there are fewer management levels and fewer managers, as is often the case, employees look for a different type of leadership. Through coaching and support, managers are expected to enable employees to manage their own work.

When Xerox cut back headquarters staff, which oversaw the work of district supervisors, it increased the power of managers in the field. District managers gained more authority to adjust prices or to extend credit to valued customers. As long as the results stayed good, corporate managers stayed away (Labich, 1989b).

Work teams need to be responsible for making important decisions, subject to the rights of management to challenge those decisions. In fact, the idea of "self-managing teams" or "autonomous work groups" implies more decision-making authority than these groups often have. Like redesigning jobs and increasing talent utilization, the emphasis on teams pushes power and control over work to a lower level in the organization. As a result, teams can take actions to improve work methods and procedures, improve talent retention, manage staffing more flexibly, improve service and product quality, and improve decision making (Lawler, 1986).

Teamwork is essential for high performance. One slogan of the quality movement is "Nobody's perfect; only teams are." Collaboration is needed to develop from a group of employees the skills, ideas, and energies necessary to solve problems and respond to competitive challenges. Leaders are necessary to unlock these talents.

The idea of a team is that people cooperate in working together to ensure each other's success. This does not require altruism, but rather a sense of common purpose and a feeling that their individual goals are compatible with this purpose. Teamwork also requires mutual trust and confidence, which result only by working together effectively.

A manager, seeking to foster teamwork, needs to find ways for people to work together instead of alone (create interactions, keep the teams small), needs to emphasize team goals and accomplishments (always say *we*), needs to build trust by delegating consistently (be predictable), and needs to focus on small successes that lead to long-term success (Kouzes & Posner, 1987).

Managers need to use creative ways in involve people in planning and problem solving. Among the most common ways, described by Edward Lawler as "high involvement management," are shifting management tasks to the team, using survey feedback, using quality improvement as a focus of team activity (like quality circles), using union-management quality-of-work-life programs, or redesigning operations (e.g., new design plants) (Lawler, 1986). Considerable experience has been developed by companies in using these various involvement processes and self-directed work teams (Gorlin & Schein, 1984; Manz, Keating, & Donnellon, 1990; Osburn, Moran, Musselwhite, & Zenger, 1990; Torres & Spiegel, 1991).

Treating teams as autonomous entrepreneurial units helps promote a sense of ownership. It also allows the teams to take actions that they believe will enhance their unit performance, without being constrained by the larger organization. Blue Cross & Blue Shield of Connecticut formed dozens of "customer action teams" to serve specific markets. These small teams combine a variety of essential skills, including sales, claims, and service. "By segmenting your organization and giving each of these units the freedom to succeed," said EVP Bud Torello, "you get people thinking about what's really important."

Federal Express used teams in its back-office operations in Memphis. It organized 1,000 clerical employees into teams and gave them the training and authority to manage themselves. With the help of the teams, the company cut service problems, such as incorrect bills and lost packages, by 13% in one year (Dumaine, 1990).

The ultimate in self-managing teams is the entrepreneurial business within a corporation. Xerox, 3M, and Honeywell are among the companies that finance start-ups by employees who have promising ideas in return for a minority share. Many companies keep acquisitions independent as subsidiaries or set up business units that are distinct, with their own profit and loss responsibility and associated financial statements. Several have even set up "internal boards of directors" to oversee entrepreneurial units.

To achieve such a transition, SEI, a financial services company in Pennsylvania, aligned its 1,100 employees into entrepreneurial units, each led by a "champion" with skills specific to the unit. Employees will receive a 20% interest in their "business," which will be purchased by the company at "market value" after a suitable period.

One way to foster team behavior is to create teams across functions or units. General Motors set up product development teams (PDTs) that allow collaboration on new products. They bridge the earliest phases in design engineering to the actual production of components for a new automobile. In this way, teams extend beyond the plant floor.

Such superteams draw together people with different jobs or functions— marketing, finance, manufacturing, etc. By putting their heads together, they gain different perspectives on the business and can solve a complex problem quickly and effectively. To do this through a traditional hierarchy would take more time and might not achieve the same positive result.

Information Systems

Because there are fewer levels of management and fewer staff resources in today's flexible organizations, information systems help employees coordinate and manage themselves. Whether in a manufacturing or a service delivery setting, individuals and teams have access to financial, production, and other needed information.

Inexpensive computing and the use of networks make it possible to have information directly available to the employees who need it, throughout the organization. Employees can share information and coordinate their activities without going through management levels or a central staff group (Naisbitt & Aburdene, 1985). Even a system so fundamental as electronic mail or messaging empowers employees by freeing them from "telephone tag" and encouraging communications. For example, memos may be electronically copied to additional individuals who may be interested, without increasing clerical burden or paper flow.

American Airlines, for example, is linking all of its employees (82,000 in 1991) through a companywide systems network called InterAAct. Through intelligent workstations, employees have access to the many information systems that may support their work, including ground services, flight scheduling, reservations (SABRE), and office automation. InterAAct consolidates and instantly updates budgets, and helps managers track costs in all areas. Through the network, employees at different airports instantly share cost-cutting tips and get updates on how well they are sticking to their budgets. Electronic mail has reduced interoffice mail by 75% to 80%, freeing up employee time and also space on jets for baggage or freight. It was introduced to achieve short-term cost savings, but has become an important tool for employee empowerment. The more people are involved in using it, "the more ideas you have and the better use you have of it." (Scheier, 1991).

Today, computing capability can be widespread in an organization, supporting as many applications as can be conceived by individuals and groups. Workstations are self-contained computers, whether desktop or notebook, and are linked to mainframe systems and other workstations. Applications are installed where they are used, some shared companywide, others local and specific.

Expert systems help people work more efficiently, freeing time from routine decisions. Such systems, based on rules taken from experience (e.g., tax deductibility of items, credit approvals, inventory replacement), help speed decisions and spread knowledge (Feigenbaum, 1989). At Digital Equipment (DEC), for example, two expert systems called Xsel and Xcon help employees configure VAX computers to serve customer needs. Xsel cuts down the time needed by salespeople to fill out an order—from one or two hours to about fifteen minutes—and it vastly reduces the chance of errors or necessary changes. DEC also uses expert systems to train salespeople about new products and their capabilities ("Smart Advice," 1989).

Information access also has symbolic meaning for employees and teams. Ready access to information promotes a sense of involvement. At General Motors, information kiosks are located in areas of high employee traffic. These give employees direct access to current company news, product information, financial updates, and so on. They also provide an ongoing employee opinion survey, using a touch-screen employee response system. Other companies have developed similar systems to make information directly available to employees when they want it.

Finally, information from customers is important in enabling employees to perform effectively. A Digital Equipment plant has an 800-telephone-number hotline from its customers directly to the team making the product. Most hotel chains have regular reports on guest satisfaction, including both statistical results and specific narrative comments and suggestions that can be acted upon. At IBM, the information system facilitates referral of customers (or referral of customer feedback) to the units and individuals who can best respond.

COACHING

An electronics company sought to improve its performance and focus its energies on the most important tasks. It had, however, all the "basics" of strategic management in place: clearly defined and communicated objectives, a sound organization, and excellent staffing and development processes. Its performance management system included a performance goal-setting and appraisal system, and compensation programs.

As part of its approach, a task force solicited inputs on how well the performance management process was working. Managers and professionals across the company participated through a survey, supplemented with focus groups and interviews. Information was obtained on how well the current processes were supporting high performance—and on perceptions of opportunities for improvement.

The study found that employees generally knew what was expected of them, received timely evaluation and feedback on performance, and perceived the rewards to be responsive and equitable. What was lacking was sufficient support from management—coaching, training, resources, and systems designed to aid performance. The enabling mechanisms were not there.

In fact, an analysis of managers' activities in the company indicated that an average of only 16% of their working time was spent interacting with their subordinates. The majority of time was spent on work as individual professional contributors (technical or customer-related work) or in activities relating to other managers and higher-level organizational demands (e.g., meetings, planning, coordination). One manager explained this by saying, "We value working managers, that's why we have so many."

Spending more time in coaching is not contradictory to the reduction of the number and levels of management, or to empowerment. In fact, with fewer managers and wider spans of management, it is essential that these managers spend more of their time in contact with their employees. The task of managing becomes an all-consuming responsibility, and coaching skills become more, not less, important.

A manager is viewed variously as a mentor, parent, consultant, facilitator, teacher, friend, partner, boss, navigator, ambassador, initiator, and even "Attila the Hun." In the flexible organization, the manager is first and foremost a coach. Coaching narrowly implies training, instructing, or guiding; but it is more than that. It is caring, listening, nudging, encouraging, advising, and nurturing others as they strive to achieve results. Good coaching is an essential feature of effective management in a high-performing, flexible organization.

At America West Airlines, midlevel supervisors are expected to lead with gentle persuasion and liberal use of praise for employee performance. They empower employees, nurturing their talents and drawing out their ideas for improvement. "When things work," says Chairman Ed Beauvais, "they get the credit. When things don't work out, you take the blame" (Labich, 1989b).

Definitions of coaching and managing have some important elements in common. In fact, sports coaches are often called "field managers" by owners and front-office personnel. Both coaching and management are people-based arts, and both focus on getting things done through the actions of others. As in sports, managers notice that individuals and teams perform better with a coach;

the better the coaching, the better the results achieved (Evered & Selman, 1990).

Face-to-face coaching "pulls people together with diverse backgrounds, talents, experiences, and interests, encourages them to step up to responsibility and continued achievement, and treats them as full-scale partners and contributors" (Peters & Austin, 1985).

Regular Contact

Good coaching relies on quality communication. A manager listens to employees and responds with encouragement and suggestions for improvement. An effective manager also provides new ideas for performance. "Great coaches communicate in a way that allows a player of a team to see the game differently than from the perspective of action" (Evered & Selman, 1990). In this way, the manager communicates a different way to do the job—and contributes to individual growth and development.

The communication is two-way. Coaches are also listening for feedback on ways they can be more effective. The effective manager solicits and respects the inputs from team members. This open dialogue between manager and employee distinguishes coaching from traditional hierarchical management. It is the crux of the participative management approach that many managers have sought to implement.

Contact is frequent. Some managers talk with their staff only in formal meetings, in performance planning and review sessions, or when there are "problems." Effective coaches know when to be in touch, through a phone call, a visit, or a meeting. They keep informed on the activities of each individual and of the results being attained, but without giving the effect of supervising closely or controlling behavior. Managers have a sense of the concerns and needs of each individual, so they can provide needed support (they "notice things"). Employees need to feel that managers are interested in them and in their work; this is readily shown through regular interaction.

Coaching calls for a relationship that is action-oriented. It is different from other types of supportive relationships (friend, teacher, counselor, mentor) in that it is focused on business performance. It is not passive, or merely aimed at developing positive relationships. "Coaching," said New York Giants Coach Bill Parcells, "is giving your players a good design and getting 'em to play hard."

Coaching is a day-by-day, hands-on process of helping employees recognize opportunities to improve their performance and capabilities. It requires the manager to analyze ways in which the employee may improve performance and capabilities, plan actions that both agree are desirable, create a supportive climate for action, and help employees actually change their behavior. To do this, a manager needs to be able to monitor an employee's performance, analyze and identify opportunities for improvement, ask employees the right questions and listen actively, and give specific, descriptive, and useful feedback (Orth, Wilkinson, & Benfari, 1987).

A study of the activities of managers provided research support for the importance of coaching in enabling high performance. The study found that the more effective managers devoted more time to managing their people and less time in administrative, networking, and information and paperwork processing (Luthans, 1988). These managers spent more time than less effective managers in listening to suggestions, asking for input, resolving conflict between subordinates, appealing to higher-level management or third parties to resolve problems, developing job descriptions, reviewing applications and interviewing applicants, filling in where needed, orienting employees, arranging for training, clarifying roles, mentoring, walking subordinates through a task, giving positive feedback, group support, conveying appreciation, and giving credit where due. Many of these activities represent coaching, as we have discussed it.

Authors Tom Peters and Nancy Austin identified five key roles in coaching (Peters & Austin, 1985). They are to:

- Educate, when new skills are needed or when goals, roles, or conditions change
- Sponsor, when an individual can let an outstanding skill make a special contribution
- Coach, for special encouragement
- Counsel, when problems or setbacks need correction or recovery
- Confront, when an individual's performance is not meeting expectations and problems persist

Coaching helps individuals become more tolerant of the difficult process of continual learning—through successes and mistakes. Through coaching, individuals develop skills and make contributions that would otherwise be lost.

SUMMARY

For decades, managers have been encouraged and trained to be more effective motivators of people—to adopt management practices that help employees perform. Emphasis has been on management style, mutual goal setting, employee participation, and the use of positive behavior reinforcement.

Enabling high performance remains an elusive goal, however. What is required is intensified and better-integrated management efforts. Empowering employees to act—giving them authority and accountability for their work—is essential and is widely pursued. Teamwork is increasingly prized and encouraged. However, more than empowerment is needed. Enabling performance means that managers ensure that jobs are structured appropriately, that employee talents and energies are utilized appropriately, and that employees have the training, information, systems, and other resources they need.

If managers are to apply what they know is true about behavior and performance, as summarized in this chapter, they need to view coaching as a primary and active, not passive, activity. Managers need to maintain regular, frequent, two-way, and action-oriented contact with employees as they strive to achieve their performance objectives. Most managers need to spend more time in coaching.

These activities are more than an array of useful management choices. Taken together, they represent an important, distinct component in the process of managing human resources. With fewer managers, fewer management levels, and heightened concern for continual improvement of performance, more attention will need to be given to the *enabling* of performance.

CHAPTER 11

EVALUATING PERFORMANCE

At Intel, we estimate that a supervisor probably spends five to eight hours on each employee's review. . . . If the effort expended contributes to an employee's performance even to a small extent over the course of a year, isn't that a highly worthwhile expenditure of a supervisor's time?

Andy Grove, president

In today's flexible organizations, performance evaluation provides an important way for managers to clarify performance goals and standards and to enhance future individual performance. It also provides a basis for decisions affecting pay, promotions, terminations, training, transfers, and other actions.

Probably the oldest technique used by managers to influence individual performance is the appraisal. Employee motivation to perform, to develop personal capabilities, and to improve future performance is influenced by feedback of past performance. Originally, feedback was by direct perception of the results achieved. Workers building the pyramids, fighting in armies, tilling the soil, and performing other work eons ago were able to see what was achieved through their efforts. Also, negative feedback, severe in some instances (for example, death), was also given by supervisors to particular workers deserving singular consideration for performance judged inadequate.

Most large companies have practiced performance evaluation for decades and have adopted various techniques in the process. Yet few companies are satisfied with the effectiveness of their appraisal processes and are alert to opportunities for improvement. Evaluations are often valued more for form than for substance. An evaluation is frequently something that must be done merely so that the company can say it has been done. And the results of this sometimes "tortured and damaging ritual" are not particularly beneficial to the company. Many managers have come to expect too little of performance evaluation, relative to the important role it plays in strategy implementation.

Effectiveness has much to do with how evaluations are conducted, by whom, and with what criteria. In flexible organizations, the process for evaluating performance changes as conditions change, focusing on the priorities and practices that fit strategies.

Accordingly, emphasis in performance evaluation practice today is on the basics—the fundamental purposes and techniques of appraising performance and planning for future performance and development. The hope for sophisticated new evaluation techniques has largely been dashed by the experience of companies that have found their implementation unwieldy, confusing, time-consuming, and costly. For most companies, more effective appraisals mean better implementation of the process, not adoption of more complex, advanced tools and techniques.

This chapter addresses ways in which managers evaluate individual and team performance. Specifically we will consider:

- Why performance evaluation is important for strategy implementation
- What makes performance evaluation effective
- How high-performing, flexible organizations evaluate performance

As in previous chapters, the issue for management is not so much how to conduct appraisals, but how to design and implement evaluation processes to support implementation of human resource strategy.

WHY EVALUATE PERFORMANCE?

As discussed in Chapter 1 (see Exhibit 1-1), managers achieve results through a series of activities that constitute the human resource management process. Expectations are shaped, the organization is built (design, staffing, and capabilities), and managers give employees the needed support. Measurement of accomplishments is a logical and necessary next step in the process.

Purposes of Evaluation

Enlightened managers see in performance evaluations an opportunity to communicate to employees what the company wants them to do. Performance evaluation personalizes company strategy and performance expectations. A Weyerhaeuser manager said, "If you want to talk about a point where a manager can exert leverage on an employee, this is it" (Kiechel, 1987).

Performance evaluation is important to employees because it answers their basic question: "How am I doing?" People want feedback, although some people want it more frequently than others. Feedback provides:

- Reassurance that they are contributing and doing the right things
- Awareness of the impact of performance on desired results (e.g., customer satisfaction)
- A measure of the adequacy of performance (quality, quantity, speed, etc.)
- Recognition of the importance and value of their performance

Evaluation is also important because it provides a basis for changing performance plans, including objectives and standards of behavior, as business plans and conditions change:

- Setting new expectation or action plans to improve performance during the year
- Establishing performance plans for the next year/period
- Affirming behavior that should be continued

Performance evaluation is used to motivate and guide the individual employee toward purposeful personal development of skills and capabilities. To some managers, this is the sole purpose of appraisal and an important tool for managing. The focus may be on development of capabilities for the current assignment or development for future assignments and responsibilities. Where it involves the latter, performance evaluation closely relates to individual development planning (see Chapter 9), which is future-oriented. A review of past performance is a potent stimulus and guide for employee self-analysis, contributing to self-development planning.

Another purpose of performance evaluation, and in many companies a primary one, is to generate information to support administrative decisions. Performance evaluations offer a sound basis for human resource decisions and actions. Promotions, transfers and reassignments, demotions, and terminations are actions based, at least in part, on performance. Similarly, changes in compensation, whether salary or wage-rate adjustments or pay contingent on performance (e.g., bonuses), are based, at least in part, on performance.

The rationale for differential treatment of employees needs to be consistent with a company's values, philosophy, and strategy. It also needs to be consistent with legal requirements, which constrain management actions in many decisions and actions. Furthermore, the rationale needs to be balanced with the desire for collaboration, rather than competition and conflict, sought in total quality management. Some people (including quality guru Deming) decry appraisals that pit employees against each other in competition for recognitions and rewards.

Dual Roles

It is difficult for managers to fulfill all of the above-mentioned purposes through a single evaluation process. On the one hand, managers need objective evaluations of past individual performance for use in making administrative human resource decisions. On the other hand, employers need tools to enable managers to help individuals improve performance, plan future work, develop skills and abilities for career growth, and strengthen the quality of their relationship as manager and employee.

Managers are uncomfortable about serving as both judge and counselor—the dual roles required by these two dimensions of evaluation. They normally

---

EXHIBIT 11-1 DUAL ROLES IN PERFORMANCE EVALUATION

Purpose	Counseling	Judging
Performance feedback	Reassurance, involvement, recognition	Making employees aware of impact measures, performance adequacy
Changing performance plans	Mutual agreement on expectations	Introducing new (higher) standards
Developing capabilities	Motivating, focusing development for future improvement	Identifying gaps and development needs
Staffing and compensation actions	Build understanding of link of performance to actions	Provide sound defensible basis for actions

---

dislike criticizing a subordinate (and having to justify criticisms) and then trying to turn the discussion around to a positive note. They usually lack the skills necessary to handle the interviews effectively, as these skills are quite different from other day-to-day contacts with the employees. Also, they are not always sure of the judgments they are making about the individual's performance and personal qualities; it is hard to take back opinions you later reverse as invalid.

Exhibit 11-1 summarizes the key roles in performance evaluation for each of the purposes identified. The dual roles of counseling and judging have been acknowledged as a difficulty in conducting evaluations for decades (Beer, 1981; Meyer, Kay, & French, 1965; Sloan & Johnson, 1968). Where all purposes are served by one evaluation process, the results are often driven by decision support needs. For example, salary administration often overrides all other considerations; hence, some managers retrofit an evaluation to justify a given salary adjustment.

Some companies focus their goal setting and review process on employee development and performance improvement. This supports company efforts to involve employees in continual performance improvement and to empower employees and work teams. A separate evaluation program establishes a rating or judgment of past performance to support administrative decisions. These companies believe that development is the primary focus for performance evaluation and that the "judging" role, together with discussion of pay changes or other actions, should be handled separately.

At one company, for example, multiple programs are used. Evaluation interviews of a subordinate's performance, potential, promotability, and salary increase are distinct from management by objectives (MBO) and appraisal sessions. The evaluations are made when the subordinate is due for a salary increase. The manager rates each subordinate's overall performance and potential. The ratings, which are shared with subordinates and endorsed by the supervisor at the next level, reflect both the whats and the hows of performance.

Other companies believe that performance evaluation should emphasize objective assessment of behavior and results attained, as a basis for pay changes and other actions. For them, career development issues are often best handled in a separate planning and review process, only loosely connected to performance evaluation, as discussed in previous chapters (Mohrman, Resnick-West, & Lawler, 1989).

Both approaches are being used effectively by companies, and some companies do, in fact, address all aspects through a single, integrated process. Following a trend set by General Electric in the 1960s, many companies have concentrated on the performance planning and goal-setting aspects, and have downplayed performance evaluation or discontinued it altogether—only to come back to doing both because they are necessary to support actions. As companies sharpen their competitive capabilities and aggressively reshape their organizations, many are giving the evaluation aspect of performance appraisal careful attention once again.

Companies continue to require evaluations and struggle to minimize the difficulties. For all their potential faults, performance evaluations are vital for the management and improvement of performance in an organization. Formal evaluations could be abolished as systems and procedures, but the guts of appraisals—the clarification of job expectations, the reviewing of accomplishments, and the planning of future performance and development efforts—are central to effective management.

EFFECTIVE PERFORMANCE EVALUATION

What makes performance evaluation effective? Many articles and studies have addressed the "requirements" for effective performance appraisals. However, requirements reflect different perceptions of the purposes served, which in turn reflect the human resource issues being addressed. These include:

- Providing employee feedback: constructive feedback that results in performance improvement
- Changing performance plans: mutual acceptance of new performance objectives or action plans
- Developing performance capabilities: mutual acceptance of development action plans
- Supporting human resource actions: valid evaluations supporting pay, promotion, and employment decisions

A single system may not address all of these purposes. More likely, however, companies will continue to modify and adapt their approaches in pursuit of continual improvement for all of these purposes. This may entail multiple systems to address different purposes, supplemented with special efforts to link them together.

For all purposes, performance evaluation is considered more effective when it is objective, uses appropriate techniques, actively involves employees, is well understood, and is an accepted management responsibility.

Objectivity

Ideally, performance evaluations are based on documented performance measured throughout the year for each defined standard or strategy-related objective for the job. Studies have shown, however, that performance evaluations are usually highly subjective, even though formal systems may be used. Managers may try to be objective in appraising individual performance and capabilities, but they may simply not have all the pertinent facts regarding job requirements, actual qualities of individual behavior, and relative standards among appraisers (Beatty & Schneier, 1988; Cascio, 1987).

To be objective, according to *Webster's Dictionary*, is to be "characterized by honesty, justice, and freedom from improper influence." This means that evaluations should be fair, impartial, equitable, candid, dispassionate, just, and impersonal. Webster also defines objective as "belonging to actuality," meaning that facts are material, sensible, tangible, substantial, physical, or based on observed phenomena.

Evaluations are more objective when they are based on carefully defined performance expectations, as discussed in Chapter 4. These may be represented as key job responsibilities, key results areas, objectives, or standards of performance. Ideally, they are linked to wider organizational objectives and, ultimately, to strategic business priorities.

To be job-related and free of bias, performance evaluations need to be based on specific, empirically derived job requirements. In many companies, job descriptions prepared for salary administration purposes serve as a starting point for performance evaluations. Too often they are the ending point as well, and the appraisers are left to "invent" applicable performance standards in the course of evaluating individual performance.

Job requirements should cover both the *what* and the *how* of job performance. They should therefore include:

- Basic activities (or roles) required in the job
- Special activities required that are unique to a given location, project, technical requirement, etc.
- Identifiable or measurable outputs or products resulting from performance

Performance requirements are more objective when they are based on some form of empirical analysis—examination of actual activities and job demands. Interviews, questionnaires, observation, or any other work-analysis technique may be used to provide empirical evidence of job-related performance standards. The results need not be lengthy, detailed job descriptions, but the relevant aspects of job performance need to be accurately defined.

Objectivity also calls for independent judgment by managers, using available indicators and measures of actual performance. While subjectivity (influenced

---

EXHIBIT 11-2 PERFORMANCE MEASURES FOR A RESTAURANT UNIT

Key Result Area	Performance Measures
Food quality	Unit index Shoppers' report scores Line checks Quality assurance manager evaluation
Employee relations, training and development	Proficiency test scores Shoppers' report scores Employee turnover Employee survey feedback
Management training and development	Unit index Training courses completed on schedule Promotions to each management level Manager and employee turnover
Clean, well-maintained stores	Unit index Shoppers' report scores Health department inspection report Audits by quality assurance manager
Customer service	Unit index Shoppers' report scores Customer feedback (telephone line)
Controllable costs	Beverage, food, and labor costs
Sales	Beverage, food, bar sales Customer counts Per customer average check

---

by politics and personal factors) may affect judgment, the onus is on managers to examine evidence of performance and make honest and just evaluations (Lawler, 1990).

For many performance aspects, measures are possible through direct observation. In Chapter 4, key result areas for restaurant unit managers were presented. Exhibit 11-2 presents examples of the multiple performance measures relating to each. For each measure, an objective is mutually set, with the circumstances of each unit taken into account (e.g., new unit, size of unit).

As reflected in this example, measures may come from different sources. Some come directly from results (e.g., sales, costs). Some come from customer surveys. Some require collection of and reporting on accomplishments (e.g., training completed, turnover, promotions, employee proficiency). Some come from external sources (e.g., health inspection reports). The unit performance index is a result of a rating process conducted by regional managers visiting the units. For the various key result areas, specific items are listed in a scoring checklist. The items are weighted to yield an overall score or index.

Objectives and other goal-setting approaches are useful; but they tend to work best where performance is geared to specific, measurable, or identifiable results that can be targeted, such as projects completed, sales, or output. Goal setting is ineffective when goals are too "easy," when goals do not constitute the total job, when goal attainment is difficult to prove or measure, and when performance is the result of team efforts. A bank lending officer, for example, can set a number of meaningful goals (e.g., new accounts, loans made), but other banking officers and staff have a hand in achieving these results. Everyone likes to take credit for a team result.

Typically, evaluations are conducted by a manager for each individual subordinate employee. Increasingly, however, many evaluation processes solicit appraisal inputs from multiple managers, from peers in the work team, and even from the customers served. This application of 360-degree evaluation, discussed in Chapter 9 as a management development tool, may be applied to many types of jobs as a way to enhance the objectivity of performance data. One system solicits inputs on both the criteria and the ratings from three to seven other raters selected by the employee; results are processed by computer and presented as a tool for discussion and analysis (Edwards & Sproull, 1985).

For example, Schreiber Foods, a cheese products company with 2,700 employees, uses a peer evaluation process at all levels. Developed with employee involvement, using teams of hourly workers and plant managers, the process is most beneficial at the hourly level. The results are used for both employee development and pay decisions, which are reviewed once or twice yearly, depending on each employee's position in a pay grade. Hourly employees are rated by their peers on attendance, attitude, safety habits, adaptability, cooperation and teamwork, and sanitation (McEvoy, Buller, & Roghaar, 1988).

Use of Appropriate Techniques

According to consultant Robert E. Lefton, "Nobody's form is all that good. We have the performance review forms of over 300 of the *Fortune* 500 companies, including GE, IBM, and 3M. We have yet to find the perfect form" (Kiechel, 1987). There is no perfect evaluation technique, nor are there any poor performance appraisal techniques. Any technique can be made to work effectively by conscientious managers. IBM's processes work at IBM because they are right for IBM and the company makes them work.

Companies use many different forms of performance appraisals, according to their needs and management preferences. Even in a single company, multiple techniques may be used, to fit the needs of different employee groups and the preferences of different organization unit managers. The fact that techniques are so varied represents the lack of agreement on the "best way" to appraise employee performance (McMillan & Doyel, 1980).

Any formal appraisal process is believed to be superior to informal appraisal, with no established form or procedure. The various techniques that have been developed represent attempts to provide more effective appraisals. How much better they actually are depends on their job-relatedness, reliability, adaptability, objectivity, and (last but not least) the cost of introduction.

Performance evaluation techniques used by companies are described in detail in various books (Beatty, 1989; Bernardin & Beatty, 1984; Carroll & Schneier, 1982; Latham & Wexley, 1981; Schneier, 1989; Schuler, Beutell, & Youngblood, 1989). The following are brief descriptions of the primary types of techniques and their applicability.

Narrative Appraisals Narrative appraisals describe the behavioral strengths and weaknesses of the employee's performance. Carefully defined performance expectations are needed to help managers make judgments under this approach. Without useful criteria for evaluating performance, narrative appraisals tend to be highly subjective and focus on the qualities of the person appraised rather than on actual performance. Also, narrative appraisals are the most time-consuming to prepare and the most difficult to analyze and interpret. Nevertheless, they are commonly used as a technique and allow the appraiser the maximum of flexibility in considering the overall performance of an individual.

Goal Setting and Review This technique relates individual or team performance to goal-based criteria. When practiced as part of a broader management-by-objectives process, the criteria (goals and measures) flow from larger work group and organizational goals. But a larger process is not essential for managers to evaluate performance relative to preestablished goals. At a minimum, the technique requires agreement between the manager and the individual on the specific goals to be achieved and subsequent comparison of actual achievements by these standards. Often, achievements are directly measurable (sales, outputs, wastage, etc.) or are easily identified by comparison with standards (for example, budget compliance). This popular appraisal technique has the advantages of flexibility and high relevance to specific job demands. Its drawback is the risk of deteriorating into subjective appraisal and focusing on only the most obvious (and easily measured) aspects of job performance.

Rating Scales Rating scales evaluate performance against established factors on a multiple-point dimension. One of the oldest formal appraisal techniques used, the rating scale has gained considerable favor because it is quantitative and reliable, and can be designed to represent empirically identified performance factors. In the past, scales typically represented personality traits (for example, integrity, dependability, sociability), which were not necessarily job-related. Today's scales, anchored with brief descriptions of desired and undesired behaviors, provide a tailored, objective basis for appraisal. The chief drawback is the cost of developing the scales based on empirical analysis of the jobs.

Checklists These specify job factors against which individual performance may be evaluated. Checklists are commonly used for routine jobs with well-defined tasks, such as clerical, food service, technician, or customer service work. They are standardized evaluation tools, easy to apply to large numbers of employees in common positions. The chief drawback is the risk of a halo bias—rating an individual on an overall basis and not evaluating objectively all aspects of performance.

Ranking Techniques Ranking techniques compare employees by relative performance levels. A straight ranking involves ordering employees from best to worst, based either on overall performance or on a number of factors. Alternation (or alternative) ranking involves identifying the very best performer, then the poorest, then the next best, then the next poorest, and so on. Paired comparisons require comparisons between randomly assigned pairs of employees, resulting (when consolidated as a list) in overall ranking. A forced distribution involves assigning employees to classes based on performance levels (similar to students in grade school). Each ranking technique is attractive because of its simplicity, but each is limited by the risk of subjective judgment. When multiple raters participate in ranking, the result may improve; but it remains a subjective consensus, and job-relatedness remains an indirect consideration.

Design of Approach

Any of these appraisal techniques may be used as a basis for effective performance evaluation. However, those techniques that have high job-relatedness provide a more realistic basis for planning future performance and development activities. Goal setting and narrative evaluations are the most widely used, largely because they fit the culture and "human nature" of managers in many companies (Levine, 1986; Mohrman, Resnick-West, & Lawler, 1989). Rating scales developed for specific job-related (or strategy-related) behaviors and results are useful, but they require more investment in development than many companies feel is justified by the added value. Also, such systems become outdated quickly as work and criteria change.

A key factor in the choice of a technique is involvement of managers and employees. Any technique developed with the active input of appraisers and employees will gain a higher degree of acceptance and support than a technique selected for them. Participation develops a sense of ownership and also educates and prepares employees and managers for the effective use of the process. However, companies have also found that good design should not be overly compromised in the interest of involvement. Project teams can invent rather cumbersome or otherwise inadequate tools.

When companies focus on "what people achieve," a goal-based evaluation is needed. When they focus on "what people do," behavior-based evaluation is needed (e.g., using ratings such as behaviorally anchored scales). When they focus on "what people are," competency-based evaluation is needed, focusing on individual development (Schneier, Beatty, & Baird, 1986).

At Xerox, for example, a task force developed a new, more flexible approach to performance evaluation, entitled Performance Feedback and Development. Objectives are set by employees and their managers at the beginning of the year; these are documented and approved by a second-level manager. After six months, an interim review occurs, which may be oral but is acknowledged in writing. A final appraisal against the objectives is written at year-end and is discussed with the employee. Emphasis is on performance feedback and improvement. Accordingly:

- The merit increase discussion occurs one or two months after the evaluation, and it addresses how the merit increase was determined.
- Summary performance ratings are eliminated, but a narrative summary is included.
- Personal development objectives are included with task objectives.

Surveys of employees and managers indicated that most employees better understood their work group objectives, considered the final appraisal to be fair and accurate, understood how their merit increase was determined, met their personal development objectives, and considered the changes to be "in the right direction." Removing the stigma of ratings was perceived to foster teamwork and to encourage the role of manager as coach (Deets & Tyler, 1986).

Employee Involvement

Evaluations are more effective when employees participate actively in them. Evaluations, and discussions of them, need not be confrontational. Feedback on performance need not (and many managers believe should not) be surprising to employees. There are several ways to involve employees in their performance evaluations.

One of the most powerful tools is self-evaluation. Employees at all levels are capable of reviewing their own performance, interests, goals, and plans in relation to stated job requirements or performance criteria. Where team performance is important, employees can examine their behavior and results relative to expectations together.

Self-evaluation communicates to employees a company commitment to disclosure about performance appraisal information, while not necessarily limiting the objectivity of formal evaluations prepared by managers. Experience indicates that employees are often more critical of their own performance than managers are.

For decades, such companies as General Electric have encouraged employees to prepare a work plan and subsequently review performance progress as part of an overall performance management process. In this way, employees help manage the process and are not merely passive when evaluations are made. Often, companies get employees involved in the up-front performance planning aspects, but then revert to unidirectional feedback in the evaluation aspects.

Effective evaluation discussions are a two-way communication between the manager and the employee. Here they compare the results of their independent

---

EXHIBIT 11-3 ELEMENTS OF A PERFORMANCE REVIEW DISCUSSION

— Review what has been achieved since the last review and examine reasons for successes and failures.
— Agree on actual levels of achievement.
— Stimulate and discuss ideas about what can be done to improve results achieved.
— Agree on future performance goals, the basis of measurement, and timing of review.
— Help the individual analyze personal performance and underlying factors affecting performance, such as skills and knowledge, job structure, standards, resources available, etc.
— Strengthen the individual's commitment to the job.
— Learn about the individual's interests, goals, and long-range career plans, and help the individual relate these to the current job.
— Strengthen the understanding between manager and individual, and foster an open line of communication.
— Discuss and resolve specific anxieties, uncertainties, or misapprehensions affecting job performance plans and directions for future career development; plan specific activities in support of these plans and directions.
— Get feedback from the individual on how well you have managed.

---

reviews and develop together an evaluation of past accomplishments and a plan for future activities and targeted accomplishments.

The discussion between the manager and the employee or team is critically important. It requires a great deal of work on the part of both to be effective, but it can provide both with a sense of accomplishment, a sense of future direction and priorities, and a commitment to specific developmental activities that strengthen both their relationship and the overall organization. Exhibit 11-3 outlines topics typically addressed in an effective performance review discussion.

Effective performance evaluation is not an event, conducted once a year, but a process that goes on all year long. Companies typically require discussions at least once a year and encourage interim progress reviews quarterly or as initiated by either the manager or the employee. A manager needs to keep an eye on progress, needs to adjust the objectives as circumstances change, and, most imporant, needs to tell employees how they are progressing. Service quality gurus talk of "catching an employee doing something right." People want prompt feedback, not a summary eight or ten months after the fact.

Understanding the Process

Performance evaluation is more effective when its purposes are widely communicated and understood across an organization. The inherent conflicts among purposes can undermine implementation of a process by confusing employees. As discussed earlier, different evaluations for different purposes provide clear focus, but also create multiple processes that are potentially confusing and unrelated. Multiple-purpose evaluations can be effectively conducted, but employees need help understanding their different dimensions.

The processes used also need to be understood. Employees need to know how the process works and how the results will be used. Performance evaluation is essentially simple; but because of the need for consistent use, job-related criteria, procedures to guide implementation, and documentation, it is often perceived as complicated and bureaucratic.

An important way to ensure understanding is through training. Managers are trained in performance evaluation techniques in most companies, at least covering the minimum administrative aspects and the overall purposes. In some companies, the training goes further, to equip managers to "model" the process and enhance its implementation. Employees learn about the process through initial orientation sessions and in the course of other training efforts.

Even when a process is designed and implemented to be objective, employees need to perceive the process as such. A judgment call is necessarily involved in any evaluation, the accuracy of which may or may not be accepted by the person being appraised. Necessary subjective judgments are based on relevant and available information. "Acceptance of the judgment is partly a result of how the appraisal was performed and partly a result of the ongoing relationship between the appraiser and the appraisee" (Lawler, 1990).

In a legal context, the courts' view is that a performance appraisal program should be job-related. That is, a judge must feel that the system is designed for specific purposes which are reasonable and clearly identified and that the techniques adopted have the capacity to achieve these objectives. Employers and employees expect no less than this for themselves.

Responsible Management

Performance evaluation is not always given the full, conscientious attention by managers that the designers of the systems assumed would be given. Often, appraisals are viewed by managers as necessary exercises to be tolerated—as paperwork requirements imposed on managers to justify salary changes and other differential treatment of employees.

Managers, as appraisers, are accountable for the performance of the people in their organizations. Accordingly, they need to see performance evaluations as an integral responsibility in their jobs. Managing and evaluating performance of staff are part of their own performance as managers and should be evaluated, in turn, as such.

Managers need to take adequate time to conduct performance evaluations. In today's fast-paced, flexible organizations, with increasingly wide reporting spans, this may seem onerous, if not impossible. But time, when allocated, can be used efficiently and can have a significant impact on behaviors and results. It is not merely how much time is spent, but whether adequate time is spent in the appropriate ways in the tasks of performance evaluation.

The courage to make sound but unpopular evaluations is another mark of a capable manager and is typically found in high-performing organizations. Effective evaluations face up to difficult employee situations. It requires courage to give poor performers their due evaluation and to take subsequent action (termination, demotion, low pay increase or none at all, etc.). It takes even greater courage to confront plateaued but seemingly adequate performers—the individuals who seem to reduce their jobs to their capacities. Effective evaluations differentiate among performers and continually seek out the lowest-level contributors.

Managers often avoid conflict that results from candid appraisals. They don't want to disrupt established relationships or trigger interruptions in work. They don't like giving employees bad news, especially "doing bad things to good people," when performance is marginal—and not obviously unsatisfactory. Managers like to keep things calm and put off tough decisions about employees. It's far easier to keep people working and to pay everyone about the same than to differentiate—and back up evaluations with defensible judgments. Yet this is an important management task that should not be shirked.

Managers can help turn around marginal performers by enabling them to recognize that a performance gap exists and to understand its causes and implications. Managers need to reaffirm original and still-desirable objectives, offer the support necessary to achieve these objectives, and set appropriate targets and timing for future evaluation. Confidence is needed that the person will respond as expected (Kaye, 1989; Schermerhorn, Gardner, & Martin, 1990).

Managers learn how to manage, including how to give performance evaluations, largely through example. They learn from those who managed them and evaluated their performance. They gain skill and confidence through experience; courage requires a definite nudge from above or a spark from within. Sadly, many managers say that they never had a performance evaluation and, at management levels, are less likely to have one because practices (and their absence) are perpetuated (Longenecker and Gioia, 1988). Evaluation capabilities, then, are often "book learned," with superiors telling them to do it but not setting the example. Effective training programs, as well as inputs from the human resource staff, can supplement the role such experience plays.

It is difficult, too, for managers to evaluate performance of individuals who are expatriates on international assignments. The evaluating manager often has little direct information that is useful in making evaluations, and may not even fully know what activities are performed and what the work entails. Significant differences among overseas situations affect performance and are not always known to remote managers. Therefore, many managers avoid evaluations of overseas talent or do such evaluations haphazardly. Special efforts are needed to train managers in evaluating performance of international personnel (Howard, 1987).

New executives and new human resource staff often zero in on appraisal programs as a great opportunity to make a change in systems that will be both widely visible in the organization and generally welcomed as an improvement. Revamping appraisal forms and procedures, along with providing new guidelines and supporting training, are surefire ways to get attention and usually have some degree of positive impact on management practices. Merely changing the appraisal forms is often a stimulus for improved evaluations, for a while. If nothing else, it sets managers off guard, and they have to stop and think about what they are expected to do. Consultants often seem to recommend that "whatever you do, change the system."

Performance Improvement Plans

The appraisal process is incomplete without a positive plan for performance improvement. While the judging role of appraisal requires managers to make an evaluation of past performance, the coaching and developing role requires a positive view toward improvement. The focus is on specific gaps or opportunities identified in the course of the evaluation.

Because the performance planning process focuses on the individual, it is often useful to view the tasks from the individual perspective. Exhibit 11-4 illustrates the logical process that individuals follow in planning for performance improvement. The employee has the option of being passive in the goal-setting process and of ignoring the efforts, however well-meaning, of managers to set challenging performance goals. At a minimum, goals for future performance reflect a continuation of past performance.

In today's team-oriented performance environment, performance planning requires examination of the strengths and improvement needs of all individuals who work on common tasks. In quality management parlance, "nobody's perfect, only teams are." Hence performance plans may begin with individual evaluation feedback and improvement planning, and then take into consideration the performance demands and effects of team participation.

Legally Defensible Evaluations

In some instances, performance evaluations have come under fire in the courts, from employees and from skeptical managers. By and large, if evaluations meet the criteria of effectiveness outlined above, they are legally defensible. Simply put, performance evaluations must be carefully prepared. A review of legal decisions will not be presented here, but several basic characteristics are important.

An evaluation needs to be *reasonable* in the view of its users and its critics. This means that the program must be generally understood and accepted as reasonably useful, fair, necessary, and objective. The purpose or purposes of the process are clearly stated, and procedures for the implementation have a minimum of vagueness. Employee participation in the design of the process and subsequent communications are also important.

A second important factor is relevance. A program is *relevant* if it covers

EXHIBIT 11-4 PERFORMANCE IMPROVEMENT PLANS

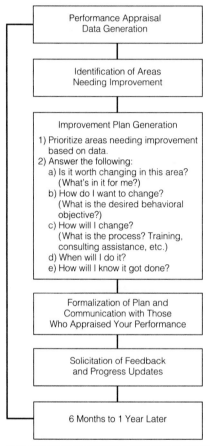

(*Source:* Leonard A. Schlesinger, "Performance Improvement: The Missing Component of Appraisal Systems," *Personnel Journal,* June 1976, p. 274.

those aspects of work that are important and only those aspects. Relevance is assured by clear statements of performance requirements and the kinds of on-the-job activities or behaviors that are necessary for successful performance. Personality traits, race, sex, and age are rarely job-related. The focus should be on how employees go about their work and the nature of the outputs or results created.

Third, appraisals need to be *reliable*. This means that they should be free of significant defects. Evaluations of performance for the same individual at the same time should be consistent among different raters. They should contain a minimum of subjectivity that leads to distortion. Direct measures of output (units produced or sold, for example) are highly reliable, but such measures are not always available or applicable. And so ratings or narrative essays are used as indirect measures, but these are highly dependent on the quality of information available about performance, the ability of appraisers to make reliable judgments, and the use of consistent standards (criteria) against which ratings are made.

In many companies, a formal appeal process provides an important recourse for employees who question the objectivity of the process and also provides another source of inputs on the effectiveness of the process. Increasingly, performance evaluations, together with the actions based on them, are subject to independent review (Bernardin & Klatt, 1985; Eyres, 1989).

Many large companies periodically review their performance evaluation programs and audit the results being obtained from them. Programs found deficient are overhauled; others are updated and reinforced for increased effectiveness. Different programs, involving various techniques, are commonly used in companies to meet diverse needs and circumstances.

At Lawrence Livermore Laboratories, for example, a monitoring system is built into a computer system, prompting employees to answer a series of questions relating to the timeliness, content, and process of their appraisals. The system tabulates the responses and presents summary data graphically. Also, a calculation of actual "yes" responses to total possible "yes" responses yields a performance appraisal index for each set of questions and overall for each department. Departments review and act on their results; a summary report is reviewed by senior management (Perry, More, & Parkison, 1987).

The courts have not indicated any process or evaluation techniques as most acceptable. Nor have they dictated parameters for the design of appraisal programs. It is incumbent on employers, then, to consider the multiple purposes being served by appraisals and to define carefully a philosophy and process that effectively serves the needs.

SUMMARY

In flexible organizations, there is no single performance evaluation approach that fits all situations. Managers need to design evaluation processes to fit specific, often changing business circumstances.

Performance evaluation processes have common elements of design:

• Involvement of employees in shaping performance plans and, subsequently, in reviewing accomplishments
• Use of appropriate techniques, with some pattern of logic and consistency
• Employee and manager understanding of the purposes and processes of evaluation (whys and hows)
• A sense of management responsibility for evaluating performance

Multiple purposes and techniques notwithstanding, the potential effect of appraisal is simple and profound. Performance evaluation gives managers a way to focus employee attention and energies on performance improvement. Through the process, employees identify areas needing improvement, generate improvement ideas, formalize and implement plans, and review progress. It is a key step in enabling employees to perform.

Performance evaluation is not a science. Neither is it intended primarily as a legal defense for decisions adversely affecting employees (e.g., terminations). In many companies, human resource staff and legal staff have promulgated policies and procedures that limit, rather than expand, management flexibility in performance evaluation. While there certainly are legal requirements, as well as a need for a degree of companywide consistency and discipline, managers should use performance evaluation as their tool—as a vital component of the process of managing human resources toward strategic ends. Managers need to address the legal constraints and risks in this areas, as they do in other management activities.

CHAPTER 12

SHARING SUCCESSES

The challenge is to align an organization's pay system with that organization's strategic direction. This is not easy to do—if it were, it would be common practice—but it can be accomplished.

Edward E. Lawler

Everyone wants their efforts to be appreciated. Flexible organizations use varied ways to reward performance and are always seeking innovations that will give them an edge in attracting, retaining, and motivating talent. By rewards, we mean anything that is offered or given for some service or achievement. In aligning employees with strategy, there is no more powerful reward than meaningful sharing in the success of the business, in both financial and nonfinancial ways.

Where companies manage their people strategically, employees understand that their pay and benefits are contingent on the success of the business. Some aspects of their rewards are determined by specific performance results, at the individual, team or unit, or organizational level. Other aspects, such as base pay and benefits, depend merely on the financial viability of the enterprise.

In this chapter we will address:

• How flexible companies use their reward systems to manage performance
• How to pay for performance
• How base salary or wages and benefits are managed within the strategic context
• How flexible organizations celebrate accomplishments using nonfinancial rewards and, specifically, recognitions

Many companies have developed elaborate compensation systems and procedures over the years with the aim of attracting, retaining, and motivating the people necessary to achieve organization goals. Special programs, both financial and nonfinancial, are used as performance incentives. Systematic programs for administering these ensure a sense of equity within the organization, external competitiveness, and efficient use of the company's resources.

LINKING REWARDS TO H.R. STRATEGY

Fundamental questions are being raised in compensation planning regarding the assumptions, strategies, and approaches being applied in various reward systems. The issues that influence compensation programs change over time. In the mid-1970s, wage and price controls, recession, inflation, and job mobility were characteristic influences on policies and practices. In the 1980s, inflation and recession together were important factors. In the 1990s, employees face continued concern for security in employment, while at the same time seeking high rewards for high performance in an exciting, competitive environment.

In this environment, rewards can motivate employees to yield the best performance results for an organization. Rewards are only as good as the effects they have on attracting, retaining, and motivating employees.

Most rewards are financial. These include pay, incentives or bonuses, cash awards, profit sharing, stock ownership, and benefits. In the context of human resource strategy, a company's aim is to design and apply these rewards in ways that maximize the performance impact for each dollar spent. At a minimum, the aim is to contain the spending on rewards that have the least impact.

Increasingly, attention is turning to nonfinancial rewards. As discussed throughout this book, employees are motivated by challenging work, opportunities for personal growth and new responsibilities, recognitions for accomplishments, and a sense of security and belonging. While not entirely without cost to a company, these rewards are more subtle ways of compensating employees for their contributions.

As shown in Exhibit 12-1, rewards may also be distinguished by their relationship to performance. Some—such as benefits, base pay, vacation, job security, and profit sharing—are only remotely related to year-to-year performance. Financial rewards that are contingent on performance include merit pay, incentive bonuses, and special achievement awards.

EXHIBIT 12-1 TYPES OF REWARDS

	Noncontingent	**Contingent**
FINANCIAL	Health care benefits	Merit pay
	Retirement benefits	Incentives/bonuses
	Employee stock ownership	Achievement awards
	Profit sharing	
	Base salary	
NONFINANCIAL	Perquisites	Advancement
	Vacation	Responsibility
	Job security	Challenging work
	Sense of family, belonging	Autonomy, authority to act
	Vacation	Recognition of achievements
	Titles	Personal growth

As noted, the most attractive and most potent motivators of performance are nonfinancial rewards that are contingent on performance: advancement, responsibility, challenging work, autonomy and authority to act, and personal growth. Simple recognition of achievements by managers, peers, and customers is increasingly acknowledged to be an important reward.

For example, scientific and technical talent seek opportunities to broaden their roles, by taking on new projects, expanding roles as team members, or setting up new ventures. Dual-career ladders offer recognition for individual expertise and contributions. For such talent, opportunities for time off the job, including education and sabbatical leaves, are also valued as rewards for performance (Gomez-Mejia, Balkin, & Milkovich, 1990).

Stock ownership plans, whether employee purchase or stock options, provide an identification with the overall success of the company, as reflected in financial markets. But this is a distant link to individual or team performance. Similarly, profit sharing focuses attention on the success of the overall company, in terms of financial results; but this, too, is a distant link. Even though they are ways that employees "share in company successes," they are not generally perceived to be easily influenced by employee performance.

Similarly, retirement, health care, and other benefits are financial rewards, but are also removed from the contingency of performance. These are rewards for staying with a company, however, and they continue to be vital elements in recruiting and retaining talent. They are expected elements of the total rewards structure that, at best, management can reconfigure to contain rising costs while maintaining their motivational value (Gomez-Mejia, 1989; Milkovich & Gomez-Mejia, 1990).

Design Criteria

Rewards need to be designed so that employees understand why they are being given. To directly support strategy implementation and business performance, rewards need to be contingent on behavior or on results. It should not be, to paraphrase Woody Allen, that "half the job is just showing up for work." Coming to work and staying with the company may be a basis for rewards, but rewards need to be related primarily to performance. Performance measures should be perceived by employees as appropriate and realistic; employees need to feel that they have an effect on these measures. Ed Lawler calls this "line of sight" or "line of influence." These terms capture the idea that employees are able to affect the performance measures through their behavior (Lawler, 1990, p. 14).

Performance at any level—individual, team, or unit—may be measured and rewarded. With increasing emphasis on employee involvement, quality management, and teamwork, rewards are being provided at all levels. Rewards need to have a strategic linkage, whether cost, quality, service, or other priority. Rewards can help sustain a shared mind-set in an organization, as through a single incentive pay or profit-sharing system. Similarly, different reward systems and payouts may be appropriate in business situations where there are different competitive conditions and strategic focuses.

Employees need to perceive rewards as within their reach—that if they do certain things, they will receive the rewards. This means that rewards are freely given, and not withheld or reduced after the fact, and that rewards are timely, given soon after the performance is achieved. Even if business results fail to meet targets, compensation promises need to be fulfilled.

Also, employees need to perceive the potential rewards as sufficiently attractive, and substantial, to be worth working for. Rewards need to fit the culture, the needs and interests of the employees, and the prevailing values. An outstanding-performance award of a fully stocked Winnebago might be a hit in the Midwest, but may not be attractive to a worker in Manhattan.

Another design consideration is equity. Employees want rewards to be allocated fairly. This does not mean equally, as employees are increasingly willing to accept differences in pay as long as the differences are reasonable and based on a fairly administered system. For example, there is increasing criticism of top executive pay as being unreasonable, when it goes up when profits go down and when it represents fifty times the pay of the first-level employee.

Finally, flexibility in compensation plans allows greater responsiveness to employee needs. Giving managers greater authority and latitude over compensation decisions affecting subordinates does much to increase the motivational impact of the plans without necessarily increasing their cost or sophistication. Getting managers to differentiate among better and poorer performers, for example, requires not only an adaptable system of merit pay but a sense of responsibility and willingness among the managers to make merit judgments.

International Compensation

Particularly in global business organizations, reward practices are flexible. International compensation practices also vary frequently, with differences among countries widening as currencies gyrate. The weakness of the U.S. dollar causes American executive talent to become relatively inexpensive on the world market. Salary differences pose a problem for multi-national companies. An executive in, say, West Germany may well earn substantially more (in U.S. dollars) than his or her counterpart at headquarters back home. Pay differences are complicated further by variations in employee benefit entitlements in different nations, including differences in perquisites provided (for example, automobiles, special allowances).

Potential conflicts arise when local or host country nationals (HCNs) are paid differently from parent country nationals (expatriates from the company's home country, or PCNs). A company can decide to reward these employees differently, the same, or according to circumstances. The approach depends on the staffing policies and the multi-national management philosophy (Dowling & Schuler, 1990).

Such problems are even more complicated for third country nationals (TCNs)—employees from one country who are working in another country for a company based in a third country. For these employees, even accruing a pension can be a complex matter, because of different pension provisions and statutory employee benefits (such as Social Security). Multi-national corporations typically maintain a multiplicity of pay and benefit programs tailored to the requirements and conditions of the various countries in which they do business.

At the same time, there are pressures to consolidate the various compensation arrangements provided worldwide into a single, common, uniform system. Just as variations may be made for cost of living in different cities within one country, adjustments could be made in other areas of compensation as well. The desire to control costs associated with staffing, particularly PCN and TCN staffing under varied economic conditions around the world, has impelled centralization of human resource policy formulation and compensation administration in some companies.

A global company typically measures financial performance in local currency terms and net of inflation. This allows comparison of apples with apples, worldwide. In addition to financial results, it weighs qualitative measures that support management cooperation and long-term strategic positioning. Three components are evaluated: teamwork within a country and with managers in other countries, achievement of specific strategic actions (e.g., market share, product launches, government relations), and sudden changes in the business environment (e.g., government-imposed controls, trade law changes).

Alternative Reward Programs

There is a variety of ways that companies can reward employees in the context of the human resource management process. In flexible organizations, multiple systems are used simultaneously to focus attention on desired performance priorities.

As summarized in Exhibit 12-2, the various programs range from an individual focus (merit pay and individual incentives) to a companywide focus (stock ownership and profit sharing). They also range in direct performance contingency (high for individual and team rewards and low for stock ownership and profit sharing). The specific results and employee coverage vary as well. This provides an exciting and potentially powerful array of reward vehicles for management to use.

The important principle is that rewards should be contingent on performance, to the extent possible. As organizations become more flexible, needs for initiative, responsibility, adaptability, innovation, risk, and results are appropriately reflected in reward programs, just as they are in other aspects of the human resource process.

VARIABLE PAY

Pay itself is of central importance to life in our society. It is the means of acquiring the necessities as well as the luxuries that constitute lifestyles. But pay is also inherently a yardstick used to judge individual worth and impor-

---

EXHIBIT 12-2 PAY FOR PERFORMANCE ALTERNATIVES

Vehile	Results	Employees Covered
Merit pay	Achievement of specific performance criteria	Individual salaried employees
Individual incentives	Specific short-term performance objectives	Individual salaried employees
Team incentives	Achievement of targeted performance	Employees, supervisors in a work group/unit
Unit incentives	Achievement of unit financial and other objectives	Unit managers, salaried employees across business unit/division
Profit sharing	Identification with company's annual financial results	All employees companywide
Stock ownership	Identification with company's long-term stock appreciation	All employees (stock purchase), executives for stock options

---

tance. From a company viewpoint, pay and other compensation elements constitute an important source of costs. In some labor-intensive service companies, payroll and benefit costs exceed 70% of the total operating costs. Even in manufacturing and other capital-intensive companies, the costs may exceed 40%.

Concern over the effectiveness of compensation programs surrounds the return on each dollar spent (or invested). As a compensation director of a large bank observed, "The most important aspect of compensation is behavioral and motivational. This is the tough part and the aspect that is ignored. In salary administration, action is totally rearguard and we end up using money with minimal effect."

In a survey by The Conference Board, 76% of 500 companies use at least one type of variable pay. The most popular were special achievement awards (40%), followed by performance incentives (36%), lump-sum merit awards (26%), profit sharing (26%), team incentives (18%), and gainsharing (15%) (The Conference Board, 1989).

A study by consultants Sibson & Company found that motivation and sharing of successes are the primary reasons companies adopt variable pay programs. Variable pay helps management focus performance on key organizational goals and priorities. Cost containment and pay competitiveness were less common reasons (see Exhibit 12-3).

Merit Pay

The principal means of adjusting salaries in American industry is the merit pay process. Once known and expected as an annual "service increase," the adjustment to individual salaries is now aimed at motivating and rewarding individual performance. It is not withheld in the future, as are incentive payments. Often adjustments are after the fact, with no clear expectation or

---

EXHIBIT 12-3 REASONS FOR ADOPTING VARIABLE PAY

Reason	Prevalence among All Nonexecutive Employees
Increase motivation to perform at a high level	79%
Share organization success with employees	68%
Focus efforts on attaining specific goals and priorities	62%
Improve pay competitiveness	27%
Reduce fixed compensation cost	22%

Source: *1990 Compensation Planning Survey* (Princeton, N.J.: Sibson & Company, Inc., 1990).

promise of an increase other than the pattern set by past increases. Cost of living, reflected in inflation, affects adjustments; competitive pay levels (and bringing people up, or down, to competitive midpoint averages) influence perceptions of pay changes.

In addition, these adjustments, whether merit-based or not, become a permanent part of an individual's salary. This means that an increase which reflects one year's performance is locked into the base salary in all future years, and thus raises the base upon which all future percentage increases are applied.

The merit pay concept requires making distinctions among those who perform and then adjusting pay to recognize these distinctions. However, adjustments are made within the limits of "ranges," which in turn reflect job worth and external labor market rates. Compression must also be taken into consideration. Hence the freedom of managers to reward performance is constrained by the other compensation variables which are considered to be important.

Employees are generally more concerned with perceived equity of pay compared with others within the organization than with external comparability of pay or even the recognition of outstanding performance. When managers succumb to this concern, they tend to make adjustments toward the norm or level the salaries toward the average. They are reluctant to give extraordinary increases to outstanding performers because of the lack of precision of performance evaluations and because increases become permanent, creating potential future equity problems.

In addition, merit pay funds are limited in the budget process and are often little more than the increased cost of living. In times of little inflation, budgets may be 4% or 5%, and individual increases, therefore, may seem insignificant. Employees may even be given smaller rates of increases or increases "stretched out" over time.

In times of higher inflation, less than full increases constitute a net realized pay decrease; but at least there are dollars to award, and high performers may be given substantial raises. Where merit pay funds represent 6% or 8% of payroll, it is difficult to persuade any employee that an increase is for outstanding performance unless inflation is below that rate. With high inflation, any increase barely keeps the employee's compensation whole, let alone recognizes performance. And to give an outstanding increase to an outstanding performer (for example, 20%), the manager is forced to give other employees less than the norm, which is really an insult in the face of widely perceived rises in the cost of living.

Nevertheless, some companies, and particularly flexible organizations, make big distinctions in the raises they give. Many companies allow increases ranging from 0% to 20%, within the overall constraint of a budgeted merit fund. Implicitly, this forces a distribution among increases. In some companies, this is formally required, as managers are expected to give increases like grades, on a normal "bell" curve. For example, only 10% of the employees receive a substantial raise, and an equal proportion receive a small raise or none. Forcing raises into such categories has the effect of guaranteeing dissatisfaction, among both the employees who question the merit basis of awards and the managers forced to make the distinctions within such rigid parameters.

Organizations need a sound performance evaluation system to support differential merit pay practices. Defending a performance appraisal process as objective and bias-free is difficult enough. Demonstrating a clear linkage of pay raises with performance, in the context of a salary administration system, is another challenge.

Often rewards are differentiated only for the few outstanding performers and for those who are clearly marginal or inadequate. Any variation in merit pay is insignificant for the majority of employees in the middle. A two- or three-point difference in salary increase results in few additional after-tax dollars in the pocket and is tough for a manager to justify. Performance evaluations rarely provide a sufficient basis for differentiating among these employees.

Clearly, the merit pay concept has value. The principal criticisms have to do with its implementation. Thus if adequate merit funds are made available, if managers are trained to make fair appraisals and reward performance fairly, if the merit portion of increases is identified for employees, and if employees are open and trusting as participants in the whole performance-based process, then merit compensation can work.

Lump-Sum Awards

Many companies are giving employees lump-sum cash payments in place of merit increases. One difficulty of granting pay raises, however substantial, is that they are spread out over a whole year as increments in base pay. After deductions, there isn't a sizable amount seen by the employee; after several months, the new base is assumed to be normal. The incentive value of a raise would be greater if a portion of the increase were given all at once.

Companies use "variable merit pay" in several ways. Where base salaries are considered high, relative to competitive levels, salaries are frozen and all increases are given as lump-sum awards. In other cases, adjustments are made to base pay, especially for individual salaries that are below competitive levels, and merit awards are given to employees according to performance. In all cases, the funds allocated for merit increases and awards are determined by company or unit performance (Kanin-Lovers & Graham, 1988; Minken, 1988). In some companies, employees are given the option of taking all or part of a merit increase as a lump-sum award.

Lump-sum awards, which are essentially performance bonuses, are most useful when salary levels are considered high and management is seeking to avoid locking in annual increases in salaries. Some companies have actually reduced employee salary levels, filling the gap with bonus programs that offer higher reward potential. The risk introduced for employees helps build awareness of business performance and treats employees as stakeholders.

AT&T gives lump-sum merit awards to managers who are outstanding performers, often 25% of a group. Merit awards, at least 3% of salary, are given equally at each level and grade to ensure equity. The program was funded by narrowing the salary ranges, limiting increase opportunities.

INCENTIVE AWARDS

Incentives reinforce the efforts of employees to improve performance, while also containing fixed costs of pay programs. They are becoming increasingly popular in companies facing heightened competitive forces and seeking ways to gain a motivational edge.

The advantage of a cash award as an incentive performance bonus is that it is held out as a promise, or possible reward, in return for some specified level of performance or service achieved. In this sense, annual merit increases often fail the test as incentives. Annual merit awards could be incentives, if the conditions are communicated. Other programs specify the standards or objectives to be met for awards to be earned.

One of the simplest and best compensation systems is that used in the sports and entertainment world. Pay is directly and immediately linked to the performance of the individual. It is not likely that industry would or even could emphasize such direct rewards, because employees need a degree of income stability and because performance is not usually so easily identifiable. But the concept of an incentive payment directly tied to behavior has appeal.

The purpose of company incentive pay plans is to encourage employees to perform or produce at extraordinary levels. In most cases, incentives are supplements to base pay based on performance and are not permanent additions to compensation. They are contingent on current performance, whether individual or organizational.

Individual Incentives

Under piecework programs, employees earn all or a portion of their pay based on measured output (sales, production, volume, etc.). Sales commissions are a form of incentive compensation, and usually a highly effective one because of the direct link to individual performance.

Individual incentives are also a factor in sales compensation plans. These plans may provide salary plus a bonus, salary plus a commission, or a commission with or without a "draw" (payments in advance of actual sales). The use of bonuses or commissions is intended to focus and direct sales force efforts while providing salespeople with competitive pay. The design of such plans needs to consider the mix of these elements (and the amount of pay "at risk"), the timing of incentive payments, and the performance measures on which they are based. If well designed, sales incentive plans can be a potent force for achieving business results. If not, employees will find ways to work around them for their own purposes (Cespedes, 1990; Moynahan, 1980).

Unit bonus plans provide a high degree of personal involvement in the unit's performance as a "team." With the increased divisionalization of companies, bonus plans of this type have become more common. A leading bank, for example, moved from a single management bonus plan to more than forty plans focused on specific units as profit centers. In a given year, the Trust Department officers may receive larger bonuses than their peers in Corporate Lending because of their superior performance relative to their objectives.

In a restaurant chain, unit performance is managed through a well-defined unit management system. As discussed in Chapter 4, eight key result areas (KRA) are defined, and standards are set in each. Specific measures are used to assess performance in each of these areas, as discussed in Chapter 10. Each year, unit managers are eligible to receive a bonus award (up to $12,000 in 1990) for measured sales improvement and a similar cash award for measured profit improvement. In addition, specific bonuses are awarded for performance in each of the other key result areas: employee relations, food quality, management training, clean and well-maintained stores, and customer service. Here, amounts up to $6,000 per KRA are awarded based on the performance measures attained. The aggregate bonus may match or exceed the unit manager's base pay in a given year. Assistant managers and other key members of the unit management team receive bonuses proportional to that of the unit manager.

Similar performance incentives are used to reward tellers, service representatives, supervisors, and officers in the branches of a major bank. Bonuses are awarded for results in selling bank products (fee-based services), much like a sales compensation plan. In addition, bonuses are awarded for branch service performance, defined as courtesy, line-waiting time, reliability (accuracy), account retention, and overall customer satisfaction. Awards are made by branch management to the employees from a fund allocated for this purpose, based on the branch's service quality relative to that of all the other branches as indicated on a composite service index. The index is calculated from data collected through ratings by bank observers, logs on wait time, ratings by independent "shoppers," surveys of customers, and branch records.

These programs represent an increasingly popular approach for providing performance-related compensation. Focusing employee attention on key performance areas and involving them in the collection of performance measures are important for performance management; the competition for bonus funds provides recognition for high-performing units (whether in restaurants or bank branches) and incentive to others for improvement.

Team Incentives

Rewards are needed to encourage cooperation, group focus, and shared achievement of objectives. In recent years, a rapidly growing number of incentive plans have been introduced in companies that focus on team performance (Dumaine, 1990; O'Dell, 1989; Ost, 1990; Swinehart, 1986).

Some work-group incentives have been used for many years in manufacturing environments. Gainsharing programs provide cash awards to employees for achievement of unit productivity or financial (usually cost reduction) goals. All gains are commonly shared with all employees in the unit according to a predetermined formula, and the payoff depends on productivity improvement.

Some of the best-known plans of this type are the Scanlon Plan, Improshare, and the Rucker Plan. In addition to these, many companies have developed their own incentive plans to fit their particular needs. In these plans, a financial performance baseline is established, and then reductions in costs are measured to compute the gain. When improvements occur, a bonus pool is created, half of which is paid out to the employees as a percentage of their base pay, on a monthly basis (Graham-Moore, 1983; Hammer, 1988; Lawler, 1990).

There are hundreds of plans and modifications tailored to other measures such as service quality or claims processing. While gainsharing usually attains positive results, its acceptance has been slow because it requires a participative work environment and other conditions for it to be effective (Lawler, 1988; Thomas & Olson, 1988).

An innovative program is used in the Fibers Department of DuPont. It's called Achievement Sharing. Initially, it reduces employee pay by 6%. If the department meets its annual profit goal, the workers receive their 6%. If the department reaches 150% of its goal, employees receive a 12% bonus. In this way, they share in both the company's gains and its losses (Ost, 1990).

In another case, AT&T Credit Corporation organized its various credit departments into full-service, autonomous teams of ten to twelve employees. The unit provides AT&T customers with financing for leased equipment. Each team works with the same field agents and customers, processing lease applications. Through a bonus plan tied to team expenses and profits, team members earn up to $1,500 additional pay a year. The plan has been effective and has vastly increased the volume of work handled, using less time and with improved service (O'Dell, 1989).

Management Incentives

Management incentive programs are often used to reward contributions to the profitability of individual units, as opposed to the overall company. These often include incentive bonuses (usually cash payments), perquisites, and long-term incentives (for example, stock options, deferred cash awards, stock awards, performance shares). While a more attractive reward than cash has never been conceived of, noncash elements of executive pay have grown in popularity. The best combination of incentives for a company depends on the preferences of the managers affected, and hence there is always a high degree of discretion applied in designing and modifying executive compensation programs.

Awards are designed to stimulate attainment of annual goals and objectives in a company. Normally, only those managers who are in positions to have a significant impact on annual results are allowed to participate, although there is a tendency for participation in such plans to expand somewhat over time. Sometimes companies have special one-shot "spot" bonus arrangements to reward outstanding performance of other managers not included in the formal bonus plan.

The bonus fund is determined by a formula which is normally tied directly to the annual profitability of the business or return on investment. The allocation of individual awards is usually determined through measured achievement of specified goals or budgets. Naturally, quantitative, financially indexed formulas are more easily administered because there is less subjectivity (except as implied by accounting practices).

Performance-based bonus plans have been widely implemented and are believed to be effective. Careful planning helps ensure that the program is perceived as equitable by the participants, as cost-effective to the shareholders, and as incentive for the results desired. Often such plans are overhauled periodically to correct problems that have emerged: eligibility is reviewed, evaluation and allocation procedures are changed, and the potential size of awards is realigned.

Among the problems that arise in bonus programs, the most difficult relate to organization. Centralized bonus awards promote corporate synergy but reward the poorer-performing managers at the expense of the better performers; decentralized awards are difficult to administer evenhandedly because the standards (target levels) may not be level and many separate management judgments are required. Also, where acquisitions are involved, it is difficult to compensate old and new employees on the same par because standards may differ.

Where entrepreneurial or venture managers are included, high reward must accompany high risk, and this is addressed in today's flexible organizations. However, traditional institutional organizations remain reluctant to do the same. Executives worry that managers will make their results look good one year at the expense of future years (for example, by cutting back on maintenance) or will not have full control over the results they are judged by (this is the situation for regional insurance managers who do not have responsibility for claims).

There has been a growing desire to relate executive pay to company financial performance. One company, McKesson, went so far as to link the compensation for its top 700 executives with stock price. The vice president of Personnel indicated that "tying management rewards to long-term stock values creates a win-win for management and stockholders." The top fifteen officers are still covered by a long-term incentive plan that consists of restricted stock grants, stock options, and cash.

At McKesson, one plan replaced two plans that treated management levels differently. The one plan unifies the opportunity for an annual bonus and fosters team effort by using the same measures for middle-level managers and the CEO. For a middle manager at McKesson, an annual bonus would reflect performance results at each company level. For example, 50% of a manager's bonus would be based on the local unit's performance, 25% on divisional performance, and 25% on corporate results. Required rates of return are set for each unit and level (Gildea, 1989).

Profit Sharing

Profit-sharing plans are designed to have a similar effect, but often lack the immediacy to yield an incentive impact on performance. They were once categorized as an employee benefit, designed to create financial security and to supplement retirement benefits. However, in many companies, they are used as an incentive tool to focus employee attention on the bottom line of the company business.

These plans are generated through company contributions that reflect year-to-year profits earned. Each employee typically receives a share of the corporate allocation based on a fixed percentage of annual pay. In some companies, the shares may be taken as cash or company stock, or may be invested (e.g., in mutual funds). In some cases, employees may also make contributions to the plans, under specified IRS provisions.

Profit sharing has the power to draw the attention of employees to the performance of the company as a whole. It generates interest in company financial performance and concern for revenue growth, expense containment, and customer satisfaction. At Hewlett-Packard, for example, the profit-sharing plan used to be a deferred program, but now provides a cash bonus to most employees for each year that profitability goals are met. Other major companies have adopted similar plans, including General Motors, Ford, AT&T, and Alcoa.

Such plans help contain wage and salary costs by making pay more variable. The companies typically slow the growth of base salaries and rely on profit sharing to provide payouts when company performance merits them. At Alcoa, the plan establishes a bonus pool of about 20% of profits earned above a threshold target, 5% of U.S. assets. In a good year, Alcoa's 7,000 salaried employees could get an award equaling 7% or more of their salaries (Schroeder, 1988).

Stock Ownership

Stock options are a common vehicle to reward executives for long-term company performance. Stock options allow long-term capital gain treatment on stock appreciation, without cost incurred to the executive until the options are exercised. They don't require performance target setting or measures but, rather, recognize executive contribution and promote identification with company performance. By another method, executives may receive restricted stock grants. Here they are given actual shares of stock which vest over time as long as the executive stays with the company. Nearly half of all large industrial corporations use this method, even though the tax advantages come and go with changing regulations (McMillan & Young, 1990).

One aim of such long-term incentive programs is to help balance the attention given to short-term results, rewarded by short-term bonus programs. Another aim is to provide the executives with tax-favorable compensation arrangements, usually involving capital appreciation paralleling company growth and success.

An increasing number of companies share stock with all employees. One survey of growth companies found that more than half of them have such programs (McMillan & Young, 1990). These organizations want everyone to focus on performance and growth and to share in the company's success. These plans include:

- Stock option plans: plans which allow employees to purchase stock at a set price at a later date
- Stock purchase plans: voluntary purchase programs in which employees can buy stock at 85% of current value, often purchased through payroll deductions
- Employee stock ownership plans (ESOPs): plans in which stock is placed in a trust for employees at a set percentage of each employee's salary
- Employee savings plans: such as 401(k) plans, in which the company matches employee contributions with stock

3Com, a computer network developer in California, offers a stock option program to all new hires. The program addresses the company's desire to share its success with employees and grew from a survey of 3Com's competitors. By 1991, 20% of all outstanding shares were granted or were available for grants.

Acuson, another high-tech company, sought to link base pay and stock incentives. Stock matrix guidelines for new employees were established based on salary grade and merit reviews. Employment offers typically include a stock option that will be matched by the company on the employee's second- and third-year anniversaries, the amount depending on individual performance.

Employee ownership has worked out well for Avis, which is fully owned by an ESOP. The 12,500 employees at Avis have succeeded in making the company increasingly profitable and have been repaying the debt obligation for the purchase at a faster rate than planned. Morale, productivity, and service have improved, according to all measures used (Kirkpatrick, 1988).

In an ESOP, employee involvement programs are especially effective because the workers are motivated to provide extra effort. Also, tax provisions are beneficial to ESOP-owned companies. About 1,500 companies were majority-owned by ESOPs in 1989, including health care companies HealthTrust

(Nashville) and Epic Healthcare Group (Dallas), Avondale Industries (ship-building), Dan River (textiles), and Wierton Steel (Kirkpatrick, 1988).

America West Airlines simply requires new employees to invest an amount equal to 20% of their first-year salaries in the company's stock. Edward Beauvais, the CEO, believes that profits should be channeled into new planes, facilities, and capital projects—and that employees should encouraged to focus on long-term success. The company finances the purchase and collects payments each month. At the same time, wages and salaries are somewhat below industry levels. While the stock has ranged from $3 to $15 over the years, it pays no dividends. The "employee-owned" airline believes that this attracts people who want responsibility, are risk takers, and will be highy committed (O'Toole, 1989).

BASE SALARY AND BENEFITS

As discussed, companies maintain a basic structure of wages (or salaries) and benefits. As organizations become more flexible, they are seeking to attune these reward systems to changing business needs and competitive conditions.

Base Salary

A traditional job evaluation program, used in most large companies, entails analysis of jobs, writing of job descriptions, evaluation of job information against a set of criteria, grouping and grading of these jobs into pay levels, development of a structure, and then pricing of this overall structure and the jobs slotted in it against comparable data from other companies.

In institutional organizations, job evaluation has served its intended purposes well. It is a formal process which provides a rational, justifiable explanation for the pay levels assigned to each position in the company. However, as companies become more flexible, they encounter difficulties. Job evaluation is a costly and time-consuming process. It arranges jobs within a hierarchical structure based largely on subjectively defined management values of what the jobs are worth (not always wholly separate from the subjective evaluations of the job incumbents). And the use of job comparisons in the marketplace assumes that jobs are fairly evaluated elsewhere. Employees may, therefore, be paid more or less than their "real worth" because of bias or error inherent in the process. Also, traditional job evaluation tends to reinforce hierarchy, by slotting each position at a level of relative value.

Job evaluation approaches have changed over the years, but the fundamental issue remains unresolved: How can we fairly and objectively determine the worth of a job? Every self-respecting salary administration system has always involved the writing of job descriptions. They are the bedrock, the basis for subsequent building of the salary structure and for pricing of positions relative to one another and the market. The basic duties or activities, responsibilities (including assets and subordinates), and accountabilities (including measures or indicators of results by which successful performance is noted) are defined.

Approaches for evaluating jobs have varied. Ranking systems and classification systems (such as that used by the federal government) tend to be global and subjective, but provide a basis for perceptions of a structured approach that has objectives of fairness and equity. Point-factor and factor-comparison methods assign points to various perceived characteristic aspects of jobs and benefit from a degree of quantification. But they are frequently no less subjective in the manner of applied judgment.

All of these approaches require learning a system and then applying "good managerial judgment" in making it work. All require periodic updating and revision, usually including the job description itself; and this implies that job evaluations are inherently always out of date to some degree. There needs to be concern for external labor market patterns in considering such jobs, to avoid the tendency to perpetuate past judgments of job worth. Evaluations always weigh the job, not the incumbent, and thus either ignore the influence of the incumbent on the job or inherently violate the rule by considering the person as well.

Job evaluation has a high degree of subjectivity: in the writing of job descriptions, in the slotting of jobs in grades, in the choice of factors to be used, in the choice of benchmark jobs to be compared externally, and in the very fact of basing job worth on prevailing pay rates. Such sources of subjectivity are seen as potential sources of discriminatory practices.

A statistical modeling approach is gaining wide use. It examines only a few key evaluation factors—selected and weighted by a company, in a multiple regression model—and allows establishment of a competitive and equitable structure without the tedious process of description writing and managerial consensus on each position's relative worth. Once established, the model is used to determine the fit or worth of specific positions (Milkovich & Gomez-Mejia, 1990).

An alternative approach, popular especially in flexible organizations, is skill-based pay. Instead of paying for the worth of the job, this system pays the people what they are worth in terms of valued skills. It has been widely applied in manufacturing settings, particularly those with high employee involvement and work team structures, as a way to encourage cross-training of talent. This permits more flexible staffing and promotes team responsibility for the total work performed. It provides increases to employees for new skills learned, usually based on training and testing. Often the skills are horizontal additions (learning other tasks and jobs), but they may also represent depth of skills or knowledge (Lawler, 1990; Krajci, 1990).

Employee Benefits

Just as executives desire perquisites, all employees like to have supplemental forms of compensation. Retirement benefits, life and medical insurance, profit sharing, and other benefits have grown in popularity over the years and are now commonplace. The expenditures by employers for employee benefits have steadily expanded and now often exceed 35% of payroll.

The particular benefits provided and the costs paid by employers vary by industry. However, the trend in employee benefits is toward higher costs, even without significant liberalization of benefit programs. Inflation alone accounts for much of the rising dollar costs of benefits.

Spiraling health care costs have affected the benefits given to employees. Where there are fixed ceilings on benefits (for example, hospitalization, retirement income), the value of the benefits may diminish.

For retirees covered by private pension plans, inflation is a severe problem, and companies must strive to upgrade the benefits with cost-of-living adjustments. Many companies are requiring future retirees to share the costs of retirement medical benefits. This move is encouraged, in part, by an accounting requirement for advance funding of such future retirement benefit costs.

Employee benefits, once viewed by employers as a gratuity to employees, are now viewed by employees as an earned component of total compensation. As a result, it is difficult for employers to modify benefits or to control the costs. Flexible benefit programs help control the costs and enhance the benefits provided. The most valuable strategy open to management is increased communication with employees regarding benefits and increased employee participation in the allocation of benefit expenditures.

Under such a program, a company provides minimum core requirements in such areas as health insurance, life insurance, vacations, and retirement income. Then it allocates a fixed amount of money, often expressed in terms of credits, to employees so that they may opt for additional benefits suited to their needs. Some employees may wish expanded medical and dental coverage; others may prefer increased vacation time. A person near retirement may wish to enrich the pension coverage.

Before Public Service of New Mexico trimmed its employee benefits, it held focus groups with employees to determine what approaches they favored. The response: "If you aren't going to give me everything I had, at least give me a choice." The result was a flexible benefits plan, including a choice of deductible on health insurance, tax-free spending accounts for health insurance and day care, and supplemental life insurance, none of which had been available before.

RECOGNITIONS

Increasing emphasis is being given to nonfinancial recognition of performance. Of course, the recognitions need to fit the interests and culture of the employees. What is a meaningful recognition for some people may not be for others.

The kind of special treatment given for individual accomplishments is limited only by the creativity of the managers and employees. Article features in company publications, local newspapers, or professional/industry media are low-cost ways to recognize accomplishments. Such recognitions may be as simple as time off from work or a round of applause at an employee meeting. They may have token financial value, such as award pins, flowers, chauffeur/ limousine service, gifts or coupons for gifts, dinners or travel, tickets to sports or other events, special designated parking, or special attire (hat, blazer).

For example, Marriott Corporation annually honors eighteen to twenty outstanding employees with the J. Williard Marriott Award of Excellence. The award recognizes outstanding employees whose performance, teamwork, and commitment to excellence are clearly exemplary. The individuals are singled out by their coworkers and are nominated by their managers. At a special awards dinner held in their honor, each receives a medallion bearing the likeness of the founder of Marriott Corporation. Each medallion is inscribed with the words of the founder's basic values: achievement, dedication, character, ideals, effort, and perseverance. The honorees are featured in an issue of the employee publication, *Marriott World*.

For teams or work units, managers make sure that everyone involved is acknowledged and that some kind of celebration is held. Some companies allocate a small budget amount to cover expenses for occasional pizzas, evening dinner parties, or outings (picnics or excursions). When a project is completed, targets are met, or other successful accomplishments or benchmarks are reached, employees appreciate recognition. Such events bring closure to a task and point out the importance of everyone's contribution.

Often, performance awards are presented to manufacturing groups to support a team concept. For example, Intecolor, a manufacturer of color graphics computer terminals, introduced a Personal Responsibility in Daily Effort (PRIDE) program in support of its quality improvement efforts. It combines teamwork and noncash rewards to encourage excellence from production workers and supervisors. PRIDE teams, consisting of a captain and twenty-five members, compete to achieve the highest improvement in monthly defect rates. The captains meet with representatives from R&D and engineering as a quality circle every two weeks to review problems and solutions. Awards include windbreakers or gift certificates for all team members and a grand prize drawing, with one team member winning a television or VCR (Beylouny, 1984).

At Convex Computer, CEO Robert Paluck tries to do things that are different. Once he paid everyone's quarterly profit sharing with 216 silver dollars. Another time he provided cruises for top-performing employees who were recommended by coworkers.

Many flexible organizations, particularly technical and research-based companies, give special awards for individual or team excellence. Awards seem particularly attractive to scientific and technical personnel. These ''Nobel''-type prizes entail special recognition, in the form of a plaque or other distinctive gift, and sometimes a cash award that is a token $500 or a substantial amount such as $50,000 (Friedson, 1985). In most cases, the recognition itself—an award pin, a picture in the company newsletter, and the attention from others—is more important than the cash.

Federal Express has its Gold Falcon program for outstanding performers selected by a special management committee. The employees are honored at a formal awards ceremony and are given ten shares of company stock. Similarly, American Express Travel Related Services rewards employees who have gone beyond the call of duty for customers. Candidates are nominated by coworkers or customers as "Great Performers." Winners are recognized locally, and regional winners are honored at the New York City headquarters as part of an all-expenses-paid one-week trip.

Of course, other types of awards and recognitions motivate employees, but are not necessarily focused on performance. Service recognition awards, awards for completion of training, awards for voluntary community service, and suggestion awards are all worthy but are not performance-related. For example, Crain Communications, a Chicago publisher, awards cash gifts to employees on their fifth, tenth, and twentieth company anniversaries. Crain also gives money to celebrate weddings or the birth of a child.

A Kadoo program at 3Com allows managers to act quickly to provide employee performance awards. Kadoo, a play on the word *kudos* (or "praise"), allows managers to nominate people from every department once each quarter. Awards include stock options (60 to 60,000 shares), cash (typically 25% to 30% of monthly base pay), and in-kind awards (e.g., weekend trips). In a given year, more than 45% of all employees receive some type of award (Radford & Kove, 1991).

America West Airlines gives its employees a quarter of their annual salary in advance when they reach each four-year anniversary. These bonuses allow employees to make major purchases. Under another program, heavily discounted plane tickets, called "guest passes," are awarded to employees with perfect attendance (as reported by employees and managers). Both awards reflect the company's trust in its people (O'Toole, 1989).

SUMMARY

Managers tend to expect and use rewards that are similar to the kind they have received and given in the past. Old practices, like old habits, are hard to break. Only by looking at rewards differently—as employees sharing in the successes of the business—will managers shake old thinking and embrace innovative, more powerful, and more relevant compensation and recognition practices.

As many institutional organizations become more flexible, significant changes are required in the use of rewards. The philosophy of and approach to compensation shift from one of consistency, predictability, and structure toward one of diversity, change, and variable performance results. Nonfinancial rewards are used more widely, more frequently, and more creatively. These shifts reflect changes in the way the company manages human resources and aligns rewards with human resource strategy (see Exhibit 12–4).

Pay for performance is more important than ever. To implement this direct link of rewards with individual, team, unit, or company success, organizations

---

EXHIBIT 12-4 REWARDS IN FLEXIBLE ORGANIZATIONS

Institutional	Flexible
Single pay plan or consistent plans	Multiple and different pay plans
Emphasis on salary, regular adjustments	Emphasis on variable pay, related to performance
Homogeneous, consistent pay treatment for employees	Differential pay treatment, but all perceived as fair and equitable
Greater emphasis on internal consistency than competitiveness	Greater emphasis on external competitiveness
Jobs defined carefully through descriptions, evaluation	Simple, changing descriptions; job focus is on clarifying roles, tasks, and expectations
Emphasis on job scope/responsibility, assets and people managed, length of service	Emphasis on results attained
Hierarchical orientation	Individual and team performance orientation
U.S. oriented	Country and globally oriented

---

use various vehicles: merit pay, incentives, profit sharing, and stock ownership. Although such vehicles have been available for years, few companies effectively use them in support of strategic change.

Compensation and benefits have been treated in many companies as specialized functions, managed by human resource and financial staff. To achieve the desired contribution in aligning employees with strategy, compensation and benefits need to be a consideration of all managers. Ideas and approaches need to be developed and implemented at all levels with employee involvement; diversity of approaches needs to be encouraged, and changes in practices need to be the norm. Consistency and continuity are fine for institutions, but may be impediments for flexible organizations.

MANAGING THE HUMAN RESOURCE FUNCTION

CHAPTER 13

MANAGING THE HUMAN RESOURCE FUNCTION

The personnel function will change drastically in the years ahead. It will have to tackle new and different tasks. It will in all probability have to behave quite differently, that is as "line" rather than as "staff."

Peter F. Drucker

As companies have sought to be flat, lean, flexible, and nimble, they have trimmed their staff functions, including human resource staff. Many have decentralized the function to put staff closer to line departments and to increase business contact and accountability. Often, companies have replaced key human resource managers, transferring line managers to the function or hiring executives from outside to help the function be better attuned to business needs.

The human resource function can and should play an important role in helping companies implement strategies. However, this requires that it play roles different from those traditionally defined.

Senior management expects the human resource function to provide leadership and support in addressing its people-related business issues. The human resource staff are being asked to help chart the course for managing human resources as conditions change. As one CEO commented, "We expect the ideas, leadership, and support we get from our best staff and consultants."

The process of developing and implementing human resource strategy, outlined in this book, is inherently a line management responsibility. In concept, a company does not need a human resource staff; managers can be self-sufficient. In practice, however, the human resource staff provide the guidance and support that managers need to understand and apply the process. Human resource staff play a vital role on the management team—to ensure that people-related business issues are effectively addressed by management.

What should management expect of the human resource function, and how should the function be managed to meet these expectations? This is a subject that warrants a whole book, not merely a chapter. In the context of human resource strategy, we will briefly address:

- The service roles of the human resource staff
- How the function may be organized to fulfill changing roles and expectations
- How the function may best be staffed and talent developed to enhance staff capabilities
- How effectiveness and efficiency of the function may be evaluated

The human resource function needs to be structured and managed in the way a company is structured and managed. The approaches in companies today are, therefore, varied. However, experience among leading companies suggests trends and points for consideration.

SERVICE ROLES

Historically, the human resource staff's primary function was to provide operational services for line managers and employees. The function—in the past variously named Employee Relations, Human Relations, and Personnel—emphasized delivery of services related to recruiting, selection, placement, training, labor and employee relations, pay, benefits, and other actions. The function developed systems, procedures, and policies, and ensured their application through monitoring or control.

The image of the function as a supportive, administrative, functionally specialized staff is changing rapidly as staff become involved with management in shaping and implementing actions addressing important human resource issues. Management expectations are changing, and human resource staff are providing services that are often directly related to critical management issues. Often, staff take the lead in defining these issues and shaping the strategies needed to address them.

Managers as Customers

Increasingly, human resource staff are viewed as providing services to their customers or clients. Human resource staffs serve multiple constituents as customers. These may include senior executives, line managers, employees, contractors, union leaders, community groups, and government agencies. The roles of human resource staff depend on the balance given to the expectations of these various constituencies. Often, the staff is viewed as allied with employees, representing their interests and serving their needs. Increasingly, however, management is regarded as the preeminent client (Tsui, 1987).

Services include all activities oriented to the requirements of their users. Services, by nature, require the clients to help define what is expected (including service standards) and to help assess whether the work performed met these expectations. Client needs, therefore, are continually assessed as they change, and the activities of the function shift to meet changing requirements.

There is a growing body of experience and literature defining ways to deliver quality services (Reif & Walker, 1991; Zeithaml, Parasuraman, & Berry, 1990). Service expectations or standards include such factors as:

- Tangible quality: communications materials, equipment and facilities, people
- Reliability: performing the promised service dependably, consistently, and accurately
- Responsiveness: helping customers promptly and in the desired manner
- Assurance of integrity: conveying trust, confidence, and credibility through employee knowledge and professional behavior
- Empathy: showing individualized customer attention; accessibility, communications, flexibility, caring

Many of the activities of a human resource function are services provided to customers, internal or external. These multiple "constituencies" have expectations of the function which shape the definition of effective performance. In these cases, the functions that are most effective are those that consistently manage expectations of their constituents in the right direction and then meet or exceed them.

In a study by Anne Tsui, the following criteria were found to be used by senior managers in evaluating the effectiveness of the human resource function:

- Level of cooperation by the function
- Line managers' opinions regarding the effectiveness of the function
- Quickness and effectiveness of responses to each question brought to the function
- Rating of quality of information and advice provided to senior management
- Satisfaction and dissatisfaction of clients, managers, and employees
- Degree to which the department has a strategy to support local management business plans in relation to human resources
- Average time to fill requisitions
- The degree to which the function is open and available to employees to deal with problems
- Employees' trust and confidence in the human resource function (Tsui, 1987)

Such a varied mix of factors indicates that customers of the human resource function define service quality in many ways. It is little wonder, then, that human resource functions vary widely in the ways they define and measure their effectiveness. Where a companywide "total quality management" process exists, a staff group can define more rigorously its internal customers' expectations and standards and then subsequently measure how well it is meeting those expectations. It also provides a basis for ongoing dialogue and negotiation among staff and client users of staff services.

The application of such standards to the human resource function requires that internal customers be identified and their requirements defined. Some human resource functions go through this process as part of their company's overall total quality management process. Other functions have introduced their own service quality program (Albrecht, 1990; Bowen & Greiner, 1986; Schuler & Jackson, 1988).

Service Expectations

An insurance company focused its human resource function directly to support a more aggressive business strategy. Its stated mission is "to support managers in their efforts to maximize the contribution of employees in achieving successful competitive performance." This view was explained as follows:

• While the function provides services to all employees and interacts with the community, vendors, retirees, and others, its primary client is management.

• The function seeks to help managers understand and implement ways in which they can best attract, retain, motivate, develop, and utilize employees in support of business objectives.

• The focus of all effort is on competitive performance, meeting customer expectations and ensuring quality of products and services. In this context, the human resource function shares responsibility for the ultimate delivery of products and services to customers.

The human resource division of a manufacturing company defined its customer orientation as follows: "The function recognizes that the primary users of Human Resource services are the managers of the organization and the Corporation itself [senior management]. By serving them appropriately, we will also ensure that all employees are equitably managed." This company was careful to stipulate that an important role of the staff is to monitor and ensure implementation of policies that are in the company interest. One example of this is necessary compliance with legal requirements relating to the management of employees.

In an oil company, the mission statement has been revised regularly over several years. It now states that the function "provides leadership and support to management by developing, integrating and implementing human resources strategies that maximize employee and organizational effectiveness in concert with the company's goals."

In these companies, the focus of the human resource function is on helping managers manage human resources effectively, in the course of achieving business objectives. The primary role of staff is to help managers understand and fulfill their responsibilities in managing people.

The human resource function exists to create value—to help the management team gain a competitive edge through the management of people. Merely bringing practices up to competitive parity—such as pay and benefits, diversity practices, or employee training and development—is not enough. An edge is needed to allow the business to excel in its management.

Staff need to manage their "client relationships" actively, involving managers in defining the services required and shaping expectations of service areas and levels. Staff need to define the specific levels and patterns of service required, and not treat all managers, employees, and other "customers" alike. They need to provide services with a competitive market mentality—charging back for costs (at least mentally), establishing service agreements, and outsourcing as appropriate. Finally, they need to obtain and act on feedback about their performance, using informal reactions, formal surveys, and tracking of performance on specific actions (e.g., recruitment speed and quality).

Some managers would prefer to be relieved of responsibility for human resource decisions. In the military, in the Catholic Church, and in many Japanese companies, "personnel departments" act with line authority and actively make needed decisions for managers (Drucker, 1986). In western companies, staff lack the authority to act and are generally more passive. They actively seek to enable managers to take action rather than act for them. In defining service, this distinction is important; service does not require staff to do everything for managers.

Through the development and adoption of human resource strategies, management at each company level addresses the relevant human resource issues. These priorities influence the roles and the skills required of human resource professionals. A business may be addressing particular priorities in managing innovation, quality enhancement, cost reduction, and other strategic thrusts, which may require human resource staff actions. In addition, the rate of change and intensity of these strategic issues affect the urgency for action, or "pain," which defines expectations.

Managers expect the human resource staff to guide and assist them in employee selection, appraisal, termination, and other actions. They recognize that legal requirements and standards of good practice impose constraints on managerial flexibility in such areas. Also, managers readily defer to staff for guidance on such matters as employee benefits plan design, labor relations, and other specialized areas. They seek inputs on competitive practices, legal constraints, tough questions of trade-offs, interpretation of values, long-term effects of actions, and new resource priorities. Staff provide the knowledge and functional expertise that managers need to rely upon.

As management staffing becomes leaner and spans wider, many managers would like the staff function to provide more, not less, administrative and specialized services. Counseling, college relations, affirmative action, payroll, benefits planning, grievance handling, tuition assistance, regulatory compliance, and a wide array of other activities are perceived as being necessary, and are believed by many managers to be more efficiently handled by central staff.

Services in some areas are being performed efficiently through the use of on-line computer systems. In this way, neither line managers nor staff need to spend undue time handling routine transactions such as pay actions, records changes, candidate searches, or job grading. Furthermore, reducing the complexity and redundancy of some activities eliminates unneeded work for managers and staff. The challenge to human resource staff is to perform necessary functions while minimizing the administrative burden on managers and the cost to the organization.

Service calls for flexibility in human resource practices. A diversified company has shifted responsibility for virtually all employee relations policies to operating divisions. In other companies, programs are being redesigned to implement more flexible management practices. HR policies and practices are designed to aid management flexibility, allowing for diversity where it is needed, yet maintaining companywide coordination where required. In many companies, staff are overhauling policies, systems, and practices affecting the ways in which employees are managed.

The strategic context of a company influences management expectations. The HR function needs to operate consistently with the developmental stage of the organization—whether it is a start-up, growing, or mature as an enterprise (Baird & Meschulam, 1988). As discussed in previous chapters, "garages" have a very limited human resource function, concentrating on basic administrative tasks and external recruiting. Institutions, at the other extreme, have strong staff functions, armed with policies, systems, and programs to ensure consistent practices across the organization (Walker, 1988).

In today's more flexible companies, human resource functions operate in different business units according to their different strategic situations and management demands. The functions' strategies and roles change to meet the different managers' expectations and requirements. In institutional situations, the function needs to ensure consistency and continuity in management practices. In entrepreneurial situations, it needs to encourage innovation and informality. In flexible situations, it needs to maintain a balance of order and informality that allows rapid change while keeping a focus on organizational strengths. According to Cornell professor Lee Dyer, this is the major challenge for human resource staffs in the nineties.

Managers also expect staff to discontinue unneeded activities, policies, and programs that consume time unnecessarily. In this way, staff may reduce time demands of routine activities and gain time for initiatives. Accordingly, human resource staffs review and improve their operations, reduce costs, reduce paperwork, eliminate activities, and contract out services, as appropriate. Not waiting for mandated cutbacks, they continually review and evaluate expenses and implement incremental changes to become and stay lean. Flexible HR functions aggressively seek to be perceived as "bureaucracy busters," setting an example for other staff functions and line organizations.

Strategic Leadership

An important dimension of service is leadership in strategic change. In flexible organizations, human resource staff help shape management expectations in the broader business interest. Senior management increasingly looks to human resource staff to help lead and implement changes relating to human resource issues and strategies. This means that the staff play an active role in organization, productivity, quality, culture, restructuring, downsizing, reskilling, mergers or acquisitions, and other management initiatives.

John Kotter, author of *The Leadership Factor,* observed that "HR people have got to stop conceptualizing their role as a 'professional' individual contributor and realize that their job is to help provide corporations with leadership on HR issues." Leadership, he wrote, "is precisely what staff HR professionals need, especially when commitment is lacking from the top to HR issues" (Kotter, 1988).

Human resource staff have the opportunity to help a company build its key source of competitiveness for the nineties and beyond: "Our people work more effectively than your people; our leaders are better than your leaders" (Reif, 1991). Once staff understand business strategies and economics, they can contribute to business discussions and decisions where people issues are important. Increasingly, these include most discussions and decisions relating to service, quality, speed, and costs.

Staff need to look for the opportunities to make a contribution and not wait to be asked to provide inputs or merely help implement a formulated action plan. They may go for the "white space"—the areas where others have not contributed fully. They may contribute by asking the right (strategic) questions and by proposing and evaluating alternative courses of action. This leadership role is a consulting role, calling for human resource staff to be on the management team, acting as peers of other managers.

Human resource staff may also change the ways in which managers manage people. Specific human resource management practices are certainly influenced (e.g., recruiting practices, managing diversity). However, the effect is often far greater, helping managers adapt their capabilities to rapidly changing demands of flexible organizations. HR staff help redesign the organization, including structure, work flows and decision processes, and job design. They help build more flexible and focused staffing. They help shape organizational, unit, and individual managerial performance expectations (KRAs and objectives). They help enable performance through teamwork, coaching, and feedback. In the nineties and beyond, the development of managers will be a key focus of human resource staff.

Finally, strategic leadership calls for focusing the human resource function on key human resource strategies and priorities. Human resource staff take leadership in addressing those needs that go beyond maintaining parity. They pursue opportunities to build distinction for the business through superior management of people. This requires focusing on the appropriate human resource strategies—people-intensive business strategies and directional plans that will truly make a difference.

Customer Satisfaction

The ultimate strategic linkage for human resource staff is directly with the external business customer. Staff may directly help satisfy customer needs

(Schlesinger & Heskett, 1991; Ulrich, 1991). This approach is being applied in a growing number of companies, particularly those focusing on service quality as a competitive strategy. For example, at 3M, the human resource staff consult with individual business units to help them meet customer expectations. By assessing employee satisfaction, developing an improved performance appraisal process, and designing employee suggestion systems, HR staff have been meeting the needs raised in the process.

At Marriott Hotels and Resorts, the human resource function spearheaded many of the initial efforts to develop a total quality program and bore a large part of the responsibility for its progress. According to Jim Moyer, vice president of Quality Improvement and Human Resource Services, "We feel that although the process of quality improvement belongs in all of the functional areas of operation, it is essentially driven by human resources" (Scovel, 1990).

Human resource practices may be used to gain customer commitment for a company. Involving customers in human resource practices such as hiring, training, development, and organization design draws them into long-term interdependence, shared values, and common strategies (Ulrich, 1989). Few companies have gone this far, but the potential exists for a direct impact by the human resource function on strategic business development.

Through innovative applications of human resource practices, the human resource staff can help a company build and sustain its competitive advantage. The sources lie in each area of the process discussed in this book, including the shaping of expectations, organization, staffing, development, and management of performance. Unifying human resource practices with the strategic direction of the business and, in turn, with customer requirements gives a company added leverage (Ulrich, 1989).

Human resource functions (and the human resource managers and professionals in them) have an opportunity to impact business performance by acting as part of the management team. Robert Galvin, former CEO of Motorola, predicts that "human resource professionals will be called on to think and act like line managers to address people-related business issues. Managers will increasingly expect HR to think and act and to view human resource activities from a business perspective" (Galvin, 1989).

ORGANIZATION

Like other staff functions, the human resource function is becoming leaner and stronger in many organizations. Some are decentralizing in order to bring human resource staff into closer working contact with line business units. While in larger companies the trend continues toward decentralization, many human resource functions are consolidating certain activities to improve cost-effectiveness and specialization.

The aim is to improve service to customers, both through decentralized staff units or teams and through central service organizations. And because the right organization is always subject to changing customer perceptions and expectations, the "best" organization is one that is continually changing and improving. Change itself is beneficial for human resource staff performance, because it challenges the status quo and stimulates new thinking and new behaviors.

Decentralized Service Teams

As companies restructure for increased flexibility, they often restructure the human resource function. The organization is often decentralized, with activities shifting to bring them closer to line management. Of course, a large company has multiple levels, and activities are aligned at each level according to the way the company is managed.

In most companies, the division or business unit is the focus for tailoring human resource strategies to business requirements. Whether the divisions are functional (e.g., refining and marketing, exploration), product (e.g., dairy, packaged goods), or geographic (e.g., North America, Europe), different requirements help shape the human resource process and, in turn, the human resource staff function.

Here, the focus is on defining and managing needed changes to support the performance of the business. The human resource function develops and adapts its programs and policies to support the needs of the organization. This represents the major shift in recent years, from a uniform, corporatewide approach for the human resource function to a more customer-focused function structured to serve the different components of the business.

In the past, companies may have had HR managers or officers assigned to business units, but they often acted as representatives of the company human resource function rather than autonomous human resource staff units designed to serve their customer organizations.

Similarly, companies have long had human resource staff assigned to specific locations, such as plants, distribution centers, or regions. Their focus has been and continues to be operational, providing direct and immediate support to managers and employees as their needs arise. While there may be opportunities to work with managers in addressing important issues and changes (e.g., organization changes, downsizing, expansion, or introduction of a quality process), the focus is on excellence in implementation, not the design of changes.

A human resource unit dedicated to each business unit provides a single point of contact for customers (managers and employees). This allows human resource staff to become closely involved with the organizations they are serving and to be highly visible and credible to employees and managers. Staff become part of the management team. In a large organization, it is difficult for managers to contact functional specialists directly, especially when they are at a remote location, in a group they contact infrequently.

Service to employees is particularly important at the local level. To the extent that all employment-related actions can be processed there, employees have a sense of caring and responsiveness that is preferable to remote services.

The use of on-line systems for processing pay changes, promotions or transfers, candidate searches, staffing requests, and other transactions empowers local staff to handle changes directly and efficiently.

The greater the delegation of authority and responsibility in an organization, the more significant the roles of local management and of their human resource staffs. As companies allow greater autonomy and entrepreneurism at the lower levels of organization, the strategic and consulting aspects of human resource staff work become more prominent. Staff do not wish to be characterized as strictly operational; at every organizational level there are opportunities to help shape human resource strategy and its implementation. The degree of influence is determined by the way the overall company is structured and managed.

Effective service teams are truly partners with managers in the organizations they serve. In many companies, this is reinforced by direct reporting relationships to their client organizations. However, even in companies where all human resource staff report functionally to the corporate human resource unit, this partnership may be achieved through informal means. Some companies have considered the reporting relationship inconsequential and have given unit managers the option of direct or functional reporting. In any case, human resource service teams live in a matrix, where both lines of relationships are essential.

Executive Resources

Many companies have a service delivery team dedicated to the executive group of management. While business units address their unique needs, management at a certain level and above becomes a client group as a "corporate entity."

At a minimum, such a team provides similar human resource staff services for the senior managers in the business units and for senior corporate executives (group or sector executives, senior staff executives, and top management). The focus may parallel the group of executives covered by a corporate executive compensation plan or those covered by corporate management succession planning. In some cases, it is limited to the group of executives who are reviewed by the Board of Directors (compensation committee) in terms of assignments, performance, and compensation, although this group is typically small.

The activities may include support in management organization design, development of executive position descriptions, and executive recruitment and selection (including relations with executive search firms). The activities may also include the design, updating, and implementation of executive compensation plans, including market surveys, job pricing, incentives, and stock ownership. Where employment contracts are used, the team may help develop them.

A major activity is the coordination of the management development and succession planning process on a companywide basis, as discussed in Chapter 9. The team provides the bridging among business units to facilitate developmental assignments and to help manage key talent as a companywide pool.

The team may merely coordinate the process, which is implemented organizationwide, or it may take an active role in negotiating developmental assignments, arranging developmental and educational experiences, and monitoring/reporting implementation progress. It may provide, as consultant Bob Eichinger says, "divine intervention" to ensure that needed executive development occurs despite near-term operating demands on management.

The executive resource team may also provide the corporate focus and staff services required for development of human resource strategy and policy companywide. The staff may define the process by which human resource strategies will be formulated, in relation to strategic business planning. They may also take the lead in developing policies guiding human resource decisions and actions companywide.

In a sense, the staff may help senior management represent the "conscience" of the company on human resource matters. Often, the staff, including the top human resource executive, are expected to work closely with top management in shaping communications on mission, vision, values, and strategic objectives. Human resource staff are a resource to the CEO and other executives as they shape and implement their approaches to managing the organization in support of strategy.

Centralized Human Resource Services

Even where companies have centralized the human resource function, this typically means establishment of solid reporting lines to the corporate level and consolidation of certain services. It does not mean the elimination or diminution of service teams. The aim is typically to gain potential efficiencies and to provide stronger functional leadership throughout an organization.

For example, some companies have consolidated such companywide activities as training and education (e.g., establishing a "company university" as an umbrella for most or all activities), compensation and benefits planning (to aid redesign and cost management), professional recruiting and college relations (to reduce cost, enhance company image, and simplify the process), and human resource information systems. But even in these areas, the result is typically a mixed structure, emphasizing policy development, focused investment, and coordination with parallel activities that continue at other levels.

The issue, then, is not so much a question of centralization or decentralization, but rather which human resource activities are best provided close to the clients and which are best provided as central, shared services. A survey by Lee Dyer, of Cornell University, found that among large companies, the placement of human resource activities varies widely. Some functions are often centralized because they serve senior management or the overall company interest, such as executive compensation, succession planning, executive development, executive outplacement, human resource information systems, and benefits. Others are performed locally, including recruiting, training, and work design. However, most activities are performed at all levels (Dyer, 1991).

The corporate role in human resources typically includes strategy and policy formulation for the human resources function, in conjunction with senior executives. In addition, the role includes providing human resource services to the CEO and senior management, as a client group, and addressing matters of executive staffing, compensation, succession, and development. In a holding company environment, the activities may require only a small staff. It may be viewed that the customer is the "corporation" and that services provided to others are incidental. The function is not intended to serve the rest of the organization.

In a company that seeks to "add value" to its businesses and provide management suport, the role is broader, and the size of the staff reflects the mandate defined. Services may be provided without charge (funded by the corporation as unallocated overhead expense) or charged to users directly as fees for services used. A few have even viewed the human resource function as an independent "for profit" business, a vendor to its customers across the corporation (Fitz-enz, 1989).

The staff functions often provided on a centralized basis are:

• Compensation: maintain a compensation policy and philosophy; maintain and monitor the use of a job evaluation system; conduct and participate in salary surveys; manage merit pay policies and programs; and consult on special incentive and other variable pay plans

• Recruiting and employment: coordinate technical, professional, and managerial recruiting, as well as college relations; manage internal job posting and placement systems; develop new-employee orientation programs, outplacement services, etc.

• Benefits: design benefit programs and policies; administer benefit program; and provide benefit communications

• Information systems: design, plan, and maintain HR information systems, including special analyses and reporting

• Managing diversity: develop communications and training programs; manage company EEO/AA programs and activities; investigate grievances; act as government and external organization liaison

• Payroll: keep records; maintain check processing and reporting systems

• Employee relations: provide or oversee employee counseling, employee assistance programs, and referral services

• Training and development: design and conduct corporate training programs; consult with units on their own training and use of vendors

• Planning: consult on human resource planning across the company; develop corporate HR strategic plans

These "heat and steam" (operational) service functions need not be centralized, but are often deemed more efficient when consolidated. Expertise, systems, and duplication of effort are usually managed more effectively. In a large organization, there may be multiple service units of this nature, depending on the management structure and efficiencies to be gained.

A number of large corporations have consolidated specialized and transac-

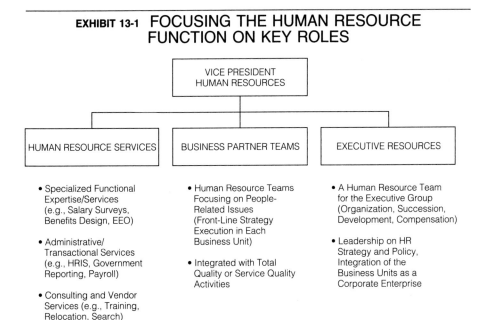

EXHIBIT 13-1 FOCUSING THE HUMAN RESOURCE FUNCTION ON KEY ROLES

tional human resource services into regional service centers. IBM, for example, established four regional personnel centers in the Eastern United States, to serve the needs of managers and employees at the various IBM locations in their areas. Under such arrangements, transactions for employment, job changes, salary administration, benefits, and other processes are handled directly with a center, usually by telephone or electronic communication. Local human resource staffs, reduced to a small team of generalist professionals, concentrate on consulting and problem-solving activities.

The purpose is twofold. A primary aim is to free up local human resource staffs to be truly business partners—to stem the flood of routine adminstrative tasks that crowd out "quality time" needed to address strategic human resource issues and actions with managers. Another is to obtain operating efficiencies through consolidation and streamlining of resources. The critical mass provided by consolidation allows re-engineering of service processes and improved use of technology.

The resulting prototype organization structure for the human resource function is presented in Exhibit 13-1. There is no specific optimal structure; this figure provides a map of three primary focal areas as a basis for designing the configuration that best fits a company.

Global Human Resources

Human resource functions in global companies have accentuated challenges in providing human resource services. Because global businesses are highly decentralized, often with autonomous operations around the world, the challenge of providing client services that fit the situation while also providing companywide "glue" is great. Once global, all human resource management systems and practices need to have a global applicability (i.e., not a host country [U.S.] bias).

Far-flung companies emphasize management training and education as a way to build global management skills, transfer technology, and build a common focus on strategies. All programs may have international dimensions both in content and in the case examples and issues addressed. Some are specifically designed to promote global management. General Electric Co., for example, conducts a Global Leadership Program, a multi-year program to help managers share technical experience while addressing important business projects. Human resource staffs are involved in finding ways to help managers in different regions interact and work together. Management succession, of course, addresses worldwide needs, opportunities, and talent.

The human resource function itself is managed globally, with rotation of talent among service teams, which are typically regional, and meetings (at least annually) of key human resource managers from around the world. Policies, programs, and systems are developed with regional and country differences (including legal constraints and cultural practices) in mind. Many multi-national companies maintain information on all management employees worldwide, and some include all salaried employees as well. Local payrolls address other employee groups.

The major challenge facing a staff in a multi-national company is international relocations. When individuals move across regions, the staff typically provide international service functions, including:

- Developing overseas compensation and benefits plans tailored to regional differences
- Providing tax and financial counsel to managers moved among regions
- Assisting with relocations, including the processing of work permits, visas, and other paperwork
- Assisting with arrangements for schools, medical care, and employment for "trailing" spouses
- Preparing managers for international moves, including training in languages and understanding of cultural differences

In large companies, expertise is justified by the number of such moves, and may be based in the central human resource services area or with the service delivery teams that have the most international activity (e.g., exploration and production in a petroleum company).

STAFFING AND DEVELOPMENT

How the human resource function is organized is usually not as important as the people in it. As one executive said, "If we wanted the function to operate differently we'd change the people and let the structure evolve.'' Effective managers shape the organization to fit the situation, build teamwork, and get on with the tasks.

Increasingly, human resource managers view themselves and are viewed by other managers as capable general managers who just happen to have responsibility for human resource management. Where human resource activities are on an equal level with finance, operations, research, and marketing, human resource staff work with management in developing strategic plans as well as implementing specific action programs.

Senior executives expect human resource staff to help management consider key issues and shape strategies for enhancing management effectiveness. In the flexible organization, human resource staff are involved in or leading organization planning, productivity, quality, culture, restructuring, downsizing, reskilling, mergers or acquisitions, and other management initiatives.

Staff Capabilities

What capabilities are needed in a strategy-oriented human resource function? Recent studies have examined the capabilities required of human resource managers and professionals in three key areas (Lawson, 1990; Ulrich, Brockbank, & Yeung, 1989).

- Human resource practices (e.g., knowledge/expertise, skills, and abilities to perform specific human resource activities as required by responsibilities)
- Knowledge of the business (e.g., business perspective, external relations, strategic perspective, financial perspective, information management)
- Management of change (e.g., vision, planning and organizing, decision making, managing performance, communicating, adaptability)

Some studies have identified more categories, but they are variations on these three key areas. These capabilities are presented as a Human Resource Effectiveness Profile in Exhibit 13-2.

Human resource professionals have often focused on specific functional activities, such as training and development, recruitment, affirmative action, career planning and counseling, compensation, benefits, or communications. Expertise in and enthusiasm for human resource management practices are important. Human resource staff are expected to bring functional knowledge and perspective to the business—just like financial, purchasing, information systems, planning, or other functional professional staff. Professional associations and conferences, accreditation and certification programs, as well as networks of professionals with similar interests and skills, foster advancement of functional practices and add to the ''bodies of knowledge.''

As the roles of human resource professionals change, however, new skills and knowledge are required for effective performance. Now staff are becoming more directly involved in business activities—company downsizing, delayering, strategy implementation, and reorganization; and they are changing human

---

EXHIBIT 13-2 HUMAN RESOURCE EFFECTIVENESS PROFILE

I. HUMAN RESOURCE PRACTICES

Involvement in the Business
    Help managers address HR implications of business plans and evolving business needs
    Help managers forecast human resource requirements (employees with needed skills)
    Assist managers in organization restructuring or job design
    Help managers to improve quality/service
    Help managers to assess and improve productivity in their organizations
    Provide HR input and support to customer/client relations activities
Building the Organization
    Identify and maintain relationships with various sources of employees
    Attract/recruit appropriate people
    Provide qualified candidates as needed
    Train managers in effective recruiting, assessment, and selection
    Help managers understand employee turnover and its causes
Developing Capabilities
    Help managers identify training and development needs in their organizations
    Provide training programs (internal or external) to meet needs
    Provide skills and tools for managers to train employees on the job
    Facilitate management development review sessions
    Facilitate developmental moves across organizational units/functions
Managing Performance
    Help managers define performance goals/standards
    Help managers develop and implement plans for improving subordinates' performance
    Facilitate performance feedback, coaching, and reinforcement
    Help managers resolve performance problems of subordinates
    Provide compensation programs that attract and retain high-quality employees and promote high performance
    Assist managers in applying salary administration programs (e.g., job evaluation)
    Help managers implement bonus incentive programs
    Provide benefits programs that attract and retain high-quality employees and promote productivity and quality service
    Help managers implement/administer benefit programs
    Design/help managers implement nonfinancial rewards/recognitions
Managing Human Resource Processes
    Help managers maintain positive employee relations (labor relations or union-free environment)
    Help managers address employee relations and communications issues (e.g., policy interpretation, work-related matters)
    Help managers manage work force diversity/differences
    Help managers develop and implement affirmative action programs
    Help managers be informed on and comply with regulatory requirements (e.g., EEO, OSHA)
    Help managers resolve issues (e.g., employee complaints or possible violations)

II. KNOWLEDGE OF THE BUSINESS

Business Perspective
    Understand all elements of the business, including goals, objectives, and operations; take an overall business point of view

---

resource systems and practices to respond to changing business demands. Staff are expected to have business knowledge, understanding, and point of view. Human resource staff need to be business-oriented to be effective in addressing human resource issues as business issues.

In the 1960s and 1970s, human resource professionals were expected to have specialized expertise, to develop new practices and programs (behavioral sci-

---

EXHIBIT 13-2   *(Cont.)*

External Relations
   Understand external forces/regulations and demands of changing customer/business rela-
      tionships; represent the company effectively
Strategic Perspective
   Think strategically; consider long-term view in decisions and actions; consider ways to gain
      and sustain competitive advantage under dynamic conditions
Financial Perspective
   Understand economics of the business, including costing, pricing, asset management, and
      other financial factors
Information Management
   Understand and use data and computer technology effectively

III. MANAGEMENT OF CHANGE

Vision
   Have a vision of future direction, goals, and priorities; build a commitment to it
Planning and Organizing
   Establish a course of action for staff and/or others to accomplish goals; allocate time and re-
      sources appropriately; establish systems and procedures to ensure appropriate follow-up
      and to monitor the activities of others
Decision Making
   Secure relevant information from different sources and accurately assess relationships and
      issues; make rational and realistic decisions based on factual information, logical assump-
      tions, and consideration of alternatives; take reasonable risks; make timely decisions and
      actions
Responsibility/Initiative
   Take responsibility for decisions and actions as situations warrant; take charge and move for-
      ward; actively influence events to achieve goals; be self-starting; take action to achieve
      goals
Communicating
   Effectively listen, present, write, and interact with peers, senior executives, subordinates, and
      customers
Influence
   Use appropriate interpersonal styles and methods of communications to gain agreement or
      acceptance or to resolve problems; achieve results without direct authority
Relationships/Teamwork
   Build and maintain working relationships with others; negotiate and resolve problems;
      achieve results without direct authority; foster cooperation within and among groups
Sensitivity
   Show genuine interest in others and sensitivity to the needs of others
Adaptability
   Maintain effectiveness in changing and often ambiguous circumstances; be open to new
      ideas and learn from others; make good decisions under pressure
Self-Awareness/Self-Development
   Have an accurate picture of strengths and weaknesses; make actions to improve skills and
      performance

---

ence applications, affirmative action and EEO compliance, organization development, salary practices and incentive plan design, personnel research, ERISA
compliance, career planning, etc.), and to be advocates of employees. In the
1980s, human resource staff roles changed. Professionals worked side by side
with managers as partners in handling reductions in force, mergers and acquisitions, productivity and quality efforts, and other activities which are not

necessarily specific to the human resource function. Human resource staff are broadening their scope of activities and are involved in a wide range of people-related management concerns.

The shift from "employee advocate" to "member of the management team" continued into the 1990s. Certainly, careful attention and empathy will need to be given to employee interests and concerns. However, human resource professionals will be called upon to think and act like line managers as they address people-related business issues. Managers will increasingly expect HR to think and act as they themselves think and act, and to view human resource activities from a business perspective.

Depending on their organizational roles, human resource staff are expected to be functional experts, capable administrators, business consultants, and problem-solvers. Management ideally would like human resource staff to "have it all." As in any staff function, administrative skills are essential for efficiency in human resource management. Specialized human resource expertise is also important, but particularly in combination with business knowledge and perspective. In flexible organizations, problem-solving and consulting skills are vital to help plan and implement changes in management practices.

Managers would like human resource staff to work closely with them to help solve their people-related problems as efficiently and promptly as possible, allowing them to give more attention to other concerns. To do this, human resource staff need to be close to the business units, understanding each business situation and the people involved and supporting managers actively. They are expected to bring technical and functional expertise to the problem, but the role of problem-solver involves more than administration or applying expertise. As staff become more capable and effective, managers seek to work with them as partners.

Staff Development

Human resource professionals and managers should have development plans, as should all professionals and managers. Some companies establish such plans as part of broader management development and succession (or performance and career management) programs. Others address these as a specific human resource staff development activity. Plans should target possible future assignments within or outside the function—with consideration given to long-term individual interests. Plans should propose on-the-job development activities, such as special projects, temporary assignments, or increased scope of responsibility. For example, staff should be encouraged to become involved more actively with quality programs, customer contacts, task forces, and other mainstream business activities.

Human resource professionals often participate in workshops and conferences sponsored by professional or industry groups. They should also participate in programs that their own functions are providing to other professionals and managers within the company (e.g., financial management, communications, interpersonal skills, negotiation skills, time management). Individuals should participate in such programs to address identified personal development needs.

Some companies—including IBM, General Electric, and Digital Equipment—are conducting programs tailored to the needs of human resource staff. Some are adapting university programs on human resource topics to their own needs, while others are designing programs specifically to address needs for increased business perspective and skills. Internal programs range from more than a week in duration to brief workshops, sometimes incorporated in companywide human resource staff meetings or conferences.

Over the past several decades, companies, universities, and professional associations have sought to develop a strong sense of professionalism in human resources. They have typically stressed the shift from administrative roles to professional roles; functional skills and knowledge have been emphasized. More recently, emphasis on human resource strategy has brought about increased attention to business, competitive, and management concerns.

As a result, many companies are providing development opportunities for human resource staff that go beyond participation in occasional professional meetings and company HR conferences. For one thing, staff participate in a variety of the company's regular management training and development programs. Some companies are providing customized programs for human resource staff, emphasizing understanding of their business issues and context, consulting skills, and roles.

Other companies recognize rotation in and out of the function as essential for vitality of the function, not merely for occasional individual development. Whereas specialization was once the primary emphasis, the flexible organization seeks more broadly experienced and skilled individuals as well. Some companies staff most of the human resource function with talent from other parts of the company to introduce business perspectives and diverse skills. When individuals are recruited and targeted for human resource staff careers, they often have assignments elsewhere in the company as they progress.

Of course, changing the organization of the human resource function is a powerful way to develop staff. It enables staff to change work assignments, it stimulates fresh thinking, and it encourages open discussion and innovation.

MEASURING EFFECTIVENESS AND EFFICIENCY

Human resource staff functions need to measure their efficiency and effectiveness. Such measures are used as diagnostic tools in managing its services. Measures, particularly information obtained from managers as customers, are useful in identifying needed improvements in human resource practices.

When companies measure the efficiency of the human resource function, they usually rely on a series of quantitative measures (e.g., cost, response time, and output volume relative to inputs) and relate results to short-term human resource activities. The measures indicate the yield of outputs to inputs (i.e.,

"Are we doing things right?") and address the relationship between key results and short-term human resource activities.

Effectiveness relates the results of activities to the achievement of objectives (i.e., "Are we doing the right things?") (Drucker, 1973). Effectiveness measures are primarily qualitative and relate results to the resolution of critical issues and the implementation of strategies. Many companies rate effectiveness of the human resource function in terms of perceptions (of employees and managers), but few adequately measure the effectiveness in relation to implementing human resource strategy and achieving specific objectives.

The focus of effectiveness and efficiency measures is on the performance of the human resource staff function as a service unit within a company. However, as mentioned in Chapter 2, measures of effectiveness and efficiency are applicable to the performance of line managers on human resource matters. Both measurement aspects are important to ensure human resource strategy implementation (Tsui & Gomez-Mejia, 1988).

Measuring Human Resource Efficiency

Implicit in human resource plans is the intent to achieve the desired results at minimum cost and at optimal speed. In companies where the performance of the human resource function has been measured, it is usually "productivity" or efficiency that is being evaluated, in terms of response time (e.g., average time required to fill an opening, time required to respond to a request for a job regrading), work volume (e.g., the number of applicants interviewed), and cost (e.g., cost per hire, cost per training hour).

Applications of cost-effectiveness measures have been a focus of research and company practice in recent years (Tsui & Gomez-Mejia, 1988). Efforts have also been made to apply utility analysis, a cost-benefit modeling process concerned with employee selection decisions, to the human resource function as a whole (Boudreau, 1988). Definition of measures, however, has not been consistent or gained general acceptance. In fact, many companies, including smaller companies, still do little if any measurement in human resource management.

By their very nature, efficiency measures are stated quantitatively, usually in terms of cost, response time, and output volume. Some companies concentrate on measures of efficiency simply because they can readily gather, analyze, and present the necessary data. It is also a common mind-set of managers to look at such measures. As one executive stated, "If you don't know what else to measure, measure efficiency."

Companies utilize efficiency measures by comparing the current value of the indicators with past values (current performance versus past performance), looking for such improvements as reduced cost, reduced response time, or increased volume. Companies also use these measures to compare performance across units (e.g., comparing different divisions or comparing a division with the company as a whole) or to compare performance with that of other companies, where there is commonality of measures (e.g., through a benchmarking process). In fact, in some industries, companies regularly share information on such measures, often through association surveys or informal contacts. The Society for Human Resource Management sponsors a survey data base on selected human resource performance measures in conjunction with the Saratoga Institute, headed by Jac Fitz-enz.

In the context of human resource planning, efficiency is expressed in terms of the results achieved in relation to the resource inputs. Various activities and programs (e.g., training, recruiting, and salary administration) are examined in light of the results (e.g., cost per trainee, cost per hire, and time needed to reevaluate a position).

To increase efficiency when necessary, companies change human resource activities or programs (for example, changing training course structure in order to reduce cost per training hour, or focusing recruiting on the most productive sources). Because companies are seeking to reduce staff expense, opportunities to improve efficiency are identified and acted upon.

Efficiency measures can be defined for each functional area of human resources. Such measures include average cost per hire, cost per training hour, and average time required to fill openings. There are numerous publications describing such measures and their application (Cascio, 1982; Fitz-enz, 1984; Spencer, 1986).

Overall measures of the efficiency of the human resource function are also used by companies. Some define trends (usually expressed as ratios) that relate human resource costs to profit, revenue, or other business indicators (Dahl, 1988). The interpretation of such measures is difficult, however. Conceptually, spending on recruiting, training, or other human resource activities could be reduced to zero (thus increasing efficiency drastically), but the effect of such reductions would be disastrous in the longer term. Another frequently used measure of the overall efficiency of the function is the ratio of professional (exempt) human resource staff to total employees in the organization. The analysis and interpretation of this measure can be influenced by a number of factors, however (e.g., differences in human resource activities performed by staff in the units measured) (Walker, 1988).

Efficiency measures help functions determine their contribution to the business, but only in terms of immediate resource utilization. Efficiency measures relate most directly to the day-to-day activities and actions of the function.

Measuring Human Resource Effectiveness

Effectiveness is defined as the extent to which the human resource function supports the successful implementation of ideas and long-term business plans and strategies. It relates results achieved to human resource issues and strategies (i.e., the effect of human resource activities on the achievement of business objectives). Results of various activities and programs are examined in terms of how well strategic human resource issues are being resolved (i.e., are the issues going away?). The definition of effectiveness in each company, therefore, depends on the focus of its issues and strategies, and this changes as priorities and conditions change.

One company study suggested that the most effective function is the one that ensures that there are no pressing human resource issues to concern management. The most proactive, strategic approach to managing resources anticipates and addresses emerging issues before the "pain" is felt. Because conditions continually change, however, there are always issues to be addressed. Through human resource planning, the function may bring these issues to management's attention and create a sense of urgency for action.

In contrast to efficiency measures, effectiveness measures are usually judgmental and qualitative. They are defined and used in terms of management expectations and perceptions. They represent a higher order of performance evaluation, but are evaluations of the performance of the human resource function, nonetheless.

Management Perceptions

One of the best ways to measure human resource effectiveness is to obtain the perceptions of managers regarding the quality of services provided by the human resource function. In many companies, human resource staff solicit the perceptions of managers regarding their effectiveness. In some organizations, formal studies are conducted involving interviews by an outside consultant. In others, discussions with managers are held on an ongoing basis to solicit inputs, concerns, and feedback. Examples of these two approaches are described below.

One company surveyed managers in detail regarding their perceptions of more than eighty defined activities of the human resource staff. The survey gathered managers' perceptions of the level of effort expended on each activity by the staff (i.e., the amount of time and resources devoted) and their opinions regarding the results attained (i.e., the extent to which their needs had been met). The survey also asked for narrative comments on opportunities for improvement (e.g., the most significant human resource challenge facing the organization, activities on which HR should spend more or less time, or the one change that should be made in the way the HR staff operate to increase effectiveness). Finally, the survey asked managers to rate the extent to which the staff had demonstrated specific capabilities "relative to your needs," against the dimensions of staff capabilities.

The human resource staff serving those units also completed the survey, indicating the level of effort that they perceived, the results they perceived, and the extent to which they demonstrated the required capabilities. The survey responses from managers were summarized by unit and compared with the aggregate response of the human resource staff serving that unit. Differences in perceptions provided a basis for staff discussion and planning at an off-site retreat. Through the survey, human resource staff gained insights into management views of the effectiveness of the function and addressed areas requiring improvement such as the need for business knowledge or increased involvement in implementing organizational restructuring.

Another company restructured and repositioned the human resource function in response to concerns raised by managers in several senior management meetings. A task force consisting of line managers and human resource representatives conducted a detailed review of the function's activities and priorities and established a series of clear expectations that would be used to assess staff effectiveness:

• Human resources are largely decentralized and oriented to the business units.
• Authority and responsibility for human resource actions are clearly defined for business units.
• Changes in employee benefit programs are effectively communicated and implemented.
• Relocation policies effectively support management moves.
• The job evaluation system gives appropriate weight to technical, managerial, and other factors.
• Management looks inside the company for talent before recruiting outside.
• Performance and development reviews are fulfilling their intended purposes.
• Appropriate and adequate supervisory training is provided.
• Appropriate and adequate information on career development opportunities is provided to professional and managerial employees.

The human resource function was then reorganized to better meet these expectations. Six months after the restructuring, the task force surveyed managers across the company to determine the extent to which these expectations had been met (i.e., "Have the concerns been resolved?"). The survey addressed the effectiveness of the function. It also gathered opinions regarding changes in the quality, quantity, and timeliness of staff services (poorer, about the same, improved, etc.) in order to assess the efficiency of the function. Specific ratings were obtained for each functional area of human resources.

The survey provided a quantitative assessment of the effectiveness of the function in terms of specific dimensions defined as important by the task force. The survey also provided a benchmark for subsequent assessments, fostering the planning of continual improvement.

Implications for Measurement and Evaluation

Companies strive to relate human resource activities and programs to their business needs. However, they measure the impact of activities and programs (and thus the effectiveness of the human resource function) in different ways, according to the business focus. Development of sales skills through training may directly increase sales. Organizational and job redesign may improve customer service, reduce the cost of doing business, or accelerate new-product development. Changes in human resource policies and procedures may lower turnover rates.

Each result (e.g., improved service, lower costs, and accelerated product development) may be measured in specific, quantitative terms. However, all measures of effectiveness or efficiency have subjective elements—in the nature of the data (e.g., opinion), in the collection of information at the source, or in the formulation or interpretation of the measure itself. Interpretation or analysis of the measure must be based on comparisons with expectations or objectives, with accepted standards (of one time to another, or among units), or with benchmarks, thus bringing an element of subjective judgment into play.

Measures may involve both efficiency and effectiveness elements. For example, hiring may be efficient and low-cost, but ineffective if new employees do not have the skills required for the business. In one company study, cost per hire was considered an inadequate measure because many new employees left soon after they started or turned out to be poor performers. Instead, the cost per "good" hire was measured, with "good" defined subjectively in terms of desired minimum tenure (e.g., staying with the organization for at least three years) or performance rating (e.g., achieving at least a "meets expectations" rating after two years).

An "efficient" source of new employees (defined in terms of cost per hire) may indeed be quite ineffective when many of them do not stay with the organization for an adequate length of time. In these cases, the cost per hire was low, but the cost per hire that reaches minimum tenure was high. Similarly, cost per hire could be low, but if those employees do not perform adequately, the cost per employee achieving an acceptable performance rating in two years could also be quite high (if the bulk of those hired are poor performers).

Other similar measures of effectiveness and efficiency include the number of employees remaining in positions for eighteen months (critical to maintaining customer contact), the number of managers capable of completing supportive, well-documented performance plans (as opposed to simply measuring the number of plans completed or discussions held), and the number of qualified backups in management development pools (as opposed to simply counting the number of candidates).

As these examples show, the analysis of even highly quantifiable meaures of effectiveness and efficiency requires subjective, judgmental interpretation. As a result, the companies studied acknowledge that there is no truly objective measure of either human resource effectiveness or efficiency. In fact, they recognize that overemphasis on measurement can cause companies to lose sight of the purpose of evaluation. Their effort focuses on scoring well and not on making substantive improvements in quality.

SUMMARY

Management expects human resource managers and professionals to be on the management team, interacting with managers at each level and sharing a common business perspective. The human resource staff function needs to be structured and managed to serve management needs effectively as they evolve and change.

Because human resource issues are inherent in people-intensive business strategies, a key role of the human resource staff is to help managers define how they want to manage differently and achieve desired changes. Senior management expects the human resource function to provide leadership and support in addressing "people-related business issues." The function is being asked to help chart the course for managing human resources as conditions change.

Human resource staff are also seeking to keep basic human resource programs current and in tune with strategies. They are striving to keep compensation, salary, incentive, and benefit programs competitively attractive and in legal compliance. New programs are developed to address such concerns as child care, benefits cost containment, union avoidance or decertification, substance abuse, and other needs.

While human resource functions are assuming a larger role in implementing management change, they are streamlining and automating their own operations and focusing services on critical tasks. The function is typically a small, high-performing, no-hassle staff function. Management wants the staff to dismantle unnecessary institutional trappings—policies, systems, procedures, etc. Staff find it essential to reduce the time demands of routine activities in order to have time to pursue initiatives.

To assess the effectiveness of the function, management needs to examine human resource management practices and results in the context of human resource strategies. Through the planning process, benchmarks are established at each step of strategy formulation and implementation: definition of issues, development of strategies, implementation of action plans. It is within this context, and not by isolated measures, that management best determines how well it is managing human resources and how well the human resource staff are fulfilling their mission.

As people-intensive strategies have become more important, managers have assumed responsibility for developing relevant human resource strategies— and managing human resources in a way that will implement them. The human resource staff function is rapidly redefining its historic roles to provide the services that managers need in this new context. Strategy formulation and implementation by line and staff together—this is the challenge of human resource planning in the 1990s.

References

Adizes, Ichak (1988). *Corporate Lifecycles: How and Why Corporations Grow and Die and What to Do about It,* Prentice-Hall, Englewood Cliffs, N.J.

Albrecht, Karl (1990). *Service Within: Solving the Middle Management Leadership Crisis,* R. D. Irwin, Homewood, Ill.

Anderson, Carl R., & Carl P. Zeithaml (1984). "Stages of Product Life Cycle, Business Strategy, and Business Performance," *Academy of Management Journal,* vol. 27, no. 1, pp. 5–24.

Argyris, Chris (1991, May–June). "Teaching Smart People How to Learn," *Harvard Business Review,* pp. 99–109.

Arvey, Richard D. (1979). *Fairness in Selecting Employees,* Addison-Wesley, Reading, Mass.

Badawy, M. K. (1982). *Developing Managerial Skills in Engineers and Scientists,* Van Nostrand Reinhold, New York.

Baird, Lloyd, & Ilam Meshoulam (1984). "The HRS Matrix: Managing the Human Resource Function Strategically," *Human Resource Planning,* vol. 7, no. 1, pp. 1–30.

Baird, Lloyd, & Ilam Meshoulam (1988). "Managing Two Fits of Strategic Human Resource Management," *Academy of Management Review,* vol. 13, no. 1, pp. 116–128.

Bardwick, Judith M. (1986). *The Plateauing Trap,* Amacom, New York.

Bart, Christopher K. (1988). "Budgeting Gamesmanship," Academy of Management Executive, vol. 11, no. 4, pp. 285–294.

Bartholomew, David J. (1982). *Stochastic Models for the Social Sciences,* 3d ed., Wiley, New York.

Beatty, Richard W. (1989). "Competitive Human Resource Advantage through the Strategic Management of Performance," *Human Resource Planning,* vol. 12, no. 3, pp. 179–194.

Beatty, R. W., & C. E. Schneier (1988). "Strategic Performance Appraisal Issues," in R. S. Schuler, S. A. Youngblood, and V. L. Huber (eds.), *Readings in Personnel and Human Resource Management,* 3d ed., West Publishing, St. Paul, Minn., pp. 256–266.

Bechet, Thomas P., & Frank P. Bordonaro (1991). "Executive Development—The Missing Links," unpublished paper.

Bechet, Thomas P. & Carole Brand (1991). "Helping Executives Shape and Implement Development Plans for Succession Candidates," unpublished paper.

Beckhard, Richard, & Reuben T. Harris (1987). *Organizational Transitions: Managing Complex Change,* Addison-Wesley, Reading, Mass.

Beer, Michael (1981, Winter). "Performance Appraisal: Dilemmas and Possibilities," *Organizational Dynamics,* pp. 24–36.

Beer, Michael, R. A. Eisenstat, & Bert Spector (1990, November–December). "Why Change Programs Don't Produce Change," *Harvard Business Review,* vol. 68, no. 6, pp. 158–166.

Bellman, Geoffrey M. (1986). *The Quest for Staff Leadership,* Scott, Foresman, Glenview, Ill.

Bennis, Warren (1985). *Leaders: The Strategies for Taking Charge,* Harper & Row, New York.

Berlinger, Lisa R., William H. Glick, & Robert C. Rodgers (1988). "Job Enrichment and Performance Improvement," in John P. Campbell, Richard J. Campbell, and Associates, *Productivity in Organizations,* Jossey-Bass, San Francisco, pp. 219–254.

Bernardin, H. J., & Richard W. Beatty (1984). *Performance Appraisal: Assessing Human Behavior at Work,* Kent, Boston.

Bernardin, H. John, & Lawrence A. Klatt (1985, November). "Managerial Appraisal Systems: Has Practice Caught Up to the State of the Art?" *Personnel Administrator,* pp. 79–86.

Beylouny, George A. (1984, October). "Pride Pays Off," *Quality,* pp. 47–48.

Blakeslee, G. Spencer, Edward L. Suntrup, & John A. Kernaghan (1985, November). "How Much Is Turnover Costing You?" *Personnel Journal,* pp. 99–103.

Block, Peter (1987). *The Empowered Manager,* Jossey-Bass, San Francisco.

Bolt, James F. (1989). *Executive Development,* Ballinger Publishing, Cambridge, Mass.

Boudreau, John W. (1988). "Utility Analysis," *Human Resource Managment: Evolving Roles and Responsibilities,* Bureau of National Affairs, Washington, D.C., pp. 125–186.

Bowen, David E., & Larry E. Greiner (1986, Summer). "Moving from Production to Service in Human Resources Management," *Organizational Dynamics,* pp. 1–16.

Branham, John (1975). *Practical Manpower Planning,* Institute of Personnel Management, London.

Bratkovich, Jerrold R., Bernadette Steele, & Thomas Rollins (1990, September). "Develop New Career Management Strategies," *Personnel Journal,* pp. 98–108.

Bray, Douglas W. (1976). "The Assessment Center Method," in Robert L. Craig (ed.), *Training and Development Handbook,* McGraw-Hill, New York, Chap. 6, pp. 1–15.

Bray, Douglas W., R. J. Campbell, & D. L. Grant (1974). *Formative Years in Business: A Long-Term AT&T Study of Managerial Lives,* Wiley, New York.

Brossy, Roger, & Carol A. Alperson (1991). "Hierarchy and Partnership: Building a New Approach to Management," *Perspectives,* vol. 3, no. 1, pp. 2–7.

Buono, Anthony F., & James L. Bowditch (1989). *The Human Side of Mergers and Acquisitions,* Jossey-Bass, San Francisco.

Burack, Elmer H., & James W. Walker (eds.) (1972). *Manpower Planning and Programming,* Allyn & Bacon, Boston.

Burns, James McGregor (1978). *Leadership,* Harper & Row, New York.

Bushe, Gervase, & A. B. Shani (1991). *Parallel Learning Structures: Increasing Innovation in Bureaucracies,* Addison-Wesley, Reading, Mass.

Butler, John E., Gerald R. Ferris, & Nancy K. Napier (1991). *Strategy and Human Resources Management,* South-Western Publishing, Cincinnati, Ohio.

Byham, William C. (1978, August). "Common Selection Problems to Be Overcome," *Personnel Administrator,* vol. 23, no. 8, pp. 42–47.

Byrd, Richard E. (1987, Summer). "Corporate Leadership Skills: A New Synthesis," *Organizational Dynamics,* pp. 34–43.

Campbell, John P., & Robert D. Pritchard (1976). "Motivation Theory in Industrial and Organization Psychology," in M. D. Dunnette (ed.), *Handbook of Industrial and Organizational Psychology,* Rand McNally, Chicago, pp. 63–160.

Campion, Michael A., & Paul W. Thayer (1989, Winter). "Job Design: Approaches, Outcomes, and Trade-offs," *Organizational Dynamics,* pp. 66–78.

Carnivale, Leila J. Gainer, & Janice Villet (1990). *Training in America: The Organization and the Strategic Role of Training,* Jossey-Bass, San Francisco.

Carroll, Stephen J., & C. E. Schneier (1982). *Performance Appraisal and Review Systems,* Scott, Foresman, Glenview, Ill.

Cascio, Wayne F. (1982). *Costing Human Resources: The Financial Impact of Behavior in Organizations,* Kent, Boston.

Cascio, Wayne F. (1987). *Applied Psychology in Personnel Management,* 3d ed., Prentice-Hall, Englewood Cliffs, N.J.

Castelli, Jim (1990, June). "Education Forms Common Bond," *HR Magazine,* pp. 46–49.

Caudron, Shari (1990, July). "The Wellness Payoff," *Personnel Journal,* pp. 55–61.

"Caught in the Middle" (1988, September 12). *Business Week,* pp. 80–88.

Ceriello, Vincent R. (1991). *Human Resource Management Systems,* Lexington, New York.

Certo, Samuel C., & J. Paul Peter (1988). *Strategic Management,* Random House, New York.

Cespedes, Frank V. (1990, Fall). "A Preface to Payment: Designing a Sales Compensation Plan," *Sloan Management Review,* pp. 59–69.

Chakravarthy, Balaji S. (1984). "Strategic Self-Renewal: A Planning Framework for Today," *Academy of Management Review,* vol. 9, no. 3, pp. 536–547.

Chalofsky, Neal E., & Charlene Reinhart (1988). *Effective Human Resource Development,* Jossey-Bass, San Francisco.

Christensen, Kathleen (1990, July–August). "Here We Go into the 'High-Flex' Era," *Across the Board,* pp. 22–26.

Ciampa, Dan (1991). *Implementing Total Quality Efforts,* Addison-Wesley, Reading, Mass.

Coates, Joe F., V. T. Coates, J. Jarratt, & L. Heinz (1986). *Issues Management: How You Can Plan, Organize, and Manage for the Future,* Lamond, Mt. Airy, Md.

Coates, Joseph F. (1987). "An Environmental Scan: Projecting Future Human Resource Trends," *Human Resource Planning,* vol. 10, no. 4, pp. 219–236.

Coates, Joseph F., & Jennifer Jarratt (1990). "Searching for Trends in the Human Resources Environment," in Manuel London, Emily S. Bassman, and John P. Fernandez, *Human Resource Forecasting and Strategy Development,* Quorum, Westport, Conn., pp. 3–14.

The Conference Board (1989, August). *The Conference Board's Management Briefing: Human Resources,* p. 1.

Craft, James A. (1988). "Human Resource Planning and Strategy," *Human Resource*

Management: Evolving Roles and Responsibilities, Bureau of National Affairs, Washington, D.C.

Craft, James A., Craig Fleisher, & Gerald Schoenfeld (1990). "Human Resource Competitor Intelligence: Concept, Focus, and Issues," *Human Resource Planning,* vol. 13, no. 4, pp. 265–280.

Crystal, Graef S. (1978). *Executive Compensation,* Amacom, New York.

Culbert, Samuel A., & John J. McDonough (1990, Summer). "Wrongful Termination and the Reasonable Manager: Balancing Fair Play and Effectiveness," *Sloan Management Review,* pp. 40–46.

D'Aprix, Roger (1982). *Communicating for Productivity,* Harper & Row, New York.

Dahl, Henry L., Jr. (1988). "Human Resource Cost and Benefit Analysis: New Power for Human Resource Approaches," *Human Resource Planning,* vol. 11, no. 2, pp. 69–78.

Dalton, Gene W., & Paul W. Thompson (1986). *Novations: Strategies for Career Development,* Scott, Foresman, Glenview, Ill.

Davis, Stan, & Bill Davidson (1991). *2020 Vision,* Simon & Schuster, New York.

Davis, Stan, & Bill Davidson (1991b, June). "The Myth of the Immortal Corporation," *Across the Board,* vol. 28, no. 6, pp. 25–27.

Davis, Stanley M., & Paul R. Lawrence (1977). *Matrix,* Addison-Wesley, Reading, Mass.

Deets, Norman R., & D. Timothy Tyler (1986, April). "How Xerox Improved Its Performance Appraisals," *Personnel Journal,* pp. 50–52.

Denton, D. Keith (1991). *Horizontal Management: Beyond Total Customer Satisfaction,* Lexington, New York.

Deutsch, Claudia (1990, December 30). "Businesses Emulate the Very Best," *New York Times,* p. 23.

Deutsch, Claudia H. (1988, July 10). "Losing Innocence, Abroad," *The New York Times,* pp. 1, 26.

Deutschmann, Alan (1990, August 27). "What 25-Year-Olds Want," *Fortune,* pp. 42–50.

Director, Steven M. (1985). *Strategic Planning for Human Resources,* Work in America Institute Studies in Productivity, Pergamon, New York.

Doeringer, Peter B., et al. (1991). *Turbulence in the American Workplace,* Oxford University Press, New York.

Dougherty, David C. (1989). *Strategic Organization Planning,* Quorum, Westport, Conn.

Dowling, Peter J. (1988). "International HRM," in Lee Dyer (ed.), *Human Resource Management: Evolving Roles and Responsibilities,* BNA Books, Washington, D.C.

Dowling, Peter J., & Randall S. Schuler (1990). *International Dimensions of Human Resource Management,* PWS-Kent, Boston.

Doyle, Frank P. (1989). "People Power: The Global Human Resource Challenge for the Nineties," Plenary paper, World Management Congress, New York.

Drucker, Peter F. (1973). *Management: Tasks, Responsibilities, Practices,* Harper & Row, New York.

Drucker, Peter F. (1980). *Managing in Turbulent Times,* Harper & Row, New York.

Drucker, Peter F. (1985a, June 4). "Playing in the Information-Based 'Orchestra,'" *The Wall Street Journal.*

Drucker, Peter F. (1985b, July–August). "How to Make People Decisions," *Harvard Business Review,* pp. 22–26.

Drucker, Peter F. (1986, May 22). "Goodbye to the Old Personnel Department," *The Wall Street Journal*, p. 16.

Drucker, Peter F. (1988, January–February). "The Coming of the New Organization," *Harvard Business Review*, pp. 45–53.

Drucker, Peter F. (1989). *The New Realities*, Harper & Row, New York.

Drucker, Peter F. (1990, May–June). "The Emerging Theory of Manufacturing," *Harvard Business Review*, pp. 94–102.

Dumaine, Brian (1990, May 7). "Who Needs a Boss?" *Fortune*, pp. 54–60.

Dyer, Lee (1984). "Linking Human Resource and Business Strategies," *Human Resource Planning*, vol. 7, no. 2, pp. 79–84.

Dyer, Lee (ed.) (1986). *Human Resource Planning Guide*, Random House, New York.

Dyer, Lee (1991). "Evolving Role of the Human Resource Organization," ILR School, Cornell University, Ithaca, N.Y.

Dyer, Lee, & Gerald W. Holder (1988). "A Strategic Perspective of Human Resource Management," *Human Resource Management: Evolving Roles and Responsibilities*, Bureau of National Affairs, Washington, D.C.

Edwards, John, et al. (1983). *Manpower Planning: Strategy and Techniques in an Organizational Context*, Wiley, New York.

Edwards, Mark R., & J. R. Sproull (1985, March). "Making Performance Appraisals Perform: The Use of Team Evaluation," *Personnel*, pp. 12–16.

Erdman, Andrew (1990, October 22). "How to Make Workers Better," *Fortune*, pp. 75–77.

Eurich, Nell P. (1985). *Corporate Classrooms: The Learning Business*, Carnegie Foundation for the Advancement of Teaching, New York.

"Europe's Women," (1990, June 30). *The Economist*, pp. 21–22.

Evans, Paul A. L. (1986, Spring). "The Strategic Outcomes of Human Resource Management," *Human Resource Management*, vol. 25, no. 1, pp. 149–167.

Evans, Paul, Yves Doz, & Andre Laurent (eds.) (1990). *Human Resource Management in International Firms*, St. Martin's, New York.

Evered, Roger D., & James C. Selman (1990, Spring). "Coaching and the Art of Management," *Organizational Dynamics*, vol. 18, no. 4, pp. 1–5.

Eyres, Patricia S. (1989, July). "Legally Defensible Performance Appraisal Systems," *Personnel Journal*, pp. 58–62.

Fairhead, Anthony J., & John H. Hudson (1989, Summer). "Leadership Template: Road Map for Managers," *Issues and Observations*, pp. 1–4.

Farish, Phil (1989). "Recruitment Sources," *Human Resources Planning, Employment, and Placement*, Bureau of National Affairs, Washington, D.C., pp. 103–132.

Farnham, Alan (1989, December 4). "The Trust Gap," *Fortune*, pp. 56–78.

Feigenbaum, Edward (1989). *The Rise of the Expert Company*, Macmillan, New York.

Feldman, Daniel C. (1988). *Managing Careers in Organizations*, Scott, Foresman, Glenview, Ill.

Fernandez, John P. (1991). *Managing a Diverse Work Force*, Lexington, New York.

Fernandez, John P., & Jacqueline A. DuBois (1990). "Managing a Diverse Workforce in the 1990s," in Manuel London, Emily S. Bassman, & John P. Fernandez, *Human Resource Forecasting and Strategy Development*, Quorum, Westport, Conn., pp. 205–246.

Finkle, Robert B. (1976). "Management Assessment Centers," in M. D. Dunnette (ed.), *Handbook of Industrial and Organizational Psychology*, Rand McNally, Chicago.

Fitz-enz, Jac (1984). *How to Measure Human Resource Management,* McGraw-Hill, New York.

Fitz-enz, Jac (1989, May–June). "HR Inc.," *Personnel Journal,* pp. 1–5.

Fitz-enz, Jac (1990). *Human Value Management: The Value-Adding Human Resource Management Strategy for the 1990s,* Jossey-Bass, San Francisco.

Fobrun, C. J., N. M. Tichy, & M. A. Devanna (eds.) (1984). "Human Resource Development and Organizational Effectiveness," *Strategic Human Resource Management,* Wiley, New York, pp. 159–168.

Forrer, Stephen E., & Zandy Leibowitz (1991). *Using Computers in Human Resources,* Jossey-Bass, San Francisco.

Forsyth, Suzanne, & Sylvia Galloway (1988, November). "Linking College Credit with In-House Training," *Personnel Administrator,* pp. 78–80.

Fortune, Special Issue: Saving Our Schools (1990, Spring).

Foulkes, Fred K. (ed.) (1991). *Executive Compensation: A Stategic Guide for the 1990s,* Harvard Business School Press, Boston, Mass.

Fraser, Jill (1989, September). "The Making of a Work Force," *Business Month,* pp. 58–61.

Friedson, Arthur S. (1985, September). "Special Award Programs: Compensating Excellence," *Personnel Administrator,* pp. 105–114.

Fullerton, Howard N., Jr. (1987, September). "Labor Force Projections: 1986–2000," *Monthly Labor Review,* vol. 110, no. 9, pp. 19–29.

Galagan, Patricia A. (1989, January). "IBM Gets Its Arms around Education," *Training and Development Journal,* pp. 35–41.

Galbraith, Jay R. (1977). *Organization Design,* Addison-Wesley, Reading, Mass.

Galvin, Robert (1989, March). "Keynote Address," *Human Resource Planning,* p. 3.

Garvin, David (1989, September). "A Note from David Garvin," *The Bean Scene,* vol. 17, no. 3, p. 12.

Gatewood, Robert D., & James Ledvinka (1976, May). "Selection Interviewing and EEO: Mandate for Objectivity," *Personnel Administrator,* pp. 15–19.

Geisler, Edwin B. (1967). *Manpower Planning: An Emerging Staff Function,* American Management Association, New York.

Gerstein, Marc, & Heather Reisman (1983, Winter). "Strategic Selection: Matching Executives to Business Conditions," *Sloan Management Review,* pp. 33–49.

Ghiselli, Edwin E. (1971). *Explorations in Managerial Talent,* Goodyear, Pacific Palisades, Calif.

Giblin, Edward J., & Oscar A. Ornati (1976). "Optimizing the Utilization of Human Resources," *Organizational Dynamics,* vol. 5, no. 2, pp. 18–33.

Gildea, Joyce (1989, May). "Executive Pay: In Search of the Missing Link," *Human Resource Executive,* pp. 1, 24–27.

Gilley, Jerry W., & Herff L. Moore (1986, March). "Managers as Career Enhancers," *Personnel Administrator,* pp. 51–59.

Gluck, Fred, S. Kaufman, & A. S. Walleck (1982, Winter). "The Four Phases of Strategic Management," *Journal of Strategic Management,* pp. 9–21.

Gomez-Mejia, Luis R. (ed.) (1989). *Compensation and Benefits,* Bureau of National Affairs, Washington, D.C.

Gomez-Mejia, Luis, David B. Balkin, & George T. Milkovich (1990, Spring). "Rethinking Rewards for Technical Employees," *Organizational Dynamics,* pp. 62–75.

Goodman, Paul S., Rukmini Devadas, & Terri L. Griffith Hughson (1988). "Groups and Productivity: Analyzing the Effectiveness of Self-Managing Teams," in John P.

Campbell, Richard J. Campbell, and Associates, *Productivity in Organizations,* Jossey-Bass, San Francisco, pp. 295–327.

Gorlin, Harriet, & Lawrence Schein (1984). *Innovations in Managing Human Resources,* The Conference Board, New York.

Graham-Moore, Brian E., & Timothy L. Ross (1983). *Productivity Gainsharing,* Prentice-Hall, Englewood Cliffs, N.J.

Gray, Barbara Jean (1989, November–December). "Motorola's Workers Go Back to School," *Human Resource Executive,* pp. 32–37.

Greenhaus, Jeffrey H. (1987). *Career Management,* Dryden Press, Hinsdale, Ill.

Greer, Charles R., Dana L. Jackson, & Jack Fiorito (1989, Spring). "Adapting Human Resource Planning in a Changing Environment," *Human Resource Management,* vol. 28, no. 1, pp. 105–124.

Gruenfeld, Elaine F. (1981). *Performance Appraisal: Promise and Peril,* NYSSILR, Cornell University, Ithaca, N.Y.

Grunwald, Lisa (1990, April). "Is It Time to Get Out?" *Esquire,* pp. 130–140.

Guion, Robert (1965). *Personnel Testing,* McGraw-Hill, New York.

Guion, Robert (1976). "Recruiting, Selection and Job Placement," in M. D. Dunnette (ed.), *Handbook of Industrial and Organizational Psychology,* Rand McNally, Chicago.

Hackman, J. Richard, & Greg Oldham (1976). "Motivation through the Design of Work," *Organizational Behavior and Human Performance,* vol. 16, pp. 250–279.

Hall, Douglas T. (1976). *Careers in Organizations,* Goodyear Publishing, Pacific Palisades, Calif.

Hall, Douglas T. (1984). "Human Resource Development and Organizational Effectiveness," in C. J. Fombrun, N. M. Tichy, and M. A. Devanna (eds.), *Strategic Human Resource Management,* Wiley, New York, pp. 159–168.

Hall, Douglas T., & Associates (1986). *Career Development in Organizations,* Jossey-Bass, San Francisco.

Hall, Douglas T., & James Goodale (1986). *Human Resource Management: Strategy, Design and Implementation,* Scott, Foresman, Glenview, Ill.

Hall, Douglas T., & Judith Richter (1990). "Career Gridlock: Baby Boomers Hit the Wall," *Academy of Management Executive,* vol. 4, no. 3, pp. 7–21.

Hallett, Jeffrey J. (1987). "Worklife Visions," *American Society for Personnel Administration,* Alexandria, Va.

Hammer, Tove Helland (1988). "New Developments in Profit Sharing, Gainsharing, and Employee Ownership," in John P. Campbell, Richard J. Campbell, and Associates, *Productivity in Organizations,* Jossey-Bass, San Francisco, pp. 328–366.

Harrison, Roger (1987, Autumn). "Harnessing Personal Energy: How Companies Can Inspire Employees," *Organizational Dynamics,* vol. 16, no. 2, pp. 5–20.

Hector, Gary (1988, November 21). "Yes, You Can Manage Long Term," *Fortune,* pp. 63–76.

Heisler, William J., W. David Jones, & Philip O. Benham, Jr. (1989). *Managing Human Resource Issues,* Jossey-Bass, San Francisco.

Henkoff, Ronald (1990, April 9). "Cost Cutting: How to Do It Right," *Fortune,* pp. 40–49.

Hoban, Richard (1987, June). "Creating a Hierarchical Career Progression Network," *Personnel Administrator,* pp. 168–184.

Hoerr, John (1990, June 25). "Business Shares the Blame for Workers' Low Skills," *Business Week,* p. 71.

Hollie, Pamela G. (1987, July 12). "Why Business Is Barging into the Classroom," *The New York Times,* p. 6.

Holusha, John (1990, August). "Unions Are Expanding Their Role to Survive in the 90's," *The New York Times,* p. 12.

Howard, Cecil G. (1987, June). "Out of Sight—Not Out of Mind," *Personnel Administrator,* pp. 84–90.

Jacobs, Deborah (1990, August 5). "Life after Wall Street," *The New York Times,* p. 14.

Jacoby, David (1989, December). "Rewards Make the Mentor," *Personnel,* pp. 10–14.

Jenkins, Steve (1988, December). "Turnover: Correcting the Causes," *Personnel,* pp. 43–49.

Johnston, William B. (1989). "Workforce 2000: Work and Workers in the Year 2000," World Future Society, Bethesda, Md.

Johnston, William B., & Arnold E. Packer (1989). "Workforce 2000," Hudson Institute, Inc., Indianapolis, Ind.

Jonas, Harry S. III, Ronald E. Fry, & Suresh Srivastva (1990). "The Office of the CEO: Understanding the Executive Experience," *Academy of Management Executive,* vol. 4, no. 3, pp. 36–48.

Kanin-Lovers, Jill, & J. D. Graham (1988, July–August). "Variable Merit Pay Program Links Pay to Performance," *Journal of Compensation and Benefits,* pp. 1–5.

Kanter, Rosabeth Moss (1979, July–August). "Power Failures in Management Circuits," *Harvard Business Review,* p. 67.

Kanter, Rosabeth Moss (1982, July–August). "The Middle Manager as Innovator," *Harvard Business Review,* pp. 1–5.

Kanter, Rosabeth Moss (1983). *Changemasters,* Simon & Schuster, New York.

Kanter, Rosabeth Moss (1989). *When Giants Learn to Dance,* Simon & Schuster, New York.

Kanter, Rosabeth Moss, Barry Stein, & Todd Jick (1991). *The Challenge of Organizational Change,* The Free Press, New York.

Kaye, Beverly (1989, August). "Are Plateaued Performers Productive?" *Personnel Journal,* pp. 57–66.

Kiechel, Walter III (1987, October 12). "How to Appraise Performance," *Fortune,* pp. 239–240.

Kiechel, Walter III (1988, July 6). "Love, Don't Lose, the Newly Hired," *Fortune,* pp. 271–274.

Kiechel, Walter III (1989, April 10). "The Workaholic Generation," *Fortune,* pp. 50–62.

Kiechel, Walter III (1990a, July 16). "12 Reasons for Leaving at Five," *Fortune,* pp. 117–118.

Kiechel, Walter III (1990b, August 13). "The Art of the Exit Interview," *Fortune,* pp. 114–115.

Kilmann, Ralph H., Mary J. Saxton, & Roy Serpa (1986, Winter). "Issues in Understanding and Changing Culture," *California Management Review,* vol. 28, no. 2, pp. 87–94.

Kimberly, John R., Robert H. Miles, & Associates (1980). *The Organizational Life Cycle,* Jossey-Bass, San Francisco, Calif.

Kinlaw, Dennis C. (1989). *Coaching for Commitment,* University Associates, San Diego.

Kinlaw, Dennis C. (1990). *Developing Superior Work Teams: Building Quality and the Competitive Edge,* University Associates, San Diego.

Kirkpatrick, David (1988, December 5). "How the Workers Run Avis Better," *Fortune*.
Kirkpatrick, David (1990, July 2). "Is Your Career on Track?" *Fortune*, pp. 39–48.
Knowles, Malcolm (1990). *The Adult Learner: A Neglected Species*, 4th ed., Gulf, Houston, Texas.
Kotter, John P. (1988). *The Leadership Factor*, Free Press, New York.
Kotter, John P. (1990, May–June). "What Leaders Really Do," *Harvard Business Review*, pp. 103–111.
Kotter, John P., Leonard A. Schlesinger, & Vijay Sathe (1979). *Organization*, Irwin, Homewood, Ill.
Kouzes, James M., & Barry Z. Posner (1987). *The Leadership Challenge*, Jossey-Bass, San Francisco.
Krajci, Thomas J. (1990, June). "Pay That Rewards Knowledge," *HR Magazine*, pp. 58–60.
Kram, Kathy E. (1984). *Mentoring at Work*, Scott, Foresman, Glenview, Ill.
Kupfer, Andrew (1988, March 14). "How to Be a Global Manager," *Fortune*, pp. 52–58.
Kupfer, Andrew (1989, June 19). "Bob Allen Rattles the cages at AT&T," *Fortune*, pp. 58–66.
Kutscher, Ronald E. (1987, September). "Overview and Implications of the Projections to 2,000," *Monthly Labor Review*, vol. 110, no. 9, pp. 3–10.
Labich, Kenneth (1989a, February 27). "Hot Company, Warm Culture," *Fortune*, pp. 74–78.
Labich, Kenneth (1989b, May 8). "Making Over Middle Managers," *Fortune*, pp. 58–64.
"Labor Letter" (1991, March 19). *The Wall Street Journal*, p. 1.
Latham, Gary P., & Kenneth N. Wexley (1981). *Increasing Productivity Through Performance Appraisal*, Addison-Wesley, Reading, Mass.
Lawler, Edward E. III (1986). *High Involvement Management*, Jossey-Bass, San Francisco.
Lawler, Edward E. (1988). "Gainsharing Theory and Research: Findings and Future Directions," in W. A. Pasmore and R. Woodman (eds.), *Research in Organizational Change and Development*, JAI Press, Greenwich, Conn.
Lawler, Edward E. III (1989, Summer). "Substitutes for Hierarchy," *Organizational Dynamics*, pp. 5–15.
Lawler, E. E. III (1990). *Strategic Pay*, Jossey-Bass, San Francisco.
Lawler, Edward E. III, & Susan A. Mohrman (1987, April). "High-Involvement Management," *Personnel*, pp. 26–31.
Lawson, Tom E. (1990). *The Competency Initiative: Standards of Excellence for Human Resource Executives*, SHRM Foundation, Alexandria, Va.
Leavitt, Harold J. (1986). *Corporate Pathfinders*, Dow Jones–Irwin, Homewood, Ill.
Ledvinka, James, & Vida G. Scarpello (1991). *Federal Regulation of Personnel and Human Resource Management*, Kent, Boston, Mass.
Lefton, Robert E. (1985–1986, Winter). "Performance Appraisals: Why They Go Wrong and How to Do Them Right," *National Productivity Review*, pp. 54–63.
Lessem, Ronnie (1990). *Total Quality Learning*, Basil Blackwell, Cambridge, Mass.
Levine, Hermine Zagat (1986, June). "Performance Appraisals at Work," *Personnel*, pp. 63–71.
Levinson, Daniel J. (1978). *The Seasons of a Man's Life*, Alfred Knopf, New York.
Levinson, Harry (1980, July–August). "Criteria for Choosing Chief Executives," *Harvard Business Review*, pp. 113–120.

Lindsey, Esther H., Virginia Homes, & Morgan W. McCall, Jr. (1987). *Key Events in Executives' Lives,* Technical Report 32, The Center for Creative Leadership, Greensboro, N.C.

Little, Arthur D. (1985). *Managing Innovation: From Vision to Reality,* Arthur D. Little, Cambridge, Mass.

Loden, Marilyn, & Judy B. Rosener (1991). *Workforce America,* Business One, Irwin, Homewood, Ill.

Lombardo, Michael M., & Robert W. Eichinger (1989). "Eighty-Eight Assignments for Development in Place: Enhancing the Developmental Challenge of Existing Jobs," The Center for Creative Leadership, Greensboro, N.C.

London, Manuel (1985), *Developing Managers,* Jossey-Bass, San Francisco.

London, Manuel, & Stephen A. Strumpf (1982). *Managing Careers,* Addison-Wesley, Reading, Mass.

London, Manuel, Emily S. Bassman, & John P. Fernandez (1990). *Human Resource Forecasting and Strategy Development,* Quorum, Westport, Conn.

Longenecker, Clinton O., & Dennis A. Gioia (1988, Winter). "Neglected at the Top— Executives Talk about Executive Appraisal," *Sloan Management Review,* pp. 41–47.

Lorange, Peter (1986). "Human Resource Management in Multinational Cooperative Ventures," *Human Resource Management,* vol. 25, pp. 133–148.

Lord, Scott (1989). "External and Internal Recruitment," *Human Resource Planning, Employment, and Placement,* Bureau of National Affairs, Washington, D.C., pp. 73–102.

Lorsch, Jay W. (1977, Autumn). "Organizational Design: A Situational Perspective," *Organizational Dynamics,* pp. 2–14.

Ludeman, Kate (1989, May). *The Worth Ethic: Eight Strategies for Leading the New Work Force,* NAL/Dutton, New York, N.Y.

Lusterman, Seymour (1985). *Trends in Corporate Education and Training,* The Conference Board, New York.

Luthans, Fred (1988). "Successful vs. Effective Real Managers," *Academy of Management Executive,* vol. 2, no. 2, pp. 127–132.

Luthans, Fred, Richard M. Hodgetts, & Stuart Rosenkrantz (1988). *Real Managers,* Ballinger, Cambridge, Mass.

McAuliffe, K., et al. (1987, June 15). "The Staggering Price of AIDS," *U.S. News and World Report,* pp. 16–18.

McCall, Morgan W., Jr., Michael M. Lombardo, & Ann Morrison (1988). *The Lessons of Experience: How Successful Executives Develop on the Job,* Lexington Books, Lexington, Mass.

McEvoy, Glenn M., Paul F. Buller, & Steven R. Roghaar (1988, May). "A Jury of One's Peers," *Personnel Administrator,* pp. 94–101.

McLagan, Patricia A., & David Bedrick (1983, June). "Models for Excellence: The Results of the A.S.T.D. Training and Development Competency Study," *Training and Development Journal,* vol. 37, no. 6, pp. 10–20.

McMillan, John D., & Hoyt W. Doyel (1980, July–August). "Performance Appraisal: Match the Tool to the Task," *Personnel,* pp. 12–20.

McMillan, John D., & Chris Young (1990, October). "Sweetening the Compensation Package," *HR Magazine,* pp. 36–39.

Main, Jeremy (1988, September 26). "The Winning Organization," *Fortune,* pp. 50–60.

Main, Jeremy (1990, December 17). "Making Global Alliances Work," *Fortune,* pp. 121–126.

Main, Jeremy (1991, July 11). "Is the Baldrige Overblown?" *Fortune*, pp. 61–65.

Maitel, Shlomo (March, 1991). "When You Absolutely, Positively Have to Give Better Service," *Across The Board*, pp. 8–12.

Makridakis, S., Stephen C. Wheelwright, & V. E. McGee (1978). *Forecasting: Methods and Applications*, Wiley, New York.

Manz, Charles, David E. Keating, & Anne Donnellon (1990, Autumn). "Preparing for an Organizational Change to Employee Self-Management: The Managerial Transition," *Organizational Dynamics*, pp. 15–26.

Manzini, Andrew O. (1986). *Integrating Human Resources and Strategic Business Planning*, Amacom, New York.

Marcus, Samuel (1991). "Delayering: More Than Meets the Eye," *Perspectives*, vol. 3, no. 1, pp. 22–26.

Marks, Mitchell Lee, & Joseph G. Cutcliffe (1988, April). "Making Mergers Work," *Training and Development Journal*, pp. 30–35.

Martin, Justin (1990, December). "Workplace Testing: Why Can't We Get It Right?" *Across the Board*, pp. 32–38.

Meehan, Robert, & S. Basheer Ahmed (1990). "Forecasting Human Resources Requirements: A Demand Model," *Human Resource Planning*, vol. 13, no. 4, pp. 297–308.

Mercer, Michael (1989). *Turning Your HR Department into a Profit Center*, Mercer Group, Chicago, Amacom, New York.

Meyer, Herbert, Emmanuel Kay, & J. R. P. French, Jr. (1965, January–February). "Split Roles in Performance Appraisal," *Harvard Business Review*, vol. 43, no. 1, pp. 123–129.

Miles, Raymond E., & Charles C. Snow (1984, Summer). "Designing Strategic Human Resources Systems," *Organizational Dynamics*, pp. 119–135.

Milkovich, George, & Luis Gomez-Mejia (1990). *Compensation*, Irwin, Homewood, Ill.

Milkovich, George T., & Jerry M. Newman (1984). *Compensation*, Business Publications, Plano, Tex.

Mills, D. Quinn (1985). "Planning with People in Mind," *Harvard Business Review*, vol. 63, no. 4, pp. 97–105.

Minken, Suzanne L. (1988, June). "Does Lump-Sum Pay Merit Attention?" *Personnel Journal*, pp. 77–83.

Mintzberg, Henry (1991, Winter). "The Effective Organization: Forces and Forms," *Sloan Management Review*, vol. 32, no. 2, pp. 54–68.

Mintzberg, Henry A. (1979). *The Structuring of Organizations*, Prentice-Hall, Englewood Cliffs, N.J.

Mirvis, P. H. (1985, Winter). "Formulating and Implementing Human Resource Strategy: A Model of How to Do It, Two Examples of How It's Done," *Human Resource Management*, pp. 385–412.

Mobley, William H. (1982). *Employee Turnover: Causes, Consequences, and Control*, Addison-Wesley, Reading, Mass.

Mohrman, Allan M., Susan M. Resnick-West, & Edward E. Lawler III (1989). *Designing Performance Appraisal Systems: Aligning Appraisals and Organizational Realities*, Jossey-Bass, San Francisco.

Moore, Thomas (1987, December 21). "Goodbye, Corporate Staff," *Fortune*, pp. 65–76.

Moorhead, Gregory, and Ricky W. Griffin (1989). *Organizational Behavior*, 2d ed., Houghton Mifflin, Boston, Mass.

Morgan, Gareth (1988). *Riding the Waves of Change,* Jossey-Bass, San Francisco.

Morgan, Marilyn (1980). *Managing Career Development,* Van Nostrand, New York.

Morin, William J., & Lyle Yorks (1990). *Dismissal,* Drake, Beam, Morin, New York.

Moses, Joseph, & William C. Byham (eds.) (1977). *Applying the Assessment Center Methods,* Pergamon, Elmsford, New York.

Moynahan, John K. (1980). *Designing an Effective Sales Compensation Program,* Amacom, New York.

Myers, M. Scott (1991). *Every Employee a Manager,* University Associates, San Diego.

Nadler, David A. (1982, Summer). "Conversation with Charles L. Brown," *Organizational Dynamics,* pp. 28–37.

Nadler, David A. (1989). "Organizational Frame Bending: Principles for Managing Reorientation," *Academy of Management Executive,* vol. 3, no. 3, pp. 194–204.

Nadler, David A., & E. E. Lawler III (1977). "Motivation: A Diagnostic Approach," in J. R. Hackman, E. E. Lawler, & L. Porter (eds.), *Perspectives on Behavior in Organizations,* McGraw-Hill, New York.

Nadler, David A., & Michael L. Tushman (1988). *Strategic Organization Design,* Scott, Foresman, Glenview, Ill.

Nadler, Leonard (1979). *Developing Human Resources,* Gulf Publishing, San Diego.

Naisbitt, John (1990, July 19). *Trend Letter,* vol. 9, no. 15, pp. 1–2.

Naisbitt, John, & Patricia Aburdene (1985). *Reinventing the Corporation,* Warner, New York.

Nathanson, Daniel A., & James S. Cassano (1982, Summer). "Organization, Diversity, and Performance," *Wharton Magazine,* vol. 6, no. 4, pp. 19–26.

Niehaus, Richard J. (1979). *Computer-Assisted Human Resources Planning,* Wiley, New York.

Ninomiya, J. S. (1988, March–April). "Wagon Masters and Lesser Managers," *Harvard Business Review,* pp. 84–90.

Noel, James L., & Ram Charan (1988, Winter). "Leadership Development at GE's Crotonville," *Human Resource Management,* pp. 433–447.

Nothdurft, William E. (1990, September). "How to Produce Work-Ready Workers," *Across the Board,* pp. 47–52.

Nusbaum, H. J. (1986, September). "The Career Development Program at DuPont's Pioneering Research Center," pp. 68–75.

O'Dell, Carla (1989, November). "Team Play, Team Pay—New Ways of Keeping Score," *Across the Board,* pp. 38–45.

Olian, Judy D., & Sara L. Rynes (1984, Spring). "Organizational Staffing: Integrating Practice with Strategy," *Industrial Relations,* vol. 23, no. 2, pp. 170–182.

O'Reilly, Brian (1990, March 12). "Is Your Company Asking Too Much?" *Fortune,* pp. 38–50.

Orsburn, Jack D., Linda Moran, Ed Musselwhite, & John H. Zenger (1990). *Self-Directed Work Teams: The New American Challenge,* University Associates, San Diego.

Orth, Charles D., Harry E. Wilkinson, & Robert C. Benfari (1987, Spring). "The Manager's Role as Coach and Mentor," *Organizational Dynamics,* vol. 15, no. 4, pp. 66–74.

Ost, Edward J. (1990, Spring). "Team Based Pay: New Wave Strategic Incentives," *Sloan Management Review,* pp. 19–27.

O'Toole, James (1985). *Vanguard Management,* Doubleday, Garden City, N.Y.

O'Toole, James (1989, October). "The Spirit of Phoenix," *Business Month,* pp. 26–37.

Pare, Terence P. (1989, September 11). "How to Cut the Cost of Headquarters," *Fortune,* pp. 189–192.

Pascale, Richard T. (1990, June). "Fit or Split," *Across the Board,* pp. 48–52.

Perry, Manuel, Joan More, & Nancy Parkison (1987, May). "Does Your Appraisal System Stack Up?" *Personnel Journal,* pp. 82–87.

Perry, Nancy J. (1990, December 17). "Schools: Tackling the Tough Issues," *Fortune,* pp. 143–155.

Perry, Nancy J. (1991, Spring–Summer). "The Workers of the Future," *Fortune,* vol. 123, no. 12, pp. 68–72.

Peters, Thomas J. (1979, Autumn). "Beyond the Matrix Organization," *Business Horizons,* pp. 15–27.

Peters, Tom (1990, May 7). " 'Hollow' Organizations Emerge as Firms Strive for Flexibility," *The Business Journal,* p. 7.

Peters, Tom, & Nancy Austin (1985). *A Passion for Excellence,* Random House, New York.

Peters, Thomas J., & Robert H. Waterman, Jr. (1982). *In Search of Excellence,* Harper & Row, New York.

Peterson, Richard B. (1985, August). "Latest Trends in Succession Planning," *Personnel,* pp. 47–54.

Pfeffer, Jeffrey, & Gerald R. Salancik (1977, Autumn). "Organization Design: The Case for a Coalitional Model of Organizations," *Organizational Dynamics,* pp. 15–29.

Pfeiffer, J. William (ed.) (1991). *The Encyclopedia of Team Building Activities,* vols. I and II, University Associates, San Diego.

Pinchot, Gifford (1985). *Intrapreneuring,* Harper & Row, New York.

Porter, Michael E. (1980). *Competitive Strategy: Techniques for Analyzing Industries and Competitors,* The Free Press, New York.

Porter, Michael E. (1985). *Competitive Advantage,* The Free Press, New York.

Porter, Michael (ed.) (1986). *Competition in Global Industries,* Harvard Business School Press, Boston, Mass.

Prahalad, C. K., & Gary Hamel (1990, May–June). "The Core Competence of the Corporation," *Harvard Business Review,* vol. 90, no. 3, pp. 79–91.

Quinn, James Brian (1978, Fall). "Strategic Change: 'Logical Incrementalism,'" *Sloan Management Review,* pp. 7–37.

Quinn, James Brian (1980a, Summer). "Managing Strategic Change," *Sloan Management Review,* pp. 3–20.

Quinn, James Brian (1980b). *Strategies for Change: Logical Incrementalism,* Irwin, Homewood, Ill.

Quinn, James Brian (1985, May–June). "Managing Innovation: Controlled Chaos," *Harvard Business Review,* pp. 73–84.

Quinn, James Brian, Henry Mintzberg, & Robert M. James (1988). *The Strategy Process: Concepts, Contexts, and Cases,* Prentice-Hall, Englewood Cliffs, N.J.

Radford, John, & Susan Kove (1991, February). "Lessons from the Silicon Valley," *Personnel Journal,* pp. 38–44.

Reif, William E. (1991). "People-Intensive Business Strategies: Sustaining Competitive Advantage in the 1990s," unpublished paper.

Reif, William E., & James W. Walker (1991). "Second-Generation Books on Service Quality," *Human Resource Planning,* vol. 14, no. 2, pp. 161–169.

Rhinesmith, Stephen H., John N. Williamson, David M. Ehlen, & Denise S. Maxwell (1989, April). "Developing Leaders for the Global Enterprise," *Training and Development Journal,* pp. 26–34.

Rhodes, David W., & James W. Walker (1984). "Management Succession and Development Planning," *Human Resource Planning,* vol. 7, no. 4, pp. 1–5.

Rose, Frank (1991, April 22). "Now Quality Means Service Too," *Fortune,* pp. 97–111.

Rummler, Geary A., & Alan P. Brache (1990). *Improving Performance,* Jossey-Bass, San Francisco.

Rummler, Geary A., & Alan P. Brache (1991, January). "Managing the White Space," *Training,* pp. 55–70.

Safire, William (1990, July 15). "Empowerment and Denouncement," *The New York Times Magazine,* p. 12.

Sahl, Robert J. (1990, December). "Probing How People Think," *Personnel Journal,* pp. 48–53.

Saporito, Bill (1987, May 25). "Cutting Costs without Cutting People," *Fortune,* pp. 26–32.

Sasser, Earl W., Jr., & Frank S. Leonard (1980, March–April). "Let First-Level Supervisors Do Their Job," *Harvard Business Review,* pp. 113–121.

Sayles, Leonard (1976, Autumn). "Matrix Management: The Structure with a Future," *Organizational Dynamics,* vol. 5, no. 2, pp. 2–15.

Sayles, Leonard R. (1990, Spring). "Leadership for the Nineties: Challenge and Change," *Issues and Observations,* vol. 10, no. 2, pp. 8–11.

Scheier, Robert L. (1991, March 11). "InterAct Network 'Informates' Users," *PC Week,* p. 12–13.

Schein, Edgar H. (1978). *Career Dynamics,* Addison-Wesley, Reading, Mass.

Schein, Edgar H. (1984, Winter). "Coming to a New Awareness of Organizational Culture," *Sloan Management Review,* pp. 3–16.

Schendel, Dan E., & Charles W. Hofer (eds.) (1979). *Strategic Management: A New View of Business Policy and Planning,* Little, Brown, Boston.

Schermerhorn, John R., William L. Gardner, & Thomas N. Martin (1990, Spring). "Management Dialogues: Turning On the Marginal Performer," *Organizational Dynamics,* pp. 47–59.

Schiffman, Barry (1991, March 3). "Tougher Tactics to Keep Out Unions," *The New York Times,* p. 8.

Schlesinger, Leonard A., & James L. Heskett (1991, Spring). "Breaking the Cycle of Failure in Services," *Sloan Management Review,* pp. 17–28.

Schneier, Craig E. (1989). "Implementing Performance Management and Recognition and Rewards Systems at the Strategic Level," *Human Resource Planning,* vol. 12, no. 3, pp. 205–220.

Schneier, Craig E., Richard W. Beatty, & Lloyd S. Baird (1986, April). "How to Construct a Successful Performance Appraisal System," *Training and Development Journal,* pp. 38–42.

Schreiber, Carol T. (1982). "Using Demographic and Technological Forecasts for Human Resource Planning," in Gerhard Mensch & Richard J. Niehaus, *Work, Organizations, and Technological Change,* Plenum, New York, pp. 39–52.

Schrenk, Lorenz P. (1988). "Environmental Scanning," *Human Resource Management: Evolving Roles and Responsibilities,* BNA Books, Washington, D.C., pp. 88–123.

Schroeder, Michael (1988, November 7). "Watching the Bottom Line Instead of the Clock," *Business Week.*

Schuler, Randall S. (1989). "Scanning the Environment: Planning for Human Resource Management and Organizational Change," *Human Resource Planning,* vol. 12, no. 4, pp. 257–276.

Schuler, Randall S. (1990). "Repositioning the Human Resource Function: Transformation or Demise," *Academy of Management Executive,* vol. 4, no. 3, pp. 49–60.

Schuler, Randall S., & Susan E. Jackson (1987). "Linking Competitive Strategies with Human Resource Management Practices," *Academy of Management Executive,* vol. 1, no. 3, pp. 207–219.

Schuler, Randall S., & Susan E. Jackson (1988, June). "Customerization: The Ticket to Better HR Business," *Personnel,* pp. 36–44.

Schuler, Randall S., & James W. Walker (1990, Summer). "Human Resources Strategy: Focusing on Issues and Actions," *Organizational Dynamics,* pp. 4–19.

Schuler, Randall S., Nicholas J. Beutell, & Stuart A. Youngblood (1989). *Effective Personnel Management,* 3d ed., West Publishing, St. Paul, Minn.

Schweiger, David L., & John M. Ivancevich (1985, November). "Human Resources: The Forgotten Factor in Mergers," *Personnel Administrator,* pp. 47–61.

Schweiger, David M., John M. Ivancevich, & Frank R. Power (1987). "Executive Actions for Managing Human Resources before and after Acquisition," *Academy of Management Executive,* vol. 1, no. 2, pp. 127–138.

Scovel, Kathryn (1990, January). "In Pursuit of Perfection," *Human Resource Executive,* pp. 25–26.

Senge, Peter M. (1990a). *The Fifth Discipline: The Art and Practice of the Learning Organization,* Doubleday, New York.

Senge, Peter M. (1990b, Fall). "The Leader's New Work: Building Learning Organizations," *Sloan Management Review,* pp. 7–23.

Shaeffer, Ruth G. (1984). *Developing Strategic Leadership,* The Conference Board, New York.

Sherwood, John J. (1988, Summer). "Creating Work Cultures with Competitive Advantage," *Organizational Dynamics,* vol. 17, no. 1, pp. 5–20.

Sibson & Company (1990). *Perspectives,* vol. 1, no. 2.

Sims, Ronald R. (1990). *An Experiential Approach to Employee Training Systems,* Quorum, Westport, Conn.

Skrzycki, Cindy (1988, October 2). "The Quest for the Best: U.S. Firms Turn to Quality as Competitive Tool," *The Washington Post,* p. H2.

Slevin, Dennis P., & Jeffrey G. Covin (1990, Winter). "Juggling Entrepreneurial Style and Organization Structure—How to Get Your Act Together," *Sloan Management Review,* pp. 43–53.

Sloan, Stanley, & Alton C. Johnson (1968, January–February). "New Context of Performance Appraisal," *Harvard Business Review,* vol. 46, no. 1, pp. 14–31.

Slocum, John W., William L. Cron, Richard W. Hansen, & Sallie Rawlings (1985). "Business Strategy and the Management of Plateaued Employees," *Academy of Management Journal,* vol. 28, no. 1, pp. 133–154.

"Smart Advice from Dumb Machines" (1989, February 11). *The Economist,* pp. 61–62.

Sobel, Stuart, & Gary Hines (1990, November). "Cray's New Focus on Customers," *Personnel Journal,* pp. 59–63.

Specter, Bert A. (1989, Summer). "From Bogged Down to Fired Up: Inspiring Organizational Change," *Sloan Management Review,* vol. 29, pp. 29–34.

Spencer, Lyle M. (1986). *Calculating Human Resource Costs and Benefits,* Wiley, New York.

Stebbens, Michael W., & Abraham B. Shani (1989). "Organization Design: Beyond the 'Mafia' Model," *Organizational Dynamics,* vol. 17, no. 3, pp. 18–30.

Stewart, Thomas A. (1990, June 4). "Why Budgets Are Bad for Business," *Fortune,* pp. 179–190.

Stright, Jay F., Jr. (1991, April–May). "Introducing CHRIS: Chevron's Human Resource Information System," *Personnel Administrator,* pp. 24–28.

Sweet, Donald (1989). "Outplacement," *Human Resource Planning, Employment, and Placement,* Bureau of National Affairs, Washington, D.C., pp. 236–261.

Swinehart, David P. (1986, July). "A Guide to More Productive Team Incentive Programs," *Personnel Journal,* pp. 112–117.

Thomas, Barry W., & Madeline H. Olson (1988, May). "Gain Sharing: The Design Guarantees Success," *Personnel Journal,* pp. 73–79.

Thompson, Arthur A., & A. J. Strickland III (1987). *Strategic Management: Concepts and Cases,* Business Publications, Plano, Tex.

Thompson, Paul H., Robin Z. Baker, & Norman Smallwood (1986, Autumn). "Improving Professional Development by Applying the Four-Stage Career Model," *Organization Dynamics,* pp. 49–62.

Tichy, Noel (1983). *Managing Strategic Change,* Wiley, New York.

Tichy, Noel, & Ram Charan (1989, September–October). "Speed, Simplicity, Self-Confidence: An Interview with Jack Welch," *Harvard Business Review,* vol. 89, no. 5, pp. 112–121.

Tichy, Noel, & Mary Anne Devanna (1986). *The Transformational Leader,* Wiley, New York.

Tomasko, Robert M. (1987). *Downsizing,* Amacom, New York.

Torres, Cresencio, & Jerry Spiegel (1991). *Self-Directed Work Teams,* University Associates, San Diego.

Tornow, Walter W., & Jack W. Wiley (1991). "Service Quality and Management Practices: A Look at Employee Attitudes, Customer Satisfaction, and Bottom-Line Consequences," *Human Resource Planning,* vol. 14, no. 2, pp. 105–116.

Tracey, W. R. (1979). *Managing Training and Development Systems,* Amacom, New York.

Tsui, Anne S. (1987, Spring). "Defining the Activities and Effectiveness of the Human Resource Department: A Multiple Constituency Approach," *Human Resource Management,* pp. 35–70.

Tsui, Anne S., & Luis Gomez-Mejia (1988). "Evaluating Human Resource Effectiveness," *Human Resource Management: Evolving Roles and Responsibilities,* Bureau of National Affairs, Washington, D.C., pp. 187–227.

Tully, Shawn (1990, May 21). "The Hunt for the Global Manager," *Fortune,* pp. 140–144.

Ulrich, Dave (1989, Summer). "Tie the Corporate Knot: Gaining Complete Customer Commitment," *Sloan Management Review,* pp. 19–27.

Ulrich, Dave (1990a). "Organizational Capability as a Competitive Advantage: Human Resource Professionals as Strategic Partners," *Human Resource Planning,* vol. 10, no. 4, pp. 169–184.

Ulrich, Dave (1990b). *Organizational Capability,* Wiley, New York.

Ulrich, Dave, & Dale Lake (1991). "Organizational Capability: Creating Competitive Advantage," *Academy of Management Executive,* vol. 5, no. 1, pp. 77–92.

Ulrich, Dave, & Margarethe F. Wiersema (1989). "Gaining Strategic and Organizational Capability in a Turbulent Business Environment," *Academy of Management Executive,* vol. 3, no. 2, pp. 115–122.

Ulrich, Dave, Wayne Brockbank, & Arthur Yeung (1989, Fall). "Beyond Belief: A Benchmark for Human Resources," *Human Resource Management,* vol. 28, no. 3, pp. 311–336.

Ulrich, Dave, Richard Halbrook, Dave Meder, Mark Stuchlik, & Steve Thorpe (1991). "Employee and Customer Attachment: Synergies for Competitive Advantage," *Human Resource Planning,* vol. 14, no. 2, pp. 89–104.

Uttal, Bro (1987, December 7). "Companies That Serve You Best," *Fortune,* pp. 98–104.

Vetter, E. W. (1967). *Manpower Planning for High Talent Personnel,* Bureau of Industrial Relations, University of Michigan, Ann Arbor.

Wagel, William H. (1988a, May). "Beyond the Plateauing Trap at KLA Instruments," *Personnel,* pp. 12–18.

Wagel, William H. (1988b, December). "New Beginnings for Displaced Workers: Outplacement at GE," *Personnel,* pp. 12–17.

Walker, Alfred J. (1992). *Human Resource Information Systems: Management Reshaping HR through Technology,* McGraw-Hill, New York.

Walker, James W. (1980). *Human Resource Planning,* McGraw-Hill, New York.

Walker, James W. (1988). "Managing Human Resources in Flat, Lean and Flexible Organizations: Trends for the 1990s," *Human Resource Planning,* vol. 11, no. 2, p. 125–132.

Walker, James W. (1988b, October). "How Large Should the HR Staff Be?" *Personnel,* pp. 36–42.

Walker, James W. (1990). "Human Resource Planning, 90s Style," *Human Resource Planning,* vol. 13, no. 4, pp. 229–240.

Walker, James W., & Glenn Weingarth (1991). "Human Resource Planning at Burroughs Wellcome Co.," working paper.

Wanous, John P. (1980). *Organizational Entry,* Addison-Wesley, Reading, Mass.

Want, Jerome H. (1986, August). "Corporate Mission: The Intangible Contributor to Performance," *Management Review,* pp. 46–50.

Watts, Larry R., & Harold C. White (1988, April). "Assessing Employee Turnover," *Personnel Administrator,* pp. 80–85.

Webster, James L., William E. Reif, & Jeffrey S. Bracker (1989, November–December). "The Manager's Guide to Strategic Planning Tools and Techniques," *Planning Review,* pp. 6–16.

Weick, Karl E. (1977). "Organization Design: Organizations as Self-Designing Systems," *Organizational Dynamics,* vol. 6, no. 2, pp. 31–46.

Wexley, Kenneth N., & Gary P. Latham (1981). *Developing and Training Human Resources in Organizations,* Scott, Foresman, Glenview, Ill.

Wheelen, Thomas L., & J. David Hunger (1987). *Strategic Management,* Addison-Wesley, Reading, Mass.

White, Harrison (1970). *Chains of Opportunity: System Models of Mobility in Organizations,* Harvard University Press, Cambridge, Mass.

Wiggenhorn, William (1990, July–August). "Motorola U: When Training Becomes an Education," *Harvard Business Review,* pp. 71–83.

Wikstrom, Walter S. (1964). *Developing Managerial Competence: Changing Concepts and Emerging Practices,* The Conference Board, New York.

Wikstrom, Walter S. (1971). *Manpower Planning: Evolving Systems,* The Conference Board, New York.

Willis, R. E. (1987). *A Guide to Forecasting for Planners and Managers,* Prentice-Hall, Englewood Cliffs, N.J.

Zeithaml, Carl P., A. Parasuraman, & Leonard L. Berry (1990). *Delivering Quality Service: Balancing Customer Perceptions and Expectations,* The Free Press, New York.

Zey, Michael G. (1984). *The Mentor Connection,* Dow-Jones, Irwin, Homewood, Ill.

NAME INDEX

SUBJECT INDEX